The Power Within

Self-exploration and psychotherapy using non-ordinary (holotropic) states of consciousness induced by psychedelic substances and non-pharmacological means has brought revolutionary, paradigm-breaking changes into the theory and practice of psychiatry and psychology. In his new book, *The Power Within*, Tav Sparks takes the readers on a fascinating journey through the territories that this work has opened, using a clear, non-technical and easily understandable style. Tav brings to his book expertise, experiences, and observations as an addictions counselor and from several decades of conducting training and workshops of Holotropic Breathwork all over the world.

Frequent references to transformative experiences of his clients and personal examples from his own spiritual crisis make his writing very captivating and alive. *The Power Within* is a treasure trove of important information for people involved in self-exploration and healing, as well as individuals who facilitate and support their process. This valuable information is described in detail not easily available in other sources. In the passages describing psychospiritual transformation and mystical experiences, Tav's language often becomes poetic, evocative, and even inspiring.

In his book, Tav Sparks makes excursions that take him far beyond the work with individuals or groups; he discusses the implications of the pivotal concept of his book, the self-healing intelligence of the psyche or the "Inner Healer," for a variety of other fields, defines what he calls the "Holotropic Paradigm" and its relationship to transpersonal psychology, and emphasizes the importance of transformative inner work and the return of authentic experiential spirituality into industrial civilization for the future of our planet.

– **Stanislav Grof,** M.D., author of *Psychology of the Future, Healing our Deepest Wounds,* and *The Cosmic Game* and co-author of *Holotropic Breathwork* (with Christina Grof)

Tav Sparks has written an ambitious and largely successful book that beautifully describes the holotropic perspective, a view of the human condition not only more expansive than conventional psychology, but also more inclusive of consciousness than transpersonal psychology. Based on substantial evidence (thousands of people) of the reality of the inner healer, Sparks gives us a whole new way to look at the human condition. He posits a far more healthy way to develop our own capacity for discovering the deepest truths within ourselves.

From this base he goes on to illustrate the power of this perspective, not only to normal consciousness, but also shows that it more accurately tracks psychedelics or entheogenic experience and other altered states as well.

Finally, he concludes that a holotropic perspective can foster a more robust methodology for addiction treatment—right now desperately needed.

A sweeping review of contemporary psychological thought through a lens of direct experience, the book also interweaves the achievements of Stan and Christina Grof's development first of psychedelic therapy and later the worldwide network of holotropic therapists and centers. A valuable and innovative book.

– **Jim Fadiman**, author of *The Psychedelic Explorer's Guide.*

In modern culture the truth that we all have a powerful Inner Healer is barely recognized. Yet it is a real force inside us that, when met with awareness, respect, cooperation and proper support, propels individuals and collectives into the fast lane for healing, consciousness, and empowerment. We owe much gratitude to Tav Sparks for teaching this truth for decades and for sharing what he knows in this fine, unique book. *The Power Within* will intrigue and motivate those who seek transformation and their own answers to life's questions.

– **Kylea Taylor,** author of *The Ethics of Caring, The Breathwork Experience,* and *Considering Holotropic Breathwork™.*

I have deep admiration for Tav Sparks. There are few who have given so many years of courageous work in the trenches of the human psyche, assisting in the transformational birth labors of so many. And this service he has rendered with unfailing humility and compassion. Both healers and seekers will find *The Power Within* a treasure of hard-won insights and observations from a lifetime of therapeutic work with non-ordinary states of consciousness."

– **Richard Tarnas,** professor of psychology and cultural history, California Institute of Integral Studies

Tav Sparks reminds us that ignoring experiential realities is as unscientific as ignoring external data. This perspective is crucial because, as Tav points out, true healing for ourselves and the planet is inseparable from the innate "urge of consciousness evolution", and may require "radical rearrangements in consciousness" that come in "expanded states of awareness". *The Power Within* shares profound insights gained from decades of teaching and facilitating Holotropic Breathwork and transpersonal psychology based on the discoveries of Stanislav and Christina Grof. It also conveys the good news that these expanded states of consciousness are more readily accessible than many of us may had suspected; in fact, in the right set and setting, expanded awareness is only a few breaths away.
– **Michael Mithoefer.** M.D. Principle Investigator

The Power Within

Becoming, Being, and the
Holotropic Paradigm

Tav Sparks

AEON

First published in 2016 by Muswell Hill Press.

This new edition published in 2019 by

Aeon Books Ltd
12 New College Parade
Finchley Road
London NW3 5EP

British Library Cataloguing in Publication Data
A C.I.P. for this book is available from the British Library

ISBN-13: 978-1-91327-415-3

Printed in Great Britain

www.aeonbooks.co.uk

Contents

Acknowledgments

I have been blessed with many meaningful relationships all over the world, both with co-workers in the field of Holotropic Breathwork™ and seekers on their own psycho-spiritual journeys. I find myself at times voicing the experiences, thoughts, and feelings of these co-workers and seekers with whom I have had the great honor, over the past thirty years, to share the collective adventure of moving toward wholeness.

And so, here, I wish to acknowledge the truth that virtually every point I make, every insight and revelation about transformation I share, is based on experiences I and these many other friends and colleagues have had on our inner journeys. When I use the term *we* throughout the text, I am using it to refer to the shared source of the insights I present.

Ongoing holotropic work, which is a central focus of this book, convinces us that in no way are our insights *the* absolute truth. Nor do we demand that you, the reader, must "buy" what we are sharing as the true and only nature of reality, or path of transformation, or anything else. Basically, the insights reported in the pages to follow represent what we have experienced, and what we have seen and heard, from seekers all over the world who have systematically applied the holotropic practice and perspective in their own daily lives—for a day, week, month, or down through the years.

In addition to acknowledging our shared insights and journey, I would also like to express my heartfelt gratitude to some of the wonderful people all over the world with whom I have had the blessing to share life-changing adventures in consciousness. I could not write another word without first honoring my beloved wife, absolute light of my life, best friend, and coworker, Cary, who began coordinating Grof Transpersonal Training in 1990, and who has nurtured its structure and expansion with tremendous agility and poise since that time. I cannot imagine this grace of a life without Cary and my two sons, Ason and Bryn, and my grandsons Dallin, Kellen, and Patrick.

For my two sisters, Tricia Lyndon and Jackie Sparks, brother Bill Sparks, and brother-in-law John Lyndon—boy did we "sign on." No way I can imagine this whirlwind of a life without you—growing up together, that kind of "love in the trenches," and the many special times that we have shared and are still sharing—I am so fortunate and blessed!

I must, of course, express gratitude beyond words to Christina Grof, whose unexpected passing in 2014 was felt across the world-wide holotropic community, and to Stanislav Grof, not only for the special, decades-long friendship, but for what they have so freely given my colleagues and me, and also for what they have tirelessly shared with seekers all over the world for nearly fifty years, and which Stan continues to do.

Their gifts have been both personal and theoretical. Not only have they spent thousands of hours on the mat with breathers, holding the space for them so each seeker could tap the power of the Inner Healer within themselves. But they also have created a body of written work that is a profound part of a global shift in the nature of science, philosophy, psychiatry, the self, the cosmos, and existence itself, as well as the perennial human journey toward wholeness, espoused by shamans, mystics, and philosophers for millennia.

Through the gestation and nurturing of the transpersonal paradigm, Stan, along with Christina and their pioneering colleagues, has, among many contributions, undertaken three responsibilities, which can be related metaphorically. First, keeping a respectful vigil through the agonizingly slow death of the long-outdated, previous worldview. Second, skillfully and courageously performing the function of midwifing the planetary psyche by providing heretical yet essential maps and experiential methodology for this era of the consciousness odyssey. And third, by continuing to scan further horizons of consciousness, with open arms and heart, from a wide-open window that reveals a frontier of cosmic evolution shifting so exponentially it has become almost impossible to conceptualize. Many of these topics will be explored in this book.

On the subject of gratitude and love, there are so many more friends and co-workers that deserve acknowledgement for this shared holotropic adventure that it is impossible to name them all. I will mention some of them, and trust in the good will and soul of the world holotropic community to *feel* my gratitude for all the others. I trust, as well, that every person who has undertaken a deep holotropic journey knows how much they are each honored in this written celebration of what we have all experienced together for decades.

We can go no further until I acknowledge two amazing people whom I trust and respect deeply—Tim Read and Keiron Le Grice. Without their support and expertise, any impeccability this book now carries could not have been possible. I first met Tim in Grof Transpersonal Training a number of years ago, and respected him from the beginning. I was impressed by both his brilliance and his commitment to deep inner work. But as much as anything, it was his passion, sincerity, and the expanse of his heart with which I was most resonated. Tim is the co-owner of Muswell Hill Press, and I am grateful and honored that he was willing to midwife this book. It has been wonderful to work with him. Throughout the project, he has always been supportive and caring, while being, at the same time, what I like to call a "straight shooter." That is, I always received the real thing from him—a compassionate truth, as well as an unalloyed sense of straightforward support.

The book is far better than it was in its earlier stages thanks to Keiron Le Grice's superb editing. He became my guide-light for impeccability, knowledge, and straight talk when I and the text needed it. I am not easily impressed with an individual's mind, or rigorous focus and magnetism toward truth and the psycho-spiritual heart of a topic. With Keiron, however, I was *always* impressed, even when he seemed to be pushing me to do better, and yet better.

And now, to some dear friends of many years. With much love to two special couples who have been both life friends and trusted mentors to Cary and me: Kate and Jack Silver; and Kylea Taylor and Jim Schofield; for all the fun, camaraderie, respect and soulful adventuring. They are impeccable people as well as carriers of the standard for Holotropic Breathwork. I honor them as well for the love and support we have shared on so many levels and the challenging moments on the holotropic adventures we have negotiated together. Thank you for every bit of it.

To Jai Uttal—there are no words to adequately express what he, my true spirit brother, means in my life. And to Matthew Stelzner, who has been like a family member for many years, thank you for all the love and real life adventures. Much love and respect as well to Carmen Scheifele-Giger, who is a life friend and has always held a unique and important place in the holotropic community.

And to Diana Medina for being my true soul sister. Girl, our connection goes beyond words.

I want to recognize Diane Haug for her exceptional and long-term commitment to the holotropic work, and for sharing the road of our early world adventures together. And also, again, Diana Medina, for her passion, dedication, and contribution. Each of these amazing women is not only a dear friend but a holotropic master teacher who has shared her wisdom and knowledge of the holotropic perspective worldwide for decades.

I send "big love" and honoring to Juanjo Segura and Sitara Blasco, for their friendship, first, and also for fostering the world holotropic adventure in Spain and beyond, and for truly carrying the soul of the holotropic in the most impeccable way. On top of that, it's been a whole lot of fun.

I am grateful beyond words for Alvaro and Dora Jardim who have for decades coordinated the holotropic training in Brazil—authentic heart friends and co-workers, whose passion and honoring of the true soul of this perspective is unsurpassed.

In this same spirit, I am honored to acknowledge other friends and colleagues who "hold space" for the training in their respective countries, impeccably representing the holotropic soul. These include Volodya and Sasha Emelianenko, Natasha Zgonnikova, Maxim Alexanian, and Alexey Shyokin in Russia; Zoya Mustava in Ukraine; Viktoria Luchetti, Gilberto Mercado, and Javier Charme in a several Latin American countries; Ole Ry and his late and much-missed partner, Susanne Andres, in Denmark; and Irena Antolic in Croatia. The amazing Vicky Nicholson has coordinated the training beautifully in Tasmania, Australia for years. And also in Australia, Donna and Dave Misso in Brisbane and Nigel Denning in Melbourne, who continue to impeccably support and expand the holotropic work there. In Germany, past training was offered with great skill and dedication by Ingo Jahrsetz and Brigitte Ashauer—who recently became Brigitte Ashauer-Grof with her marriage to Stan. We wish to acknowledge Father K.C. Thomas for his unending enthusiasm and commitment to bringing training to India, and to Holly Harman and Marianne Murray for the hundreds of hours and more that they've donated to that program.

It is an honor to acknowledge Holly Harman in another context, and her partner Debbie Dunning as well. Though she is in England and we are in California, Holly handles a great deal of the crucial administrative work that goes on behind the scenes of the Grof Transpersonal Training organization around the world, and we don't know what we would do without her. Both Holly and Deb wear two more hats—close friends and excellent facilitators—always carrying the truth of the holotropic spirit wherever they travel around the world. Closer to home, Cary would be hard-pressed to manage GTT's worldwide outreach without the loving, dedicated support of Angel Cassidy and Janet Kingsley. And much gratitude to Jeannie Claire for her unfailing support for Holotropic Breathwork, and her help with this book and other projects.

We are blessed to have as heart friend, co-worker, and elusive holotropic ninja spirit, Stacia Butterfield. Somehow she manages to be in the right place at the right time, helping to seed the holotropic perspective in a variety of previously less connected but ever more related communities. Among others from the US teams whose work thoroughly honors the blueprint established by Christina and Stan are close friends Mireya Alejo and Michael Stone in California; Sharanya Naik, a true leader in the US community, in New Jersey; and Pam Stockton, Christine Calvert, and Rob Park in Texas. They all play pivotal roles in the unfolding of the holotropic perspective, including Christine's and Rob's work to continue bringing the holotropic vision into the recovery arena. By the example of each of these people—and we could mention so many more—the world community is well served. We also wish to honor two more couples, Ashley and Chuck Wile; and Annie and Michael Mithoefer—for friendship, impeccability, as well as their important contributions to the holotropic perspective.

Authentic facilitation of Holotropic Breathwork throughout the world, to a substantial extent, owes its quality to the benchmark/blueprint established by some of the original training teams, from the early nineties onwards. In this context, I must mention both the friendship and the dedicated workshop presence of Laurie Weaver, from the very beginning, and Nienke Merbis and Jean Farrell for their decades of contribution and for always being the closest of friends. And the list would be far less complete without mentioning my Irish co-conspirator Geoff Fitzpatrick.

They and too many others to mention hold space for breathers across the world. These friends and co-workers are the embodiment of caring, loving, impeccable holotropic support, as well as fierce keepers of the deepest, most authentic holotropic practice. They walk their talk, and always model the best of what the holotropic perspective has to share. A few who come to mind not mentioned elsewhere are Tom Francescott—an integral part of the US certification team; Ben Allen, Cal Parrott, Dory Perry, Kirstin Kairos, Tom Dann, Rosan Hepko, Dorothy Hopkins, Lincoln Scott, Lila Pesa, Wendy Eveleigh, and Ashley Wain. This incomplete list is "the crew in the trenches" at training events—always in deep contact with breathers, offering love, safety, honoring, and support—day-in, day-out, and deep into the night when called upon.

We would like to acknowledge also Jay Dufrechou, for his multi-leveled skill set and support; Lenore Reinhart for nurturing so many seekers through her presence and her amazing cooking; Daniel Terres and Vinny Harrington-Terres, two close friends and fellow practitioners who, through their revolutionary medical/spiritual approach, have upgraded the lives of hundreds, including myself; and for Byron Metcalf and Mark Seelig for gracing us with their wonderful music for decades. I must express gratitude, also, for Cait Branigan, who has been my guide into deep relationship with Mother Earth.

There is no way to bring to mind or to honor all those who have been instrumental in nurturing the holotropic perspective for so long. There are so many who have deeply mattered to us, and to seekers they've worked with and inspired, who have taken the inward journey of a lifetime towards wholeness through Holotropic Breathwork. So, here we honor all those who have not been named. May the spirit of the love we feel here reach you in your heart of hearts, that you may also be uplifted gracefully, in the manner of those you have helped to uplift all over the world. And we also apologize for any glaring oversight we have made—our hearts are here, even if our minds have not kept pace. Thank you.

This brings us full-circle in our celebration of the world holotropic community—back once more to the reason we are all here. This is the power of our individual and collective relationship with Christina and Stan Grof. From all our hearts, to yours: may you feel, no matter where you are, at least a hint of the depth of our love and gratitude. Thanks for all.

T. S.
Novato, California
August 2016

Introduction

It is our nature to forever seek fulfillment in life. We pursue this goal with tremendous passion, and with as much desire and life force as we can summon. Yet our longings and dreams seem endless. Sadly, our dashed hopes and disappointments can often seem just as never-ending. But there is good news. We all have the power within us to become free—to be liberated from the personal and collective psycho-spiritual dream that binds us and keeps us separated from our true self and our most fulfilling place in the planetary and cosmic scheme.

The perennial philosophy—what I call the "wisdom of the ages"—is often considered to be the inner core of truth described by the world's religions, spiritual disciplines, and mystical philosophies. It seems, however, that most seekers—even if they "hear the piper calling" from beyond—begin by looking over their shoulders, into the misty past. Yet, we live in a fascinating era, where it is easy to lose what we think of as our *selves*. Despite our trying to "be here now," as teacher Ram Dass recommends, somehow the present appears to whirl through us, even as we struggle to establish a beachhead of insight in each ephemeral moment.

But, in this epoch, all bets we have made concerning our personal and collective future are off. Our understanding of perennial philosophy seems to be morphing before our psyches quicker than we can grasp it, mold it, write about it, or package it for the world as the latest revolutionary paradigm. In the midst of this dance, *point omega*, Pierre Teilhard de Chardin's teleological beacon of *apotheosis*—his words for radical individual and planetary transformation fueled by psycho-spiritual death/rebirth—burns brighter than ever, compelling us to make a leap of faith, or, as Ralph Blum puts it in the *Book of Runes*, an "empty-handed leap into the void."

To be fanciful, one might imagine the power of consciousness blossoming as a wondrous tree with a thousand fruits of unique flavors, nourished by the one sun and sky above, and roots intertwined in one earth below. There are so many mesmerizing tastes to beguile us with the notion that, "This is *the* truth, the one that is going to finally do it for us, once and for all."

However, it seems that, at least so far, one of these fruits, in the end, has always proven to be sour. As we habitually look for fulfillment, most of us will experience, almost like Tantalus of Greek myth, the bitter taste of disillusionment in a relentless reaching—a futile craving for lasting happiness—always *outside* ourselves. Fortunately, there are other fruits within our reach. Among the core tenets of nearly every psycho-spiritual practice in the world—past, present, or those that flirt with us at the outer rim of our future dreams—lies a solution to this universal human dilemma. The answer is either specifically addressed, or it may be veiled and merely hinted at.

The sweetest promise of these philosophies is that the power of true fulfillment for any individual can actually be found by *turning inward*, through searching the core of our own deepest selves. Driven by unfulfilled desire, as the Buddha said, we are likely to experience such ills as chronic dis-ease, craving, addiction, or ceaseless longing. The fundamental urge to change, to grow, to be transformed in some authentic way, eventually drives us not outward but inward to the depths of the psyche, toward a mystery, an unknown wholeness, that we sense must be latent here.

An inquiry into the wellspring of this mysterious *power within* is the overarching aim of this book. In the chapters to follow, we will introduce and explore a perspective that many of us feel may come to be known as a holotropic paradigm. This is a field of inquiry that in many ways is a fruit of the transpersonal paradigm, with roots in that paradigm's approach to science, psychology and spirituality—much of it based on the work of Czech psychiatrist Stanislav Grof and his late wife Christina Grof.

Originally emerging from LSD research in the 1950s and 1960s, the holotropic perspective is the child of a powerful experiential method of self-exploration known as Holotropic Breathwork™. Having been involved in this field for over thirty years, I have been able to experience for myself and witness in thousands of others the therapeutic and healing power of the Grofs' method and model.

This book presents a distillation and summary of the work of my friends, colleagues, and myself within the holotropic milieu. In addition, it also unveils a further horizon of the holotropic perspective that may prove to be a culmination of its radical power. Many of us feel that this revolutionary power has the potential to catalyze a host of world psychospiritual disciplines by taking a leap forward into new frontiers of service to individuals, humanity, and the planet itself.

Interlude: Some Backstory

A little backstory seems called for, so let me explain how I became so passionate about helping to foster the holotropic perspective. In 1984, I was working in an addictions recovery center in Macon, Georgia. I was immersed in an environment on the cutting edge of treatment philosophy and strategy, with a strong emphasis on the psycho-spiritual power of the Twelve Steps of Alcoholics Anonymous. Having been clean for five years, I felt miraculously freed from the grip of a powerful addiction that had almost killed me, and had wreaked havoc on the lives of nearly everyone I had ever known.

I was deeply committed to my psychological and spiritual growth; by all rights, living in what some fellow recovering addicts called the "bonus round." Here the power of gratitude for rescue by what we called the Higher Power should have left me "wearing the world like a loose garment," as they say, where every day, no matter how tough, was golden compared to life as an addict. Instead, I was restless and spiritually hungry. My mind seethed with contradictions. My body felt chorded with hot steel tendons. Every painful emotion I had ever experienced visited me daily with an intensity that felt diabolically more profound than when I was powerless and in the grip of my addiction.

It was a crisis. Here was the dilemma: On the one hand, I was totally committed to my recovery. My "program," as we called it—my sadhana, my yoga—was the central dynamis of my life. Spirit, the Higher Power, or what philosopher Rudolf Otto called the *numinous* power of the psyche, had been a vital force in my evolution for almost fifteen years, even all through my active addiction. But I was experiencing what seemed to be an unbridgeable gulf between two halves of my being—two warring forces, each of which seemed indispensable on my journey toward wholeness.

One force was the life-changing, ego-shattering power of psychedelic substances. When I was twenty, having already, for a number of years, been ingesting entheogens—another name for psychedelics—I took a powerful psychedelic substance and went into a movie theater with some family and friends. It seems, now, to have been no accident that, two weeks previously, I had finished reading an amazing text by psychedelic pioneers Timothy Leary, Richard Alpert, and Ralph Metzner, called *The Psychedelic Experience*—a modern re-telling of the *Tibetan Book of the Dead* and a manual revealing to modern seekers a clear path to profound psychospiritual transformation, or death/rebirth.

When I emerged from the womb of darkness a couple of hours later, I was no longer the same person as the one who had entered the theater. To put it simply, I died there—not my body, of course, but my entire sense of self, of who I thought I was. To use recovery terminology, my Higher Power came to me, and seemed to have obliterated my current, false self. It awakened me to what was to become the central focus of my life: a conscious journey into numinosity, the tremendous and fascinating mystery and power of the spirit.

Over the next ten years, even as my addiction progressively worsened, I underwent a series of powerful psychedelic experiences, which verified and enhanced that first radical dispensation of numinosity in the temple of the cinema. Nearly all of these took place in secluded natural settings, with the support of trusted friends. During this strange and contradictory time, where forces of self-destruction vied with a cellular urge to move toward wholeness, I managed to immerse myself in the wisdom of the ages.

I was convinced even then that my meta-purpose was to embrace as wholeheartedly as possible this odyssey toward wholeness. I was to do this, even if it meant confronting on a regular basis the ongoing death of all that I thought I was. It also entailed an unfolding of incremental rebirth into a more all-encompassing revelation of whatever this evolution was calling me toward, like a lighthouse on a darkened, stormy sea. Then another fierce, powerful death occurred; the unbidden experience of grace that brought me, against all personal resistance, into recovery, and my dedication in earnest to what I call a Twelve Step yoga—or commitment to the deepest, most rigorous dimensions of transformation at the core of the Twelve Steps themselves, one day at a time, or even one moment at a time.

But back to my dilemma in 1984, just prior to my first Holotropic Breathwork experience. I felt completely caught in a double bind. It was as though two essential halves of my being—on the one hand, the revelations from my psychedelic experiences, and, on the other, my total commitment to my recovery, to be drug free, one day at a time—could never, ever be reconciled. It seemed to be a soul-torturing irony that would leave me forever grounded, my wings clipped. I despaired that I would be powerless to fly towards what I know was a vital horizon of my own life destiny, and not a part of my active addiction at all.

On my birthday in 1984, I had my first experience with Holotropic Breathwork, the tremendously powerful psycho-spiritual practice developed by Christina Grof and Stanislav Grof at the Esalen Institute in Big Sur, California, in the middle seventies. I will have much more to share about these two wonderful people who became my teachers, co-workers, and friends. But there, in that darkened room, with my eyes closed, breathing deeply to a profoundly sacred set of music, I was once again graced with an experience of numinosity quite beyond my own personal ability to create.

Through the breath, I experienced what aboriginal elder Uncle Bob Randall, who has been an important mentor to me, calls *kanyini*, or connectedness, or oneness with all that is. When this occurred, almost miraculously, these two seemingly irreconcilable halves of my life dreams—the power of the psychedelic experience, on the one hand, and my recovery odyssey, on the other—came together in a freedom and a wholeness of which I had never even dreamed.

Now I truly knew that the same deep dimensions of the psyche that were available through entheogens were also totally available through the ancient, multi-cultural tradition of breathing practices. And I also had the insight that this method, Holotropic Breathwork, was exactly what was missing in traditional addictions recovery and in many other therapeutic settings.

In the prevailing treatment system, we did effective work with the physical disease aspect of addiction, and would get better at it as the years went by. We also made a good beginning in working with the power of emotions in the life of an addict. But what was often overlooked was the unavoidable truth that the modern recovery movement began with the mystical experience of Bill W, even before the birth of the Twelve Steps.

And what had always been missing in traditional treatment—in its role as a helpmate to the Twelve Step tradition—was what I have been calling, for over thirty years now, *language, method, and structure* for the mystical or numinous dimensions of the psyche. The story of what happened next, and continues to happen to this day, will be a thread winding itself through the tapestry of this inquiry into the holotropic paradigm.

Two Octaves

To enter the holotropic universe is like embarking on a mythic, cosmic odyssey in the manner of those described by Joseph Campbell in his powerful explication of the Hero's Journey. Specifically, we are looking forward in this adventure to exploring two dimensions, or octaves, of the almost universally agreed-upon truth of a readily accessible, internal source of fulfillment.

1. The first octave unveils the way that the workings of this power within has been deftly explicated throughout what many are now calling a holotropic perspective, or perhaps even a holotropic *paradigm*. At this level, we are referring to a therapeutic worldview, psycho-spiritual in nature, and the inner practice at the core of the worldview, which may eclipse the healing power of many others that have come before.

   Within this worldview, many are now envisioning a holotropic approach applied in a range of ways: therapeutic work with seekers engaged in the use of psychedelic substances, addiction recovery, support for those in psycho-spiritual crises or spiritual emergencies, the implementation of a wellness model of mental and psycho-spiritual health, and even as a radical enrichment to traditional therapies.

2. The second octave envisions the holotropic perspective as a panoramic, revolutionary lens through which to envision global, some may say universal, consciousness evolution. The term *"holotropic"* means *moving toward wholeness.* "Moving toward wholeness" seems to be a perfect depiction, as well as trajectory, for what mystics and philosophers often call the Becoming, in its eternal dance with the other half of this perennial dynamic, known as Being.

To the First Octave

Among the thousands of healing stories we have heard from seekers who have experienced Holotropic Breathwork, the method developed by Christina and Stanislav Grof, one particular fruit of this deep inner work is consistently reported: the sense of authentic *personal empowerment* they have received as they embrace the mystery of the journey toward wholeness—not outward, but inward, *within* themselves.

Seekers consistently relate that every aspect of healing they have encountered in their holotropic journey has been generated, not by the fiat of some external individual, group, or technique, but from a mystery at the core of their deepest selves. They share with us that, whatever this mystery ultimately is, for them this experience is the true heart of the holotropic practice. In our work, we often call this profound power within by a most humble name: the *Inner Healer.*

For those of us whose life adventure involves working with others through Holotropic Breathwork, it is the cultivation and protection of this foundational principle, this inner healing source, that is our sacred, fundamental responsibility when supporting those who come to us with openness and trust. If we as helpers fail at this, either consciously or unconsciously, then our holotropic work becomes just one more bead on the rosary of disempowerment in the lives of seekers.

As we have suggested, at this point in the unfolding of the holotropic perspective, it feels like the right time to at least introduce the idea of a holotropic paradigm. Holotropic work and its associated worldview have not been presented through the lens of a holotropic paradigm in any systematic way so far. For the most part, when we speak of the holotropic, or its underpinnings, we relate how it was birthed from elements within transpersonal psychology, as well as psychedelic research. This is essential information for an in-depth understanding of a holotropic perspective. Yet, at this point, the term "perspective" does not seem to be wholly adequate. We are beginning to sense that the holotropic perspective might possibly be viewed as a *paradigm* related to, but in fact distinct in important ways from the transpersonal paradigm.

For thirty years, many of us have journeyed deeply, via Holotropic Breathwork, resulting in rich, life-changing rewards, for which we are forever grateful. We have also had the great blessing to support seekers all over the world—those in Grof Transpersonal Training, as well as those engaged in inner work solely as seekers. During these adventures, we have rigorously addressed certain essential components of the holotropic perspective that, though similar in many ways to many transpersonal modalities, are in fact unique and specific to Holotropic Breathwork.

We will continue to emphasize throughout this inquiry that the most vital of these components is a total honoring of the individual seeker's power within. Such an honoring radically redefines the role of all helpers, as we will point out by gazing through a number of lenses as we proceed through our inquiry. Yet we hear from many people whom we have supported that it has been often difficult for them to absorb at a cellular level the principles that make Holotropic Breathwork truly one of a kind. In addition, we have experienced a similar difficulty in impressing upon practitioner trainees these nuances unique to the holotropic work. This seems to be particularly true of many excellent therapists rigorously schooled in other modalities who wish to do the additional training to become certified as Holotropic Breathwork practitioners.

Those of us working within the holotropic milieu tend to agree that the reason for this confusion is not so much theoretical as it is experiential. The principles of the holotropic perspective are, for the most part, not too difficult to grasp intellectually. They all center around a core principle which cannot be mitigated in any way whatsoever. This is the inalienable power of the seeker's own truth-revealing inner healing intelligence—what we call the Inner Healer, or perhaps even a power within. The total honoring of the Inner Healer requires that all support people rigorously uphold this tenet. They accomplish this by functioning almost as midwives for seekers, as these inner explorers discover and bring on line for themselves this life-changing dynamic.

Yet to truly operate from the elegant therapeutic poise of these specific nuances often seems to be far more challenging for practitioners-in-training than understanding the rigorous theoretical positions supporting the experiential work. It is this issue—a type of core, experiential blind spot—that, among other related topics, we wish to stress in this inquiry. It is a principal reason why many of us also feel that it is time to be thinking, not only of the transpersonal paradigm and Holotropic Breathwork, but also of a holotropic perspective, and perhaps even a holotropic paradigm. A further motivation for this is that these unique characteristics are what set

Holotropic Breathwork apart from other modalities, even many which are characterized as transpersonal. In fact, these exclusive principles themselves *are* the true indentifying foundation of a holotropic paradigm.

As a workable reference point, it is within the meta-framework of a holotropic paradigm that we will be able to accurately address the profound, indispensable qualities that are the heart and soul of this powerful healing methodology. Many of us feel that a text highlighting the core truths of this perspective may play at least a modest role in ensuring, at this relatively early stage of this method's growth, that Holotropic Breathwork can be nurtured and preserved in its original form and power for many generations to come.

To the Second Octave

Another level of our inquiry reveals an even deeper, more all-encompassing potential within a holotropic paradigm. It is true that such a perspective or paradigm would, in part, owe its character and power to the principles encompassing the transpersonal paradigm. Later we will outline in more detail the basic principles of this revolutionary world view. Yet, in envisioning a holotropic paradigm, at its heart are also those truths unique to a holotropic perspective alone. We have witnessed how transformative the method has been psycho-therapeutically for thousands of people worldwide.

Many breathers regularly report a fascinating phenomenon: that the expansive, inner vistas they have experienced through deep work in nonordinary, or some say meta-ordinary, states of consciousness, are shifting so quickly that none of us dares at this stage to conceptualize just how powerful a revolutionary paradigm may yet be unfolding. Nor have we, until recently, considered what such a far paradigmatic horizon might actually be called. But we are nearly all convinced that the essential value of Holotropic Breathwork lies in one unalterable characteristic innate to this type of deep inner work. This dynamic, as we have said, is the principle we call the Inner Healer, or the power within.

The main question before us, as we take the journey of this inquiry, is this: "In what ways can core reliance on an infallible inner healing resource common to everyone—a power within—be valuable within a global context, potentially involving every facet of the human experiment, both individually and collectively, in our planetary evolution?" The answer to this vital question can be found in two parts: a singular, radical transformative experience; or an incremental process of the death of our false selves; or both—*an ongoing unfolding of in-depth, universally realized self-empowerment*. Many believe that this perspective holds bright promise for humanity, as well as for the biosphere to which we owe our very existence.

Allowed to reach its zenith, the essence of a holotropic paradigm is commensurate with a consciousness shift that could bring to light new facets of what it may really mean to be human. It is, as well, a re-imagining of the very nature and source of *power* itself. It directly addresses the manner in which we human beings wield this power in the individual search for fulfillment, in how we treat each other, and with what positive commitment and regard we may hold the earth and human evolution.

Even though what we are suggesting seems to be, in some ways, new in this current epoch, paradoxically it has been espoused and explored by almost every spiritual tradition in history, including practices passed on from the planet's indigenous cultures. It is a core focus of many modern, unique, yet interrelated movements. These disciplines seem to have emerged from a collective desire to be of service to human beings as well as to Mother Earth, herself. They honor ancient wisdom, but stand on their own in the light of fresh, modern renditions of psycho-spiritual power.

Even with this heartening news, it is ironic how few psychological modalities truly define themselves by highlighting, much less thoroughly relying on, a power within. Even though many therapists and people-helpers profess to be honoring an inner healing source, all too often prevailing therapeutic interaction unconsciously, if not consciously, disempowers seekers. Even though most of these therapists are honorable, loving, and caring individuals, this disempowerment occurs in myriad ways, which we will examine in detail later. But, based on what we have heard from thousands of seekers worldwide, an unalloyed commitment to the empowerment of our true deepest self—not a repeated aggrandizement of our surface or egoic nature—truly seems to be where the next planetary psycho-spiritual adventure—what we may call the holotropic paradigm—may be headed.

This shift offers a priceless opportunity for individuals to radically reset certain self-limitations. These restrictions have been systematically imposed by a core belief that our power, happiness, and fulfillment almost always comes from some outer, or other-directed, source. One of the most prevalent of these outer sources is the current climate of individual and group therapy.

Such a shift as we are now proposing would signify an awakening to, and recognition of, the innate condition in which every human could recognize and fully accept that *the true source of all healing as well as evolutionary power always already resides within themselves.* This can only materialize if we as people-helpers reframe our roles as experts in a host of particular modalities, to simply one of total support and reliance on the power of the seeker to heal herself. This perspective will truly flower when helpers and those who are helped fully recognize, and operate from, the baseline that we all are heir to an infallible power within.

We have heard exciting stories from many who have discovered deep wellsprings of personal empowerment through Holotropic Breathwork, entheogens, and other related modalities. Seekers consistently report how this consciousness shift may well be one of the most significant, revolutionary upgrades for humanity in all of history. It is exciting to know that what mystics have been writing about for millennia is now, through Holotropic Breathwork, potentially available in another sophisticated, modern method of self-exploration.

Even with our excitement about the expanded possibilities within the holotropic arena, it may come as a surprise that we are just not overly invested in the formal establishment of the name the *holotropic paradigm*. It is ultimately irrelevant what such a focus as we are highlighting will be called. What matters to us is that it become as globally available as possible. Our real passion lies in the healing, transformative power of Holotropic Breathwork and the core underpinnings of the perspective itself.

After years of supporting seekers through the breathwork, we are convinced that most holotropic principles are readily transferable to a number of therapeutic settings which traditionally have been labeled incompatible with the holotropic perspective. These would include supporting various groups and individuals in a briefer, yet still viable, frame of time—all without sacrificing the power of the original Holotropic Breathwork. We are also excited that, as far-fetched as this may sound, the holotropic perspective may even have the power to revolutionize a traditional, office-oriented, one-on-one psychotherapy.

Finally, it is our honor and pleasure to invite you on this journey of what we hope will be a valuable adventure of self-discovery. We trust that it may be a gift of knowledge and support on your odyssey toward wholeness, as we delve deeply into the mystery of the Inner Healer, or a power within. We also hope that this text may be a valuable support for the journeys of all those who undertake an adventure into Holotropic Breathwork, the profound gift the Grofs have shared with seekers world-wide for years. With this in mind, we offer you the greeting we often extend to seekers, as we come together in our opening circles: "Welcome aboard!"

PART I

The Transpersonal Paradigm: Language, Method, and Structure for the Numinous Experience

CHAPTER I

On Maps, Methods, and Paradigms

Our inquiry into the power of the holotropic perspective begins with a very brief, general overview of a radical yet ancient way of envisioning reality. To explore in depth this ancient, and at the same time, modern way is just not the focus of this book. There are already many texts available which serve this purpose thoroughly. However, I *will* share a favorite of mine—the first book by Stan Grof I ever read, and one which changed my life.

This amazing text is called *Beyond the Brain: Birth, Sex, and Death in Psychotherapy*. For me, it was a kind of "one-stop shopping" for an in-depth understanding of the transpersonal paradigm, as well as the breathing practice he later named Holotropic Breathwork. For a quick yet thorough exposition on the foundations of transpersonal psychology, I invite you to explore this text.

The perspective Grof shared is the philosophical and experiential womb out of which the holotropic paradigm may be birthed. This womb has also nurtured the fertile beginnings of the latest revolutionary blueprint for planetary evolution: the transpersonal paradigm. Yet, as one may imagine, the early years of this new paradigm, which came into existence in the 1960s, have not proven to be smooth. Transpersonal perspectives have not been readily accepted by the mainstream academic and scientific communities. Many of these, in some respects, still subscribe to worldviews opposed to what a transpersonal outlook implies. History will likely show that this era has been a flash-point of worldviews in collision, the full implications of which will not be apparent for decades.

It's been stated that Stan's work within transpersonal psychology, as well as his and Christina's contribution of Holotropic Breathwork, will not be fully accepted by mainstream seekers, therapists, or researchers for at least fifty years. Perhaps a wider recognition may come sooner, based on what some physicists suspect may be, at this stage of cosmic evolution, a kind of "speeding up." If this were true, it might facilitate, among other things, a shortened cycle of paradigms.

Many seekers—and non-seekers of all kinds as well—often report that "everything is moving so fast." If various modern controversial theories of time hold any weight, we may be in for an even wilder ride than ever before. In this case, our vision of a soon-to-manifest therapeutic norm might very well include Holotropic Breathwork, and an array of modalities derived from the core of a holotropic paradigm—one of which we might even soon be calling a holotropic therapy.

Furthermore, could we perhaps witness an eclipse of the transpersonal paradigm's current incarnation in the not-so-distant future by an even more radical revolution in consciousness? Or, if not eclipsed, might not the transpersonal perspective, sooner than historically expected, reveal break-throughs which even more elegantly refine its own power and influence?

Such possibilities are not as far-fetched as they may at first appear. Systematic work in expanded states of consciousness seems, almost always, to lead us to the edge of wider, more fulfilling vistas of therapeutic and transformational evolution. One of these vistas, which we are referring to as a holotropic perspective, may ultimately prove to be a philosophical and experiential "golden child" of its transpersonal parents.

Before we begin to chart a holotropic frontier, we should touch on the current transpersonal revolution and the radical implications it has had for planetary evolution. We begin with a brief baseline for the nature of para-digms in general, and for the difficulties that attend the occasion of para-digm collision or "paradigm wars," as they have sometimes been termed. Many feel that this is the predicament in which current world civilization seems to labor, as we evolve toward new horizons of consciousness. His-torically, this kind of upheaval is systematic of world cultural shifts. It also seems to be an inherent characteristic of the evolutionary current within the holotropic perspective known as *moving toward wholeness*.

The Curious Case of the Elephant in the Living Room

When they have outlived their time, or when applied inappropriately, para-digms often display an eerie similarity to dysfunctional family systems. We see this in a metaphor used in the recovery and codependence tradition, where, in addressing addiction/recovery, we often speak of the *elephant in the living room*. This metaphor refers to the tendency of a family, or any group, to unconsciously or consciously overlook what is, to an outsider, an astoundingly obvious dysfunctional situation. In the recovery tradition, the elephant is some kind of addiction—chemical, process, or relational. We refer to this tendency of ignoring dysfunction, or the inability to accept it, as *denial*, or the process of being *in denial*.

Not only are addicts within the system in denial, often everyone else in the family is too—those to whom we refer as codependents. Each member of the system is trying desperately to feel better or to get free, as they consciously or unconsciously attempt to help the addicted person recover. Each, again unconsciously, develops a compensatory survival strategy, which frequently backfires and results diabolically in the perpetuation of the addiction. The addiction/codependency dynamic continues unabated until some major crisis—often an illness, legal or social intervention, or a death—shocks at least one member of the system to break free.

When this occurs, there can be a shifting of the tectonic plates of the denial system, which often results in emotional and psychological upheaval within the crystallized family tradition. Over time, either collectively or one by one, family members can then break through their denial and begin the journey of recovery. When this happens, it is as though everyone has emerged from a psychological trance, enabling them to make new choices about their own wellbeing, as well as that of the so-called "identified patient."

These observations mirror our inquiry into a new paradigm, such as the transpersonal, or even a holotropic world view. For any group, this mesmerizing interrelation among various members—in its circle, or outside the group, including humanity at large—often results in a systemic denial of philosophical or scientific breakthroughs, or anomalous data that cannot be explained in terms of the established dominant paradigms. Just as we see this repeatedly in family dynamics, we can also observe it in world cultures. "Buying into" sacrosanct scientific, philosophical, and even religious ideologies, a specifically defined system of thought—what we now call "reality"—can mesmerize a large portion of humanity. This is what we call a *paradigm*.

An octave of this phenomenon occurred in the addictions treatment movement in the late 1980's. A number of us, including Christina and Stan Grof, attempted to provide a broader horizon in recovery and in treatment potential. We sought this by exploring the possibility of a *wellness*, or *transpersonal* paradigm, based on language, method, and structure for the numinous experience and its enhancement of the Twelve Step philosophy. Holotropic Breathwork and transpersonal psychology were also at the center of this possibility, as the most effective "help-mates" to the therapeutic power of the Twelve Steps. We were all excited about the possibilities of this revolutionary paradigm as we moved toward the new millennium.

Unfortunately, the majority in the field chose to relax within the comfortable domain of the status quo. Metaphorically, they elected not to leave the old secure classroom, where the blackboard had already been filled with the equations of the old paradigm. Treatment professionals using strategies, like the Hazelden and Johnson Institute models, stuck to what they knew best. This included rather confrontational group therapy, work on family-of-origin issues, family treatment, codependence work, and, for the addict, Twelve Step meetings in the evening.

Most accepted the traditional medical model and welcomed each new finding about brain chemistry connections to addictions, and the possibilities of new miracle substances that will heal addiction by rewiring the hardware of the brain. However, they chose to ignore the chance to venture into a brand new auditorium, where the whiteboard or computer screen was empty—a *tabula rasa*. They also failed to capitalize on the fresh, and by-and-large, spiritual insights which could have led to a revolutionary, system-wide upgrade. Treatment had become big business, and, as we all know, attractive financial possibilities are often hard to pass up.

It is true that the rank and file of the current recovery paradigm *appeared* to become more sophisticated, but something else actually transpired. In their microscopic exploration of over-specialized nuances in treatment dogma, many leaders succeeded merely in focusing "more and more on less and less." They became even more specialized in the details of so-called axiomatic, unassailable truths. All of this exploration into deeper levels of minutiae occurred while overlooking the richer horizons of a new paradigm altogether.

But there is good news. Today, there are a significant number of recovery pioneers radically challenging the status quo. Building upon a baseline established by Kylea Taylor in the early nineties, dedicated holotropic practitioners Rob Park and Christine Calvert are bringing the holotropic perspective, including breathwork, into treatment centers. The idea of a true transpersonal recovery center is no longer a fantasy, but a viable option being discussed in many mainstream treatment settings.

As in the recovery movement, it has become painfully obvious that, even with the benefits provided by science in the past two-hundred years, almost none of these findings have come without a toxic shadow side. Many well-respected scientists, teachers, and philosophers would currently suggest that through a wide array of economic, military, and political decisions, governments and societies have become addicted to the perpetuation of strategies that may ultimately threaten all life on the planet.

The double-bind for world cultures is that facing the emergence of these painful truths by contemplating alternate ways forward—or thinking outside the box—would probably precipitate a radical destabilization in the global system's prevailing addictive strategy. As we pursue our inquiry into personal and collective empowerment, we should point out that, where the *lack of power* seems to be the problem for the individual, it is often the *addiction to power* that is the issue for big business and government. This strategy seems to have become almost inescapably mired in a colossal, multi-national struggle for wealth, power, or a fanatic religious supremacy.

What was needed was a shift from the addictive focus on unconscious power drives—a selfish or destructive use of egoic power—to the kind of transformative empowerment inherent in reliance on a deep source of power and inspiration at the core of what has become known as our "true self." Through some sort of explicit, implicit, or wholly unconscious agreement, this scientifically and philosophically-based denial, precisely as in addictive family systems, appears to be stifling much creativity and innovation within many bureaucratic systems, governments, or multi-national businesses. However, there is one crucial difference: In this case, the dysfunctional family to which we are referring is a substantial portion of *humanity* itself.

Be that as it may, through philosophical and scientific breakthroughs based on an explication of the transpersonal paradigm, proponents of many disciplines have already embraced radical information powerful enough to liberate us from the paralysis within many intransigent disciplines, organizations, and governmental systems. There are already millions of people worldwide who champion this trajectory of intellectual, scientific, and spiritual creativity. They embody the vanguard of an enlightening trend emerging more profoundly during this current global paradigm collision.

It makes sense why those in power might feel deeply resistant to change of this kind. Confronting the possibility of profound change is often just too threatening. We see this in the case of addicts. Really breaking free of denial can be so painful that it may even feel like some kind of death. Many champions of particular paradigms seem to have staked their reputations and livelihoods on an eternally stable set of scientific and philosophical assumptions. It is as though these paradigms are *entities* possessing a life and power all their own—forces for which they will fight quite creatively, as well as vehemently.

With this in mind, what can we say about this particular elephant in the living room of planetary culture? For our inquiry into the emergence of a holotropic paradigm, based on a radical definition of personal and transpersonal empowerment, this elephant could very well be the critical evolutionary force called *spirituality*, or *numinosity*. It seems essential for planetary survival that there be a deep psycho-spiritual shift in world culture. If so, what might this elephant be trying to communicate to us?

It is fascinating that this presence actually resembles closely the Hindu elephant deity *Ganesha*. Ancient texts reveal that Ganesha is sometimes known as a destroyer of obstacles, or as a fierce advocate of the arts and sciences—even as a deity of wisdom, as well as a lord of new beginnings.

All these are relevant, dynamic attributes that the birth of any new paradigm would certainly welcome.

Yet we usually think of the "elephant in the living room" as a negative force—the power of suffering and denial. Although having a shadow side, this particular elephant may also represent something quite positive. It could be the power required to initiate a moving toward healing, an evolutionary shift from the current malaise causing so much physical, psychological and spiritual suffering globally.

In this current context, the Ganesha theme seems to offer a radical new message of hope: the *power of expanded consciousness for radical change*. Viewing a paradigm collision in a positive context appears essential for us. It will validate our inquiry into what many are referring to as a *wellness model of transformation*. Moreover, many seekers suggest that the principle of wellness must play a central role in any inquiry into a holotropic paradigm.

Throughout the history of the paradigm now coming to a close, we have, for the most part, operated within a *sickness,* or *disease model* of the human psyche. The shift from the disease paradigm to a *wellness model* of human evolution is a cornerstone of our inquiry. The wellness perspective mirrors and affirms an ancient, cross-cultural tenet—that death and rebirth are often intertwined dynamics. These seemingly polar opposites are two integral sides of one powerful healing dynamic, which we might encapsulate as follows: *Through systematic self-exploration, the seeds of stagnation, addiction, and disease can blossom into the flowers of awakening, wellness, and wholeness.* This is the power that the symbol of Ganesha seems to promise as the elephant in the living room of planetary evolution.

Through this bright lens, as opposed to the disease-oriented focus of the elephant in the addictions metaphor, the Ganesha metaphor brings an elegance and sense of hope to all who are concerned with the denial of so many wielding destructive egoic power today. Out of our disempowering addictive behaviors as a species, the symbol of Ganesha appears to promise that through this overwhelming dysfunction can emerge remarkable healing. Out of our ignorance can come wisdom, and out of a pervasive impotence can emerge a radical display of authentic personal empowerment. This is a dream that millions might find hopeful in light of what many all over the world feel is a crisis of current planetary evolution.

The Nature of Reality

Here are a few typical sacrosanct pronouncements characteristic of the prevailing worldview. Proponents of this paradigm often see these as virtually unassailable truths, or scientific facts:

1. The material universe is all that exists, having come into existence through a Big Bang.
2. Consciousness is an epiphenomenon, or by-product, of the brain, and happened to emerge during the course of an extremely long evolutionary process when matter became sufficiently organized and sophisticated for it to appear.
3. If scientists even posit the possible existence of a spectrum of consciousness—such as the extended cartography of Stan Grof, including biographical, perinatal, and transpersonal dimensions, the great majority of what has come to be called non-ordinary states of consciousness—these states of consciousness, whether sane by traditional measurement, or pathological, by similar measurements, arise from biochemical or electrical reactions in the brain.
4. There are no further dimensions to the psyche beyond the personal, or biographical domain, such as a memory or record of biological birth. Nor is there any validity to a realm of consciousness that includes spiritual or archetypal experiences. All these experiences, and the belief systems that are a result of such fantasies, are signs of pathology, which psychiatric and medical experts alone can treat effectively.
5. Spiritual experiences are frequently signs of psychosis, or mental disease. Any evidence derived from experiences of wellness and wholeness acquired by using so-called deep experiential methodology has for the most part not been quantitatively measured by research, and therefore cannot be valid.
6. Appropriate treatment and therapeutic strategies unequivocally reduce descriptions of these experiences to issues arising from within the post-natal, or biographical domain of the psyche—i.e. the moment of birth, up to the present.
7. Spiritual experiences are fantasies, or delusions, and either have a post-natal origin psychologically, or are physically based products of aberrant brain chemistry. They are misguided human urges employing escapist and avoidance strategies, which reflect a basic level of pathology. Licensed mental health and medical experts are the only ones qualified to treat people who are thus deluded.
8. The only effective treatment of these pathological conditions is an astonishing array of psychotropic medication used to chemically alter the hardwiring of the brain and consequently the behavior and mental function of the individual, plus an occasional foray into personal early or later post-natal history by qualified mental health professionals.
9. Beliefs in the existence of other, non-corporeal realities or dimensions of consciousness beyond the basic orientation toward physical reality are deemed to be signs of pathology, as is the belief in the therapeutic

value of non-ordinary, or meta-ordinary, states of consciousness that include expansion or modification of brain-based physical reality.

10. Questions of dissatisfaction with the nature of human existence and the search for fulfillment reflect, and can for the most part be logically reduced to, issues arising from our biographical experiences.

11. Any testimony from individuals who claim that their quality of life has been greatly enhanced by psycho-spiritual experiences is only "anecdotal" and not scientifically valid.

12. There is no real evidence or basis for the experience of multiple dimensions of reality, the power of the spiritual experience, or that consciousness could exist independently of the brain and uses the brain to orchestrate a certain limited experience of reality.

13. There is a belief in a number of scientific and psychiatric schools that, since emotions cannot be scientifically measured, it is questionable whether they actually exist.

Finally, these guiding assumptions also negatively frame our understanding of the journey towards wholeness, which is at the heart of the holotropic perspective. They do this in a number of ways:

14. By inference, then, each of the following can be explained by a number of recognized pathologies and diagnoses, and therefore represent delusional fantasies: the Hero's Journey, as described by Joseph Campbell and others, Carl Jung's model of the individuation process, the one-hundred-thousand-year history of indigenous wisdom, the extended cartography of the psyche put forth by Stan Grof, spiritual practices, and the maps, systems, and experiences chronicled from the so-called mystical systems of the world.

15. Any attempt to move toward wholeness that supports an experiencer to feel that what lies beyond traditional conceptions of reality may also be real and valid, is a misguided, quixotic quest doomed to failure or psychological dysfunction.

16. Any so-called insights derived from such approaches are false, unmeasurable, unscientific, and potentially pathological.

Nearly every conceptual development and experiential practice of the transpersonal paradigm, or its possible offspring, the holotropic perspective, challenge these assumptions, which are at the heart of the prevailing scientific and psychological worldview.

CHAPTER II

The Influence of the Transpersonal Paradigm

The current paradigm collision has been a source of confusion for many seekers. To cover the full implications of this era's adventure with the ongoing shift in worldview is not the focus of this book. However, a quick overview may provide us with a foundation and validation as we explore the possibilities of a holotropic perspective, and the re-envisioning such a perspective may require. Our primary focus here–in alignment with our emphasis on a holotropic perspective and in-depth psycho-spiritual transformation—will be the implications of such a paradigm for the individual seeker.

At one time or another, most of us have had some kind of "false self" or ego-deconstructing, experience. These were either the results of planned explorations into our psyches, or spontaneous episodes that have taken us by surprise. In most instances, these episodes have not led us into pathology, but have actually been the impetus behind a profound life upgrade. It is a blessing that today we can find many sources of psycho-spiritual support as well as scientific validation for our inner adventures.

Over the past half-century, the revolutionary transpersonal paradigm has emerged, which now co-exists with the dominant scientific/psychological worldview of the past two-hundred years or more. Christina Grof and Stan Grof, along with colleagues from all over the world in science, psychology, philosophy, religion, anthropology, mysticism, art, and other disciplines, have written many groundbreaking books on these new frontiers. Pioneers have conducted remarkable research validating what we sometimes call *meta-realities* or *meta-truths*. It is significant that much of this research also reflects perennial validation from the *wisdom of the ages*.

The International Transpersonal Association (ITA) has been one of the most powerful vehicles for the dissemination of this information and research. This organization, founded by the Grofs, has for decades held conferences all over the world, helping to establish a rigorous scientific, psychological, and numinous base for the unfolding paradigm. Verification of the insights derived from the experiences of seekers and scientists alike has the potential to provide the underpinnings of strategies that may eventually support an era of wellness and wholeness for all of humanity.

The new paradigm has cycled through a number of names: It has at times been called "holistic," or "integral." In addition, it has also been presented as a wellness model of transformation. But, one of the most influential designations has been the transpersonal paradigm. "Transpersonal" was the name preferred by Stan Grof when he was working with Abraham Maslow, Anthony Sutich, Jim Fadiman, and others as they sought a revolutionary breakthrough in psychology, science, and other disciplines.

The term *transpersonal* implies, among other things, an intellectual worldview and direct experience of dimensions of reality in which there are no exclusive or arbitrary boundaries between the individual empirical self, or the ego, and the universe at large. In order to be whole psycho-spiritually, we must address both the individual, personal self, as well as our trans-personal, or collective self. With this expanded worldview, we may entertain an entire range of revolutionary perspectives in science, as well as the meta-scientific, or even numinous, nature of reality, the individual, humanity, and the cosmos.

At some point, most sincere seekers arrive at a shared conclusion: If we pursue systematically any psychological or spiritual practice, or any comprehensive method such as the Twelve Steps, the Diamond Approach, the Arica School, the use of entheogens, or Holotropic Breathwork, we will eventually encounter what philosopher Rudolf Otto called the *numinous*, or sacred, dimensions of existence.

In opening to numinosity, seekers also become heir to what seems to be a blessing. This gift is *radical self-empowerment*. True self-empowerment—as opposed to egoic empowerment—emerges through deep work in which the seeker's realizations are recognized as having emerged from within her own deepest authentic self. The companion principle to this realization is that self-empowerment should never be co-opted, or directed by any outside healer or source of support. It is always, already, the seeker's own. This is a cornerstone of our inquiry into a power within, and we will explore this dynamic in many ways throughout our inquiry.

We hear from many seekers the insight that science, psychology, and indeed a number of academic disciplines could be transformed by a universal infusion of these dimensions of numinosity. To implement a new perspective in psychology, these endeavors must be centered in a worldview that includes the sacred dimension as a sign of *meta-health*, not pathology—a point stressed by Grof, Maslow, Assagioli, Jung, and others. Re-visioning many of these disciplines can quite possibly initiate an important upgrade by opening to a radical new *language, method, and structure* for the numinous levels of existence.

As a global culture, it seems clear that, despite the continued entrenchment of many powerful old-paradigm *modi operandi*, we are systematically
implementing a viable experiment in transformation. This multi-cultural
evolution toward a transpersonal perspective has for decades acquired a
heartening level of momentum. It is our hope that an in-depth exploration
of a holotropic perspective can play some small part in helping to midwife
the birth of new transpersonal worldviews.

In addition, if a holotropic paradigm does emerge, its focus on a centerpiece of radical self-empowerment may provide another facet in the diamond of global psycho-spiritual transformation. Many feel that it may
shine a light on an ever-deepening transformative vision of wholeness,
wellness, and personal empowerment for peoples of all cultures.

Whether we are scientists, psychiatrists, or lay people who have done
years of Holotropic Breathwork and/or any of the many other powerful
practices, we are seekers who quite likely have had very effective, life-
changing experiences through our focus on inner work. Many of us might
have also had the great blessing to be witnesses and support for people
around the world in their inner journeys.

Almost without exception, seekers report that the freedom, power, and
wholeness they have realized by engaging in these kinds of practices absolutely cannot be understood in terms of any traditional paradigm. More
importantly, it just does not always seem necessary, or even possible, to
force these meta-truths into an old paradigm way of thinking. When this
has occurred, in many cases, profound psychospiritual experiences quite
likely have been misdiagnosed as pathological.

We hear other fascinating insights from seekers who are embracing
this new worldview. As one takes this journey toward wholeness, the issue
of whether a past life, an experiential identification with the Divine Mother,
humanity, or the cosmos, or whether a reliving of biological birth or a
racial memory is real or true in a scientific or empirical sense, is often not
the most relevant issue any more. To many seekers, what matters for true
inner wellbeing is not its traditional, scientific reality, but its *experiential*
validity. It is important for a seeker because of its transformational power.
Whether it can be externally validated or not, it is a very real experience—
for the one who has it.

When a seeker reports that she has experienced herself as the power of
lightning or become identified with a hawk, a quark, or an oak tree; or has
experienced the grief of all humanity for all time, it can be very empowering for her to, first and foremost, trust herself. This can be true, even though
she may sometimes feel the need to be validated by various disciplines of
a leading edge of science or psychology, such as those provided by the
transpersonal perspective.

Ultimately, she may come to trust deeply that these experiences may not be factually true, but are absolutely *experientially* true for *her*. What is often important, however, is that, along with the support of growing edge scientific research, she feels validated by other seekers who have made the journey before her. They can be people she has met, or she can receive much support from time-honored texts of spiritual practices chronicling the same kinds of experiences she may be having here in modern times.

For example, there is a shamanic and indigenous heritage of powerful psycho-spiritual relevance that has existed in global cultures for at least 100,000 years. Based on what has been handed down from generation to generation, these practices have survived the ages still vibrant in their actual, literal experiences and applicability in modern transformational settings. Many of these practitioners hold no formal degrees. They often recognize no external bureaucratic authority to "certify" or validate them for the power of their inner experience and learning. Nor are they regularly given degrees to verify their ability to support others in their own inner work. Their sources of validation are the realized truth of their inner experiences, coupled with the affirmation they have received through the healers and teachers in their own particular lineages for thousands of years.

A modern seeker in current psycho-spiritual settings often arrives at the realization that the experience she undergoes is vaster, more multidimensional than that recognized by the traditional scientific community, with a level of authenticity that sometimes can be independent of outside validation. She has opened to a level of, what is for her, deep, uncommon truth for which there may be no name or reference point in any source upon which she may have previously relied.

But by far the most relevant truth is that, whether empirically real or not, these experiences have changed her life in a fundamentally important way. She feels better. She may even feel that she *is* better. She feels more whole. Her life experience has perhaps been upgraded in lasting and profound ways. The capstone realization is often a gift of a foundational self-empowerment sometimes independent of the need for outside validation from teachers or therapists. She has found her Inner Healer, or power within.

It is the task of her "helpers, guides, and allies"—to quote Byron Metcalf's CD title—to be supporters and co-adventurers with her on her journey—her midwives, if you will. What many seekers ultimately learn from this kind of support is perhaps the most important element of any spiritual practice. As we will often stress through our inquiry, this vital element is the *empowerment* that emerges through the ever-more-profound trust each seeker has in her own deepest self—what we call, to keep it simple, her Inner Healer, or a power within.

She knows she can seek outside help at any time when guided by her Inner Healer. But at some point, she often comes to believe that she no longer needs to continue the self-worth-reducing practice of always turning her psyche over to so-called experts when many of the solutions to her life challenges she can now find deep within herself. She also recognizes that this sometimes seemed to further cement what has been for her and many others a lifelong, systematic episode of disempowerment.

Many opponents of a transpersonal, comprehensive, integral, holistic, wellness, or holotropic paradigm will argue that this seeker's experiences are not real or valid because they have not been sufficiently researched. Nor, in fact, can they ever actually *be* measured. However, supporting evidence does exist. Though not always essential for everyone, verification and validation through the findings of consciousness research is without question valuable for many people. This is particularly true for seekers who seem to be standing at a critical crossroads of their own personal evolution.

There may be millions who are "on the fence" or "on the cusp" of powerful internal change. For these seekers, it may be that research is the critical jump-start they needed to begin the inner journey. People will often read or hear about so-called "groundbreaking" research, "proving" that a certain theory is the final word of truth. Unfortunately, for many, theories can actually attain a false aura of irrefutable validity. These "facts," which almost always turn out to be, in truth, nothing more than metaphysical assumptions, can tragically create a disempowering reliance on so-called external experts.

Historically, we seem to have a selective memory. If we look back through any traditionally defined record from the past, nearly every pronouncement or theory "verified" during that era has been rejected in light of new findings. At some point, the wondrous latest insight almost always gives way to new research and the pronouncement of a new true worldview. These so-called "true truths" then negate once again the last *final word*, which came before.

However, on the heartening side of this perennial issue, there has been, for at least fifty years, a substantial body of groundbreaking research in many different disciplines, even the so-called hard sciences. The historic Spring Grove work, done by Stanislav Grof and his colleagues, using LSD for the treatment of a variety of conditions, including alcoholism and drug addiction, were the path-finders of this validation. With the re-emergence of psychedelic research here in the modern era, these studies will have proven to be absolutely seminal.

Currently, evidence-based research validating breathing practices such as the Vipassana approach from the Buddhist tradition has also been incredibly valuable in a number of modern therapeutic settings, including the treatment of addictions. It is also a real validation for consciousness pioneers that research in the use of entheogens has once again found a place in a number of university settings and various clinics throughout the world.

Some of the most exciting present-day possibilities are a timely continuance of the work done by Grof and his colleagues decades ago. These current efforts have been funded and supported by the vibrant organization MAPS, the Multidisciplinary Association for Psychedelic Studies, founded by Rick Doblin. It has increasingly become a powerful world force for establishing the efficacy of the kinds of strategies we have been discussing. Much of MAPS's success is the result of Doblin's irresistible passion and keen intellectual rigor through decades of reaching out to proponents of traditional science and psychiatry.

A Psycho-Spiritual Therapeutic Synergy Comes Full Circle

As I pointed out, when I was twenty, I had a life-changing experience with a psychedelic substance. I had already been ingesting these substances for a few years, and would for ten years more. If it were not for this experience, and other life-changing episodes in expanded states of consciousness over that period, I could not be sharing this expression of my gratitude for the miracle of transformation, my power within, and of course, entheogens, Holotropic Breathwork, and Christina and Stan Grof.

From here, we will explore another encouraging phenomenon that holds much promise for the emerging holotropic paradigm, including a holotropic therapy. There is already substantial multi-cultural validation for the use of breathing practices to facilitate meta-ordinary states of consciousness. Unquestionably, Holotropic Breathwork holds a legitimate place within the lineage of these practices. In preparing to unveil a holotropic therapy and other holotropic possibilities, we should first focus on the synergy between entheogens and Holotropic Breathwork—two powerful methodologies, born from the same womb.

Many seekers report excitement for the unfolding of this powerful new therapeutic paradigm. We will share a few of the revolutionary possibilities inherent in a psychedelic and a holotropic therapy based on the core principles of a holotropic perspective. As we know, the holotropic strategy is already used to support seekers in their work with entheogens. Many journeyers, including those holding space for others in their psychedelic exploration, are engaged in both Holotropic Breathwork as well as exploration with entheogens. Considering both methods, then, we appear to be looking at a modern inner practice with enormous potential.

The deep connection between therapeutic use of entheogens and the holotropic perspective began in the Prague laboratory after Grof's first LSD experience. He initiated his entheogen work with others, knowing, in a sense, nothing. Out of this unknowing—this fertile emptiness—emerged, first, a deep trust in the psyche's ability to heal itself. He correctly intuited that, just as his own deepest self had been the unerring guide on his profound inner journey, this same inner guide within each person would be the healing force for those with whom he and his colleagues would subsequently work.

He knew that the journeyers themselves would show him how their transformation and true in-depth empowerment occurred. The insights he garnered from his own inner work, and from those hundreds for whom he "held space"—providing non-directive support for their inner explorations—would be the source of his teachings and the many books he subsequently wrote. This unknowing would continue when his entheogen research was ultimately declared illegal. It was from this setback, however, that Holotropic Breathwork would emerge as the serendipitous child of the long but ultimately temporary hiatus of psychedelic research.

Grof has never failed to champion the Inner Healer, or as we are also presenting it in this inquiry, a power within. Nor have the core practitioners of authentic Holotropic Breathwork failed to honor the revolutionary transformational power already at work within seekers the world over. The therapeutic strategy has always been the same for both methodologies.

As entheogen work is becoming once again a legal force for in-depth psycho-spiritual work, the critical power of trust in the seeker's own inner resources remains the benchmark of authentic deep self-exploration. What began with entheogens, and proceeded to be honed and perfected with Holotropic Breathwork, has once again become the benchmark for working with others in expanded states of awareness.

For example, with the support of MAPS, psychiatrist Michael Mithoefer and Annie Mithoefer have done exciting, leading-edge research using the compound MDMA for sufferers of PTSD, or Post-Traumatic Stress Disorder, and have met with paradigm-changing clinical success. The Mithoefers have now recently completed a successful study, applying the same practice and criteria with returning Iraq and Afghanistan war veterans who also suffer from PTSD.

And with MAPS, they will be starting larger studies around the country in 2017, in order to apply to the FDA for MDMA-assisted psychotherapy, using the holotropic approach, to become an approved legal medicine for clinical use. In addition, they are in the process of completing a program for veterans, fire fighters, and police officers with PTSD.

Their successful outcomes are opening wide the doors on a more universal acceptance of the healing potential of work in expanded states of awareness, beyond the methods espoused by the prevailing paradigm. It is worth noting that the Mithoefer's strategy in working with their clients is, they report, based on their experience as certified Holotropic Breathwork practitioners. It was in this transformational milieu that they worked systematically with the holotropic strategy for their own growth and to support the growth of their clients for many years.

It is important to also acknowledge the work of Diane Haug, one of the original holotropic pioneers, and a close friend and colleague. She and I, along with Kylea Taylor, Laurie Weaver, Jim Frazier, Cary Sparks, and others, spent many hours together facilitating in the early days of the Holotropic Breathwork training in the U.S.

Among the modules Diane teaches as a part of the Grof Transpersonal Training program is *The Psychedelic Experience: Promises and Perils*. Diane is an instructor in the "Psychedelic-Assisted Research and Training" certificate program started in 2016, at the California Institute of Integral Studies (CIIS). In this context she introduces participants to Holotropic Breathwork and the holotropic perspective as part of their training and preparation for becoming the psychedelic therapists and researchers of the future. Her important contribution is a validation that the synergy between Holotropic Breathwork and work with psychoactive substances is a realistic, viable transformational partnership.

Seekers who have supported others in their own inner work often report a profound realization, as valuable for them as psychological research. This is, that the more we work on ourselves, through any kind of deep psycho-spiritual practice, the more fulfilled and authentically empowered we will be. Through this sense of profound personal empowerment, many feel that we would have a greater chance to address the almost insurmountable problems our world cultures face. These would include the very real scenario of the extinction of the human race, and quite possibly the destruction of all life on the planet.

The perennial philosophy, transpersonal psychology, a wellness model of the psyche, and a new holotropic perspective, can, and have already, become part of a viable, realistic strategy for addressing world problems. These perspectives are particularly valuable when their experiential components occur in safe, supportive sessions midwifed by helpers who are themselves dedicated seekers and who absolutely know that they are *not* the directors of seekers' processes. These support people hold to the inherent truth that all real and lasting growth is mediated by the inner healing resources of the individuals doing the deep experiential work.

Seekers' Choice: Entheogens or Holotropic Breathwork

It is well known that entheogens have been an integral part of world culture for millennia. Ritual use of psychedelic substances is often touted to be a true deep root of the perennial philosophical tradition. When we consider that Holotropic Breathwork has been an influential practice for less than a half century, it seems irrelevant to attempt a comparison of these two approaches—breathwork and entheogens—from the perspective of longevity. However, because they both seem to have blossomed from the same deep roots, it may be helpful for seekers if we delve a little deeper into what seems to be a powerful therapeutic synergy.

Psychedelics have been recognized perennially as one of the most powerful transformational tools on the planet. What thickens the plot is that modern seekers report that through Holotropic Breathwork, they are able to access many, if not all, of the same dimensions of the psyche as are available through entheogens: the biographical, perinatal, as well as the transpersonal or the collective domains. Nevertheless, there is a relatively common belief that the breathing practice is just not as powerful as entheogens. However, this perspective may be changing.

To illustrate this, we will share a few of the revolutionary possibilities inherent in a psychedelic/holotropic therapy based on the core principles of a holotropic perspective. As we pointed out, the holotropic strategy is already supporting seekers in their entheogen work. Many journeyers, including those supporting—or holding space—for others in their psychedelic exploration, are also engaged in both Holotropic Breathwork and exploration with entheogens. We appear to be looking at a modern inner practice with enormous potential. Seekers are already reporting a significant overlap in transformational power between entheogens and Holotropic Breathwork.

In the last decade, comparisons between the two methods—entheogens and Holotropic Breathwork—are more nuanced and well informed than when the breathing practice was in its infancy. As opposed to the one-dimensional *either/or* perspective we often heard early on, what we now hear appears to be much more of a *both/and* situation. Actually, a "comparison" between the two disciplines—especially to determine which is "better" or more powerful—does not seem to be the relevant issue. It feels more important to share a few stories, and to open a dialogue where seekers can begin to envision a mutual spirit of exciting, powerful healing possibilities. A beneficial outcome of such an inquiry might be a cooperative level of enthusiasm and camaraderie on our individual and collective adventures of self-discovery.

Here is a cross-section of what some seekers have reported: Some say that with Holotropic Breathwork, they just could not get to the true depth of inner experience that they reached with psychedelics. At the other end of the continuum, seekers share that with entheogens, they sometimes "flew right by" many pressing, relevant issues and patterns, and spent their sessions in a glorious, light-filled, but psychologically less focused world. Although these points seem to represent extremes—and are of course not true for all seekers—there is also broad common ground for many journeyers.

An age-old truth relates that no two seekers are alike—in life experience, psycho-spiritual makeup, or what has come to be known as karmic unfolding. Every voyager has a unique life trajectory. Each seeker is blessed with an infinite capacity for individual preference. Each choice she makes is perfectly correct and relevant within her own individual experience and her understanding of the inner and outer universe. Once again, this highlights the centerpiece of our inquiry: that the only true trajectory and value of any seeker's life path should be orchestrated by her own power within.

For years, there was a baseline belief that, although psychedelics and Holotropic Breathwork opened consciousness to all three dimensions of the psyche—the biographical, perinatal, and the transpersonal—for sheer, dynamic inner exploration, nothing seemed to surpass entheogens. A comparison between the two is all the more difficult due to the large variety and dosages in entheogen use. Many are naturally occurring, with little or no need of laboratory synthesizing, such as certain species of mushrooms. Some are laboratory-synthesized from naturally occurring plant substances, as well as a few derived from the animal kingdom.

Experienced inner voyagers often report quite a few similarities between many of them. But they also share that there are fascinating nuances that render each unique. All of this indicates that we probably have only scratched the surface of psychedelic potential. With this in mind, it is difficult to make an all-encompassing comparison between Holotropic Breathwork and psychedelics. Yet, we can relate a few observations that seem to be relevant.

Many entheogen users share that when they try breathing practices, even though they open to meta-ordinary states of consciousness, they often just do not seem to get as "expanded." Or if they *do*, it just seems to take a lot longer. Many report that the ease with which most substances act makes them preferable to utilizing a practice often involving quite a bit more systematic physical effort, such as sustained deep breathing.

To put it colloquially, with entheogens, one just gets "more bang for the buck." Yet, this type of comparison strikes many seekers as being overly simplistic. Many seekers report that they have had just as powerful, life-changing experiences with Holotropic Breathwork as they have had with psychedelics. In nearly every case, they recognize that they were able to experience their own deepest healing dimensions—the Inner Healer, or power within.

Whether psychedelics are more powerful depends on exactly what we mean by "powerful." If we are referring to the often explosive, rocket-like blasts into the mysteries of an inner space or the far frontiers of consciousness that are often characteristic of experiences under certain entheogens, then psychedelics can definitely be termed extremely powerful. In addition, in terms of sensory vividness, many feel that psychedelics are unrivaled.

However, over the course of decades, we have supported many seekers who have systematically worked with entheogens as well as Holotropic Breathwork. And what we hear from these adventurers covers a broad spectrum of experiences and opinions about the intense nature of their healing experiences in *both* milieus. All comparisons aside, it is clear that entheogens represent a powerful initial catalyst for a psychedelic or holotropic therapy. A story from Stan's early history highlights his recognition of what we might call the therapeutic "cross-over" power of psychedelics to Holotropic Breathwork and, ultimately, to a possible holotropic/psychedelic therapy.

When he was working in Baltimore, he heard in London a lecture of two psychoanalysts, Pauline McCririck and Joyce Martin. In their work, which they called fusion therapy, they would give their clients a high dose of LSD. Then, for the entire session, they would hold them in a nurturing fashion. Intrigued, Stan visited them, and decided to experience their method of working. He took LSD, and for the entire session, he was held by Pauline. According to Stan, this was one of the most powerful therapeutic experiences he had had with entheogens, and opened an exciting new frontier for him.

He experienced an extremely positive episode of symbiosis, or union, with the feminine. There were several levels to his journey. One was a biographical experience of being nursed by his mother and having a deep, loving connection with her. In another, he experienced a deeper octave of the same experience—connection with his mother already in her womb. In both of these experiences, the contact was mediated by the flow of life-supporting liquids—milk flowing through the breast and blood flowing through the placenta.

The third component involved an expansion into the transpersonal domain, where he had an extremely powerful experience of being nurtured in the arms of the Divine Mother. During this dissolution of boundaries, he was able to absorb a profound sense of connection and union with the divine—a mother/child archetype of oneness that was tremendously healing for him. Afterwards, he had the insight that this kind of work had enormous therapeutic potential for seekers who had experienced compromised relationships with the original mother figure. He had witnessed from his work with entheogen clients how common this kind of trauma was.

This is what he termed a "trauma of omission," as opposed to "traumas of commission." By this, we mean that, in the first case, a journeyer has not received the nourishment she needs as an infant or young child. In many cases this absence of a loving atmosphere was also an experience in the intra-uterine episode. Among the most important of these healing powers is the profound connection—both physical and emotional—with the mother.

Instead of leaving the seeker with a trauma that needs to be excised by deep work—a trauma of *commission*—she experiences a powerful emptiness that can only be filled by the experience of connection—by being physically held by someone while in the expanded state of awareness and regression to either the womb or the earliest post-natal. Or it can also include a transpersonal dimension associated with separation from the Divine Mother.

Or perhaps it could be an archetypal experience of what it would be like to be every child at once, in separation from every mother. On the other hand, a trauma of *commission* leaves a wound that must be removed through deep work. In this case, the correct intervention often involves a number of sessions with holotropic focused release work to clear the psyche of the traumatic overlay. We will explore these two kinds of trauma in more detail later as we outline the extended cartography of the psyche.

However, this was one of the first opportunities Grof had to understand how the psychedelic experience might be translatable into a therapeutic milieu without entheogens. Of course, the most obvious alternative—and one of equal therapeutic power in this context—would be Holotropic Breathwork. We have been overwhelmingly validated in working with *traumas of omission* hundreds of times in the world-wide holotropic training. In fact "the power of *holding*" a breather is one of the most profound applications of the healing potential of Holotropic Breathwork.

To continue, another interesting interlude comes to mind—this one from the very earliest trainings. During that era, a few seekers would take

LSD during the regularly scheduled breathwork sessions in the modules. This came to be known as "power breathing." It was supposed to be a secret, because Stan and Christina had made it a rule that there would be no psychedelic use during the modules. One reason was because Stan was, at that time, "on the radar" of law enforcement agencies due to his world reputation as a proponent of psychedelics. He and Christina just did not want to do anything that would jeopardize the training, thereby depriving many seekers of the healing potential of meta-ordinary states in a safe and legal space through Holotropic Breathwork.

They also felt that, since this was a breathwork training, the strategy should be to focus on the use of the breath—to see just how powerful this methodology might be. It was clear at that time—although this has really changed in the last few years—that the public might be more likely to embrace a non-drug method than they would one derived from ingestion of psychedelics. Also, Stan felt that, to do both at the same time was, in a sense, "mixing metaphors." Since he already knew how amazing psychedelic work could be, he was really excited to find out just how powerful the use of breath might also be in accessing deep states of consciousness. So, he was adamant about keeping the training substance-free.

We also witnessed on a number of occasions in the training a rare, rather tragic, and disconcerting phenomenon relating to the dance between entheogens and Holotropic Breathwork. Since Stan's earliest work in Prague, there was a "diaspora" of psychedelic methodology all over the world within a wide variety of settings. One of these was the work of a pioneer whose approach to psychedelic therapy was absolutely the polar opposite of how Stan worked with his clients.

This teacher's modus operandi was to create for seekers—while they were under the influence of the psychedelic—a quite violent and frightening scenario. For example, he might play discordant music, specifically chosen to be upsetting. In addition, he would show movies with violent, bloody, or otherwise frightening imagery. His strategy was to orchestrate an external setting in which the ego, or false self, could be radically shattered, thereby setting up an experience of transformation.

The external manipulation of a seeker's psyche goes against *everything* we hold sacrosanct about our strategy with either psychedelics or Holotropic Breathwork. To begin with, the holotropic strategy *never* involves an attempt to manipulate the client from the outside. The goal is to create an environment that fosters a seeker's reliance on her own Inner Healing power. From our perspective, there is absolutely no reason to orchestrate the ego death externally.

The Inner Healer is quite capable of setting this up in Her own time, from within. Death and rebirth are intrinsic qualities of the human psyche, as well as the archetypal journey toward wholeness. There is nothing we can add that could enhance the inherent benefits of this internally empowered, natural process. We would add that, without question, to subject seekers to violent external attacks is totally unethical and, quite truthfully, should be considered criminal.

In our training, we had the unfortunate opportunity to witness the psycho-spiritual damage this kind of approach had created. A few seekers came to us, quite wounded, whose lives in the world had become nightmarish, after their experiences with these types of practitioners. Instead of becoming liberated through the death/rebirth process, they had been violently traumatized. To make things even worse, they left those settings with inner processes unfinished—wide open.

One reported feeling like a ghost in the outside world, each waking moment a horror of the late third matrix in an archetypal overlay of torture and pain. The third matrix is the last stage of the perinatal process before physical birth, or psycho-spiritual death/rebirth. We will go into more detail on this and other stages of the birth experience in a coming chapter.

Their experience with us first involved a reliving and a healing of the compounded trauma they had experienced in the previous setting. This repairing of trust and a re-establishment of safe boundaries must take place before a seeker can once again open without fear to the unconscious material compounded during the previous unethical episodes. In our work—whether it is with psychedelics or Holotropic Breathwork—the core, unassailable baseline is safety and protection. The benchmark is that our setting should always be the safest haven in the world. We devote ourselves wholeheartedly to keeping seekers spiritually, physically, mentally, and emotionally safe.

On a different note, stories we have heard and episodes we have witnessed may be surprising to some inner adventurers. In the late eighties, a couple of close friends in the holotropic community and I had the opportunity to "sit for"—or support—a former colleague of Stan's in Baltimore, Maryland, during his first Holotropic Breathwork session. This man was a researcher, and worked as an integral team member in the program Stan led at the Maryland Psychiatric Institute. The research in which they were engaged was the basis for much of Stan's groundbreaking theory on the power of expanded states of awareness.

The journeyer was quite awed by his holotropic experience. He reported that it was as powerful as any of his experiences with LSD. His session took him through the perinatal and into the transpersonal domain of consciousness. In addition, he had a powerful numinous episode, for which he was extremely grateful. It had been many years since he had taken psychedelics.

He reported that having the breathwork experience was a serendipitous renewal of his faith in the healing derived from contact with the far reaches of the psyche and his own Inner Healer. He also felt surprised that these states could be accessed simply by doing deep breathing with evocative music. In addition, he was grateful for the presence of caring people who supported his journey without trying to be directive in any way.

The purpose of sharing a spectrum of experiences occurring in expanded states of awareness serves to demonstrate just how unique all seekers truly are. It also offers a choice for journeyers, who may have previously thought that psychedelics or breathwork alone were the only methods that could be of therapeutic value for them. In the adventure of self-discovery, there appears to be no exclusive, or sacrosanct truth, no dogma etched in stone, to determine the relative power of one strategy over another. As always, the one true director of a seeker's choice is the Inner Healer. First and foremost, if we have any inclination toward transformation, we must listen to that inner voice, trust, go seeking, and find our own truths, as well as the methods most suited for each of us.

It becomes clear that there are just too many variables in human predilection and experience to state unequivocally that one strategy is better than another. In the broadest sense, every experience is, of course, an individual one—a tableau perfectly orchestrated by the individual's inner healing resources, and specifically relevant for that particular moment in time and space. We must always take into account a number of factors. First, of course, would be the life history of the individual. And when we speak of "life history," we would have to include the seeker's individual astrological chart—both the natal chart and the transits at the time of the session.

Even though to bring it up, out of the blue, as they say, we cannot stress enough how valuable archetypal astrology has become for those of us working within the transpersonal or holotropic perspective. It has emerged as one of the most effective transformational support strategies for seekers working in meta-ordinary states of consciousness today. We will go into greater detail about the power of this psycho-spiritual treasure house later in our inquiry, when we focus on an explication of a holotropic therapy.

However, we must mention the groundbreaking work of Rick Tarnas, begun at the Esalen Institute with Stan four decades ago. The archetypal astrological perspective has become an essential adjunct to transpersonal/holotropic work and is being taught today by Rick and many colleagues, including my close friend and fellow Holotropic Breathwork practitioner and training teacher, Matthew Stelzner. I am happy to mention, as well, Keiron Le Grice, who I am tremendously grateful to have as the editor for this text. As an aside, we can almost guarantee that any seeker who attends a lecture given by Stan will hear at least a mentioning of the power of archetypal astrology to enhance any type of psycho-therapeutic undertaking.

These examples offer just a cursory glance at the issues and experiences of seekers using either psychedelics, Holotropic Breathwork, or both, in their systematic practice. Our inquiries into these frontiers appear to affirm one essential observation: that both entheogens and Holotropic Breathwork are very powerful and effective for individuals on the journey toward wholeness.

Of course, we have barely touched on the subject. There are so many fascinating nuances yet to report. To fully honor this synergy would be the work of many books. However, it seems worth-while that we mention it here, particularly in light of Michael and Annie Mithoefer's work, as well as Diane Haug's, within the holotropic support framework that we mentioned earlier. Many of us are really looking forward to how this fascinating synergy will unfold in the years to come.

CHAPTER III

Stanislav Grof and the Birth of the Transpersonal Paradigm

A universe vista that includes, and is in fact born from, the numinous dimensions of existence—plus language, method, and structure for this numinosity—is an essential element of the transpersonal paradigm. Yet the *Rosetta Stone* at the core of this revolutionary perspective may not yet be totally deciphered. Through one lens, it seems reasonable to suggest that the transpersonal era may be largely grounded in Stan's initial LSD journey in the Prague psychiatric clinic. His first psychedelic episode was an experience of profound numinosity. When he shares this experience with groups, it appears to be as powerful as any such episodes recorded in many of the world spiritual systems or chronicles of individual, transformative episodes.

Many of us also feel that this is the heart and soul of our inquiry into a holotropic perspective. As unscientific as this may sound to some, Stan's first psychedelic experience seems to have been visionary. As a result, his life work, which blossomed from this experience, has been guided by a worldview as expansive as that of any of the world's great psycho-spiritual systems.

Recently a colleague from the Spring Grove era introduced Stan at a conference, referring to him as, among other things, a mystic. To be clear, Stan himself has *never* presented himself to the world in this fashion. Nor has he ever considered himself to have played such a role. But many of us feel that future chronicles of this era will, one day, validate the truth of this possibility.

A perhaps more palatable reframing of this proposal might be that his life work has involved presenting *the power of numinosity within a scientific, philosophical, and psychological framework*—or, as we say, providing *language, method and structure for the numinous experience*. If this sounds unscientific, yet at the same time carries a ring of truth, then you are in good company. Undoubtedly, the essence of what Stan has taught and written about—and what he continues to share wherever he goes—can be, to use a line from *The Matrix*, a "splinter in the mind" of many from within a host of traditional, old-paradigm disciplines.

A certain spiritual tradition aptly points out that, "A pick-pocket only sees pockets." A metaphor we employ frequently through this text reflects a similar notion. When speaking of an individual's worldview, or her understanding of the human personality, or one's personal take on any aspect of life or cosmology, we have often used the phrase "through the lens of." Here is a simplified example to demonstrate how this lens metaphor works: "Looking at the world through a lens colored by a personal, perinatal, and transpersonal pattern of love and wellbeing, an individual has a good chance of believing that this is true of her universe, as well as then experiencing an external environment full of love and wellbeing." In short, the lenses through which we look help to define our reality.

This mechanism—how we at least co-create our reality based on the condition of our conscious or unconscious inner motivations and latent psychological material—also applies to how a group of thinkers views an innovator, or psycho-spiritual revolutionary, such as Stan Grof. Through the years of ITA conferences for which my wife Cary and I have worked, as well as through many interactions we have witnessed between Stan and other teachers and seekers all over the world, and including the books I have read of his work, this "pick-pocket" metaphor seems to be valid. By this, I mean that, in many instances, for scientists, Stan is essentially a scientist. For psychologists, his contribution has been psychological. For philosophers, he will be remembered as a philosopher. And for psychedelic yogis, well, he is the cosmic cowboy "par excellence."

It seems that, as we embrace our teachers, we often, consciously or unconsciously, reshape their messages to specifically validate our own worldview. But when we do this, we often diminish the richest profundity of these pioneers' gifts—the breadth of their influence, and the authentic power of their messages. We often internalize only what we are capable of understanding, or what validates our own entrenched positions.

The rest—that which we cannot quite accept, or just plain do not understand—we ignore, or consign to triviality or to a twilight world of mere tangential relevance. It can be just too threatening to give up our hard-won credentials, as well as the kudos from admirers in which we revel. Few of us relish questioning what we think we know. It is more difficult still to actually embrace the fullest, iconoclastic implications of what another pioneer may be offering us.

When we evaluate our teachers primarily through lenses already colored by what we cellularly hold to be true, we can sometimes lose substantial impeccability in our inquiry. Through our fear-generated rigidity, we might unconsciously attempt to "pigeon-hole" revolutionaries into worldviews with which we are comfortable. When we do this, we could be reducing the true power of their teachings, instead of allowing ourselves to open without judgment and resistance to theirs. Nowhere is this dynamic more glaring than when we confront the great mystery of numinosity—that farthest horizon of human potential that always looms ahead, challenging us to dare the unknown. Even more, embracing the "mystery" often spells the ongoing death of who we are and what we think. Here once more is our old friend, Ganesha, in the living room of our consciousness—the always greater truth we are staring in the face, but are reluctant to acknowledge.

This situation underscores an historical truth: For many lineage-holders of any status quo, the periodic presentation of revolutionary philosophical upgrades can frequently lapse, after a number of years, into a kind of sterile, stodgy, repetitious, comfortable, and non-threatening orthodoxy. This observation, in turn, presages the occurrence of what we have referred to as a paradigm collision. If we read chronicles of scientific or psychological revolutionaries—or any renegades of the human potential era—we will almost always get a picture of their travails in communicating their inspirations within an idiom that forces, or at least nudges, proponents of traditional worldviews beyond the boundaries of their own safe, sacrosanct ideologies.

However, when we scan our current paradigm collision—between a primarily materialist/scientific perspective and a worldview centered in numinosity—we find that we may now be in territory significantly more disconcerting than any other time in the history of paradigm collisions. Before the current epoch—the one birthed from Stan's first experience with LSD and the work of other pioneers—many crises of difference seemed to have been based more on contrasting *philosophies*, each defended by so-called uncontestable scientific discoveries and facts. Of course, Jung also struggled with the theological and scientific establishment (and with Freud), trying to accommodate the numinous. In addition, Teilhard de Chardin was forced to contend with the Jesuit order because of his revelation of the inherent spirituality of matter and evolution.

In reality, all of these supposedly "scientific" pronouncements are theories masquerading as unassailable truths—and often nothing more than metaphysical assumptions. Among these many assumptions, two seem particularly relevant for our current inquiry. The first is that matter is the fundamental basis of existence. A second untouchable tenet is a psychological perspective limited to the unquestioned basis of a human postnatal history alone. This would include the so-called "truth" that consciousness is an epiphenomenon, or by-product, of human brain development.

Debate in support of any of these past paradigms-in-conflict seems to have been authenticated by whoever might present the most convincing *intellectual* argument or paradigm-circumscribed research. This entrenched orthodoxy of "assumption-become-truth" has, for the most part, relegated numinosity to the realm of pathology. Or, at best, numinosity is branded an unprovable fantasy devoid of intellectual or scientific gravitas, and consequently not worth studying. However, in the world at this moment, all bets are effectively off. The truth is, the entire modern game changed, that day in the Prague laboratory, where Stan first took LSD.

From that moment until now, within the world of paradigmatic debate, the stakes seem to have become infinitely higher. The search for truth is no longer about differences of opinion, no matter how elegantly supported by rational, intellectual rigor they may be. It has ceased to be a mere theoretical conflict, no matter how cleverly proponents of the traditional paradigm may seem to affirm various, ever more infinitesimally circumscribed points within the current litany of their so-called unassailable scientific facts.

Nor does it seem any longer relevant or, for that matter, valid, to propose a dialogue highlighting the comparison of minutiae under either a physical or mental microscope in order to justify an opinion or a belief, no matter how strongly it may be felt emotionally. On the day Stan returned to the hylotropic, or matter-oriented dimension, from his inner experience with LSD, the issue no longer concerned whose blackboard seemed to be filled with the most complex, paradigm-bound justifications. Finally, once and for all in our current epoch, the most profound focus of inquiry could no longer actually fit into *any* classroom, or upon any blackboard, at all.

Many feel that our current paradigm collision operates like the old story of the traveler who was lost, and who then asked a passer-by for directions. With much good will and considerable detail, the passer-by described, one after another, a host of ways for the traveler to arrive at her destination. After each set of directions, he would say, "No, wait a minute—that's not quite right." Then he would offer an alternative path; and each time, he realized that the new route he proposed was not going to get her there either. Finally, he seemed to brighten up—to arrive at an important conclusion. He smiled, and turned to the traveler, and said, "You know, come to think of it, you just can't get there from here."

This is exactly the problem that proponents of a new paradigm have when they attempt to make a case for their new perspective with someone entrenched in a worldview so long established that many see it as reflecting an unalterable truth. Believe it or not, most people will not see the elephant in the living room, even when it is sitting right next to them. You just cannot "get there" through mental gymnastics alone. As we said, this collision can no longer just be about changing peoples' minds—about "out-intellectualizing" them—or simply presenting a better argument.

From another angle, a true, in-depth psycho-spiritual understanding of this current transpersonal or emerging holotropic perspective cannot be gleaned from reading a book, or from merely studying this, or any form, of psychology or science. It can only be truly grasped by a *radical change of consciousness*—one that will bring about a whole new way of being, thinking, and feeling altogether.

Transformation is just not about belief. It is about *experience*. This is why this paradigm collision has been so vehement and so difficult. "One just cannot get there from here"—not without a revolutionary rearrangement of consciousness. Even if this latest transpersonal paradigm, or our proposal of a holotropic perspective, sounds intellectually rigorous—even if they appear intriguing and entertaining—this will almost never be enough. It just will not effectively mobilize this in-depth shift of consciousness in the entrenched majority—in those who champion the latest orthodoxy and who are lulled to sleep by comforting metaphysical assumptions.

However, it is heartening how many individuals, who later report that they have been "on the cusp" of this radical shift for some time, have been able to open experientially to numinosity—intellectually, philosophically, as well as intuitively. After these seekers have experienced their breakthroughs into the new paradigm, upon looking back, they often recognize the "splinter in the mind" that had been plaguing them. They share that by scanning the past through the clear spotlight of their new state of consciousness, they see how they had been preparing themselves through their life experiences for the culmination they have recently achieved. They have the core recognition that they have undergone a life-changing paradigm shift—an upgrade in consciousness much more profound than a mere change of mind.

Deep inner work reveals that the universe is not a mere mechanism. Instead, it appears to be *ensouled*. But it is extremely difficult, through mere belief alone, to absorb this in-depth, life-changing realization. Many of us have been rudely confronted with the fantasy that the systematic acquisition of what we consider to be new ideas, or greater levels of physical comfort brought about by ever more refined manipulation of the physical environment, have been the most relevant purposes of human evolution.

It has often felt altogether too threatening to entertain the notion that consciousness is the fundamental fabric of existence. To a host of seekers, this possibility can seem like a fairytale. The idea that life flows with an intelligent trajectory, guided by this uncannily powerful, wise, and loving evolution of consciousness, can only be the babble of a delusional dreamer.

Many leading transpersonal teachers, in a sense, "scratch their heads." They report being simply bewildered by how difficult it has been to even get others' attention, much less to create a rigorous base of evidence supporting the reality of an ensouled universe. They often share that it has not been easy to witness their life work being dismissed as fantasy, or even psychosis. Yet, their task has been absolutely essential, and an authentic labor of service and love.

However, for those of us "in the trenches" with seekers, authentic transformation often appears to be coming from primal, mostly uncharted human resources altogether. A seeker just cannot always get "here from there" without some powerful shift in consciousness encompassing, not just a change of mind, but a *change of heart* as well. After deep experiential work, journeyers often report that they are no longer looking for the latest theory, but for a continued, fertile relationship with the inner and outer cosmos. This is what aboriginal elder Uncle Bob Randall calls *kanyini*, or *interconnectedness*. For many, a fresh, radical appreciation for in-depth personal, psycho-spiritual and emotional experience becomes more valuable than the acquisition of knowledge alone.

Of course, seekers feel gratified and supported by the rigorous scientific foundation created by transpersonalists over the past decades. Many are excited because the only validation they could find previously occurred, not in a college curriculum, but from the wisdom of the ages. This body of numinous knowledge has frequently validated what they have experienced in Holotropic Breathwork, or through entheogens and other experiential methods. To have found kinship in sources derived from what many teachers are calling modern yogas, spiritual practices, or mystery schools has been a real blessing. Now that research and university curriculums are "catching up" with perennial philosophy, seekers seem to be entering a golden age of psycho-spiritual inquiry.

To sum up this stage of our inquiry: One can rarely, if ever, "get there" through the head alone. Most seekers report that they can only undergo in depth psycho-spiritual change through inner experiences capable of accessing all levels of human and supra-human consciousness. Many also feel that they are beginning to hear the siren call of traditions yet to be born. They intuit that they themselves may have a part to play in the greater consciousness that is evolving. This is also what we are referring to by the emergence of a radical, multi-leveled *self-empowerment* for individuals and humanity.

In the past, it might have been easier to negotiate a paradigm shift by simply a change of mind, in the ability to *think about* existence differently. However, ideas or thought-forms are just not sufficient to transform a transpersonal or emerging holotropic worldview into a viable reality. This will take *experience*. But, in the case of true change, experience is just not something that we *do*. It is something that *happens within* us. This is what separates the emerging paradigm from all that have gone before. It is also why the collision we are currently experiencing has felt so difficult, threatening, and at the same time profoundly exciting.

As we turn to Stan Grof in the Prague clinic, here is a fantasy, simplifying what actually took many years to unfold. After the radical dispensation of numinosity he encountered during his first LSD experience, he returns to *hylotropic*, or matter-oriented, consciousness. He opens his eyes . . . it is the same laboratory. He sees the same machines to drive brain waves and various instruments to perform other experiments on the human brain. This is the brain, incidentally, which was *known absolutely* at that time to be the physical basis and originator of consciousness. This is the consciousness that, according to the scientific status quo, just *happened* to emerge—like magic—at some point in evolution.

Stan flashes through the teachings of Freud and his followers—the rigorous training he has had in the psychoanalytical perspective. He is wide open. He sees the world with new eyes. He thinks and feels with radically transformed faculties. With acute clarity, he is confronted with those principles of his training which seem to have been etched in stone—what he now begins to see as a kind of sacrosanct pathology. These assumptions, which are called scientific facts, include the axiom that the human psyche is limited to post-natal biography—that birth memories, archetypal experiences, and spirituality are indications of serious pathology.

He recognizes that the philosophical and therapeutic bases for these so-called facts have become totally unassailable—that there is no place whatsoever for the possibility that he may have actually undergone an authentic, transformative experience. Nor would these experiences be recognized in psychiatry as radical healing mechanisms with unlimited potential for consciousness evolution. He scans the standard psychiatric practices of his day. For perhaps the first time, he is amazed that anyone might consider electro-shock, lobotomy, and other horrific practices as standard operating procedures, or as safe, legitimate, and humane strategies to ensure optimal psychological functioning.

After undergoing this profound experience—one, incidentally, for which he could only find validation later in ancient mystical texts—just where was he to go from here? With whom could he share the truth of what he had experienced? To whom could he turn for camaraderie, support, and validation? In what current modern psychiatric tome would he find a grounded validation for what he felt might not only *not* be a sign of psychosis, but might in fact be an indicator of an optimum psychological health undreamed of before then?

How could he even hint at the possibility to his mentors and peers that what he went through might augur recognition of an unlimited numinous inheritance available to all human beings? How might he orchestrate a way to present the unparalleled psycho-spiritual implications of this kind of experience as a valid strategy for all human beings in what he saw was a natural, inherent evolutionary trajectory toward wholeness?

The rest, as they say, is history. From this initial revelation—and moving through the overwhelming resistance of an entrenched orthodoxy of psychiatric and scientific assumptions masquerading as uncontestable truths—these are the questions for which he and his colleagues found answers, and the changes they proceeded to make. With fifty years of research and the publication of many ground-breaking texts; through the intimate, life-changing encounters he has had with thousands of seekers in holotropic and psychedelic sessions; supported by the camaraderie he developed with his peers; and the sharing of himself with millions all over the world, we have the answers to "where he went from there."

It is natural and inevitable that scientists, looking through their own particular educational lenses, have said he is a scientist. Psychiatrists, looking through their's, will avow that he is, of course, a psychiatrist. Philosophers and proponents of many diverse disciplines have sought to make him the "poster boy" of their own visions. They have done this through a ubiquitous human inclination: Most of us seem to cement our interpretation of *reality* through lenses colored by our own paradigmatic frameworks and life experiences.

Yet, there is, without a doubt, an elephant in this living room. Its presence represents a wide, crystal-clear vista that encompasses, and transcends, the breadth of these circumscribed lenses we have mentioned, and hundreds more as well. Stan, and many of his colleagues, have always sought to view existence through the clearest, brightest, most all-encompassing lenses as possible.

Any seeker may clearly see, in every text he has ever written, the meta-truth, the unlimited lens through which shines every nuance of his vast, comprehensive revelations on the nature of human, planetary, and cosmic evolution. It is through this widest of lenses we are all invited to gaze, as we outline the transpersonal paradigm, and unveil the extraordinary implications of the holotropic perspective as yet another catalyst for planetary evolution.

The Birth of the Modern Psychedelic Era

As we gaze through one of these lenses, we can make a compelling case for how the transpersonal paradigm blossomed from the early psychedelic research of Stan Grof and his colleagues in Prague, Baltimore, and other centers of this new frontier of the consciousness revolution. In terms of the therapeutic potential of transpersonal approaches, an important breakthrough for Stan was that healing happens in what he called *non-ordinary states of consciousness*.

The second milestone presents a revolutionary lens through which Western psychology might view the human psyche. By observing for years the process of clients in psychedelic sessions, Stan concluded that the traditional biographical understanding of the psyche was inadequate and did not reflect the full spectrum of consciousness and healing potential that becomes available during a psychedelic session, or any form of deep, systematic inner work powerful enough to access expanded states of awareness.

The result was the formulation of an extended cartography of the psyche, based upon repeated observations from these psychedelic experiences. This map included the personal, post-natal biography espoused by Freud and his followers. It also included a dimension that contained the record of biological birth, along with an experiential continuum of what he called psycho-spiritual death and rebirth. Moreover, there was a third, or transpersonal, dimension similar to, yet more comprehensive than the collective unconscious as presented by one of Freud's most famous colleagues, Carl Jung. We will go into much more detail on the extended cartography of the psyche as mapped by Grof soon in our inquiry into a holotropic paradigm.

The third major component of effective psychedelic work concerned the therapeutic strategy adopted by the guide who supported, or "held space" for, the client. This radical alternative to traditional therapeutic support suggested that every important healing mechanism from psychedelic work is a function of the journeyer's own psyche, and not the result of any therapeutic intervention from the outside. In other words, *the role of the therapist changed from being the director/healer of the inner process, to that of supportive guide and co-adventurer.*

This radical shift resulted in a profound sense of personal self-empowerment for the seeker. Secondarily, it has often fueled an inner crisis for many therapists who had been taught that they were the experts in relation to their clients. This was a central catalyst for the paradigm collision in the psychological arena we discussed earlier. We will revisit these insights in greater detail later in our inquiry.

This chapter leads us closer to the emergence of the holotropic perspective from psychedelic research and its parent, transpersonal psychology. It was a breakthrough for Stan to leave Czechoslovakia, and to play a central role in the groundbreaking psychedelic exploration taking place at the Maryland Psychiatric Research Center, and at John Hopkins University in Baltimore, Maryland. Here, he carried out much of his historic research into the efficacy of psychedelics as a potent tool for psychological, or psycho-spiritual, growth. It is well documented how, through government regulation and a culture-wide, fear-based backlash, the program was ultimately shut down. Things seemed bleak at this point for the future of psychedelics and consciousness research.

Yet, it was exactly because of this potentially disastrous situation that the holotropic perspective would emerge as a viable, non-drug co-strategy side by side with psychedelics. This emergence helped to ensure the continuity of the triple healing dynamic we mentioned above that had blossomed from the psychedelic work. The new incarnation of that strategy was a perspective using breath instead of an entheogen as the catalyst for transformation. This takes us from Baltimore to Big Sur, the Pacific coast, and the Esalen Institute. It was here that Holotropic Breathwork was born.

The Inner Healer: The Pearl Beyond Price

To state a holotropic mantra: *The most essential foundation of any authentic psycho-spiritual practice is the experience that all true power of transformation comes from within.* We cannot stress this enough. It is the cornerstone of our exploration. It is the lynchpin of a holotropic perspective. Seekers using any deep method that opens them to non-ordinary, or as we mentioned, meta-ordinary, or expanded states of consciousness almost unanimously report that everything we need to heal—everything—always already exists within us.

This is a core principle of virtually every spiritual system in the world. It appears to be valid, even if a select few misguided teachers of these ancient traditions periodically co-opt and misuse these truths for their own personal gain. It is the very heart and soul of Holotropic Breathwork—the nucleus around which every other holotropic strategy revolves. It is the principle that may elevate Holotropic Breathwork, from its function as a modern strategy alone, into the domain of world spiritual practices.

The existence of an internal source of healing and transformational power common to all human beings is certainly not something Stan Grof discovered. It has been an integral part of psycho-spiritual systems, philosophies, religions, and practices for millennia. However, he experienced this source's action within the psyche, through his own inner work and his support of his clients using LSD, and later through the Holotropic Breathwork. He repeatedly saw, in himself and others, that the psyche seems to have an intrinsic ability to make available to seekers what is physically, emotionally, psychologically, and spiritually relevant for their healing.

This dynamic functions as an inner "radar," or as a spotlight, which throws light on, or brings into awareness, what is essential for a seeker's transformation at a particular time.

He also observed how, from a complementary angle, unconscious material becomes available through the function of *consciousness* itself. It seems that, before the activation of the inner healing mechanism, unconscious contents of the psyche exist in varying degrees of stasis, or "coagulation." Unmanifest, and in some way "free agents" behind the scenes of our lives, and seemingly beyond our control, they are wellsprings of unconscious motivations. These motivations in turn seem to order the evolutionary unfolding in our lives.

A psychoactive substance, or a breathing practice, activates the inner self's inherent healing power. This power then mobilizes the unconscious contents of the psyche. When activated by whatever strategy is employed, these previously immobile or static contents can be converted into what we might call a "stream of energy." At this point, this stream of energetic, intra-psychic material emerges into consciousness, or the awareness of the experiencer.

The ability of the experiencer to become conscious of, or aware of, this unconscious material, plus the complementary ability to embrace, surrender to, or accept, whatever emerges, constitutes the healing or transformational dynamic for the individual. Healing seems to occur through an inherent "cooperation" between the inner healing source and consciousness itself. *In fact, it appears that consciousness and the Inner Healer are one and the same dynamic.* They are two poises, two interrelated complementary characteristics, of the same process—like water and wetness, or fire and heat.

This Inner Healer, or power within, has been repeatedly referred to globally through the centuries, in virtually every mystical text and metaphysical treatise. It goes by a host of names, many metaphorical or even anthropomorphic in nature. Among the most often used are terms such as *soul, Higher Self,* atman or *jivatman.* In his Integral Yoga, Sri Aurobindo refers to a dimension of this force as the *psychic being.* By this, he did not mean the more pedestrian definition of the word "psychic." In so-called occult circles, *psychic* refers to a supraordinary, yet still limited, extrasensory dimension. However, Sri Aurobindo chose the word "psychic" to refer to a structure of consciousness that was a function of soul, in an alignment with its classical definition, which comes from the Greek, and, in fact, means *soul.*

For many in the helping profession, the designation Inner Healer may sound simplistic, unscientific, unsophisticated, or even quasi-anthropomorphic. For something to be this important in such a revolutionary psycho-spiritual system as Holotropic Breathwork, it seems that the term ought to be more clinical or technical, or at least have a more profound moniker. For those who prefer a more rigorous, clinical basis for our inquiry, in his original findings, instead of just calling it the Inner Healer, Grof sometimes spoke of this power as an "inner self-healing intelligence."

Yet even this nod toward an academic and scientific "rigor" was not convincing enough for him to use it in every setting. In the principles of Holotropic Breathwork—the blueprint for the Holotropic Breathwork training—he and Christina once again returned to the straightforward, unambiguous roots of this powerful dynamic. In this training document, they call the primary transformational force the Inner Healer. This name is so minimalist that many professionals seem to have a difficult time, either to understand it intellectually, or to internalize it deeply enough to put it into practice with seekers.

It feels impossible to overstate the pivotal role that the Inner Healer dynamic, or a power within, plays in the holotropic domain. After outlining the birth of the transpersonal paradigm, and unveiling the holotropic perspective, we will continue to revisit the Inner Healer in a variety of essential contexts. Among the issues we highlight will be the priceless gift of personal empowerment. These gifts represent the core of a radical perspective, both for seekers as well as helpers, who themselves undertake the holotropic journey. In addition, it is essential to address the challenging paradigm collision that therapists will often face when confronted with the power of the Inner Healer in their work.

The Gestation of Holotropic Breathwork

At Esalen, where he became scholar-in-residence, Stan recognized that, even if the use of psychedelics was problematic, this did not spell an end to the healing potential in working with meta-ordinary states of consciousness. Through his study of world mystical systems, mystery schools, shamanism, rites of passage, and other practices, he knew that there were many alternatives to psychedelics effective enough to benefit seekers. With these alternatives in mind, he developed a fascinating, powerful transformational strategy that took place in a month-long format.

Esalen is an absolutely magical setting. It is one of two places in the world that remind me of the mythic land of Rivendell, a home of the elves in Tolkien's masterpiece *The Lord of the Rings*, which Peter Jackson recreated with such astounding beauty in his movie trilogy. The other is the mountain haven Montserrat in Spain, one of the homes of the Black Madonna, a mother goddess figure known all over the world. The Esalen landscape is so powerful that a seeker often need just be there, and partake of its beauty, without engaging in any other transformational practice, to be transformed in some uplifting way.

Stan's strategy was to organize a theme for a month-long seminar—for example, shamanism, Tibetan Buddhism, or new findings in modern physics. He would invite world-famous presenters in these fields to teach throughout the month. In addition to the educational material and specific practices teachers would offer, he also provided one standard modality—a *breathing practice*. This practice evolved, in a quite unlikely fashion, into the Holotropic Breathwork we know and use today.

His first inclination to use a breathing practice at Esalen emerged from his work with psychedelic journeyers in hospital research settings. Particularly toward the latter half of a session, a client might report that he was feeling physical tension. He might ask Stan to work with him to help relieve the tension. Under the direction of the client, Stan would offer supportive physical contact that seemed to intensify, and most accurately reflect, what the seeker was requesting.

Later, the client would share that, after the body work, he once again went more intensely into his inner process. There, he would often access deeper levels of whatever physical, psychological, emotional, or spiritual patterns he had been confronting when he initially asked for Stan's support. Stan noticed, and the journeyer would report, that, at first, the seeker's symptoms intensified.

Next, after the intensification, there would be a release from the symptoms. Stan also noticed during these times that the journeyer would often engage in spontaneous episodes of a deeper, faster breathing. When he brought this to the client's attention after the session, the client reported that the deeper breathing seemed to intensify, and then ultimately help to resolve, whatever issues were emerging at that time.

These personal observations, secondarily validated by the historical precedent of the use of breathing practices to facilitate non-ordinary states of consciousness around the world, solidified for Stan the transforming power of the breath. These reasons, coupled with the fact that psychedelics were now illegal, convinced him to offer a deep-breathing strategy during the month-long residentials to enhance the power of the natural environment and the theoretical presentations offered in the groups.

Christina Grof and the Alchemical Foundation of the Holotropic Perspective

Before Christina met Stan, she was in the vanguard of two important lineages that would play an essential role in the underpinnings of Holotropic

Breathwork. First, she was a close friend of world-renowned mythologist Joseph Campbell, with whom she had studied at Sarah Lawrence College. This friendship fostered her deep connection with, and ready access to, transpersonal dimensions of the human psyche.

Second, she was a favorite disciple of Swami Muktananda, a master of Siddha Yoga, which was known to be one of the most sophisticated, powerful spiritual systems to emerge from India and take root in the West. Through the yogic practices derived from Kashmir Shaivism, the foundation of the Siddha system, Christina was already well acquainted with the process of embracing deep unconscious material, as well as the power of the numinous dimensions of the psyche.

Yet other important life experiences she was undergoing magnified even further her role in the birth of Holotropic Breathwork. When she met Stan, she was engaged in an extremely powerful psycho-spiritual event that, although virtually unknown in the West at the time, was well known in India and other countries. This process is called a *Kundalini* awakening, an overwhelming confrontation with what can aptly be described as the central, primal spiritual force and source of all creation.

Christina was not a scientist of the new paradigm. She was already *living* the new paradigm within her being. This intimate acquaintance with the forces of psycho-spiritual birth, death, and rebirth enabled her to be the perfect co-creator with Stan for the birth of the holotropic paradigm. One of the cornerstones of the esoteric tradition derived from *alchemy* is a union of the feminine and the masculine principles. This union has been called the *sacred marriage*. The individual, in this case, is the holotropic perspective. And of course, the two complementary principles that are "married" are the contributions of Christina and Stan. It is also interesting that later, Swami Muktananda would refer to the couple as *Shakti* and *Shiva*, or the two primal creative forces of the feminine and the masculine in the Hindu tradition.

Christina, Stan, and the Birth of Holotropic Breathwork

With Christina and Stan together, the breathwork and holotropic perspective began to take deeper root, in preparation of its ultimate flowering. Along with her exquisite presence on the floor with breathers, Christina imbued the process with a rich depth of artistic expression, which became essential to the integration process of the breathwork. Yet she was also blessed with an aesthetic sensitivity to music and a deep connection with, and understanding of, world symphonic and rhythmic sources. With these gifts, she was able to fashion the musical accompaniment to the holotropic journey that in such a profound way upgraded the transformational possibilities of the deep breathing.

However, there was one final piece of the holotropic mosaic that was about to fall into place. This capstone would signal the true birth of Holotropic Breathwork and would indelibly imprint the strategy as a radical, revolutionary philosophy, methodology, and paradigm, as well as a unique contribution to perennial philosophy. Here is how a breathwork session was set up, prior to this breakthrough:

The breathers would lie in a circle, heads toward the center. The Grofs would play the music, and participants would begin the deeper, faster breathing. When someone would go into process, the Grofs would assist him or her with whatever was emerging from the psyche. Often, this work would be a catalyst for another participant to go into process. And the Grofs would then work with this other person. When everyone was complete for that day, the group would take a break, do some integrative artwork, and then return to session later for further integrative sharing.

Now, in the middle of one month-long group, an amazing serendipitous crisis occurred. Before the morning session, Stan was working in his garden, and there he injured his back. He was in such pain that he did not believe he would be able to support participants that afternoon in the scheduled breathing session. So, he and Christina devised an alternative, emergency plan.

Instead of every participant breathing at the same time, they asked the breathers to pair up. One member of the pair would be the breather in the session, and the other would be the "sitter," or the protector of the breather's space. Then, in the next session, the roles would reverse. And the one who was the sitter first would be the breather, and the one who was the breather would be the sitter.

When they experienced the breathing this way, participants were astounded by what happened. They each felt that the process had been way more empowering than before, for a couple of very important reasons. First, as sitters, they touched a much greater level of responsibility for the care of their breathers, whereas before they knew the leaders, the "experts" Stan and Christina, would support them. This experience of "holding space" was just as transformational for many of them as the breathwork itself.

When they were breathing, they found that something similar also happened. They discovered that they were relying on deeper healing resources within, as opposed to looking toward someone outside themselves, like Christina or Stan, to be the fixer or the healer. It was also very moving how deeper connections and more profound relationships flowered between the breathers and the sitters. In short, the whole session seemed transformed, enriched, and upgraded.

What was the difference, then? The most profound change was that the power within, which came to be called the Inner Healer, irrevocably emerged as the primary healing mechanism in the work. As we continue to highlight, this is a truth known by most of the world's powerful spiritual traditions. And, an absolute commitment on the part of facilitators to safeguard this truth—the power of the *Inner Healer*—has been, and will always be, the most profound principle of this work.

It remains the component that indelibly separates Holotropic Breathwork from so many other methods in traditional as well as even transpersonal psychology, and even in modern renditions of perennial philosophy. As we move toward a holotropic paradigm, it is also the essential cornerstone of our inquiry here, including the unfolding of a holotropic therapy, or any of the holotropic applications we will address later in our inquiry.

We are essentially exploring the domain of *personal empowerment*, one of the most sacred, irreducible components of true individual transformation. We are not referring to the power of what has been called the ego, or false self. In this case, we are speaking of the empowerment of what may be termed the authentic self, or even the soul self—what seems to be a personal dispensation of the "Unlimited Divine." This empowerment can only occur through a radical awakening to the presence of the Inner Healer within ourselves.

This leads us undeniably to this fact's companion requirement: a fierce commitment from all helpers to recognize and honor this power in their clients. The shift must take place that we, as supporters, understand thoroughly and operate from this poise. Furthermore, we must come to believe, absolutely and authentically, that we, in no way whatsoever, will ever know what is best for anyone else.

Now that we have recounted the birth of Holotropic Breathwork, we can focus on some of the principles we touched upon in the last few paragraphs. It is also the time to take a first look at the extended cartography of the psyche, which offers an unlimited field of transformation available to seekers as they engage in these kinds of deep experiential work.

Breath

Breath, of course, is the medium, the driving force, of the holotropic perspective. If we examine any of the psycho-spiritual strategies that make up the *wisdom of the ages*, we will find some focus, whether substantial or tangential, on the power of breathing practices to change consciousness and to mobilize the healing power within a human being. It is fascinating that there are also a number of root words from various cultures demonstrating an intimate connection between breath, spirit, and life force, all of which are variously recognized to be essential components for transformation.

For example, the Greek word *pneuma* means both *soul* and *spirit* and *breath*. The word *psyche*, of course, is the root of psychology. Yet an earlier connotation has been translated as *soul*. An even deeper, original meaning of psyche was the *breath of life*. In the Hindu tradition, there is a powerful breathing practice called *pranayama*. Pranayama is a derivative emerging from two Sanskrit words: *prana*, which means life force, or vital energy; and *ayama*, which means to extend, draw out, or control. Chinese systems have the same word, *chi*, for both breath and life force. These are just a few of the amazing, nearly identical, cross-cultural connections on the nature of breath and transformation.

This is clearly no historical anomaly. These similarities are a strong validation for a globally coherent body of wisdom of the power of breath within perennial philosophy. They represent a direct thread linking Holotropic Breathwork with world mystical and philosophical systems. Breathers in our work begin to experience for themselves what they have read about in various schools of yoga and transformation.

They often get the insight that, as humans, we seem to operate through multiple interrelated life systems within what we call our body. Some of these are not physical but energetic. They are often referred to as *subtle bodies*. And we often hear from many who do Holotropic Breathwork systematically that the power of breath operates somehow on a continuum, interacting with these systems.

At the outer, surface level of the continuum, breath is a carrier of oxygen and nutrients for the maintenance of physical wellbeing. Obviously, without breath, the body dies. At a more subtle level, breath becomes *prana*, or what some traditions call vital force. This level has often been called the astral body, or the vital level in certain systems. This subtler force seems to comprise another body somehow interpenetrating the physical body. At a still deeper level on the continuum, seekers are able to experience in the meta-ordinary state more energetically or refined bodies, or sheaths, as well.

Ultimately, many feel that they discover access to, or awareness of, even more subtle, and some say more spiritualized levels. These strata have been variously termed the causal body, or the mental body, or sometimes the psychic or soul level of consciousness. Seekers often report a sense that breath is the medium for carrying various streams of activating force that, guided by our Inner Healer, transform, revitalize, and basically upgrade the evolution of the individual.

There are as many interpretations of what the breath is, and how it functions, as there are seekers. These interpretations change almost as fluidly and as often as one experiences the meta-ordinary state. It is in no way necessary that any of these experiences we are recounting here be deemed essential for transformation. When all is said and done, the bottom line is: *"Breath works."*

We have learned that, even though there are hundreds of quite sophisticated breathing practices from perennial philosophy, many of which have been modified and are being utilized today, it is clearly not necessary to make the holotropic breathing too complicated. Just by lying down, closing the eyes, and doing some simple, regular breathing—a little bit faster and a little deeper than we ordinarily breathe—healing can happen for us in ways we cannot possibly imagine.

Non-Ordinary States of Consciousness

Through our discussion on the nature of paradigms, we have already explored the theme of non-ordinary, or meta-ordinary, states of consciousness. However, we did so rather peripherally to our central purpose. So, for clarity, and to demonstrate the crucial role it plays in our inquiry, we will bring the concept into sharper focus here.

Healing happens in meta-ordinary, or expanded states of consciousness. This truth straightforwardly reveals the most vital relevance of this principle for the purposes of a holotropic perspective. To define what we mean by a non-ordinary state of consciousness, it is first helpful to explain what we mean by an *ordinary* state.

In the early days of our association with Stan Grof, he often purposely offered a rather pedestrian definition to "keep it simple," as they say in Alcoholics Anonymous. He called an ordinary state the "hamburger stand, rush-hour state of consciousness." This amplifies this state's "ordinariness," and the fact that it is by far the most prevalent way the vast majority of human beings consistently operate in the world, and for the most amount of time in their everyday lives.

There are many observations, some quite technical, on the difference between ordinary and non-ordinary states of consciousness. But here is a fairly simple one that helps to clarify these dissimilarities. In an ordinary state of consciousness, we are more or less exclusively identified with our bodies and our egos, or our separate, or what are sometimes called our false selves. The boundaries of what or who we are as human beings extend to an experience of our physical bodies, coupled with, for the most part, self-centered, individual thoughts and emotions that we experience as being generated by the hardwiring of our brain and central nervous system complex. In addition, we also seem to be bound by time and space.

It is important to interject again a few words here on our use of the term *ego*: By ego, we are not referring to its clinical Freudian definition. In that system, the ego is part of a triple dynamic composing a structure and function in the human psyche. The components of this structure are the id, the ego, and the superego, where the ego, in simple terms, is the principle that enables us to function in everyday life. In our context here, however, the ego refers to what we call the *false self*. It is a term used frequently in transpersonal and spiritual systems.

We often speak of the tremendous importance of the *ego death* in deep experiential work. For obvious reasons, we would not want the Freudian principle of the ego to die. Yet, the incremental episodes of the death of our *false self* open us to greater and greater octaves of wholeness, which is our objective for this holotropic paradigm in the first place. We will spend much more time on the nature of the ego death later, in many different contexts.

Based on what we just covered on the nature of an ordinary state of consciousness, we might then say that a non-ordinary state implies a consciousness where we are no longer exclusively identified with our bodies and egos. In these states, our consciousness, unfettered with the exclusivity of a self-focused limitation, is free to identify with any part of, or the totality of, existence. This implies an experience of all that is known or unknown, in so-called existence, or not.

It also would include experiential identification with any level of what we commonly call imagination, inspiration, philosophy, metaphysics, mystery, fancy, or hallucination. And we could even go so far as to envision it containing what is called in Buddhist parlance *tathagata*, or, in essence, that one, or thing, which has gone "beyond the beyond." In short, this would imply identification with "all that is."

In essence, we may experience that consciousness and awareness seem to be synonymous. However, there are those who, in the pursuit of a more rigorous specificity, sometimes view what we think of as awareness, particularly its personal focus, as being simply a function, or subset, of a larger field of consciousness. Another metaphor may be helpful: States of consciousness, whether ordinary or meta-ordinary, are like distinct, or sometimes overlapping universes.

Each of these universes exists within a certain set of observable, experiential laws or parameters. They are recognized by what we *think, perceive, or emotionally feel* about them when we experience them. In short, they are known by their qualities, or characteristics. So, we humans, in a sense, either spontaneously or through the use of various experiential strategies, can become voyagers, or explorers, of these various realms or universes—these states of consciousness.

In addition, freeing ourselves from our exclusive identification with the body and the ego, and opening to the possibility of countless other universes, or realms of consciousness, would definitely be essential to our goal of *moving toward wholeness*. With these thoughts in mind, we are naturally led to one more issue essential for an understanding of a holotropic paradigm. This concerns our opening line on this topic: *healing happens in meta-ordinary states of consciousness*.

In order to understand this aphorism, we should address what we mean by *healing*. This is a crucial line of thought. It will reveal itself throughout our exploration to have multiple, ever-unfolding levels of nuance and insight. By healing, we are referring to an individual evolutionary process of psychological and spiritual—not just physical—unfolding that leads to ever more expanded levels of wholeness. The question is, "What is the basis for our suggestion that healing is associated with meta-ordinary states of consciousness?"

Our justification comes from the personal experiences reported by seekers everywhere, who have confirmed this to be true for themselves. This truth is based upon their examination of the dynamics of every significant upgrade they have undergone in their wellbeing—whether it was a spontaneous, single episode, or one that occurred over a period of time. Upon self-inquiry, they realized that, in virtually every situation, in the moment of the upgrade or the healing, their perspective of consciousness was radically realigned in some significant way.

In short, the consciousness realignment was extra-ordinary, or supra-ordinated to their everyday awareness. This realignment was so profound, that from one moment to the next, they experienced that they did not seem to be the same person they were before. The shift in who they thought themselves to be from one moment to the next was often a convention-shattering episode. What's more, they felt that the consciousness shift itself, and the experience of greater wholeness, were somehow inextricably interrelated.

In a sense, these two seemed to be functions of each other. This unified function was nearly impossible to describe without including both elements of the dynamic. The most valuable insight was that this radical shift unveiled profound new vistas of consciousness on how they saw themselves and the universe around them. To be metaphorical, the healing experience and the non-ordinary state of consciousness were two poises of one essential manifestation, like, as we said once before, water and wetness, or fire and heat.

A Disease Model of the Psyche

A holotropic perspective, or paradigm, paves the way for a wellness model of the psyche, as well as a system of revolutionary psycho-spiritual healing strategies. We know of no other perspective, that, for all intents and purposes, treats every emergence from the psyche as an opportunity to heal, presented to the awareness of the seeker by her own deepest inner healing resources—what we may call a power within. As a prelude to this radical unfolding, and the healing possibilities inherent in such a revolutionary return to the psyche's psycho-spiritual roots, it is not far-fetched to suggest that psychiatry as we know it today has been inherently flawed from its inception.

By making, from the very beginning, such metaphysical assumptions as the "fact" that consciousness is an epiphenomenon of matter, or the brain; that spirituality is a sign of psychological dysfunction; and that the psyche is a totally post-natal affair, pioneers in psychology appear to have stripped the psyche of its cosmic status. Seekers can discover that the psyche is so much more than our every-day process of mentation, or our personality, or even what we believe to be irrevocably true.

Ultimately, it seems as though we have the ability to experience the psyche as commensurate with the farthest horizons of consciousness itself—in essence, equal to all that is. This is what we mean by our "cosmic status." As such, it will always dare us to be open to the ultimate mystery of existence itself. It is the full embracing and celebrating of this realization—plus a radically self-empowering transformational strategy like Holotropic Breathwork—that may separate a holotropic paradigm from virtually all of its evolutionary predecessors.

As a result of the loss of the psyche's cosmic status, when viewed through some current psychiatric lenses—which often reframe what is merely an interesting belief system into a scientific fact—a tragic shift occurred: A host of psychological and physical phenomena, which for centuries had been considered natural signs of the psyche's urge to move toward health and wholeness, began to be seen and treated as mental diseases. These have, in addition, been variously termed, in modern parlance, illness, dysfunction, delusion, illusion, or as symptoms of deep underlying biographical aberrations. What's more, most, if not all, of these are thought to have a fundamental physical basis in brain chemistry and, in most cases, must be treated pharmacologically to reset or repress such chemical dysfunction.

There are, of course, a number of mental health issues that appear to have a strong physiological basis. Yet this, in and of itself, does not irrevocably prove that physiology alone is *the* cause, or *only* cause of the condition. An entirely different possibility always seems to arise: Is it not possible, that, as we view these so-called aberrations in brain chemistry, might they not have been orchestrated by meta-influences pre-existing the changes in the gray matter—in fact having an existence "beyond the brain," as Grof would say?

Moreover, could it be possible that these types of conditions seen as totally brain-based may in fact have an actual *psycho-spiritual* basis that deserves to be addressed, along with, or as a substitute for, certain medical or pharmacological interventions? In short, could the physiological conditions primarily be signposts of—if not the actual result of—original non-physiological problem? Or might these conditions be—as we term them in this inquiry—an indication of the psyche's intrinsic healing trajectory toward wholeness?

In any event, it seems shortsighted to rule out a psycho-spiritual foundation for a number of conditions that are now seen as entirely brain-based. Of course, at least so far, many of these conditions require medical/psychiatric treatment, including hospitalization. But it seems clear that further study would be valuable as an alternative to the standard practice of lengthy hospitalization, including a "life sentence" of often mind-numbing, or some may even say, "soul-killing" medication.

Modern consciousness research, as well as a wealth of insights from perennial philosophy, reveals that quite a few of these pseudo-sophisticated psychiatric disciplines have actually severed themselves from many, more time-honored and critically important, psycho-emotional and spiritual underpinnings. In addition, these questionable disciplines may also have served to separate a substantial portion of psychology from its perennial spiritual foundations. As a "disease model" of psychological health, much of the current psychiatric approach has become, among other things, a profound backlash or repudiation of a much more ancient holistic perspective on the nature of psycho-spiritual wellbeing.

For the last century and more, modern psychiatric approaches espouse the strategy, either unconsciously or consciously, of practitioners and researchers to assign a diagnosis of pathology, or wrongness, to a substantial portion of human thought processes or behaviors existing "outside the norm," or even some of those considered inherently socially unacceptable. It is ironic that many of these now-termed aberrant philosophies and behaviors had, for millennia, flourished in societies as legitimate signs of moving toward wholeness. As opposed to being relegated to pathology, they had often been seen as optimum states of wellness, or wellbeing.

It also seems to have become almost customary for modern psychiatry and society itself to assign a label of "wrongness," abnormality, disease, or aberration when juxtaposing the prevailing set of customs and worldview embraced by modern psychiatry with other, more ancient psycho-spiritual beliefs and practices. This label also includes the "diseasing" of many segments of society—both present and past—engaging in lifestyles or behaviors considered foreign, bizarre, anti-social, revolutionary, radical, or outright insane.

The natural tendency for the prevailing culture seems to be to seek in a variety of ways to "fix," or even homogenize those people manifesting these so-called abnormalities of thought, emotional response, and behavior. This need to label and treat psychiatrically such idiosyncratic phenomena naturally occurring in previous world cultural and social structures appears to be generated by an amalgam of arrogance, ignorance, and fear. The rallying cry of many espousing a worldview can sometimes feel generated by an underpinning of feeling threatened by that which is neither comfortable nor easily understood.

It is interesting that modern societies' inability or unwillingness to embrace those threatening aspects of individual or collective human evolution appear to intensify as humanity approaches what are termed by society to be greater levels of psychological sophistication. In more ancient cultures, there was often reverence for the "holy innocent," the dervish, the shaman, or the fool. It seems that in these past eras, before the birth of what some may call modern Western civilization, many members of societies often honored those who lived outside the cultural norm, and would turn to these pioneers for revelation and inspiration in times of need. Today, these segments of the population would often be considered pathological, irrational, or even psychotic.

From philosophy to practice, it appears that whole segments of the human population have been relegated to the status of "disturbed," sick, or even insane. One of the greatest travesties of this malignant trend has been the pervasive world tendency to presume that a large portion of what were previously known as spiritual experiences have become indicators of deep psychological pathology. It is ironic that the more culturally or psychologically sophisticated we seem to have become, the more narrow-minded, intolerant, and unforgiving we are toward psycho-emotional idiosyncrasy and creative individuality.

With these philosophical musings in mind, we may suggest that, for the most part, the early foundations of modern psychology could be characterized by what many often call a disease model of the human psyche. Most Freudian approaches and their offshoots focused on examining unconscious dynamics, particularly issues stemming from the early postnatal history, looking for the roots of pathology. To paraphrase Freud, he was supposed to have said something like this: "The goal of psychoanalysis is to restore those who are suffering a great deal to the ordinary level of everyday human suffering." This is not the brightest, most hopeful outlook on the nature of the human condition.

The prognosis for positive human development, or a possible *wellness model* of psychology, was definitely more heartening in the teachings of some of Freud's followers, who broke away from psychoanalytical orthodoxy and founded their own schools. In particular, Jungian and psychosynthesis approaches, with their powerful basis of a transpersonal and numinous, or sacred, dimension of the psyche, brought psychology fully into the realm of ongoing spiritual practice and the wisdom of the ages.

The school of psychology known as *behaviorism* has been characterized by some almost to have been a backlash and antithesis to psychoanalytical approaches. It was also a reaction against introspection, as well as an attempt to make psychology scientific and thus put it on an equal footing with the hard sciences. Either purposely or incidentally, it appears to relegate the unconscious motivations of the human psyche almost into non-existence, or at best, non-relevance. In fact, it seemed to have actually bypassed the psyche altogether.

This school's founders and early champions, including Ivan Pavlov, John B. Watson, and B. F. Skinner, sought to describe virtually all psychological manifestations, including thoughts and feelings, in terms of their resultant *behaviors*. They were not concerned with thoughts and feelings. Psychology was seen as the study of human behavior—the "black-box" approach. Thus, the therapeutic plan led basically to strategies for changing what were seen as these unproductive behaviors through external conditioning, and the development of new strategies enabling the client to function at a more optimal level in everyday life.

Behaviorism has ultimately made way for cognitive-behavioral therapy (CBT), which has been the most prevalent approach in psychotherapy of the last half-century. Through the work of this school's pioneers, the rejection of the power of inner psychological patterning was mitigated by approaches combining systematic introspection with behavioral strategies, a kind of cognitive reprogramming. This marriage of two approaches was bolstered by research demonstrating its efficacy, particularly with the nearly universal and constant inclusion of long-term, and often permanent, use of psychiatric medication, which has unfortunately become the "therapy of choice" today. In essence, the overwhelming method of support today is a scientific psychology, with the primary focus on the scientific and medical dimensions.

This most disturbing tendency of the modern medical/psychiatric/scientific culture's use of medication to suppress psychological symptoms stems from the entrenched paradigm that tends to view almost all pathology as a product of aberrations in brain chemistry. Our hope, however, is that we, and the thousands of teachers and pioneers before us, are beginning to present an alternative to this view. That alternative includes, among others, what is offered by a transpersonal paradigm, and, in particular for our exploration here, a holotropic perspective.

It is not as easy to point to any obvious underpinning from behaviorism, or cognitive/behavioral approaches, that directly support either a wellness model of psychology or a transpersonal vision that includes the realm of the numinous as a vital, necessary component of human development. However, in this context, it is worthwhile mentioning some studies done in the past, which attempted to ascertain what were the most effective therapeutic modalities.

Interestingly, findings seem to suggest that no therapy was actually statistically more effective than any other. However, what appeared to make the difference was not the therapy, but the *therapist* herself. What was most important was the *relationship* between the client and the therapist. The relevant indicators were actually more difficult to measure, and included such factors as empathy, trust, compassion, and non-judgmental positive regard. With this in mind, we would suggest that any approach on the continuum between cognitive/behavioral therapy on the one end, and Holotropic Breathwork on the other, can be effective, if it occurs within the timeless, universal dimension characterized by true caring, love, and support. This is what the client will "take home" with her. This is what she will remember in her heart of hearts.

Finally, we must mention a diamond in the crown of the holotropic perspective, which we will explore in much detail later in a number of contexts. This jewel is the power that in this work we call *presence*, a nearly indefinable attribute that is an essential component of holotropic support and for those working in any modality involving meta-ordinary states of consciousness.

We would suggest at this point that the development of presence—in essence, the atmosphere, or consciousness, within which a therapist or practitioner "holds space" for a seeker—should be the single most essential aim or goal in facilitator training, no matter what the goal or strategy of any particular school may be. At this juncture of our inquiry, it is important to emphasize that, regardless of method, it seems quite likely that it is this presence—generated by a therapist from in *any* school—that fosters the most positive impact on a seeker in that school. As we proceed with an exploration of how many approaches are often a "set-up" for the disempowerment of seekers, we must always honor the genuine, heart-felt commitment of people-helpers *in all schools* who work deeply from a nurturing, empowering space with their clients.

On the Nature of a Wellness Model

Parallel with cognitive approaches from the 1950s onward, there was another school called humanistic psychology that deeply influenced the field of psychotherapy, and was a forerunner of the revolutionary transpersonal paradigm. In a sense, the humanistic movement has been a rebirth of a wellness perspective on human potential that has extremely ancient roots. This timeless heritage is commensurate with, as you might expect, the wisdom of the ages. Among the disciplines that make up this foundation are shamanic practices, rites of passage, the use of psychedelic plants, mystery schools, and the world's mystical traditions.

The humanistic era is often spoken of in the same breath as the human potential movement. It was founded by Abraham Maslow and others, as an alternative to the previous practices of behaviorism and the traditional Freudian approach of looking into the early post-natal for the roots of pathology. Certainly, this earlier endeavor was worthwhile. However, followers of the humanistic schools believed human beings were more than merely a product of pathology. They were also heir to what was known as a *teleological* dimension—a blueprint of future wholeness with a more Jungian underpinning that acts almost like an inner lighthouse, or a homing beacon, to help guide individuals toward wholeness. Hence, they often used the term *self-actualization* to designate this focus upon wellness.

In the context of a holotropic paradigm, the groundbreaking work of Carl Rogers has a valid place. He is one of those pioneers credited with the development of a *client-centered* approach, where it was the responsibility of the therapist to trust the healing attributes naturally inherent within the seeker. This approach radically altered the role of the therapist from director of the process to that of co-journeyer with the client. This is quite similar to a foundational insight that emerges for those of us who have experienced Holotropic Breathwork ourselves, and who are working systematically with other seekers using this method.

One of the most famous developments from the humanistic pantheon was the school of Fritz Perls known as Gestalt Therapy. Gestalt is another seminal client-centered modality, which some feel can be characterized as a forerunner of the holotropic approach. The essential strategy in Gestalt is, in a sense, to follow the client—not direct or lead her. The practitioner's role is to encourage the seeker to focus on and intensify whatever it is she is already experiencing or reporting.

It is interesting that when Stan was invited to leave the Maryland Psychiatric Institute to become Scholar-in-Residence at Esalen in Big Sur, his forerunner in that position was Fritz Perls. It was there that he and Stan met and over the years shared their work. For Stan, it became quickly clear that

Gestalt was of a similar mold to Holotropic Breathwork, which relied so emphatically on the inner healing resources of the seeker as the soul orchestrator of a seeker's process. Although different in a number of nuances, including a greater reliance on verbal communication between the therapist and the client, Gestalt has for years been one of the most important supportive modalities in the holotropic milieu—both *before* and *after* a holotropic session.

However, during the 1960s, even the founders of humanistic psychology began to feel that the horizon of human potential was too small to encompass all that human beings were heir to. For example, Maslow, to whom we have already alluded, had begun to research what he called *peak experiences*—spontaneous or systematically pursued episodes that resulted in radical rearrangements of consciousness. In traditional psychology, most of these kinds of episodes were considered pathological.

Yet Maslow felt that they were signs of a greater, meta-level of wholeness. He had already developed what he called his *hierarchy of needs*. But with the inclusion of the benefits of peak experiences, he concluded that human existence encompassed not just personal health, but transpersonal health as well. And this health included the fulfillment of what he termed *meta-needs*. These needs are *wholeness, perfection, completion, justice, richness, simplicity, liveliness, beauty, goodness, uniqueness, playfulness, truth, autonomy*, and *meaningfulness*.

Can we imagine a practice, a yoga, in which the pursuit of these kinds of needs would be considered the inalienable rights of all human beings? Or furthermore, can we envision that there are actually strategies available to us capable of facilitating this level of transformation? Holotropic Breathwork is just one of the methods which are able to support this type of journey. Ultimately, the wellness model inherent in a humanistic perspective paved the way for this era's iconoclastic worldview—the transpersonal paradigm, and its psycho-spiritual upgrade, transpersonal psychology.

As we focus more directly on a holotropic perspective—a central theme of our inquiry—it will become increasingly evident just how important the implications of a wellness model of transformation actually are. It would be, as they say, a game-changer. The principle inherent in the term *holotropic*—that is, *moving toward wholeness*—wholeheartedly represents the essence, not only of a wellness approach to psycho-spiritual growth, but also of a radical re-envisioning of the human planetary adventure. We look forward to exploring the profound implications of the wellness model with more rigor later in the text.

The shift from the disease model to a wellness model does not become a grounded experiential reality within the human psyche by mere acquisition of a new thought form garnished through intellectual study alone. As is so often the case—especially during a paradigm collision such as the one in which we are now engaged—new ideas are presented that challenge the status quo.

We are apt to overlook the fact that many of these new ideas are not just interesting oddities to be bandied about as a parlor game for mere pseudo-psychological and scientific debate. It is essential to realize that by the time these fresh insights have become a valid force in scientific inquiry, they have frequently already been the revelatory outcome of deep psycho-spiritual work. They are the mental descriptions of powerful *experiential realities* that cannot be theoretically framed in the current scientific or philosophical idiom.

For example, the term *holotropic*, or *moving toward wholeness*, reveals itself to be the inheritor of a powerful perennial pedigree. It represents experiences that have been mapped, codified, and validated, often by centuries of experiential methodology as well as scientific research. Modern consciousness study and exploration are often "re-explorations" that have been undertaken and chronicled by proponents of many of the world's most sophisticated psycho-spiritual disciplines. What's more, the realizations and findings they present can be re-experienced—here and now, in our modern era—by any seeker who chooses to engage in deep inner work powerful enough to access expanded states of awareness.

Yet, it cannot be over-stated that these often revolutionary findings are based on powerful inner realizations. Two observations seem relevant: first, as we have shared, their validity cannot be affirmed or discredited simply by some process of intellectual debate alone, especially one that uses, as a baseline of so-called unassailable truth, the current assumptions of the latest paradigm. And second—an observation representing some good news—what is now occurring in our world augurs a scientific validation and justification of the realizations preserved from the inner work and subsequent writings of many of our forebears. Many of the scientists and philosophers who are the founders of this new paradigm have themselves experienced, here in modern times, the same types of realizations as those preserved in many ancient spiritual and philosophical sources—what I call the "wisdom of the ages."

It is helpful to remember that, as Pierre Teilhard de Chardin so wisely pointed out, there is more to transformation than looking back into either the personal or collective past. Ahead of us, in our Becoming, is what he calls "Point Omega," a future goal of wholeness—or Being—toward which individuals and humanity are always moving. It is deeply satisfying to reflect in this moment on the essence of the term *holotropic—moving toward wholeness*.

Perhaps we feel this way because we recognize that, although we can receive many blessings and much validation from the wisdom of past ages, we are not bound by the past. Instead, we are, to a much more profound degree, the co-creators of our future. This future gives a gracious nod to what has gone before, yet at the same time it beckons us like the siren call of Odysseus toward the unfolding of our own inner-directed, self-empowered creation of a radical numinosity never dreamed of before. This is one of the promises of a holotropic perspective.

Spiritual Emergency—A Wellness Approach to Psychosis

Christina Grof's own life was a laboratory for the development of a revolutionary alternative to viewing a whole continuum of psychological symptoms and conditions currently known as psychosis here in modern times. As we shared earlier, she was supported by the famous mythologist Joseph Campbell, as well as Stan Grof, in her journey through an extremely powerful psychological and spiritual upheaval that in modern times would have been without question labeled as psychosis by the prevailing, so-called modern medical/psychiatric system.

She and Stan were pioneers in reframing psychosis as a dual structure of human evolution which they called *spiritual emergency* and *emergence*. Based on a multivalent worldview, which included the standard strategies outlined in our current inquiry, they chose to de-pathologize many psychological conditions, which in the past one-hundred years had come to be seen unequivocally as psychosis. The central underpinning of their revolutionary approach was based on experiences available through a host of methods accessing expanded states of consciousness.

Among these findings was a radical insight into the sacred nature of reality and existence itself. By this we mean that, whether physical, emotional, or mental, virtually all human inner experience represents a signpost, or a certain reflection in time and space. This signpost points to an inherent, natural tendency for all of human psycho-spiritual and physical evolution to move toward optimum wholeness and wellbeing. This is what we may call *spiritual emergence.*

On the path toward this inherently available fulfillment in wholeness, there may be a host of psychological manifestations that represent challenging stages of this evolution and are difficult to negotiate in so-called normal everyday functioning and interpersonal interaction. These belong within the category of what we may call spiritual *emergency.* However, just because these are challenging in no way requires us to view or label such manifestations as psychosis, whose healing prospectus is to be treated, repressed, or subdued with a range of powerful substances designed to medicate the symptom, leaving the emergence from the psyche unsupported, except as psychosis.

The radical alternative to this labeling and so-called therapeutic approach was highlighted by the Grofs as representing signals of a possible stage of exceptional evolutionary development or meta-levels of psycho-spiritual functioning. Their alternative proposal for supporting such conditions included an extremely ancient tenet of perennial philosophy. This tenet states that all of human existence is a "Becoming," an inexorable evolution of physical existence as well as consciousness itself toward a pinnacle of wholeness. This pinnacle of wholeness derives its nature from an all-encompassing display of perfection in what was known perennially as "Being" itself.

To thicken the plot, seekers using all kinds of practices can have the experience that human beings are *always already* whole, from the womb, to death of the body, and beyond. This seems to be the point where Being and Becoming are one. Yet most of us still function in the ever-shifting evolutionary process we call *time*. Thus we may discover at various times an intersection of our Being and Becoming.

This Becoming goes by many names in spiritual literature, such as Maya, the dream of brahma, or the great play. In any event, the Becoming seems to be a relevant poise of evolutionary development that, for all intents and purposes, constitutes life itself on the earth and in this cosmos. This is true, even as the basis underlying the Becoming is none other than Being itself.

On the evolutionary trajectory toward this level of wholeness or being, various manifestations of human behavior and emotional as well as psycho-spiritual development may manifest as quite challenging indications of a current but temporary "incompletion." A crossroads of tragic proportions and implications occurred with the development of certain aspects of modern psychiatry, based primarily on a disease model of the human psyche. From that point onward, no longer were the temporary signposts on this evolutionary trajectory toward wholeness seen as manifestations of Being in our evolutionary Becoming that should be supported. Instead they were seen as signs of psychosis and treated as, for the most part, brain-based physiological abnormalities.

The intermediate re-awakening to the ancient underpinning of "spiritual emergence" has been the great work of Christina and Stan Grof toward a recognition of the condition they have termed "spiritual emergency." That it has been called *spiritual emergency* reflects, perhaps, humanity's temporary sojourn on its journey toward wholeness. A culmination of this human psycho-spiritual odyssey may include the truth that we are facing the possibility of an inherent revisioning of psychology itself. This revisioning would allow us to freely employ the term "spiritual emergence" as opposed to mental disease.

In fact, as we have already alluded to, it may be possible at some point to envision this wellness strategy as applying to all cases—even those conditions that we term organically or physically based. We also might begin to believe that we can, at some point, virtually do away with a disease or sickness model of the human psyche altogether and inaugurate a whole-hearted radical return to a wellness perspective encompassing every facet of human psycho-spiritual development. Time, of course, will eventually reveal to us how possible this may be.

This radical return to a wellness perspective, which is always already inherent within the teachings of world perennial philosophy, is a lynchpin of our inquiry into how humanity may refocus itself on the personal and collective psycho-spiritual treasure we are calling the Inner Healer, or a power within. Many of us who have been blessed with a vestige of this refocusing on our innate inner power are dedicated to sharing this ancient wisdom with others through the holotropic perspective or paradigm.

We are already fascinated by the possibilities we see unfolding within a host of psycho-spiritual disciplines and practices. As we have pointed out, these include those working with Holotropic Breathwork, as well as those exploring the universal psyche through entheogens and other indigenous practices. We work in the addictions/recovery field, with those in spiritual emergency, and with the surge of humanity who are seekers on the road to wholeness in every human endeavor on our planet. We each, in our own way, feel deeply that a holotropic paradigm may play a vital part in the evolution of our Becoming toward the mystery of a wholeness of Being, written about for millennia as the birthright for all of humanity.

PART II

Reawakening to the Mysteries of the Unconscious

CHAPTER IV

The Sensory and Biographical Dimensions of the Psyche—Preparing for Our Journey Through the Mysteries

Deep work via psychedelics, meditation, shamanic practices, or Holotropic Breathwork inevitably requires us to see the human psyche and the nature of reality within a much larger framework than we have before. For this era's exploration into a fresh, even revolutionary therapeutic approach, there are, as we have stated, a number of exciting possibilities.

The power of a wellness model of psychology; an optimally effective strategy for psycho-spiritual self-exploration using entheogens; an expansion of therapeutic power of spiritual emergency; an effective framework for deep addictions recovery practices; and even a revisioning and restructuring of traditional forms of individual and group therapy, are among the most relevant of those contexts. What's more, they all seem to characterize Stan Grof's revolutionary breakthrough for modern psychology that he first unveiled in his masterpiece *Realms of the Human Unconscious*.

It is not that Grof *discovered* deeper dimensions of the psyche. Mystics and shamans have always known of these. The importance of Stan's work was, first, to further open the Western psychological tradition to the wisdom of the ages that others, including Richard Maurice Bucke, William James, Aldous Huxley, Carl Jung, and Roberto Assagioli, had already established. Second was his absolutely compelling case for the healing capabilities in using practices powerful enough to access the deepest dimensions of the psyche. And third was the gift for modern humanity in developing an extended cartography of these crucial dimensions of what it means to be a human being. As we have said, his first focus was psychedelics. And his second one was through Holotropic Breathwork.

Our current task will be to outline this extended map of the psyche, with the knowledge that this sketch can be enhanced by going directly to many of Stan's and Christina's publications, as well as the work of a leading teacher in the holotropic community, Kylea Taylor. It is also validated by hundreds of sources from transpersonal psychology and world mystical traditions. Keep in mind a number of points we have already made: What I write here is, as we say in the Twelve Step tradition, my own "experience, strength, and hope," as well as that of many of my colleagues.

I have chosen this particular metaphor, based upon two things. First, and most importantly, what follows is derived from more than three decades of witnessing, supporting, and listening to reports from thousands of others who have done work in meta-ordinary states of consciousness. Second, it also reflects the understandings and insights with which I and my colleagues have been graced through a gradual opening to our own Inner Healers.

Our understanding of this subject is anything but static. It seems to be one of the functions of any deep healing capacity to act in the unending, relentless manner of waves breaking upon a shore. For many of us, the purpose of this eternal wave cycle is to forever wash away whatever daily sand castles we have constructed which represent this moment's partial dispensation of truth. Furthermore, this systematic shattering of our illusions, or partial truths, keeps us from becoming too fossilized and hopelessly mired in "how we think it all is." It is important to remember that each topic we cover frequently invites a fresh outpouring of expanded truth, which can always emerge from the Inner Healer-guided work of any passionate seeker.

Every insight, example, or description we include of the extended cartography we are exploring, including the strategies used to access these dimensions, and the value this exploration has for seekers, is entirely based on what we, as facilitators, have seen from journeyers, or heard from the stories they have shared with us. Of course, it also includes what we have experienced ourselves. As a capstone, seekers have reported that every one of these experiences, having been made conscious and fully embraced, has been healing for them in extraordinary, life-changing ways.

Finally, there is a lens, particularly helpful, through which one may wish to view this material. We are inspired, in this text's inquiry, to explore the revolutionary possibilities inherent in a *wellness model* of the human psyche, discussed above. With this in mind, it is distinctly possible that *every* experience we may all undergo in our own epic journey through the realms of the human unconscious—no matter how intense—is motivated and orchestrated by a power of infinite compassion and love inherent and fundamental to all human beings. As we have seen, this is the principle known to us in Holotropic Breathwork as the Inner Healer, or a power within.

You will find that we have gone into considerable detail on the nature of this extended cartography. This is by no means a pedantic self-indulgence. So many nuances of the cartography—particularly including the perinatal and its octave of psycho-spiritual death/rebirth—are totally relevant to our unfolding of a holotropic perspective for psychology, therapeutic entheogen work, a holotropic therapy, and the further development of a healing strategy for spiritual emergency. Our primary objective is to provide a document wherein seekers may find multiple ways to understand, initiate, expand, or nurture for themselves the emergence of a radical self-empowerment, as well as for integration of their particular journeys toward wholeness. In addition, the details over and over again reaffirm the essential nature of this authentic self-empowerment for true, in-depth transformation.

In his first few books, Stan made reference to four dimensions, or levels, to the psyche, or *bands of consciousness*, as he often called them. These bands were the *sensory*, the *biographical*, the *perinatal*, and the *transpersonal*.

A Note on the Sensory Level

In his later works, Stan tended put somewhat less focus on the sensory level, for a number of reasons. The sensory band is essentially a dimension of expanded sensory awareness. Here, there does not seem to be quite as much access to relevant psychological material. For example, a journeyer may have vivid inner experiences of color, sound, and heightened sensual or body awareness. In colloquial counter-cultural terminology, this level may refer to what was called a "good trip." This is an experience quite common for many breathers, in particular (but not exclusively limited to) seekers in the early stages of their exploration.

We have, however, noticed a number of important psycho-spiritual outcomes of experiencing this dimension. On the one hand, the sensory band seems to act as a barrier to deeper levels of the psyche. However, once they begin to access these more personally relevant realms, breathers realize that they had been receiving a gift from their Inner Healer by not being unduly forced to face something for which they are apparently unprepared. They often have the insight that this "wise, inner timing" demonstrates certain qualities of gentleness, love, and safety that are inherent components of their psyches.

In becoming aware of this compassionate inner quality, breathers often feel two things. First, they are able to embrace acceptance for themselves and for their own timing in facing the often-arduous adventure of inner exploration. And second, they may notice that they are being carefully afforded the opportunity to develop a trust in their own inner healing intelligence—a power within. They see that they will not be forced to face something within themselves they are not yet ready to make conscious. They are able, as the saying goes, to "get their feet wet" before taking the big plunge.

We should also emphasize that even though, by its very nature, the sensory level is often empty of deep psychological material, nevertheless, an experience of expanded sensory awareness often proves to be, in and of itself, quite transformational. Seekers often report that, because of the myriad manifestations of introjected trauma, they have spent their lives feeling constricted, separate, and isolated.

This isolation can extend to the inability to feel anything, either emotionally or sensually. With the experience of expanded sensory input, even though there may be little if any underlying psychological material associated with it, nevertheless they still feel emotionally renewed and expanded. This experience of positivity and uplift is often due directly to their recognition that they are more whole than they had previously thought. And this wholeness often seems to be based upon the Inner Healer's revelation of a heightened awareness of their sensual and sensory capabilities. The healing power in opening to and deepening our relationship with the physical body often elevates this dimension to its rightful place alongside all other realms of consciousness.

A Note on the Biographical Level

The biographical band is the realm of our post-natal history—everything that has happened from the moment of our birth to the present. This includes both what we are aware of and those things of which we are unconscious. One of the healing mechanisms of Holotropic Breathwork is that the breathing brings into our awareness what is relevant for our transformation. *Consciousness, or awareness itself, is a function of the Inner Healer.* The gift of most forms of traditional Western psychotherapy is the exploration of this important biographical dimension. The curse of all traditional Western psychology is its belief that this is the only dimension of the human psyche that exists, and that all psychological causation and outcome stem from this dimension alone.

What emerges, here, into our awareness from the unconscious, via the breathing, certainly includes what we would expect from traditional psychotherapy and developmental psychology. Work in meta-ordinary states validates the traditional understanding of the primary importance of very early post-natal history, childhood, and every subsequent level of physical, emotional, and psychological development addressed by prevailing systems. In similar fashion, all subsequent trauma and other repressed memories, which are explored in many well-known psychotherapies, all become available through conscious deep breathing.

However, there are a couple of areas where traditional exploration in the biographical dimension and deep experiential work do not totally overlap. Those issues that contain prominent elements of physical insult or trauma, particularly when it involves powerful abuse, or a life threatening or near-death situation, are frequently dynamics that have the most powerful charge. In this case, these kinds of dramatic issues will often take center-stage in the work of the breather. Breathers repeatedly confirm that it is the fear of death due to a life-threatening situation that almost always has the most relevance.

This observation is crucial to work in non-ordinary states. It appears that the fear of death, both physical and psychological, as in the case of what we call the *ego death*, is one of the most powerful issues human beings ever face. Its power is not just limited to biographical experiences— either as actual events, or as levels of nonspecific fear that cannot be singled out as having any direct physical basis. The issue of death is like a *gateway experience*. By this, I mean that it has a powerful resonance across all levels of the psyche—not just the biographical, but also the perinatal, or dimension of birth, and the transpersonal, or collective, dimension as well.

The second important difference relates to the manner in which unconscious material comes into the client's awareness. In traditional biographical work, what seems to be the most prominent medium is a faculty involving memory. The client is supported to bring to mind memories of past psychologically relevant episodes. However, in non-ordinary states work, seekers seem to frequently activate a deeper octave of memory function. Their healing occurs, not just from recollecting what was previously unconscious, and then exploring the implications of the memory.

Instead, seekers can actually *relive* the event, make it conscious, physically, emotionally, as well as psychologically. I do not mean that the traumatic event again occurs in this physical reality. However, with eyes closed and having turned inward, it can have tremendous power and the sense that it is very real. In fact, one of the challenges for facilitators at this point is that a breather may be making conscious a memory of trauma that feels so real that they will open their eyes, and fight the imagined, threatening perpetrator.

This external person is in fact there for total support only. However, for the breather the support person is perceived no longer as an ally, but as an abuser. The correction in this instant is to vigorously encourage the breather to "take it inward," or "stay with the breath," or even a reply such as "you are safe." This is one of the reasons we highlight the need for there to be as deep a development of trust as possible between breather and "sitter," or facilitator, as a prelude to the inner breathing experience.

Often, unconscious events are found to be interrelated in some way, but they are also autonomous enclaves within the psyche. They are, in a sense, "gestalts"—a sort of internal "energy ganglion"—which must be excised, or re-experienced fully by the breather, for there to be optimum functioning for the individual. The strategy involves a surrender to, and a full embracing of, what has emerged into awareness. This would include, as much as possible, a conscious *reliving*, not just remembering, of the original event and a full release of the pent-up energies trapped in the unconscious and manifesting as blockages in the physical body and psyche.

At the end of this section on the bands of consciousness, we will begin an inquiry into a principle crucial at all levels of holotropic practice. These levels include holotropic breathing when it is done once, or periodically but sparingly, or systematically as part of a regular, frequent practice. Ultimately, this mechanism will prove to be absolutely critical, as the holotropic perspective reveals itself to be the possible basis of a daily, or moment-to-moment, or even second-to-second practice. This principle, or dynamic structure within the psyche, is what we call a *COEX*, or a *system of condensed experience*.

For now, it is sufficient to say that COEXs deal with the nature of physical, psychological, and spiritual *pattern*. Through deep work, we learn that these patterns tend to be pan-dimensional. They operate throughout the psyche on all levels—the biographical, perinatal, and the transpersonal. And the experience of facing death is one of those issues that has powerful cross-band relevance for our healing.

CHAPTER V

Birth and Rebirth—The Perinatal Level

It is at the perinatal level that seekers really begin to navigate what seem to be, in most psychological systems, uncharted waters. The word *perinatal* is derived from two roots. *Peri* comes from the Greek, and means "of, or through, or around." *Natal* comes from Latin, *natalis*, meaning "birth." Hence, together, these two imply a dimension having to do with birth. Among the fascinating characteristics of the perinatal dimension, several deserve to be mentioned at the outset because of the pivotal role they play in a holotropic paradigm.

In the first case, it is helpful to imagine that the perinatal level acts as an interface, or a "dimension doorway," between the biographical and transpersonal levels. In this work, seekers can have the realization that, in order to move toward wholeness, they must open to the reality that we have both a *personal* and *transpersonal* nature. It then becomes clear that, as human beings, we are not just what Alan Watts called the "skin-encapsulated ego." But we are also beings who are heir to a level of self and consciousness equal, in a sense, to "all that is"—our personal as well as our transpersonal nature.

In a very real and functional sense, the perinatal is a true *gateway dimension*. But the picture is more complex than it seems at first glance. In the initial stages of Stan's research, he and his colleagues typically administered lower doses of LSD than became the norm at later stages of the research. Even though clients frequently accessed deeper dimensions of the psyche, a substantial part of the work occurred within the biographical domain. This early strategy was known as *psycholytic* therapy.

When the seekers' work transcended the post-natal biography, there was frequently a kind of linear trajectory—from the post-natal history into the, for the most part, uncharted spaces of the perinatal and transpersonal domains. At this point, it began to be clear that, in addition to holding the record of biological birth and the possibility of psycho-spiritual death/ rebirth, the perinatal was also the gateway to the transpersonal, or collective realm. Stan also observed that a client's accessing of the transpersonal would often augur a radical spiritual awakening and an accompanying core shift in the seeker's perspective on self and existence.

It was not until later, however, when the therapeutic doses were typically stronger—what became known as *psychedelic* therapy—that there often seemed to be an additional trajectory added to the healing work. The original findings were more often based on a therapeutic or psycho-spiritual journey from the biographical into the perinatal, with the perinatal as the gateway, or doorway, into the transpersonal domain. Instead, with the higher dosages, what began to emerge more frequently were experiences akin to the insights derived from cosmologies within the most influential spiritual traditions in planetary history.

Many of these would describe an evolutionary psycho-spiritual episode, or series of episodes, which seemed to originate in what we might call a Being level. In a sense impossible to define, this Being level has often been described as *tathagata,* the "beyond the beyond" or sometimes the "great mystery," or the realm of "no mind." For seekers, it appeared to be a dimension of consciousness, unmanifest, yet at the same time, pregnant with infinite potentiality. Or it was the eternally elusive *subject,* in which all objective phenomena were latent. Even for a seeker to think of what this subjective foundation might be, or attempt to describe it, would hurl the experience into an objective realm and be the annihilation of its "subject nature" altogether.

These kinds of experiences are often reported throughout perennial philosophy. From this Being level, many systems describe a kind of nuclear blast of creation, or universal "birth," which typically has its origins in, and emerges from, what we may call a "cosmic womb." It is from this cosmic womb that, according to Sri Aurobindo and others, an *involution* occurs, where Being, or Spirit, involves itself in various, ever-denser gradations of creation. Seekers can also experience this involution of Being into creation, the Becoming—this down-stepping, if you will, or this specific focusing of the creative impulse.

According to these systems, this focusing culminates in the formation of the human being, or individual soul, or unit of consciousness—a specifically *individual* level of creation. In addition, this unit, or any unit of consciousness can also be experienced to encompass the entire manifestation of all creation. But, at this point, the individual unit of consciousness would now be living in a Becoming—what Aurobindo calls the *evolution*—in a journey toward wholeness or, once again, Being.

Please keep in mind that the goal of creation and life itself, as described by many of the world's most respected spiritual teachers, frequently emerges as a reality for seekers doing work in expanded states. This can be true, even if these seekers report that they have rarely given a thought to metaphysical issues, or may have in fact ridiculed such beliefs earlier in their lives

Most seekers report that the various goals of their inner exploration have changed as often as the experiences they have undergone. This seems to be a basic characteristic of the evolution of our interaction with this force or power we call consciousness. In addition, these insights seem to point to a great mystery—almost as though our Becoming is orchestrated somehow by a wise but playful trickster. On this note, nearly every seeker I have known who has embraced wholeheartedly what we call moving toward wholeness comes to feel that rich humor in some form is without question a characteristic of our inner healing power.

Yet there is another equally as powerful therapeutic dimension of the transpersonal that plays a critical role in seekers' transformation. The transpersonal is also the domain of what is known as *archetypes*. Archetypes can be experienced in a number of ways. To name but two of these ways, they can appear to seekers to be core, ordering principles or powers representing the blueprint of forms in material or psychological dimensions. And they can also be recognized as gods or goddesses, a kind of anthropomorphic experience of universal emotions, thought forms, or trans-human presences. We often hear from journeyers that, in a sense, every form in material existence also lives as a primordial archetype—in essence, its non-material program, from which springs the actual form into objective manifestation.

As we already mentioned, one of the most exciting contributions to modern perennial philosophy comes from the work of Rick Tarnas in archetypal astrology. His work has been perhaps the most powerful, relevant, and useful support and resource for seekers doing systematic work in expanded states of awareness. His findings validate the power of the archetypal dimension as an ongoing, multivalent blueprint for any explorer of the psyche. It is an unsurpassed tool for interconnection between the outer and inner domains.

Rick's and Stan's work, recognizing the almost unbelievable connection between the four outer planets (Neptune, Saturn, Pluto, and Uranus) and the four perinatal matrixes, has been a discovery of monumental philosophical and therapeutic value for all seekers. It also represents a kind of elegant yoga, or spiritual practice, that totally supports the universal human dynamic of moving toward wholeness. Having the experience, for example, that one's personal feelings of love are connected with a great cosmic realm of love is a powerful force for the healing essence in moving toward wholeness. Later, we will have more to say about this amazing perspective and the strategy one may engage in to support a holotropic therapy.

This dance between the forces of Becoming and Being seems to echo quite elegantly the nature of "moving toward wholeness," or the holotropic trajectory. And this is a primary reason why Stan gave this name to the breathwork. He wished to reflect, as accurately as possible, the entire psycho-spiritual odyssey, or the primary as well as ultimate purpose in human evolution. Yet even here paradox is at work.

I am reminded of a final scene in director Ridley Scott's underrated film *Kingdom of Heaven* about the Crusades and the wars for Jerusalem between Christians and Muslims. Near the end, the Christians surrender the Holy City. The two main characters—one Christian and one Muslim—who had come to respect one another, are in a ruined temple room alone. The Christian, played by Orlando Bloom, asks, "What is Jerusalem worth?" The Muslim, played by the brilliant actor Ghassan Massoud, says, "Nothing—Everything." This seems to reflect beautifully the confounding nature of our purpose of life here in the Becoming. Is it real? Is it ultimately without reality or value, and Being all that matters? Many seekers would respond the way the Muslim king did, and state as precisely what they think: The journey toward wholeness means everything, and at the same time, it means nothing. The amazing accuracy and specificity of the term *holotropic* will be vitally important for us later as we explore the possibilities inherent in the evolution of paradigms.

However, let us return to the perinatal dimension and its multi-leveled importance for psycho-spiritual transformation. During the experience of this down-stepping of the realization of cosmic oneness, unity, or Being, it is possible once again for a seeker in expanded states of awareness to open to a kind of bivalent level of the perinatal band of consciousness: These two levels would be, as we have said, the experience of biological birth as well as the possibility of the experience of psycho-spiritual death/rebirth.

With these findings, we now recognize the therapeutic availability of a dual trajectory—an Inner Healer-directed process—inherent in the experience of the perinatal domain. One is the emergence of the individual consciousness, soul, or self from the biographical dimension into the realm of birth, or the perinatal dimension. In this situation, the perinatal becomes the gateway, or the open window, to the transpersonal level—or the domain of "all that is"—what we may refer to as *wholeness* or Being itself.

The second possibility is the original experience of Being, or oneness—a universal, undifferentiated consciousness—as it propels itself into an evolutionary process of down-stepping or, if you will, a gradual focusing of its infinite nature into individual incarnation, or the Becoming. Or, we might say that there is an involution from the macrocosmic to the microcosmic—from perfect potentiality, or "all that is," into manifestation—the focused dimension of the incarnated individual. Once again, in both of these healing trajectories, the perinatal acts as the gateway, the dimension doorway, the two-headed Janus peering in both directions— between the personal and the collective realms. In this case the perinatal is the gateway—not just into the transpersonal realm—but into the biographical domain as well.

How all of these transformational trajectories are possible for breathers and other seekers brings us to another defining characteristic of the perinatal band of consciousness. As we have made clear, the perinatal is definitely about birth. But what do we actually mean by birth? What are the true implications of such a pronouncement? For one, the perinatal contains the actual biographical record of our biological birth. For our healing, and for a comprehensively valid experience of moving toward wholeness, it appears we must include the necessity of making conscious this biographical record. In doing so, we confirm a triple healing dynamic open to us through deep experiential work. This would be, of course, making conscious our *personal* and *transpersonal selves*, and all that this implies. But now it includes making conscious the record of our *biological birth* as well.

However, when seekers access the perinatal dimension, they discover that the actual record of biological birth is but one aspect of birth available or necessary for their transformation. In fact, the biological component assumes almost a "lower octave" of the implications of birth. What ultimately emerges for them is recognized by spiritual systems the world over as one of essential cornerstones of authentic transformation. This is the possibility of undergoing the radical experience known as *psycho-spiritual death/rebirth*. These two—biological birth and psycho-spiritual death/ rebirth—are unique, individual, yet experientially interrelated dynamics. One of Stan's greatest contributions to the fields of psychology and perennial philosophy is his explication of the four stages of these two dynamics and their universal relevance as a personal and collective trajectory for evolutionary transformation.

Here is a brief outline of these four stages of birth, and death/rebirth, and the elegant nature of the psycho-spiritual dance between the two. Bear in mind, these do not directly correspond to academically or medically recognized stages of clinical birth. Rather, they represent observable experiential matrices containing physical and psychological clusters of related material whose healing potential has been reported by thousands of seekers. It is our purpose, as we go through them, to weave biological birth and psycho-spiritual death/rebirth into a coherent synergy with, as much as possible, an unmistakable experiential logic. In a later section, we will also direct ourselves more exclusively to the nuances and transformational implications of the ego death.

The First Matrix

The first matrix represents the fetus's intrauterine experience. Depending on medical and biological factors and on emotional and psychological circumstances involving the relationship between the mother and the fetus, this creates a continuum between what is called a *good-womb* or *bad-womb* experience. Breathers relive, and find to be psychologically relevant, a host of issues, from conception, through gestation, and a range of other circumstances up to the onset of delivery. An influential factor is the physical health of the mother, which, if precarious in some way, can in many cases adversely affect the fetus.

Other factors include the presence of twins, or multiple fetuses, or whether the birth was a planned or emergency Caesarian. We should also mention the dietary factors, including drug, alcohol, or tobacco intake of the mother, and in rarer cases, life-threatening issues surrounding blood-type incompatibilities. This latter situation virtually renders the intrauterine episode a "near-death" experience for either the fetus or the mother, and frequently for both of them.

All those elements that constitute a good womb, such as safety, connectedness, wellbeing, nourishment, love, meaning, purpose, and identity, depend upon a type of positive symbiosis and synergy in the relationship between the mother and the fetus. Likewise, all those components of a bad womb, such as sickness, fear, vital threat, starvation, lack, disconnectedness, alienation, victimhood, and meaninglessness, emerge from another nuance of the compromised synergy, or absence of positive symbiosis, between the fetus and the mother. The two central currents of this synergy, or lack thereof, are physical and emotional.

Let us imagine that the expectant mother is physically healthy, enjoys a wholesome diet, and does not smoke or drink excessively, or take addictive or system-damaging drugs. This is hugely important for the fetus, for obvious biological reasons. Whatever the mother takes into her system is transferred to the fetus via the umbilical cord, the placenta, and the flow of blood that delivers all nutrients from the mother to the unborn child. In addition, let's imagine that she is anticipating the coming birth in a positive way. She really wants her baby. She feels supported by those around her, who are creating a safe, caring environment in which the baby can be born.

The entirety of these two kinds of support for the unborn child—both the physical and the emotional—can be relived by seekers who access the intrauterine, first-matrix universe in their work in meta-ordinary states. By casting the spotlight of consciousness on these intrauterine memories via the breath or some other method, they get all kinds of insights on the importance of this stage of their history and how it has affected the experience of their post-natal life.

Now let us imagine the opposite scenario. In this situation, perhaps the expectant mother is physically unhealthy. She is a heavy drinker and smoker. She may be involved with other addictive substances, or have neither the ways, the means, nor the inclination to eat healthily. Add to this a whole array of negative emotional scenarios. She is ambivalent about her pregnancy, or actively does not want to be a mother. She conceived in an inopportune environment, and has no support from the father, or other possible avenues of caring and wellbeing to which she can turn. Perhaps she herself has experienced powerful physical or emotional abuse. She is fearful, unhappy, and alone.

In the exact same way that the child is the direct inheritor of the positive physical and emotional environment created by the mother in the first scenario, the fetus is the victim of the mother's difficulty in the second tableau. In this situation, the oxygen-deprived blood supply through the umbilical and the placenta carry toxins and poisons to the fetus. In addition, the mother's emotional pain is unwittingly transmitted to, and inherited by, the unborn child. Again, any or all of this can be re-experienced by seekers at some stage in their inner holotropic work.

In either case, whether the biological or emotional influence of the intrauterine is toxic or positive, seekers have the insight that their womb experience deeply affects their lives. It is even more fascinating that these insights often turn out to be higher or deeper octaves of inner work they have already been doing in traditional systems of psychology that focus on the post-natal biography alone. It is not that the insights they receive from their post-natal work are inaccurate. It is just that, in the light of what they have learned from the intrauterine experience, and of course, from the birth experience itself we will soon describe, what they had learned about themselves so far is incomplete. It represents only part of the picture.

When breathers relive their intrauterine, or first-matrix experience, or when they relive the dynamics of any matrix, for that matter, they do so from the possibilities of three poises. One, they directly relive, as a biological living entity, what happened physically. Or, two, they have some kind of metaphorical experience of the emotional and physical history. Or, third, they experience something from both of these perspectives at the same time. So far, we have looked at the first scenario: the re-experiencing of intrauterine events in what appears to be a more or less direct remembering and reliving of actual events.

But what do we mean when we say that the reliving of physical phenomena can occur within a metaphorical context? These kinds of experiences are the basis for our understanding of the perinatal dimension as an interface, or *dimension doorway*, between the personal and transpersonal domains. So what are some of the forms this higher octave, or metaphorical overlay, of physical experiences might take? First, we will relate a few examples from seekers' inner exploration that demonstrate this interplay of biographical experience and metaphorical, archetypal, or transpersonal overlay.

It seems experientially logical to do this within the contrasting amniotic environments of the *good womb/toxic womb* context we already established. So, let us envision a situation where a breather experiences herself as the fetus in a good womb, where there is a healthy, life-enhancing, nurturing transmission of biologically supportive nutrients through the umbilical and the placenta from the mother to the unborn child. In addition to this, she might then also experience herself as an aquatic creature, like a dolphin or jellyfish, basking and floating in a pristine oceanic environment. Another possibility would be the experience of life in an earthly paradise, where every physical or emotional need—food, shelter, health, love, and nurturing—is effortlessly, naturally, and irresistibly met.

At the other end of the continuum, along with the biographical components of the toxic womb, a seeker may experience what it is like to be immersed in a polluted swamp or cesspool. Instead of peace and safety, this can be accompanied by a sense of dis-ease, anxiety, or paranoia. When the physical and emotional deprivation was particularly viral, breathers can feel that, as fetuses, they are in mortal danger, or under attack by dangerous, or even demonic entities, mythic creatures, or phantasms. The atmosphere can seem drenched in vital anxiety, mortal fear, or even hysterical panic. Instead of experiencing the feminine energy as that of loving, nurturing protector, she may experience the mother force as a dark presence of fear and evil, a sorceress, a witch, or vampire-like being.

Studies of the cosmologies and mythologies of world cultures reveal that there are numerous realms from which these kinds of images, beings, and experiences may emerge. As they manifest in a session, they may take on the personal, mythic nuances characterized by any one or more unique systems. So, the central issue before us is to fathom the modus operandi and logic whereby a personal biographical memory will often be accompanied by frequently recognizable cross-cultural, transpersonal, and mythic structures.

Most journeyers receive a consistently convincing demonstration of this logic through what we have referred to, in somewhat less than scientific terms, as the Inner Healer, or the power within. For those of you with the need for a more rigorously clinical explanation, one may choose to call this action a *mechanism*. Virtually all endeavors toward explaining the results derived from work in non-ordinary states of consciousness follow what we call *experiential* logic. In this context, seekers have insights and revelations based on what they undergo in their journeys. With an inherently inalienable reliability, the internal events themselves, in an *experiential* fashion, seem to contain their own validation.

It is well known that the value of inner holotropic sessions is often defined by the experience of powerful *insights*. The most transformative of these insights, those that have the capacity to shatter the ossification of a less comprehensive, outdated *imago mundi*, tend to emerge from a stratum of mentality beyond the rational level. This deeper dimension of truth is known as *intuition*. Yet, it comes as no surprise when seekers also report that it is their *physical* and *emotional* experiences, which most often indelibly catalyze deep change. This deep change tends to catapult them from the personal to the transpersonal domains of the psyche. In addition, this trajectory ultimately results, as it moves them toward wholeness, in a deepening of the spiritual impulse crucial to authentic, in-depth transformation.

Physical and emotional experiences have a great power to shape causal impressions in the human psyche. As we said, breathers are often surprised at, and sometimes overwhelmed by, a confrontation with the perinatal level of an emotion they have already explored in traditional therapy. They seem to access an expanded level of power and vividness way beyond what they felt in their post-natal inquiry. When they first open to the transpersonal domain, including the metaphorical and archetypal levels of the personal experiences they have undergone in their biographical or perinatal work, a similar deepening occurs. Once again, it is the impetus of the *emotion* and the *physical sensation* that seems to carry the explosive power necessary for the breakthrough to the next level.

We should emphasize that *transformation is not linear*. When we do our inner work, there is no inherent or compelling reason why our process will begin with our post-natal biography, proceed to the perinatal, and then ultimately open to the transpersonal, or collective dimension. It certainly *can* happen this way. But just as often, seekers' work tends to be "all over the map." It may be initiated by a powerful transpersonal overlay, and then proceed to a systematic uncovering of more personal material from the perinatal or biographical dimensions. Or one's initial episode may be a biological birth experience, and from there blossom into biographical and transpersonal revelations.

However, it is difficult to present this cartography of the psyche without at least paying minimal homage to a linear trajectory. Yet we can also make other erroneous assumptions if we employ this kind of linear evaluation to the transformative potential offered by the different dimensions of the psyche. For example, there is a tendency to think that the perinatal level is "deeper," or more important, than the biographical. And, with similar specious logic, we conclude that the transpersonal level is thus more powerful or valuable than the perinatal or the biographical.

We often see breathers, and even the facilitators supporting them, give biographical material short shrift. There is an implication that, when they really "get it together," breathers will be ready to access the deeper dimensions. The possible result is that participants might somehow feel better about themselves in a more egoic and less authentic way when they access the perinatal or transpersonal. As facilitators, we must be diligent not to consciously or unconsciously support this attitude. It is a dogmatic interpretation not shared by those who have done this kind of work with rigorous integrity over time.

Many breathers report having the empowering experience that the biographical domain—far from being the least important dimension therapeutically—can sometimes be the most powerful and relevant. This is true for them, even though the emotional and physical intensity of previously experienced perinatal and transpersonal material may sometimes feel greater than an initial reliving of biographical material from within a pattern, or COEX.

It seems that, at this point, a powerful "meta-layer" of insight and healing has become available. Breathers have reported that, after doing deep work in the perinatal or transpersonal dimensions, their Inner Healer or power within will take them into the biographical domain—either for the first time, or for another post-natal episode. However, this time, they have an extremely powerful experience, in which *all levels of the psyche*—biographical, perinatal, and transpersonal—are fully present in one biographical amalgam. The power of each dimension seems to be simultaneously superimposed over the others in a dynamic cluster of extraordinary emotional and psychological intensity.

It is as though an entire COEX is experienced—not just sequentially, but all at once. And when this occurs breathers have the insight that they have attained a core, in-depth level of healing of that particular pattern. In addition, along with the reliving of the previously unconscious material, they now get an added "meta-insight." This meta-insight effectively focuses and summarizes the linear trajectory of the material into one supreme episode.

These insights are often accompanied by a sense of celebration and freedom. Breathers realize that the biographical life—based on its presence and availability as the current earth operating platform—is the playing field for the seeker of all dimensions of universal existence. They get the mystical insight that the whole journey of Becoming is "here, now," in an always already presence, or sense of Being. Ultimately, this experience reveals as well as validates a wonderful, cosmic relevance for the earth incarnation, and an exciting attunement to the perennial philosophical tradition.

Our own personal experiences, coupled with our observations of many in their processes, lead us to trust that each emergence from the psyche during Holotropic Breathwork comes with impeccable timing and has a perfect relevance for our transformation. Without this trust, we denigrate the central healing mechanism operative in the method. It just does not seem to be therapeutically logical to imagine that the Inner Healer works with any kind of linear intention. When this insight is not immediately obvious for a breather, it is the task of a facilitator who deeply trusts a more non-linear working of inner healer dynamics to validate the journeyers' experience, within the framework of the inherently irrefutable perfection of the gift of consciousness they have received.

One of the profound characteristics of the perinatal dimension, as we said, is its *gateway capability*, its function as the dimension doorway, or interface, between personal and transpersonal experience. To reiterate, the physical and emotional experiences of birth are often so powerful that they can be disconcertingly overwhelming to breathers. There seems almost no way to prepare oneself for their particular intensity.

An interesting phenomenon frequently occurs at this point of emotional and physical confrontation. This power can assume the characteristics of a *magnet*, or a *homing beacon*, directed toward the transpersonal domain; a realm that we have said is basically commensurate with all that is. This beacon will attract, from the infinite realms of the transpersonal, other physical and emotional experiences of the same *quality* as those that are being experienced within the perinatal domain.

This magnetic, gateway capability would account for the frequently occurring dynamic whereby, when seekers relive the record of their biological birth, this experience is often accompanied by transpersonal phenomena. What validates the attractive power of emotions and physical sensations is that the transpersonal experiences relived in conjunction with the perinatal material share the same or similar *experiential* qualities. The difference is that, for individual breathers, the experience is personal to them alone, being an accurate record of the birth experience they underwent.

However, the kinds of experience that enter the spotlight of consciousness from the transpersonal domain are somewhat dissimilar, in one important aspect. Although they are of the same experiential quality, they tend to be what we call archetypal. That is, they emerge from fields of experience common to humanity at large—from any historical or mythic period—not just an individual manifestation, such as karmic memory.

In addition, not only can these experiences represent humanity, both historically or mythically, across space and time, they also can include *any* kind of experience from supra-human realms, including any way that birth or creation occurs within nature, be it of animal or plant origin. But it would include as well the nature of birth, in all its ramifications derived from non-physical dimensions, including archetypal, spiritual, or any realm of meta-physical manifestation imaginable or unimaginable. The thread that binds them all into a therapeutic whole is woven from the physical and emotional concomitants of the record of individual birth.

With this understanding of the phenomenon of experiencing archetypal/metaphorical as well as biographical information when reliving biological birth, it should be easier to proceed with our unfolding of the rest of the first matrix, and the subsequent three matrixes of the birth process. We should be able to dance back and forth between the biological and the metaphorical without confusion. We will look at the experiential trajectory of *Caesarian birth* in a few paragraphs. But for now we will focus on a small cross-section of the elements of a *vaginal birth*.

The Second Matrix

The walls of the uterus contract; this along with the various chemical messages being sent from the mother through the umbilical chord and the placenta, coupled with the transmission of a range of emotional messages, signals the beginning of the birth. Biologically or emotionally, it could be felt as a disturbance, an interruption, and any one of dozens of levels of distress or discomfort. Archetypally, if it has been a good womb, it could be experienced as what we might call "trouble in paradise." It could take on the mythic power of "expulsion from the Garden of Eden," or other similar motifs.

If it has been a toxic womb, it can be experienced as another octave of an already familiar deprivation and danger. In either event, it represents a separation or threatening disconnection from the mother. The disconnection, although very frequently emotional, has a solid biological component. As the walls of the uterus contract, the blood supply through the capillaries in the walls becomes crimped. This cuts off the flow of blood, vital nutrients, and oxygen that have been the living, physical connection between the fetus and the mother. Of course, this biological deprivation has its emotional octave too. Life support experienced by the fetus transcends the merely biological. It includes the sense of emotional separation as well.

The fetus is now leaving the safety of the womb, or whatever the experience the fetus has had of that environment. This is the shift, then, from the first matrix to the beginning of the second matrix. Physically, the fetus is now being propelled by the contractions toward the entrance to the birth canal. But at this stage, the cervix is closed. This is now the second matrix, what we call the "No Exit" situation.

The fetus is unavoidably caught in a biological and metaphorical/emotional double-bind. On the one hand, irresistible muscular pressures are compelling the fetus forward. On the other, an equally powerful biological situation thwarts this ability to proceed. What was frequently experienced as an Edenic environment is fast becoming an introduction to an agonizingly slow descent into a hell born of entrapment, monumental impediment, separation from the source, and the cessation of linear time.

The enormous physical pressures of contraction and compression can be accompanied by a host of biographical and transpersonal phenomena imbued with the same experiential spirit. As seekers explore themselves biographically through traditional means, they often work with memories involving depression, futility, powerlessness, guilt, shame, low self-esteem, anxiety, hopelessness, emptiness, loss of love and connection, or aloneness. When these seekers access the perinatal alone, or as the gateway to the archetypal domain, they often get the sense that they are finally confronting the powerful, creative roots of their process. Through the experience of this higher, or deeper, octave of their post-natal emotional/psychological/physical material, they are beginning to get in touch with the full implications of a journey toward wholeness. All of this information supports our viewing transformation through a lens of wellness or wholeness, as opposed to disease or pathology.

Sometimes opening to these deeper dimensions of formative causality can feel overwhelming. It is as though, all of a sudden, the experiential spotlight of the power within has become brighter and more acutely focused. Yet paradoxically, the unexpected opening to this expansion of underlying motivations can also feel strangely validating. Seekers report feeling that, instead of wondering why they just cannot seem to reap the benefits they need from their traditional therapy, all of a sudden, what they have been feeling so intensely, and what has been so difficult to negotiate, now makes perfect sense. In other words, they at last are becoming acquainted with the *experiential logic* born from a promise of future wellness.

The second matrix also has a unique relevance for those in recovery from all kinds of addictions who are working the psycho-spiritual path known as the Twelve Steps. A profound confrontation with the state of consciousness we know as *powerlessness* is the foundational first step of this powerful yoga. Over the years, we have supported hundreds of recovering addicts in Holotropic Breathwork experiences. For many of these, the Twelve Step yoga has been effective, yet quite a few have found the recovery process to be difficult.

However, most of these seekers report that, when through holotropic work they access the sense of powerlessness that the fetus feels in the second matrix of the birth process, their recovery paradigm expands dramatically. They finally understand the most profound implications of the Twelve Step yoga's first step: *We admit we are powerless over our addiction, and that our lives have become unmanageable.* And at this point, they really begin to absorb the life-changing healing potential inherent in the surrender experience.

We also frequently witness invaluable realizations from deep self-exploration in those who are dealing with depression. Even after extensive work in their early biographical history looking for the roots of why they feel so depressed, the insights they receive just do not seem to accurately reflect the intensity of their daily suffering. However, when they first access the second matrix, and relive themselves as the fetus stuck in the canal after having been expelled unceremoniously from the safety of the womb, all of a sudden, their overwhelming depression makes perfect sense.

Moreover, when the Inner Healer brings up archetypal clusters associated with depression, for the first time hope can begin to dawn, in what has felt for so long like a timeless hell of hopelessness. Reliving the transpersonal components of the second matrix ultimately opens them to the insight that, even if they are feeling alone, *they are not so alone in their aloneness.* These excruciating feelings reveal themselves to be common to all humanity, or archetypal. Spiritual teachers have referred to these states of consciousness throughout history, and relate that this experience is a challenging yet integral stage of transformation and moving toward wholeness. Once again, seekers report feeling relieved that there is nothing "broken" within them, now that they understand the healing trajectory of such difficult states.

The Christian mystic St. John of the Cross wrote about the existential crisis he called the *dark night of the soul.* We sometimes wonder, for example, how a cosmic experience of engulfment, isolation, or depression, though initially unbearable, can at some stage feel better than the personal levels of these emotions we have felt in our everyday lives. By the very nature of the transpersonal/archetypal dimension, we are opening to a seemingly limitless, or at least, greatly expanded, level of the pain with which we are all too familiar.

Yet this insight, that the torture many have personally felt is an experience common to all humanity, elevates seekers to a higher, more expanded sphere of life-function and understanding. This collective, higher, universal sphere includes *connection.* The good news is that this connection and identification with something larger than our individual selves can be extremely healing. It is a vital component of moving toward wholeness.

This is one of the immeasurable benefits of doing work in meta-ordinary states of consciousness. We find ourselves *part of ...* in a way we have never been before. Later, when we address the transpersonal dimension directly, along with collective dimensions of the other birth matrices, we will give more examples of the cosmic nature of the second matrix. It is through this dimension that what we heretofore thought of as *my pain, my depression, my aloneness* becomes *ours*, or *all of humanity's* experiences of these conditions. This shifting of our focus from *my* to *our* always represents a significant therapeutic and/or spiritual milestone on the road to wholeness and wellness.

The Third Matrix

Most of us have never met any seeker who says she likes the second matrix. By its very nature, its essence encompasses the absolute negation of, as well as the inability to experience, any joy whatsoever. However, nearly everyone agrees there is one stage of the second matrix worth experiencing. And this is getting out of it.

Biologically, the cervix opens, so that now there is a way for the fetus to begin in earnest the journey toward birth. The dynamis of this journey will be the contractions of the uterus catalyzed within the mother. Contractions can generate quite incredible force, sometimes reaching fifty to a hundred pounds of pressure per square inch. It is interesting that in traditional therapy, clients often report that depression, a hallmark of the second matrix, is an episode of total absence of power, energy, will, force, or motivation. In addition, there is widespread agreement among many therapists that depression is *anger turned inward*. Based upon what we see in deep work, these therapists are actually onto something.

Even though the breathers' experience is one of having no energy, once the cervix opens and the fetus is free to move, the real truth of the dynamic actually emerges. It is not that there is no power or force in the second matrix. It is just that at this stage, power is unavailable. In fact, the seeker is "sitting on," or repressing, an enormous reservoir of power and energy. It is just not accessible yet. It is turned inward, or introjected somehow. The physical constrictions of the second matrix seem to demand such an introjection. There is no way to expand when biology relentlessly forces constriction. As a result, journeyers often interpret this unavailability of personal power as a proof that there is no power in the universe. No wonder we are depressed!

However, with the opening of the cervix, the *depression* of the second matrix often morphs into the *power* of the third matrix. This power is frequently experienced by seekers as rage. In light of this experiential reality, the belief of post-natal therapists that depression is anger turned inward is experientially quite valid. But rage is just one way breathers experience third matrix energy. Other nuances in the same vein include *biological fury*. In traditional therapy, anger carries quite a stigma and a charge. This makes sense, given the tragic results of so many forms this force takes in the lives of human beings. However, in the birth canal, biological fury carries no such stigma. In fact, the opposite is true. Here it represents a heroic, often life/death struggle for existence by a being who is virtually helpless and at the mercy of relentless external pressures and forces.

The archetypal/transpersonal content involving aggression, anger, or biological fury which becomes available in the reliving of the third matrix is incredibly rich, and can even be awe-inspiring. Drawn from the infinite collective dimension, as though magnetized by the "tractor beam" of the emotional/physical power of the birth episode, this transpersonal material deepens and enriches the power of the third-matrix experience. For example, seekers' rage may take on universal proportions, as they find themselves experiencing ferocious war sequences as real personages from history, or as mythic warriors reliving noble yet terrible battles, or undergoing hand-to-hand combat to the death in a wide array of cross-cultural contexts.

On another level, seekers find themselves actually fully becoming the pent-up rage they may have endured and barely touched in face-to-face talk therapy when it was associated with abuse, punishment, ridicule, and systematic disempowerment in familial or social situations. We hear from breathers repeatedly that when they access the third matrix, it is almost impossible to be prepared for the outpouring of intensity these kinds of energies assume at this level. They often find it amusing as they recount the "anger reduction" techniques they underwent in some traditional therapies, in contrast with the raw, straightforward purity of rage and biological fury they encounter in meta-ordinary states.

We should also mention another fascinating healing phenomenon that we often see in breathers who for the first time embrace both the perinatal and the archetypal level of aggression. As we pointed out, the second matrix includes the reservoir of emotional and physical experiences where humans have identified themselves as victims. Almost everyone who has done any kind of deep work reports at least some experience of victimhood in their lives. In processing the uncovered material associated with victimhood, seekers seem to arrive almost unanimously at an interesting admission: As painful as being a victim is, they would rather be a victim in their lives than a perpetrator. They also report that it seems to be a lot easier to admit to being a victim than it does to confront the possibility that they are also perpetrators.

Now, as we have pointed out, the third matrix is the repository of "perpetrator energy." So, when breathers hit this level of the psyche, they have some interesting reactions. First, they can find it to be tremendously rewarding to emerge from the shackles of victimhood by accessing this powerful, warrior-like rage. And, "while on the mat," it often feels quite satisfying to then punish intra-psychically, or even annihilate the abuser in their lives, or to wreak havoc upon the entire archetypal field of abusers for all time.

On the other hand, it is also common to experience resistance to perpetrator energy, because of breathers' natural reluctance or abhorrence at seeing themselves as an abuser. Ironically, though, it is well known even in more traditional therapeutic modalities, that getting in touch with rage is a necessary early stage of coming into personal power, as a precursor to opening to the experience of a true power within. Consequently, facing the dilemma of whether to embrace the abuser in the meta-ordinary state often becomes one of the great lessons to be learned at this stage of personal transformation.

We should also mention one more permutation of the victim/perpetrator dynamic. In traditional therapy, seekers are often taught that the reliving of the trauma followed by forgiveness of the perpetrator constitutes full healing of abuse. However, those who do Holotropic Breathwork frequently report something a little more nuanced. They also attest to the fact that one must fully relive and discharge the pent-up energies associated with the victim episodes. Next, they too confirm the empowerment in being able to muster a third-matrix energy and respond with their own newfound, and in fact refreshing, level of aggression and power.

Yet, deep work in this level of the psyche reveals another fascinating stratum of healing that seems much less available if the work only takes place in what we call the hylotropic, or ordinary, everyday level of consciousness. In third-matrix work, breathers often at some point confront the possibility of actually identifying with either the one person or group who actually violated or abused them. What's more, they then find themselves confronting the possibility of becoming, not just an individual perpetrator, but the archetypal perpetrator as well. And it is from this disconcerting, yet profound experiential *identification with the perpetrator* that the deepest level of healing seems to actually emerge for them.

Breathers also realize that they have taken quite a leap beyond forgiveness once they have become the perpetrator. In the act of forgiveness, one sees oneself still as a victim who is separated from the perpetrator. But in actual identification with the perpetrator, or even the archetype of "perpetratorness," all boundaries are superseded. It is no accident that most mystical traditions recommend letting go of arbitrary boundaries in favor of an emerging oneness as a necessary and important stage in the journey toward wholeness. What's more, the recognition that everyone carries perpetrator energy within, as part of their universal archetypal heritage—even if they may have never felt that they were a perpetrator in this life—totally reframes the dynamic in such a way that it seems to maximize the deepest healing.

For seekers who are accustomed to viewing themselves through traditional therapeutic lenses, reliving the birth struggle radically reframes their personal reactions to aggression. In the same way they felt some kind of validation for their depression after experiencing deeper perinatal and archetypal levels of this condition, experiencing rage in the birth canal can be healing, and add a sense of wellness to the gestalt. What we often hear is that for the first time the power of the rage they feel in everyday life finally feels validated and somehow congruent. To relive it without the lens of social stigma, but as an inevitable component of birth survival, not only frees the pent-up charge, but also heals deep levels of guilt and shame. In addition, the connection they access by the realization that rage and aggression are archetypal to all humans can greatly reduce previous levels of isolation, shame, and guilt.

To continue, the power/anger/biological fury motif is by no means the only important dynamic of the perinatal level. It is the addition of the forces of sexuality and spirituality that make the third matrix such a compellingly rich, complex well-spring of healing power. The energy of aggression in terms of biological fury is fairly straightforward. But what about sexuality? How is the third matrix a causative level for the emergence of human sexuality? A number of factors come into play here. First, most journeyers, whether through the breath, some type of substance or other practice, the birth struggle can be a trial of great physical pain. It is well known historically that heightened physical pain can morph into powerful experiences of sensual and even intense sexual pleasure.

This blurring of the boundaries between pain and pleasure appears to have a physical baseline that can experientially translate into a psychological and emotional counterpart. One of the chief components of the physical situation is strangulation and oxygen deprivation caused at this level by the enormous pressures of the birth canal exerted upon the fetus. There are also other specific biological nuances, such as the umbilical chord being wrapped around the neck. It is interesting to point out that many men who are executed by hanging have an erection during the experience, and even ejaculate during the death throes. However, we can most persuasively validate the psycho/physical/sexual connection between pain and pleasure by examining the underpinnings and motivations operable in the practice of sado-masochism.

To slightly digress, we should point out that many of Freud's and others' observations, at a certain level, seem to be compatible with what we see in the experience of breathers. However, this is almost exclusively true when breathers access biographical information. For example, what we see in the breathing as regards the experience of the newborn, for the most part, reflects Freud's understanding of early post-natal dynamics. His observations are also frequently validated by breathers' experiences of sexuality, both at the adolescent as well as the infantile level.

But it is much more difficult to feel a resonance with, or an experiential validity in, his attempts to explain other psychological phenomena, including sado-masochism, through early post-natal dynamics alone. However, when breathers themselves experience the third perinatal matrix, or witness others reliving certain sequences within this matrix, all of a sudden, these kinds of life sexual behaviors or identifications take on a whole new meaning.

Traditional psychology teaches us how unconscious, unprocessed biographical experiences can be acted out in everyday life and become the source of substantial distress. This is also borne out by the holotropic perspective. But we have also seen how breathers garner other levels of motivational stimuli in the same manner. It is clear to many that the unconscious record of the birth process accounts for a substantial degree of the dynamics that focus and shape the psyche and the choices humans make. This can absolutely include seekers' sexual predilections, and in some cases, an experience of at least temporary sojourns of one or more sexual identities.

Here, in the third matrix of the perinatal episode, with its experientially logical mixture of sexuality and aggression, lies a related, yet deeper and more relevant octave of the sado-masochistic tendencies encountered in human sexual behavior. We have already reported that in the case of the discovery of deeper roots of depression in the second matrix, as well as anger in the third, seekers can feel overwhelmed at the intensity of these levels. But they can also experience a certain sense of validation and ultimately a reduction in shame. This validation emerges in discovering that what they thought was an illness or aberration may have in fact been a natural and logical way that the psyche attempts to heal itself by bringing into consciousness some hint of deeper dynamics.

Over the years, we have supported a number of breathers who in their everyday lives not only regularly engaged in sado-masochistic practices, but actually became obsessed with, or even addicted to, to these particular life experiences. Upon an experiential encounter in the breathwork with the sexual and aggressive feelings and sensations of the third matrix, they often reported how they could finally understand where the desire for much of their sexual preferences originated. This once again underscores the process of how seekers can reach a deeper octave of healing through doing work in meta-ordinary states of consciousness.

We can amplify, and put in a slightly different context, some of what we have already discussed as part of the basic holotropic strategy: First, the Inner Healer appears *always* to be orchestrating healing dynamics that move seekers toward wholeness. Even without individuals' paying any attention to this orchestration whatsoever, the healing trajectory is more than likely occurring anyway. This takes place through the emergence of unconscious material, gradually or suddenly, into the consciousness of individuals in their everyday lives.

We witness over and over again how that which is unconscious naturally and inherently seeks to become conscious. Moreover, this healing dynamic is operative for all. It is true for seekers who are attempting to bring intra-psychic material into awareness through deep practices. But it is also true for those who are merely engaging in their everyday life process, more or less unconscious of underlying motivating dynamics, and at the same time having no desire whatsoever to pursue inner growth.

The most common difference is that the evolutionary process of moving toward wholeness proceeds at a much more gradual pace, punctuated by more episodes that are difficult to understand or to integrate when individuals are unconscious of the process and are making a choice not to do inner work. The continuum of experiences individuals can undergo in everyday life, whether positive or negative, either healing or reinforcing of dysfunction, seems to be directly related to the intention, or lack of intention, including opposition, with which they face or deny the presence of the emerging material.

Even if one has no inclination to engage in deep work, or no idea of this transformational process at all, it is almost inevitable that at some point the Inner Healer will thrust intra-psychic material into one's life field. When this occurs, the lack of context, understanding, or desire to do inner work can create a sense of dysfunctional, or to some degree even pathological, situations that further bring confusion and a level of suffering into the everyday life. The emerging material becomes just one more unacknowledged issue or pattern that directs the behavior of the person into more and more self-defeating outcomes.

On the other hand, if one engages in deep work, in the holotropic manner or in any number of other practices, it is much more likely that these emergences can occur in a safe, healing context capable of midwifing a rich spectrum of insight, empowerment, and self-compassion. This can often result in a state of freedom and healing, giving the seeker an opportunity to make more creative, empowered life decisions. Furthermore, it can initiate the impetus for the individual to begin a practice with which she/he resonates in order to continue the growth already attained. These essential insights will be covered in much greater detail later when we explore a holotropic therapy. But even without a day-to-day, or moment-to-moment holotropic practice, these dynamics have most often been more readily accessible within healing milieus afforded by the holotropic breathing, ingestion of entheogens, or any method capable of accessing meta-ordinary states of consciousness in a safe setting.

Thus far in our outline of the third perinatal matrix, we have covered two aspects of the three intertwined components of this stage of the birth process—aggression and sexuality. But what about spirituality, or as we have proposed, *numinosity*? Even if combining the dynamics of aggression and sexuality requires us to make a few emotional and intellectual leaps, adding spirituality to the mix definitely "thickens the plot." To accomplish this, we will explore an already mentioned centerpiece of the holotropic perspective.

Ego Death and Rebirth

What we call the *ego death* is one of the most powerful of all transformational experiences. We have already made the distinction between the ego in psycho-spiritual context, and the ego in the Freudian tradition. To reiterate, in psychoanalysis, the ego was Freud's term for that part of our psyche that enables us to function in the everyday world. However, in many spiritual and philosophical traditions ego is used to denote the *false self.*

Most psycho-spiritual systems offer nuances on the origin and makeup of this false self. It is nearly unanimously agreed upon that, no matter how it is formed, most human beings live in this ultimately unsatisfying poise. Even more vital to our inquiry is that the ego is almost universally recognized as the root cause of our suffering in this world. All of these psycho-spiritual systems suggest, in their own metaphors, that a primary characteristic of the false self is the sense of separation, disempowerment, and isolation it engenders in our lives.

This crucial alienation from any fundamentally revitalizing sense of connectedness plagues most of us. It seems to be the source of most existentially dissatisfying cravings, attachments, or addictions we humans have. Our false self motivates us to always look in vain for fulfillment *outside* ourselves, or as some like to put it, "looking for love in all the wrong places." We do this, not knowing that, as many mystics tell us, the only source of any absolute satisfaction comes in a recognition of our identity with a true, whole self, or unifying state of consciousness *within* each being.

In addition, they share that our empowerment and fulfillment begin with the recognition that it is the birthright of all of us to return to our numinous origins and sense of wholeness—as well as a recognition of our own power within. It is worth noting that many of those who use Holotropic Breathwork or a path with entheogens relate that it is the accruing of unconscious material not just from the biographical dimension of the psyche, but from the perinatal and transpersonal bands of consciousness as well, that is often the source of our alienation we often feel in our lives.

As we pointed out, there are two octaves to the perinatal. One is the actual historic record of our biological birth. Making conscious this life event has powerful relevance for optimum psycho-spiritual health. The second level is an intra-psychic structure, or matrix, containing elements of the powerful transformational experience we call the *ego death*. In meta-ordinary states of consciousness, we can have the experience that the four stages, or matrices, of biological birth also directly correspond to four cross-culturally and historically recognized stages of psycho-spiritual death/rebirth. Or, metaphorically expressed, we could say that they represent four *seasons of transformation*. In the same manner that the perinatal can act as a gateway to the transpersonal domain, the ego-death episode is also magnetized by, and becomes focused within, the perinatal.

The physical birth process seems to be a perfect medium for the ego-death experience. It is ironic that, in order to be born, we often face what can be a life-threatening situation—physical birth. Second, birth is a dimension that combines, not just physical suffering, but intense emotional states that seem to be the quintessence of their biographical counterparts.

The perinatal can also act in the metaphorical manner of Janus, the two-headed god of the Roman pantheon. Like Janus, the perinatal—in its gateway capability—scans, and has a power of experiential attraction, in two directions. It can magnetize the transpersonal domain. But it can also attract material of similar qualities from the biographical dimension. The perinatal is, in a sense, the open, invitational playing field of transformation. To be poetic, it is the Burning Man, or the Kumbh Mela of the psyche, where experiences from all dimensions of the unconscious are welcomed to co-mingle or celebrate in Inner Healer-directed gestalts. For many seekers, these experiences somehow attain the zenith of their healing power and relevance in the death/rebirth experience.

We will have more to say about the death/rebirth process in other contexts. At this point, it is important to explain the dynamic whereby we can experience this mixture of aggression, sexuality, and spirituality. The dance between aggression and sexuality should already seem fairly straightforward. But why the spiritual, or numinous component?

To answer this, we must briefly focus on the essence of the fourth matrix. Simply put, the fourth matrix is the birth itself. The fetus emerges from the birth canal into whatever environment is at hand. Therefore, the third matrix is the final transition, or stage prior to physical birth. It is at this turning point, or on this cusp, between the third and fourth matrix where seekers report that they often experience the ego death.

The third matrix can also be surprising. Sometimes the power experienced by seekers may not be as all-sustaining as a fetus close to birth might need in order to complete the journey. Many breathers report that, in reliving the late stages of the birth, there comes a moment, or an experiential eon of moments, where they feel physically and emotionally spent, broken, and defeated. To put it colloquially, the fetus just seems to "run out of gas." At the emotional level, this exhaustion can assume devastating proportions, including a sense of profound powerlessness, annihilation, and defeat. It is as though, here, at the final stage of the struggle, where the freedom of the birth is so near, all feels lost, or diabolically just out of reach.

This stage of the perinatal episode then becomes the fertile ground for a breather's physical/psychological/spiritual experience of the ego death. The physical and emotional concomitants attract the transpersonal archetype of death/rebirth, so that breathers may find themselves in any of three poises. First, they could be reliving only the episode of their actual biological birth. Second, they may experience themselves, not as a fetus, but as a soul, on the universal journey of the ages, described in so many different ways in world mystical traditions: the arc of transformation, from alienation from self and cosmos and finally, through death to rebirth. Or third, they may undergo an experiential overlay of these two themes, experiencing simultaneously, or one level after another, the transpersonal and the biological perinatal. Sometimes one element will dominate, and the other fade momentarily out of consciousness. And then, in some kind of staccato rhythm guided by the Inner Healer, the other dimension will predominate for a while.

At this juncture, we should relate an interesting phenomenon for seekers who find themselves on the cusp between matrixes. For the most part, the transition from one matrix to the next is not abrupt, nor is it sharply delineated. Instead, this movement from one to the other occurs on a gradually shifting experiential continuum. The change in emotional, physical, and numinous content acts very much like what we hear when two sources of music are manipulated in response to engaging the fader mechanism on a sound system's mixing board. Listeners experience that one track gradually shifts *out of* focus, and the next tract gradually *comes into* focus.

During this transition, the two tracks can be heard to overlap, sometimes harmoniously, and sometimes dissonantly. In a similar fashion, for a breather, the content of one matrix often blends for a period of time with the fading of the energy of the previous matrix. As a result, there can be a period of conflicting and contradictory psycho/physical/spiritual material. Or there is also the possibility that the experiential mixture can create a wholly new phenomenon, neither one nor the other, but, in a sense, more powerful or meaningful than the sum of the parts.

We often see this phenomenon in the shifting from the second matrix—the stage of immovability and powerlessness—to the third matrix—a stage of consciousness full of power, fury, and irresistibility. For example, we have seen many breathers experience identification with an animal caught in a trap. After some integration, they get the insight that they were on this cusp between the second and the third matrix. Here, they report reliving the dilemma of the animal ferociously fighting for freedom from the constrictions of the trap.

The trap, of course, represents the confining energies of the second matrix. The savage animal reflects the onset of the biological fury of the third matrix. In this case, neither matrix is pure and undifferentiated, but shares predominance with the energies of the other matrix in the shift, creating a whole new experiential gestalt. Reliving this kind of transpersonal experience gives breathers amazing insights into biographical patterns, especially within the realms of personal relationships. These kinds of bi-matrical perinatal experiences can accurately foreshadow what happens in the transition between the third and the fourth matrix as well—or between aggression, sexuality, and spirituality.

In a few paragraphs we will amplify the nature of spirituality, or the numinous in its pristine fullness, as we continue our exploration of the ego death. At this point, we can say here that the introduction of a prominent spiritual component is the primary concomitant of the resolution of the death/rebirth episode. To reiterate, this occurs at the border between the third and the fourth matrix, where the fourth matrix is the birth experience itself. However, in the bi-matrical fashion, when the fetus is still predominantly under the influence of the third matrix, there can often be a taste, a foreshadowing, of the approaching numinosity.

In this first glimpse of numinosity while still in the third matrix, the true clarity of the spiritual dimension will not be available, nor will this flavor have the potency that may emerge later in the birth. But it will begin to be felt, in the manner we just described, like the metaphor of the fader on the mixer being shifted slightly from the third matrix energies into the border-domain of the numinous. Without the fullness and the purity of the completed death/rebirth episode, the power of the numinous is mitigated, and becomes mixed with the predominant energies of aggression and sexuality. The result provides a fascinating lens into the archetypal domain, and activates a magnetic attraction from there, resulting in the downloading of a rich experiential amalgam.

As the manifestations of aggression, sexuality, and incomplete spirituality mix and merge, we frequently see situations involving the shadow, or darker side of the numinous. One of the most common and striking examples is an experience, a part of which might be universally referred to as the Sabbath of the Witches. Here we have a situation where the spiritual impulse has been glimpsed but egoically perverted, including elements of classic horror tales involving vampires, the demonic, ghosts, and interdimensional dark spirits. These beings enact episodes of orgiastic rites involving perversions of religious rituals, such as experiencing a festival with Christ crucified upside down. Or it can also include the stark irreverence and so-called blasphemy of saints, angels, animals, demons, and other infernal beings participating in wild, quite complex variations on sexual and aggressive themes.

One of the most amazing examples of this phenomenon comes from Walt Disney's classic movie *Fantasia*, the episode called *A Night on Bald Mountain* by Mussorgsky, where the demon lord orchestrates a phantasmagoric celebration, a classic ecstatic orgy of the profane. Most of these experiential situations include a wild, dark sexuality, involving, in a sense, a more intense octave of the sado-masochistic element we have already described. What gets added is not a celebration of spirituality in the usually perceived sense, but a festival with a kind of shadow spirituality, or numinosity's mirror opposite. This creative, yet unorthodox sexual, aggressive, and quasi-spiritual milieu is the form the mitigation of numinosity often takes before it reaches its pure opening and zenith in the final stages of the death/rebirth episode.

I would like to mention, in this context, an experience shared quite a number of years ago by a breather who worked with us on a number of occasions. In her everyday life, she was intimately connected with a community regularly engaged in sexual practices with a predominantly sado-masochistic flavor. After one of her holotropic sessions, she reported that, as we have mentioned before in the case of other breathers, she really understood a deeper and more complete level of her predilection for this particular life choice.

But she added another, more exalted dimension as well. She shared that, in her community, these practices were not engaged in for sexual satisfaction alone. For her, and for her fellow practitioners, it was a religion.

She related that it was common during these rituals for her and her partners to experience powerful ecstatic states of consciousness involving energies of light, expansion, and connectedness, all with unmistakable numinous qualities.

In her own breathwork, it was when she was approaching the birth, toward the end of the third matrix, that she recognized the connection between sexuality, aggression, and spirituality. She also had the insight that her Inner Healing source had been affording her opportunities to heal her perinatal, as well as other unconscious dynamics, by the repetition of the these practices she underwent in her everyday life. The realization that this urge to repeat experiences in our lives is an attempt by our psyche to heal itself is something we will cover in greater detail later, when we unveil the possibility of a holotropic therapy.

The crucial nature of the evolutionary continuum inherent in our individual awakening to spirituality is where we have been headed all along. However we will now, in a sense, "up the ante" and directly address what is an absolute cornerstone of our entire inquiry. Here is a brief preview of what will ultimately prove to be a lynch-pin in the holotropic perspective. Numinosity has a powerful, central relevance in the death/rebirth process available through all perinatal unfolding. To put it simply: *If we work on ourselves systematically with any method, our path inevitably becomes a spiritual journey.* To reiterate: At this point, we must have a *language, method, and structure* for this numinosity.

As a vibrant component of the transpersonal paradigm, the holotropic perspective, through the methods and maps we have been exploring, offers for many just such a language, method, and structure. What seekers seem to be responding to is its comprehensive ability to bridge traditional science and psychology with the wisdom of the ages. The paradigm succeeds at this, in part, through the expansive, coherent, and logical way it supports the needs of our current humanity, which has been fostered and shaped by a much more secular, scientific, and technological constellation of metaphors.

Without actual methods, such as those provided by spiritual systems, psychedelic exploration, and breathing practices like Holotropic Breathwork, we might still only be dancing around an authentic shift in personal and collective consciousness.

Except in the situations of spiritual emergencies or cases of being "blinded by the light," as some call radical awakening—both of which, if supported properly, can result in amazing healing—we would most often be relying on theory, philosophy, science, and traditional psychology, as well as religious dogma. But what we have learned, and heard reported hundreds of times, is that true numinosity is not just a system, a theory, book, belief, or behavior change alone. It is an *experience*. It is the *radical, consciousness-shifting experience* that is transformational and potently productive of progressive individual and planetary evolution.

We are logically led to focus on the language and structure of one of the most powerful healing dimensions in Holotropic Breathwork—this spiritual opening, or numinous experience. First, think back to the meaning of the name holotropic—moving toward wholeness. We also recently alluded to the diamond-like clarity of perennial wisdom's teachings on the underlying, fundamental causes of human suffering. To summarize, we seem to suffer because of an inherent sense of smallness, or, we could say, our exclusive identification with what Alan Watts called the "skin-encapsulated ego."

It appears that we become preoccupied with, hypnotized by, or even addicted to, this separate self that ultimately and existentially isolates us from all else that is. A defining characteristic is an inwardly focused auto-obsession. We can have the experience through deep work that this auto-obsession, and the ego as well, are ultimately nothing more than a self-referentially created expediency. This expediency is not only limited, but ephemeral, groundless, and inherently false. Its modus operandi is to compound this initial error by a persistent drive for an ill-conceived, wrongly glimpsed, and ultimately perverted sense of what the individual thinks of as wholeness. It creates this false wholeness by obsessively adding to itself a host of coveted external objects and characteristics, in an effort to become enlarged, or greater, in some way.

Ironically, the false self is onto something, but just going about it wrongly. Unwittingly, it is responding to a very real and valid urge of consciousness evolution. This urge is, as the Indian philosopher/mystic Sri Aurobindo has taught, the natural evolution of all humanity and creation—a Becoming—back to the Source, wholeness, or Being. But in this case, the false self is only attempting to enlarge itself, as though a bigger false self is in some way more real or whole. Mystics will tell us, as well as the insights derived from an experience of the Inner Healer in our own exploration, that this strategy is doomed to failure. What we end up with is a greater, more "engorged," and isolated ego, rather than a more whole, connected, and authentic self.

However, if we are lucky, or blessed, we may at some point confront a crisis in our lives, where we hear the deep, clear, chords from the song of the Inner Healer echoing its way through our suffering, sorrow, and relentless craving. Many feel that the following statement is a truth of transformation: *Any episode that allows us to experience ourselves as more whole than we were before, or to see ourselves in an essentially more expanded way, constitutes a spiritual experience. Likewise, any experience accompanied by a sense of expansion, connectedness, freedom, empowerment, and a greater level of fulfillment and joy, also is indicative of an authentic opening to numinosity.*

Bringing these musings to bear on perinatal dynamics, there are at least two poises from which seekers will more than likely experience this level of perinatal consciousness. First, we can be more or less identified with our selves, or the human being, the person who has already been born. We are the one who is now the seeker, who chooses to lie down, close the eyes, take a few deep breaths, and listen to some evocative music. As we go through the holotropic session, we may never lose this sense of the outside reality in our inner experiences, whatever they may be. We may always primarily, or even exclusively, feel that we are this person, who is having an experience of our own birth, or whatever else the episodes may be.

Our consciousness may still focus in two dimensions here. One, we are the consciousness of the *witness* of the perinatal event. Or two, we may lose touch with being this person, this witness consciousness altogether, or at least much of the time, and actually fully experience ourselves as the fetus in the canal. In a sense, we actually *become* the fetus, and lose all touch with our "experiencer-self" on the mat. These two poises in being with our breathwork experience seem to hold true throughout all inner experiences, not just in the perinatal.

Beyond this, there is another set of dual experiences available to breathers when we are in the birth canal. Here, we have access to two possible scenarios, linked by an undeniable, experiential logic. Remember, by scenarios, we also mean states of consciousness, or experiential dimensions or universes. In one of these, we are the *fetus*, unbearably confined, separate, and suffering, longing for relief, freedom, release, and connectedness. Or in the second realm, we may discover ourselves to be the *"soul of the ages,"* perhaps in the Bardo dimension of the Buddhist tradition. Or we may experience this birth passage as though through any mythic tunnel of light, a before-death or after-death plane, or some dimension where death is immanent and rebirth a distant goal.

On one level, we may find ourselves heading toward the archetypal Clear Light. On another, we may be experiencing struggling toward the opening of the vagina and blessed release in the arms of our mother. But, toward which mother might we be moving? Is it our actual birth mother? The answer is of course in the affirmative, in many cases. Or could it in fact be the Divine Mother, or some other representative of the Higher Power cross-culturally? Are we the ancient wanderer, the lost soul, or as the rock band the Moody Blues might say:

A gypsy from a strange and distant time

Traveling in panic all direction blind

Aching for the warmth of a burning sun

Freezing in the emptiness of where he'd come from

Left without a hope of coming home

Or are we the fetus—biologically and emotionally—completely immersed in the birth struggle? Are we the helpless one, exhausted, in pain, perhaps drugged, suffering the agonizing suffocation and torture of the birth pressures, feeling as though we will die and never make it to the safety of our mother's arms? Perhaps we have struggled beyond all endurance, and yet here, at the gateway to freedom, we can go no further.

Or might we be the soul who has been annihilated by great cosmic forces, burned to cinders in some unholy conflagration? Have we been left alone on the last battlefield, wounded, our life blood seeping into vast, empty desert sands, or on the steps of some blasted, torched and bloody temple ruin on a mythic world, in another dimension, or on a planet light years away? Or are we both, or all these beings, fading back and forth like music manipulated on the mixing board of our Inner Healer?

Using the metaphor *"Burned to cinders in some unholy conflagration"* compels us to add a word here about fire in the context of the ego death. Two parallel but distinct impressions emerge at this point, in the late third matrix and on the cusp of the fourth. First is the nature of fire as a quite definitive and striking destroyer. This would make it a perfect offering from the Inner Healer for the destruction of the false self.

Yet there is a second elegant nuance on the nature of fire that focuses this force on the character of rebirth. This is what we call in our work *pyrocatharsis*—a word coined by Grof. "Pyro," of course, has to do with fire. And Aristotle used the term "catharsis" to mean the powerful emotional and psychological cleansing that could occur for the viewers of intense, dramatic stage presentations of his day.

In this context, pyrocatharsis is a perfect name for the experience of radical purification, encompassing a devastatingly thorough obliteration of the old self as the gateway for the emergence of the perfectly cleansed, renewed, and reborn self. As we have pointed out, this experience can be individual, or it can be collective, and even cosmic. Beyond personal ego death and rebirth, we have seen experiences of global annihilation through nuclear cataclysm and other forms of fiery apocalypse. On a wider universal stage are experiences of intergalactic warfare involving mega-atomic weapons of unimaginable destructive power. All these are different octaves of a pyrocathartic transformation with the experiential logic of the often life-threatening intensity inherent in biological birth.

There also seems to be evidence of a physical logic to seekers' experience of fire as part of late stage fetal transition in the birth canal toward birth. Stan Grof reports having heard from mothers who, during delivery, experienced sensations in the vagina akin to burning during the final stages of birth. When Cary and I were attending classes in preparation for the home birth of our son Bryn, our coach surprised us by referring to the point where the baby's head crowns as the *ring of fire*. So, once again, it appears that there is experiential validation for this experience of fire, as well as any number of other perinatal experiences reported by breathers. This validation is cross-matrical, as well as multidimensional, containing evidence from the physical, emotional, mental, as well as numinous levels.

In whichever way we may experience this cusp between the third and the fourth matrix, there is one pivotal event, one thing all beings seem to ultimately face: the very real possibility of defeat, death, and the end of our existence. Both beings, the fetus and the soul wanderer, whether it is one or the other or both that we are experiencing, in most instances, must face the awful possibility of giving up, failing, and never reaching the goal. At another octave, we may confront the necessity of what feels like the impossible: the experience of *surrender*, the moment where we truly accept this death of who we think we are.

It is in this surrender that the miracle happens. If we are the fetus, then it is this moment in which we are born. Beyond the strength or will of any last surviving personal effort, as if by grace, we emerge into our new life. We are not dead; we are life itself. And if we are the archetypal or individual wandering soul, we die. We die to the identity we previously thought ourselves to be. And at this death, we are somehow miraculously reborn.

We may experience ourselves as the phoenix rising from the ashes. Or we may be like Frodo and Sam, alone on a crag in the volcanic collapse of Mt. Doom, having given up the false self of the Ring, miraculously rescued by Gandalf and the eagles, the solar birds of rebirth from the shamanic tradition. Beyond all hope, past any final personal resources, we are magically and cosmically saved. Or perhaps we are both, the fetus and the soul wanderer, our consciousness shifting poetically back and forth between these two poises in the elegant dance of birth, death, and rebirth.

Breathers consistently report that these experiences, of physical rebirth and psycho-spiritual death and rebirth, can be absolutely pivotal in their lives. These are episodes that go beyond thinking, beyond the mind. They are visceral, primal, core-reaching, and worldview-shattering. We feel them in multi-leveled fashion—through the body, the mind, the emotions, the psyche—what we refer to sometimes as our true self, higher self, or perhaps even as the soul. Some say it is as though we are the butterfly emerging from the cocoon, or a saint walking from the tomb.

We are simply not the same person who, once upon a time, it now seems, lay down to have the breathing experience. We are more whole than we have ever been. Our boundaries can seem thinner, lighter. We can be filled with a freedom, peace, empowerment, and connection such as we have never known. It might also be helpful at this point to remind ourselves that, as we have pointed out, the ego death can be a once-in-a-lifetime experience, yet for most of us it is an incremental episode on the journey of our Becoming, as we move toward wholeness, or Being, under the guidance of the power within.

This is what we mean by the ego death being an opening to the numinous dimensions of the psyche. We have sloughed off an outworn cloak, a way of thinking, feeling, and being we now see was false, limiting, and powerless to free us. We become clothed now in a new way of sensing and perceiving ourselves, who we are in relation to our selves, others, the world, the cosmos, and to Spirit. We have let go in a way we could only have imagined before. To put it in a counter-cultural idiom, we are, for all intents and purposes, the *grateful dead*. We are, for the moment, not the same person we once were. That person just no longer exists.

There are of course numerous important experiences that mediate amazing life upgrades for seekers in Holotropic Breathwork and other methods accessing meta-ordinary states of consciousness. Often, they afford journeyers the personal platform of still being a separate self, yet a self that is by all accounts different as well. In a sense, powerful healing experiences become part of a fresh, new personal makeup, outlook, and operation kit of life skills. These provide for a heightened ability to find freedom, empowerment, and wholeness while negotiating a world of other separate selves. Yet breathers consistently report that nothing can quite take the place of the experience of becoming someone absolutely new, with the old self truly nothing but the ghost of another incarnation past.

To reiterate, where we see this episode involving a total change of personhood most often is in the perinatal, on this cusp, this vast, yet often ephemeral borderland between life and death, just prior to physical birth. It seems that it is here, as we are catapulted into the transpersonal domain, that our being, our consciousness, our self, our soul, faces the depths and the heights of spiritual rebirth in the manner described by perennial philosophy for all time. Many of us feel that this is one of Stan's and Christina's greatest contributions: That here, in modern times, even on a hotel ballroom floor, in the heart of a great city, we can experience what mystics and saints have been describing for thousands of years.

The Fourth Matrix

The fourth matrix is the final stage of the birth experience, where the fetus emerges as the newborn into an external environment. We have spent the most time so far covering the fourth matrix experience that seekers report of the archetypal death/rebirth level. To reiterate, this can be an autonomous episode, the one particular way seekers relive the birth in a given session. Yet the experience can also come in a harmonic resonance with a reliving of the actual physical birth.

In addition, the birth experience often assumes the same dual characteristics that reliving of any other memory in the psyche offers. That is, it will involve the historic record of birth, as known by external records and observation, through doctors, nurses, midwives, and so on. Yet it can also include the re-experience of fascinating nuances of the episode almost universally considered inaccessible through physical memory, yet experientially recovered by seekers in the meta-ordinary state experience.

With a few exceptions, it has become generally accepted that there can be no memory record of biological birth, because the portion of the brain responsible for memory is not sufficiently developed at this stage. This widely held position notwithstanding; this is not what we see in Holotropic Breathwork. Breathers report being able to access and re-experience many extremely detailed nuances of the birth, regardless of whether the cortex is sufficiently myelinized, or despite any assertion by members of the medical and scientific community that such memories are impossible.

We have touched on this issue in our brief discussion of paradigm collisions in the second chapter. The entire controversy seems to originate in the nature of the origins of consciousness itself. If we believe, as traditional scientists tell us, that consciousness is an epiphenomenon, a by-product, of the brain, then, as we said, the thousands whose lives have been irrevocably upgraded by the experience of so-called irretrievable psycho-physical data are for the most part either deluded or psychotic.

However, mystics have posited for millennia—and some pioneering brain researchers have presented credible evidence to the effect—that consciousness pre-exists and is independent of the brain. They are inclined to believe that consciousness uses the brain as a kind of reducing valve, as Aldous Huxley believed. Or they suggest that the hardwire of the brain may serve as a medium, one of whose primary functions is to orchestrate the nature of external reality itself.

If these sources are correct, then the majority of the experiences that seekers have had in the meta-ordinary state cannot be so easily dismissed. Moreover, there would be certain scientific bases and validity for them, even if that validity transcends the parameters and purview of traditional science. But as we said before, the most relevant truth of this conflict for most seekers is the fact that, regardless of scientific justification, these experiences have proven to be life-changing and pricelessly rewarding.

What we hear from seekers in terms of the experience of their actual birth is fascinating and incredibly detailed. In addition, they consistently report a quite comprehensive continuum of experiences, ranging from the most blissful to the most challenging. It is also compelling that many of the experiences breathers report, which traditional science and medicine say are impossible to retrieve, are validated by accessing, after the fact, existing records which corroborate the internal experiences they have related.

We begin with what many seekers feel is the ideal birth by referring once again to the intrauterine history. Another look at the womb episode makes it clear that there is a deep experiential connection between the first and the fourth matrix. By this, we mean that both of these are different octaves of the same crucial dynamics that have an indelible impact on not only birth, but also subsequent post-natal history.

The first matrix, in what we might refer to as a good-womb situation, may create a blueprint of wellbeing and connectedness for the fetus. This blueprint contains variations on the theme of a healthy, physically nourishing situation transferred through the placenta and umbilical chord connecting the mother and the fetus. Moreover, the nourishing blueprint will contain the mother's positive energetic attunement with the pregnancy, and the creation of a loving, caring, and emotionally supportive environment in which to envelop the fetus. The keystone, here, is *connection*. It is impossible to overstate the importance for the fetus, physically, emotionally and psychologically, of this positive symbiotic relationship mediated by the experience of connection.

For an optimal foundational beginning, almost all traditional psychological systems stress the necessity of a loving, caring environment of connectedness for the early post-natal situation. If this is not present, they almost unanimously point to its absence as one of the primary causes of later life dysfunction. Work in meta-ordinary states bears this out as well. However, once again it seems that analysis of post-natal factors paints only a partial picture—only one octave, if you will—of important dynamics within the foundational mother/child relationship.

What we have seen is that, in terms of octaves, the intrauterine experience and the experience of birth, along with the early post-natal environment, may share similar components of connection, both biologically and emotionally. Where the fetus in a good-womb situation is dually connected to the mother via the umbilical and the placenta, including her enriching emotional environment, the newborn is in an optimum early post-natal situation. It has the opportunity to be positively connected to the mother, both biologically, through the breast, and emotionally, through her loving support, nourishment, and touch as well. This dual sense of connectedness then creates the optimum baseline and opportunity for the future psychological and emotional wellbeing of the developing, unfolding self.

However, as many of us well know, standard birth practices over a period of at least the last half a century involve a powerful traditional medical presence. It is also well known that, historically, birth practices have been considered a natural, nurturing ritual experience of mother, newborn, midwife, family, and extended community for thousands of years. And it has only been in the 1900s, with the emergence of a powerful, entrenched, primarily Western medical model, that birth has come to be seen as a medical issue which can only be supported by doctors who have for the most part been men. What has been gained by the positive presence of timely good medical intervention during emergencies has been largely overshadowed by the dehumanization of the millennia-long, cross-cultural, natural process. This results in a situation where medical procedures have become the norm, not just during delivery and in the post-natal period, but all through the pregnancy as well. However, there is heartening news. In many more instances, there are doctors, nurses, and midwives representing the best of both birthing worlds—a deep orientation with ancient birthing traditions, supported, as well, with the benefits of modern medicine.

We often hear from seekers that the sometimes sterile, impersonal environment created by an overzealous medical presence can contribute to the disempowerment of the mother. It may also, through no fault of the mother, foster a sense of alienation between her and the baby during the pregnancy, birth, and the early post-natal. The result is a greater likelihood of a situation lending itself to trauma and dysfunction causing significant dissatisfaction in later life experience. It is not surprising, then, that when journeyers are reliving their births, they have the insight that much of the stress and difficulty, both physically and psychologically, has often been caused by these sometimes unnecessary medical interventions.

The mother's receiving of anesthesia at some stage of the birth is a frequent intervention reported by breathers. This powerful experience can be the cause of many complications for a fetus or newborn. It also can create a unique double-bind for seekers when they are reliving an anesthesia situation during a session. Breathers often remark about the healing power of a natural, organic synergy between themselves, as the fetus, and their mothers with which the journey through the canal often seems imbued. Conversely, one of the most invasive, confusing, and destabilizing experiences, characterized by a diabolical ability to derail the natural trajectory of the birth, turns out to be reliving the onset of the anesthesia episode.

There are basically two intertwined dimensions in which the anesthesia difficulty can be experienced. The first is the actual historical record of what the mother and fetus underwent during the event, which of course can be relieved by breathers. The second involves an interesting, as well as ironic, double-bind created for these seekers whose Inner Healers bring them the anesthesia experience in their sessions.

In the first scenario, anesthesia, by its very nature, can greatly inhibit the mother's natural contraction rhythm. When this happens, the next medical intervention often involves the administering of another drug to counteract the inhibited contractions, thereby frequently setting up a vicious cycle. This cycle effectively takes the main responsibility of the birth from the mother and places it in the hands of the medical attendants. Moreover, it serves to amplify substantially the presence of negative emotions by the mother, including fear, anger, frustration, panic and stress. These are often transmitted unwittingly to the fetus, creating trauma with significant negative consequences for foundational, early post-natal development and beyond.

Now, let's look at what is happening to the fetus, when the breather is reliving this while on the mat. We will share it as an amalgam of experiences reported by seekers who have relived anesthesia in their births. This composite represents stories we have heard in slight variations hundreds of times during integration sessions following the meta-ordinary episode.

We might imagine a situation where the fetus was two weeks late. The breather reports that, in reliving herself as a fetus, she knew what was coming—the kind of powerful life she was to have—and was having difficulty facing it. However, when she finally was ready, she was *really* ready. She was like a female Frodo, just about to venture into her own Mordor. In the film, when Frodo was looking down on all those orcs they would have to sneak by to get to Mount Doom, Sam turned to him and said "We have to go in there, Mister Frodo. There's nothing for it." Just like Sam and Frodo, she knew she had to go.

So the process began, and she was off, and moving pretty smoothly, it seemed to her—on the mat, through the canal, heading for the light. It was at this point that her mother—she learned later—had a dose of a narcotic. Remember, as an adult, at the time of her breathwork, she did not know this. She learned about this experientially first, and much more later by asking her mother. In the beginning, she was just totally involved in her inner experience. After she experienced the narcotic, she just faded out into unconsciousness. The next thing she knew, she came back into consciousness, on the mat, feeling totally drugged up, as though she had a bad hangover. She did not know where she was or what had happened. She felt lost, alone, nauseated, and very depressed.

She managed to intuit later, in another session, that she had actually experienced her birth that first time. Yet she had totally missed the entire experience. At this point, she began to put all the pieces of the puzzle together and to remember things her mother had said—like what an easy birth she was. She had shared that the doctor had given her Demerol, and she, the mother, was in bliss through the entire delivery. However, this was definitely *not* the breather's experience at all. For her, it had been traumatic.

Most importantly, the breather not only missed her birth experience. She had also missed connection and bonding with her mother. Her mother was drugged—totally in her own world—and she herself was drugged as well. Her mother told her that she—the newborn—had been taken away, and, she found out later, allowed to be with her mother once in a while for a bottle, on the hospital's time.

This was a long time ago—the era of the Dr. Spock babies—where the strategy was to put the babies in cribs, only receive nourishment from a formula, just be allowed to cry, and be fed on the mother's schedule. She and her mother were just never allowed to truly connect, or to experience the critical episode of bonding, which she, the breather, had read about in Stan Grof's books. She also realized that, even more painful, she and her mother could never connect after that, for decades, until she was able to actually experience her rebirth consciously in one of her sessions. She reported that this set the stage for a beginning to a true mother/daughter relationship.

As we can see from this short account, the bottom line was the absence of the most vital emotional and physical component: *connection*. When breathers continue to work on uncovered issues, such as the anesthesia episode, most of them come to the realization and acceptance that what they went through was not the mother's fault. For the most part, mothers are simply following the doctor's orders, participating and trusting in the prevailing birth strategy at the time. This story is not unique, but quite common in this work.

Many breathers have particular difficulty in reliving, and ultimately healing, the anesthesia episode. Remember, consciousness itself is a co-function of the Inner Healer. Breathers heal by making issues conscious. So, it would seem logical that in the meta-ordinary state, all that seekers would need to do is keep breathing, and when the anesthesia episode arises, stay with it, or, as we say, embrace it, or relive it. As is the case in all other emerging dynamics, when the unconscious material becomes fully conscious, it is released and ceases to have a negative hold upon the psyche.

However, there are some unique, even peculiar nuances of this anesthesia situation. For all intents and purposes, we are proposing that we must *make conscious unconsciousness*. This is because unconsciousness is actually the nature and essence of anesthesia. It suppresses the ability to feel, creating scenarios somewhere on a continuum between a slight numbness, or lack of local sensation, all the way to total unconsciousness. But what happens in a session if the experience of *unconsciousness* or the *inability to feel* emerges into breathers' awareness? What will they begin to experience? Well, often, quite frankly, *nothing*.

How is this possible? The reason is that, if breathers are embracing an experience of unconsciousness—that is, the fetus *feeling nothing,* or *being unconscious*—as this becomes present in their awareness, they will lose the ability to be aware or conscious. They themselves then become *unconscious*, which is the result of the emerging gestalt. When that happens, they will no longer be able to "stay with it," as we encourage breathers to do when they are becoming aware of an emerging experience.

This is one of the most diabolical double-binds that breathers will face in the perinatal experience, or in any of the breathwork experience, for that matter. The inherent nature of the emerging process itself actually short-circuits and shuts down the psyche's ability to make that emerging process conscious. Often, breathers simply go to sleep. Or they will find themselves waking up, or "coming to" some time later, not knowing what has happened. The only thing they know is that they feel groggy, nauseated, dizzy, or any of the other common after-effects of anesthesia.

They also often experience disappointment, confusion, loss, and disorientation. Or they even feel that they have failed at the breathing. All of these situations add another dimension to their process, even if they may discover later that these feelings may be concomitants of the emerging pattern in some way they have not yet fathomed. The good news is that facilitators themselves are familiar with this double-bind, either through working with this issue in their own processes, or because they have already seen this phenomenon frequently during other sessions as they facilitate.

The further good news is that there is a very effective strategy in making conscious that which, as it emerges, perpetuates unconsciousness, or as in this case where another octave of the same intra-psychic problem actually gets created for the breather in the external reality. The solution involves systematic, persistent, ongoing support on the part of either the sitter or the facilitator in helping the breather stay awake and as alert as they can while they are on the mat. This is often a slow, arduous process, one that is definitely not fun for the breather. But gradually, after much commitment and a good deal of effort, this steady work can be very effective.

Another irony around the anesthesia experience is that, for somewhat unknown reasons, it is quite often one of the very first issues to come into a breather's awareness early on in sessions. So, in the same manner that the fetus was experiencing "giving up" in the birth canal, the breather also experiences this futility. She often wants to quit the breathing experience altogether before she really becomes engaged in the flow of the process. This futility is not just an emergence from the birth episode, but is also reflective of the difficulty in the external environment. For breathers, even if they are courageous and desirous of completing the birth, just the effort to breathe or to stay awake becomes an ordeal that can seem to have nothing to do with the internal process. Nevertheless, with persistence and support, it can be worked through. But the often exasperating effort ironically underscores the power that anesthesia has for the fetus, and how it exacerbates the already extremely challenging process of birth, as it is being relived by the breather.

Caesarian Birth

Caesarian and vaginal birth are so clearly biologically different that we can readily expect seekers' re-experience of these births to be radically dissimilar as well. In Caesarian birth, the fetus is taken from the womb or the birth canal through a surgical procedure. Looking through the holotropic lens, which would be, in this case, based on the physical and emotional elements relevant for the fetus and later the developing person, Caesarian births are of two types: planned and emergency.

The physical, psychological, and emotional circumstances surrounding these two methods can be markedly different for both the mother and the fetus. As one would expect, the experiences of journeyers' reliving these two forms of birth also clearly reflect the stark contrast between the two. This contrast includes both physical mechanics of the mother's body, the emotional environment resulting from her reactions to what may be happening externally in the medical milieu, and of course what the fetus is experiencing as well.

Breathers who report reliving any dimension of the unsafe or toxic-womb situation often relive a planned Caesarian as a "magical or miraculous rescue." They have the sense of themselves as the fetus being lifted, against all odds, from a dangerous and otherwise extremely unpleasant situation. One seeker reported an archetypal overlay that involved experiencing herself as Atlantis rising from the ocean. This adds an ecstatic, transpersonal rebirth element to the episode, which takes the journeyer far beyond the feelings of simple relief.

On the other hand, if the seeker's experience is one of a safe and nourishing womb environment, then the planned Caesarian can be horrendous. We hear many stories with two contrasting chapters. First, there is the

Edenic incarnation, the nourishing experience of safety and protection. And second, there is a sudden invasion, a horrific shock from out of nowhere. This shock escalates into an often precipitously violent, bloody snatching of the fetus from the safety of the mother's womb into the delivery room—a harsh, blinding, environment bereft of connection and protective boundaries.

We should emphasize that an emergency medical procedure such as the Caesarian strategy almost always involves the protocol of separating the mother and the newborn for whatever further medical interventions need to be administered. All of these interventions tragically prevent that crucial episode of bonding between mother and child so necessary for healthy emotional and psychological development.

As one would expect, the inner environment of the fetus is also quite different with an emergency Caesarian. This type of birth is almost always a highly charged situation, often involving life-threatening elements for the mother or the fetus, or for both of them. In this scenario, the atmosphere is already fraught with dis-ease, panic, threat, and danger. These and other sensations and emotions are transmitted both emotionally and chemically through signals from the mother to the fetus. It goes without saying that if the fetus is in a life threatening situation, the fear of death will be prevalent through this stage of the episode, and will also be relived by the breather as well.

What aggravates and deepens the emotional and physical complexity of the emergency Caesarian is that frequently the fetus will not just have had an experience of the first matrix, the intrauterine experience only. It will also have had at least some kind of precarious contact and interaction with negatively charged, painful elements of the second and even the third matrix. It is also experientially logical that, if the fetus is taken out of the mother during this stage—after contact with the second and third matrix—we would come to expect a whole range of reports on this recurring theme of magical or miraculous rescue.

There is another component of particular relevance for both the fetus and the seeker reliving the perinatal episode, and one we have discussed in a related context already. The Caesarian birth process, whether planned or emergency, whether involving the first matrix alone, or an amalgam of the second and third, is once again rendered more complex, stressful, and challenging by the obligatory use of some form of pain medication and/or anesthesia. As we have seen, this complicates the breather's ability to work with the emerging material, not to mention what the fetus must endure in the actual episode.

We have often alluded to the wide array of important insights breathers get from reliving their births and that are directly relevant to some crucial aspect of their post-natal lives. It should come as no surprise that a Caesarian birth could prove to be the wellspring, or seedbed, of important motivations and life tendencies that might make themselves known during the birth episode. For example, some breathers who in their everyday lives have noticed a seemingly groundless optimism, or the sense that everything will end positively, feel validated after reliving their Caesarian birth. By making conscious the magical rescue motif and having the insight that it is a deeper root of their positive life perspective, they now recognize an experientially logical reason why they have always felt that way.

Yet seekers also discover challenging dynamics that have deeper roots than biographical underpinnings alone. Breathers who are Caesarian-born often relate that, after reliving the birth, they now understand why they have always felt somehow cheated by life. They get the further insight, and relive the emotions connected with this insight, that that they never have had the opportunity to fully experience any kind of hard-won victory that vaginally-born seekers have often experienced. In addition, now that they have at least an understanding of the powerfully aggressive nature of the third matrix episode, they realize that they have never been able to fully experience any of the freeing and cathartic nature of rage. Or they report that they have never had the experience of fully coming into their own power.

In a sense, the unconscious record of the actual physical birth, with all the possible complications of a physical and emotional nature, frequently seems to inhibit, or stand in the way somehow, of full realization, freedom, and the ability of humans to function in optimum fashion in everyday life. However, as these gestalts of associated inner material are being made conscious and released, the healing power afforded by the experience of the *archetypal nature of birth and death/rebirth* becomes an experiential possibility for the seeker. As breathers clear the actual history of their biological birth, gradually the transformative aspects of the archetypal birth become more available for them. This gradual emergence of these positive aspects of the birth episode is one of the main indications of true healing in this work, as well as a signpost of substantial progress on the journey toward wholeness.

With this is mind, it should be easier to see how the gradual clearing of the birth record, and in this case Caesarian birth, can transform the core complications inherent in this type of perinatal episode. Take, for example, the situation we mentioned, where a breather reports that she just could not get in touch with her power. A birth experience filled with drugs, stress, fear, disconnection, trauma, and medical intervention is inherently very disempowering. However, once these issues have been made conscious, the road to wholeness is cleared of a significant level of obstacles, as further healing dimensions latent in the psyche now become available.

When the negative aspects have been released, there is in essence what we may call a *figure/ground reversal*. The trauma that was in the forefront of consciousness recedes and deeper healing mechanisms begin to take center stage of the awareness. Consequently, the breather, who in her Caesarian birth has been disempowered, can suddenly gain access to emotional connection, bonding, validation, and support. But she can also access and embrace boundless creative energy and power, which then becomes available for her use in her everyday life.

In this way, deep work does more than just get rid of traumas. It actually corrects them by activating creative traits that were somehow overshadowed by the birth record. The historical concomitants of the birth that have been blockages and obstacles to optimum health are cleared. When this happens, the way is open for the heretofore latent positive attributes to take their place and become the foundation of the currently emerging whole and authentic self.

CHAPTER VI

The Transpersonal Level

In order to do justice to the transpersonal band of consciousness, we will first revisit the nature of the psyche itself. As we pointed out, the term *psyche* has a number of meanings. In modern psychology, it has come to represent the individual mind and the faculty of individual consciousness. Deep work reveals that this personal consciousness is but one function of the psyche. Originally, the word itself came from the Greek, and means *soul*. This core definition gives us a much more comprehensive and accurate picture of what the psyche is. If one studies the characteristics of soul described in mystical traditions, it is interesting to see quite similar correlations in breathers' experiences of the newly reborn true self with which they identify after the false self/ego death experience.

Understanding the psyche this way leads us again to a profound truth of depth self-exploration. *If we work on ourselves systematically, we will inevitably confront the numinous reaches of the psyche.* When this occurs, by the reality-shattering nature of the inner experiences we have had, we are required to completely revision our previous view of the psyche. We realize that the original root meaning of "soul" as psyche seems to much more accurately reflect what we discover about the numinous underpinnings of existence and reality.

Carl Jung was famous for opening Western psychology to this groundbreaking frontier. Through envisioning the collective, archetypal realm of consciousness, he paved the way for transpersonal psychology to begin to assume its rightful place as a spiritual system, one that can provide maps and methods with which to open to the wisdom of the ages. For him, the psyche's healing trajectory was on a continuum from the *personal* to the *collective* in that, when facing the unconscious, we first encounter repressed biographical material and then have to come to terms with the archetypes behind our personal complexes. This was certainly a revolutionary upgrade for the Western psychological tradition, although Jung remains a peripheral figure in mainstream academic psychology. Many feel that it would be hard to overstate just how influential Jung's model of individuation has been on contemporary spirituality. However, as will always be the case of pioneering breakthroughs, there were still uncharted territories.

Many feel that it has been one of Stan Grof's major contributions to embrace the Jungian worldview, as well as many others. Of course, their approaches are different, although overlapping. One lens through which to view a comparison of their approaches might be to suggest that a portion of Grof's work is based on direct experiential encounters with the realm of the Jungian collective unconscious.

Grof's explication of the three levels of consciousness—the personal, the perinatal, and the transpersonal—accomplished much more than just a revolutionary advance in traditional psychological theory. By providing language, method, and structure for the numinous experience, his system actually elevates transpersonal psychology into the domain of the great mystical systems of the world, or perennial philosophy, and positions him alongside other pioneers, including Roberto Assagioli and William James.

In the medical, scientific, and academic circles in which it has been one of his life tasks to operate, he does not often publically characterize his contribution in quite this fashion. His in-depth Western psychological pedigree, and the service he has committed himself to in this world, have necessarily shaped how he has presented this Ganesha in the living room to those who are, if not unable, then unwilling to see the unlimited numinous dimension lingering behind the theory. This elephant, as we have said, is *spirituality*. And it roams the furthest frontiers of all psychological inquiry, breaking down all barriers to the truly unlimited realms of the human psyche.

With this in mind, our definition of the psyche must expand, even further than its original Greek origins. Here is the holotropic perspective: Under the infallible guidance of our inner healing capacity, we are able, through powerful methods, to heal our personally circumscribed state of consciousness, what we call the individual self. We are also able to heal what we initially feel belongs exclusively to the realm of biological birth. This in itself would have been quite enough to send a shockwave through the traditional psychological community, if not simply be rejected outright as nonsense. Yet as radical as access to the biological birth experience is, ultimately it turns out to be just the gateway, or a curtain on a much larger stage.

The biological perinatal episode becomes the opening act of this epic drama: the experience of psycho-spiritual death and rebirth. Even beyond this event, the transformation play has another act: the experience that we are not just limited individual beings, but heirs to, in essence, an unlimited field of awareness and experience. This awareness could come before the death/rebirth process—an initial spiritual awakening, or other experience of expansion or numinosity, followed by either biological birth or spiritual rebirth, or both types of birth at the same time.

So far, one of the most expanded cartographical representations of this unlimited field for Western psychology is the *transpersonal* domain. It becomes clear that healing and transformation always involve a dance of interconnection between "evolution and completion" or "moving toward wholeness" or "Becoming and Being."

As we embark on this odyssey from the personal, through the perinatal, and into the unbounded dimensions of the transpersonal, our definition of the psyche also undergoes an evolution. We experience that the psyche is not just the personal consciousness. Nor even is it the personal individual soul. What we learn from our inner exploration is that the psyche is commensurate with all that is. It is in the transpersonal domain that seekers can experience how what we have always imagined as the individually limited soul is also equally limitless. Consciousness, psyche, and soul become both *one* as well as *all that is.*

Based on the holotropic perspective, then, we could imagine that the triple dynamic of the extended cartography—the personal, the perinatal, and the transpersonal—represents three poises in a Becoming that the conscious, unlimited field of the psyche, or Being, might take. In essence, this holotropic system we are exploring is a Western way to describe what many of the great mystical systems have espoused for millennia. That is to say, within an unlimited field of consciousness or psyche, individual human beings have different possible modes of expression or operation.

On one level, the psyche can be experienced as this limited field, which of course has many operating platforms. At another level, it seems to have unlimited bandwidth containing multiple, diverse perspectives. The gateway between these two fields is the perinatal. It is in this realm that we can experience the total destructuring of our attachment to the limited empirical self, thereby opening us to the priceless gifts of the unlimited domain of the transpersonal.

In a sense, one poise, or operational point of view, is not better than another, provided that our personal experience is not circumscribed by the false self, or ego alone, but comprised of our true self, or, some say, the soul as Self, which has emerged through the ego death. At some point in our deep work, we also learn, then, that this true self or the soul is not bound in any way by the limited field in which the ego operates. But it in fact functions as a fluid operating system, a mode of consciousness designed by the Inner Healer to orchestrate a certain level of personal and interpersonal experience and reality. Yet the true individual self, which is the outcome of the death/rebirth experience we have just described, becomes a functional vehicle in the Becoming with which to operate within the unlimited field of psyche that is equal to all that is, or Being itself.

Here is a look at some of the experiences breathers and other seekers have had when they open to this unbounded dimension. Keep in mind what we discussed earlier about the danger of limiting ourselves to linear thinking. If at all possible, we should abandon one problematic assumption: that is, that the only valid trajectory of evolutionary transformation entails that we linearly evolve from a personal mode of consciousness, through the death/rebirth experience, and then, from there, finally open to the transpersonal.

As we said, it is just as likely that a breather can lie down, take a few breaths, and immediately find herself in the transpersonal domain, all this before she has had any biographical and perinatal experiences. As we will amplify later in our inquiry into the holotropic perspective, this does not necessarily mean that she is avoiding deeper work in the other two dimensions. It simply means that her Inner Healer has unerringly guided her to this dimension, where at this particular time she can access the healing experience perfect for herself.

We should emphasize that the perinatal, death/rebirth episode, while being a crucial spiritual opening, is by no means the only valuable experience of numinosity or healing mechanism available to seekers. In fact, numinosity is what the transpersonal is all about: an adventure of limitlessness in realms mapped by perennial systems. These systems of thought have chronicled the vast range of episodes that voyagers have embarked upon in ever-widening dimensions of connection, freedom, power, and wholeness. Such episodes, in countless guises, are what the transpersonal dimension offers the explorer of the deep psyche.

We have already covered elements of the transpersonal domain, including the death/rebirth process centered in the dual perinatal episode. Of course, there are countless possibilities, which represent the collective octave of their counterparts in individual human experience. From the archetypal, into further reaches of the transpersonal, we are basically voyagers on an ocean of infinite possibilities. To use another metaphor, we are cosmic wayfarers in unlimited space, or non-space, traveling through a boundary-less expanse of stars and forms of light. The celestial entities we focus on always depend on the unerring guidance of our cosmic navigator, the Inner Healer, or a power within.

One important category involves experiential identification with anything that has ever existed in the physical universe. This includes, but is not limited to, anything we have ever become aware of, actually experienced, or touched upon tangentially through some external source of scientific inquiry. Breathers may identify with any element of the natural cosmos—animal, plant, or mineral, organic or inorganic—in whatever form—as a solid, liquid, gas, element, or microscopic entity, including the molecular level, atoms, and subatomic particles. To expand the canvas, one may experience any element of the entire physical universe, including planets, stars and systems, matter and anti-matter, and any astronomical phenomenon known to humanity, including black holes, worm holes, quasars, and many more.

The list is as endless as existence, or our ability to envision. In short, we have in the meta-ordinary state the ability to become conscious of, or to identify with, *all that is*. This may sound far-fetched, if not ludicrous, from our customary level of consciousness. Take, for example, a seeker who, after doing some deep work, reports that she became a blue whale. This does not mean that if the breather were to get on some giant oceanic scale, she would weigh one hundred tons. She has had what we call an *experiential identification* with a blue whale.

The type of identification to which we are referring is not merely about the physical form itself, but about gaining clear experiential access to *information*. Nor is this type of information something that the breather may have learned, or experienced at some point in her life, either remembered or forgotten. We are referring to information to which she has had absolutely no access at any level, whether indirectly, subliminally, or in any other way. Yet, even without any traditional form of knowing, or strategy to gather information whatsoever, she can have direct, infallible availability to information about what it is like to be a blue whale. This would include actually *experiencing* how they see, eat, sleep, procreate, swim, communicate with other whales or different life forms, what it feels like to weigh what a blue whale weighs, to navigate the oceans, use their flippers and tails, take care of their young, or in many other ways.

Yet even experiential identification can be more nuanced than this. One could have the experience of being a *specific* whale, involved in unique life or death scenarios. Or one may gain access to the *archetypal* dimension, i.e., a core ordering principle of the blue whale. There may be a type of species identification reflecting an evolutionary capacity, such as phylogenetic memory. These are three related, but distinctly different experiences. But they all have two important things in common. One is specific, and the other is more universal and applicable to every other example of experiential identification in the transpersonal domain. The first commonality is that each is about some form of "blue whaleness," or what it is like to be a blue whale. And the second is its relation to a dimension of *information* itself.

It is not just the realm of physical beings or entities that seekers access in the transpersonal domain. They may also experience a virtually unlimited array of *natural processes*. This includes such phenomena as evolutionary trajectories, weather and the change of seasons, photosynthesis, and complex interactions of molecular and chemical elements. Seekers have related identifying with or accessing information about any number of evolutionary patterns of organic species and inorganic substances, as well as any bio-chemical reactions that account for the physical basis of what we call life.

Journeyers even report observations about which they have had absolutely no prior contact or information. Even more fascinating, they can also access information that seems impossible to obtain as a human being to begin with. For example, any encyclopedia contains a section on how a swan sees, or an elephant remembers, or an earthworm experiences sex, or why swallows always return to their previous home. All of this knowledge is based upon scientific observation, followed by rational processes such as deduction and inference, which arrive at what is assumed to be truth, fact, or "what something is." This is the basis of virtually all human knowledge.

However, experiences in meta-ordinary states reveal a radically different mode of access to knowledge than this type of traditional scientific inquiry. In this new manner, information is gained by *experiential identification* with a life form, a process, or an inorganic compound. For all intents and purposes, the seeker *becomes* that thing. It is in this identification— this Becoming—that true knowledge seems to be acquired.

History is full of the accounts of scientists who are credited with forging paradigm-changing breakthroughs. Many of these reveal that these pioneers reached their conclusions based on an inexplicable, traditionally unscientific episode of what can only be called meta-ordinary awareness. All of these scientifically unverifiable observations are available to anyone who lies down, closes her eyes, takes a few breaths, and pays attention to what emerges into her awareness. It just depends on what the power within reveals in any particular episode.

At this juncture, we should mention the work of Rupert Sheldrake in biology involving the existence of *morphogenetic fields* as a creative dimension preceding the evolutionary emergence of different species. We should also address the *psi field* postulated by Ervin Laszlo, and its fascinating similarity to the metaphysical conception of the *akashic record*. In both these instances, we are referring to a non-physical dimension supraordinated to physical reality containing constellations of information that appear to have a vital, essential creative capacity in terms of what manifests in physical time and space.

If we add to this the suggestions of systems theorists such as Gregory Bateson, a close friend of Stan's and Christina's during their Esalen adventure, as well as the experiences seekers have in deep inner work, we can extrapolate a few compelling assumptions. First, the universe is *not* exclusively made up of a physical dimension. And second, the universe, or existence itself, can be envisioned, at least in part, as a realm of *information*. This information becomes accessible through meta-scientific observation via strategies that are capable of opening observers to enhanced states of consciousness.

Bateson made another incisive as well as humorous observation on so-called scientific truth and the power of outmoded paradigms. He said that in almost every discipline, scientists rely on what he calls *explanatory principles*. Take, for example, the question, "Why is it that a certain species of California swallow always returns to its exact same nest year after year?" According to Bateson, scientists would proclaim that they know why this happens. They would state definitively that the cause, or reason, is *instinct*. Most of us nod, and say, "Oh, yes! Of course. Now I get it! It's instinct." Then we blithely go about our way, confident in what we think of as knowledge. This so-called knowledge then settles into the collective psyche as an almost unassailable truth.

But according to Bateson, this is not real knowledge at all. It is really only an *explanatory principle*. We have arbitrarily labeled what is essentially a cosmic mystery *instinct*, and by naming it, have decided we know what it is. We could have named this phenomenon anything. We could just as well have named it *jitharoaxis*. This would have had just as much scientific validation as the name *instinct*.

Both of these names are really just a way to *label* some thing, or a phenomenon. In so doing, we commit the profoundly delusional error that, by naming it, we actually believe we *know* what it is. This is absolutely ludicrous. Yet, it is humbling to recognize the astounding self-delusions in which we often live by forcing the wondrous complexity of universal phenomena through the narrow bandwidth of certain internal search engines, such as ratiocination.

That the universe is multi-dimensional is not a pronouncement for which perennial philosophy has been waiting with bated breath for millennia to see verified by modern science. Shamans, mystics, healers, philosophers, and practitioners of transformational systems all over the world and throughout history have always experienced this truth. They have also provided for future generations sophisticated maps and methods with which to verify these truths.

The transpersonal dimension is infinitely more comprehensive and diverse than what can be categorized within a scientific, or even meta-scientific inquiry alone, no matter how sophisticated such a science might be. Once again, we turn to the Ganesha in our cosmic living room—the power we have been taking such pains not to overlook thus far in our exploration. Of course, we are referring to the dimensions of *numinosity*, or *spirituality*. We cannot stress this enough. As the death/rebirth episode opens us to a new, truer self, and a more permeable, pliant, and responsive operating platform from which to access that which is beyond the personal, it is in the transpersonal domain that this platform of the new self truly fulfills its numinous destiny.

Through another lens, religious or mystical systems see the numinous, or the Godhead, as *transcendent* or *immanent* realities. Many view the Divine as a transcendent entity, power, or force. That is to say, the divinity of these systems is an entity, force, or power that supra-ordinates, or dwells *outside* of creation. We see this in a number of world religions, where God is a supreme deity or a spirit, who created, and then "stepped back" and proceeded to observe creation. Or God becomes almost the puppet master, directing players on the stage of life.

Others perceive divinity as immanent, or *within* creation, as the very substance of existence itself, where, for all intents and purposes, God or Goddess *is* none other than the universe or the totality of existence itself. There are also those who imagine a divinity or numinosity both transcendent and immanent, where there are only apparent, and at best arbitrary, degrees of differentiation between matter and spirit, and where in the final analysis, all is spirit, or the divine.

When seekers touch the realms of the numinous in meta-ordinary states, they often report experiences of both an exclusive transcendence and exclusive immanence. Yet, if they pursue a holotropic inquiry systematically, many arrive at a worldview where they see the Divine as both transcendent as well as immanent. The power of this inclusivity, particularly in awakening to the immanence of divinity, is that it breaks down the barriers of traditional science and presents us with a cosmos that is not only physical, but *ensouled*. This is a fundamental, invaluable realization for seekers in this work, in that it fosters an ecological, evolutionary perspective with the potential for a whole new healing era in planetary evolution. We will spend more time on this later in our exploration of this new vision of a holotropic practice.

To sum up, in the transpersonal, a seeker has access to an absolutely unlimited field of experiences and realizations. All of these are capable of widening the horizons of the self, and of moving the individual consciousness toward greater and greater levels of freedom, empowerment, and wholeness. Every spiritual system, truth, or level of realization; every mythic interpretation of the spiritual journey; every plane, realm, or dimension; every order of the various denizens who reside there, including gods, goddesses, including once-human, but now ascended spiritual hierarchies; demons, angels, jins, nature spirits, and beings of any order or magnitude—all these possibilities are available to the seeker for experiential identification.

A comprehensive exploration of every possible phenomenon in the transpersonal, or any other dimension, cannot be the primary focus of our inquiry. But even a limited cross-section of the type of experiences we see in this work would include planetary and cosmological evolution, racial and collective memories, psychic phenomena, and karmic, or past-life and ancestral memories. It would also encompass all kinds of psychic phenomena, including encounters with spirit guides, mediumistic experiences and communication, UFOs, extraterrestrial episodes, angelic communication, recognition of the reality of other planes of existence, and the acquisition of supernormal powers.

All of these, plus everything we think we hold knowledge of, and then all that about which we have no knowledge, but can imagine, yet have not done so yet; everything that is knowable, but yet currently unknown; and ultimately any conception, or non-conception, of what can only be called the Great Mystery—all these identifications are possible for the seeker in the transpersonal dimension. In short, it is a dimension of infinite creativity and possibility.

This leads us to a core healing experience reported by the majority of seekers with whom we have worked. It is one we have already mentioned as being foundational to perennial philosophy the world over. When confronted with the power of what can only be viewed as an overwhelming Mystery, Socrates was supposed to have said something to the effect that the first step toward true knowledge is to *know that we do not know*.

To Close

Once again, *everything* we have shared in these sections is based on the inner experiences of seekers—past and current—who have undertaken the journey toward wholeness. They represent what we hear over and over again. Who of us could know the answer to the ages old question, "What is truth?" However, it is our hope that through this inquiry, seekers may feel moved to take the epic inner journey under the perfect guidance of their own power within.

Such a journey needs only the validation and justification of the one who takes it. Of course, it will be wonderful when science and other disciplines one day validate what many inner voyagers already know. The most relevant truth is that these kinds of realizations can be absolutely life changing, even without the validation of an external philosophy. But there is a truth we may all rely on now. This is, that we can each truly be the living proof of our own inner sacred hypotheses. And the infallible mediator of such a realization is our own Inner Healer—the power within.

CHAPTER VII

Articulating a Holotropic Perspective and Paradigm

The Holotropic Dynamics of Power

Many of us have had the realization that an unlimited power within is paramount for any authentic trajectory toward fulfillment within the universe drama. The holotropic perspective consistently addresses this critical catalyst for a sustainable evolutionary upgrade toward wholeness. There are many lenses through which to view power—each with a specific focus and nuance in our lives. In the training, we offer a presentation called "Power and the Perinatal," pointing out the dynamics of power throughout the spectrum of consciousness, from our biography, through our birth and the perinatal matrices, including the death/rebirth process, and into the transpersonal domain.

Power is one of the intricate, artistic threads winding its way through the human and cosmic tapestry. Through holotropic work, we are able to make conscious the operative dynamics of power through the explication of various COEXs, systems of condensed experience. These COEXs, or core patterns with a similar theme uniting all dimensions of the psyche, are either challenging or supportive, or both. They highlight how we may be disempowered, or in what manner we are empowered, or both. Our own deep experiences, and what we have heard from hundreds of seekers, help to clarify the power dynamic. Perennial philosophy validates our search in three dimensions. These are, first, power's influence in our individual lives; second, power's effects on the collective adventure of humanity; and the third involves our relationship to and interaction with power at the cosmic level.

From a metaphysical point of view, power is an attribute of the cosmic mystery, of divinity. In this inquiry, we define power as the *impetus or dynamis of creation*, or the *ability to effect change*. It seems to be an inherent force within all beings—either latent or active. It is a neutral force without an abiding moral compass, which may be wielded, at one end of the continuum, by a sociopathic will toward abject ego-centeredness. At the other end of the spectrum, it may be put to use within an enlightened, heart-centered, and service-oriented focus for the furthering of the evolutionary human/cosmic adventure. In the holotropic milieu, power is an effective orchestrator of our healing. *Power is the principle dynamis of the Inner Healer*. To take it one step further, *the Inner Healer is in fact our power within*. It is the universal, numinous, and conscious creativity that resides within each individual.

Many seekers feel that the acquisition of a true inner power, independent of external influences, is the essential attribute of an effective, optimal life functioning. This includes our personal evolution, the fulfillment of our life dreams and interpersonal relationships, and the ability to negotiate the myriad twists and turns of our evolution toward wholeness. This evolution is what addictions recovery pioneer, Bill Wilson, called the *Broad Highway* of human existence.

Here are just a few of the experiences reported by seekers, concerning the experience of power in their deep inner work:

1. The personal or transpersonal process of "coming into personal power."
2. Awakening to the power of sexuality and aggression in the third perinatal matrix, including Joanna Macy's term, *power over*—an egoic third-matrix dynamic.
3. Opening to or identifying with a personal or impersonal force of numinosity, such as an experience of the Higher Power or the Divine, in any of its names and aspects.
4. The experience of *power with*, another of Macy's terms—usually experienced as a fourth-matrix, or transpersonal phenomenon, based upon an opening of the heart and an experience of true caring and good will for others.
5. The ability to access previously unavailable dimensions of consciousness, including the sense of, and ability to, awaken to our true self.
6. Identification with any archetype of personal or collective power for the accomplishment of endeavors within our life evolution.
7. The ability to make some form of personal use of the creative urge derived from identification with certain multi-cultural deities, mythological personages, animals, spirit guides, or impersonal forces from the transpersonal or shamanic dimension.
8. The radical transformation of biological birth, or psycho-spiritual death/rebirth, affording the individual access to an up-graded ability toward personal and transpersonal fulfillment, as well as freedom from the constriction of unreleased trauma in the birth canal.

9. The life-changing experience of the serendipity of power as *grace*, or, as Benedictine monk Brother David Steindl-Rast might say, the power inherent in a profound sense of gratitude.

10. Experience of identification with the *superman* or *superwoman*, in a Nietzschean sense.

11. The transformative power of love and acceptance for oneself, or the relinquishing of a constricting, debilitating overlay of low self-esteem.

12. The freeing power of forgiveness for oneself and others, including a relinquishing of the toxic overlays of shame and guilt.

13. The power in recognizing that we are infinite beings, and not just a limited, constricted "skin-encapsulated ego."

14. The yogic powers acquired through specific psycho-spiritual practices, such as those outlined in the *Yoga Sutras* of Patanjali.

15. The power of the so-called "dark forces," either experienced in non-ordinary states, or accrued through other ritual means for the expressed purpose of wielding that self-focused power in the world for one's own real or imagined need.

16. The power in accruing brute physical strength.

17. The power of personal magnetism and charisma.

18. The power in new-found courage, and freedom from the contractions of fear.

19. The transformative power in awakening to the great mystery of an egoless love.

We have mentioned but a few ways that empowerment profoundly upgrades our lives. It becomes ever clearer that radical self-empowerment is key to optimum fulfillment in life, and is a central principle, in one form or another, of many elements of the perennial philosophy. Lest we forget, the power to which we refer is not the aggrandizement of the false self, or ego. Instead, we are spotlighting the empowerment which is a result of our experiencing what mystics often refer to as our true or authentic self—that portion of the great mystery individualized as a soul, or unit of the one consciousness. Through systematic inner work, the healing of disempowerment culminates in the recognition that a total power of transformation always already resides within the seeker herself.

Systematic deep inner work often leads us to the conviction that there are two poises, from which every manifestation of a holotropic dynamic has its origin and purpose. These poises are derived from two dimensions of the word *holotropic*. They are *moving toward* and *wholeness*. In perennial philosophy, they constitute two yogic, spiritual, or metaphysical dynamics that reflect the human exodus toward an omega of fulfillment. These are, as we have said, the principles of Becoming and of Being.

Within the holotropic perspective, Becoming relates directly to the process of *moving toward*. Being refers to the state of consciousness known as *wholeness*. Nearly all systems, including shamanic/indigenous, yogic, meditative, or philosophical, operate within these two dynamics. Many spiritual traditions point to a kind of apotheosis—becoming godlike, meta-human, or divine, including a culmination resulting in the realization of an all-encompassing, unitive condition, or state of "oneness."

In some schools, this apotheosis refers to a cessation of the "play of opposites," or the cessation or transcendence of duality itself. This results in what has metaphorically been called "going beyond the beyond," or *tathagata*, or, metaphysically, the *realization about which naught may be said*. There is a reason nothing can be said about it. This level of transformation is simply beyond the realm of words, or even traditional mentation. Words and description owe their very existence to a communicative process, which requires two necessary components—*subject* and *object*. Without these two, "naught can be said."

To attempt to name or describe the Mystery automatically voids the truth of the mystery itself. Yet, the irony is that the term *Mystery* seems to be the only way to describe the meta-cosmic dimension of wholeness—to define the cosmic conundrum that "some thing ceases to exist in any attempt to name it." However, we *can* speak and write about the Becoming. But *wholeness* seems to disappear in the light of the beacon which forever summons us toward itself—the thing which cannot be named, but which we, nevertheless, often call Being.

Many feel that the possibilities these musings suggest represent one of the greatest cosmic mysteries. It is an experience beyond description. It is one of the most beautiful gifts from the numinous level of unnamable power that, as seekers moving toward wholeness, we are able to receive. The Christian tradition often simply refers to this ultimate level of power as the experience of *grace*. In myth or other sacred texts cross-culturally, there are references to the divine boon or gift bestowed graciously and freely from a transcendent source, even when there was not corresponding effort by a seeker or non-seeker toward the receiving of such a gift.

Each of these particular "musings" on the dynamics of power represent experiences seekers have reported as a result of deep work accessing meta-ordinary states of consciousness through Holotropic Breathwork. They are, of course, only a minimal cross-section of the possibilities inherent in systematic deep work. Yet, it seems that power—and in particular a *power within*—will always play a central, crucial role in our individual and collective evolution, or our Becoming in its inexorable journey toward wholeness or Being itself.

To Dispel a Possible Misconception

With the preceding foray into the metaphysical nature of a whole-hearted self-empowerment, we can continue to explore the efficacy of a holotropic perspective. One of its most important underpinnings, of course, has been transpersonal psychology. But this focus on the holotropic perspective's transpersonal roots can be confusing. The problem is that when we speak of this particular leading edge of psychology, we often use the name *transpersonal*—including the versions as articulated by Grof, Wilber, Washburn, Wade, Assagioli, and others—and the name *holotropic* interchangeably, as though they each represent the same paradigm. With an initial, superficial glance, these worldviews might actually appear "of a piece" or "from the same mold." But the transpersonal paradigm in general and the holotropic perspective are *not* identical.

We may assume they are identical, based on some of their overlapping, compatible nuances. For example, with similar metaphors, both highlight a critical foundation of this leading edge: that is, *language, method, and structure for the numinous experience.* Yet it is essential to clarify how the *transpersonal* paradigm and the holotropic perspective are, *in one unambiguous, fundamental way, actually quite different.*

Even though they overlap in their underpinnings and share much of the same historical bases, to equate the two paradigms, and to use these designations interchangeably, can be quite misleading, particularly within their *therapeutic applications*. This confusion may sometimes contribute to an intensification of the emotional and psychological problems that seekers are attempting to alleviate in the first place. They may be opening to healing or psycho-spiritual methods they do not fully understand and which ultimately may not support them in the manner they had hoped.

This confusion can also be problematic for potential therapists, who might choose to study and employ modalities of both transpersonal approaches and Holotropic Breathwork, or any of the modes of holotropic therapy that are likely to emerge from the holotropic paradigm in the coming years. If therapists do not understand the core difference between these philosophies, which are the underpinnings of the modality they represent, then they themselves can become part of the problem for seekers, rather than the solution. It is essential to explore how this confusion may arise, and to highlight where the two paradigms diverge.

Toward this end, we will focus on two primary components of each: the *theoretical* and the *experiential*. This brief, cursory comparison between certain transpersonal and the holotropic dynamics is in no way meant to determine which is more effective for seekers or for practitioners offering specific modalities from these schools for their clients. The differentiation between these perspectives is actually quite easy to understand theoretically.

However, just because it seems fairly simple to see the difference intellectually, this does not mean that it is equally as easy to manifest the difference in actual practice. To implement a core, fundamental level of the holotropic perspective within the precise spirit of where it diverges from the transpersonal approach requires more than understanding. It requires a *change of consciousness*. We have already addressed this truth in our discussion of the problems many old paradigm proponents faced when confronted with the fledgling transpersonal perspective.

It may help to highlight this divergence by juxtaposing just a few therapeutic strategies from a transpersonal and a holotropic perspective. To begin with the obvious, many transpersonal therapists have been trained to view the seeker as a being with personal as well as meta-needs, or someone with an individual, personal, as well as collective, or transpersonal self. This perspective is extremely effective, and represents a radical expansion of traditional psychological practices. It also paves the way for many new modalities, or modern renditions of practices from the perennial philosophical tradition.

To facilitate the dynamics associated with this perspective, transpersonal therapists could, of course, employ the best of traditional modalities, as they deemed appropriate in any specific therapeutic scenario. These may include gestalt, or any other from humanistic psychology. Or they may bring on line in the moment any strategy from any school that feels relevant for the situation in which they may be engaged. They would also have at their disposal any methodology or interpersonal skills derived from perennial philosophy—or the wisdom of the ages. These may include the creative use of therapeutic interventions based on the world's mystical traditions.

Transpersonal strategies may also include the contributions of traditional pioneers in psychology, at least for an initial exploration of postnatal issues, such as Freud and any modality that followed in this vein for many decades. All of these could then be employed as part of an overall, yet initial biographical stage of a strategy that may eventually require methodologies that access the perinatal and transpersonal dimensions of the psyche. This category would include theory and practice of other humanistic strategies, or those from an array of other schools as well. They might especially draw inspiration from pioneering, paradigm-changing teachers, such as Carl Jung, Roberto Assagioli, Otto Rank, and Wilhelm Reich. Of course, Stan Grof's contributions from within the psychedelic arena and Holotropic Breathwork would be classic foundations for an effective transpersonal therapy.

If we now juxtapose the holotropic perspective with the above descriptions of a transpersonal philosophy, it is clear that holotropic work shares many of the same underpinnings, and belongs within the categories of transpersonal modalities. The holotropic perspective does not, as a matter of "dogma," exclude any relevant system within seekers' post-natal biography. The essential requirement, however, definitely includes a core holotropic dynamic—an unequivocal honoring of the seeker's Inner Healer, or the power within.

Therefore, any choice of modality must be based specifically on a need expressed by the client, either directly or indirectly. In addition, how the therapist responds to the client—whether she directs the process in any way, or merely supports whatever emerges from the seeker's psyche— would determine if this intervention should be designated as holotropic or not.

Holotropic Breathwork practitioners, or proponents of a holotropic therapy, would view the client's experiences through the lens of the extended cartography explored by Stan Grof, including, along with the post-natal biography, the perinatal and transpersonal domains. Of course, this would include language, method, and structure for the numinous experience. These perspectives would also be nourished by the holotropic perspective's deep roots in many of the world's spiritual systems and disciplines—particularly, those that utilize some kind of breathing technique for transformation.

We have already explored transpersonal psychology, the fundamentals of Holotropic Breathwork and the extended cartography of the psyche. But we have not yet highlighted the one distinction which would cause a strategy to be deemed holotropic, but *not transpersonal*.

This principle, as you may have guessed, is the elegant, paradigm-shattering power of what in colloquial terminology we often call the Inner Healer, or a power within. The authenticity of the individual's inner healing resources is the central, unalterable tenet of the holotropic worldview. Absolute reliance on the Inner Healer is what clearly distinguishes the power of the holotropic paradigm from almost every other system, even including many other transpersonal modalities.

This distinction is essential for all individuals seeking the therapeutic milieu that resonates most deeply for them. Although a transpersonal strategy may claim to be based on some partial, or even complete, reliance on an inner healing mechanism, there is no compelling requirement within the transpersonal domain that this mechanism be the non-negotiable power. Even if something akin to the Inner Healer is acknowledged, this does not guarantee that this truth will actually play the authentic, central role, or any role whatsoever, in a therapeutic interaction between helper and client.

Later, we will cover how easy it is for us as people helpers to be misled by our own unconscious motivations. We will paint a vivid picture of the insidious delusion to which we frequently fall prey in believing we are actually following a client's Inner Healer. We can believe we are actually doing this, when in fact we are still unconsciously directing the therapeutic interaction. This often results in merely re-enforcing what may be a client's life-long sense of multi-leveled disempowerment.

By Inner Healer, we definitely do not mean any anthropomorphic entity or spirit that magically resides within seekers. Our use of the term is simply a colloquialism, a convenient way to describe what we call an inherent inner healing source. It is an innate, natural component of the individual human psyche. This power within human beings is not a fantasy, a meta-phor, a theory, or an intellectual construct. *It is a life-changing reality that is experientially available to any seeker doing deep work in expanded states of awareness.* Furthermore, we should point out that none of us came up with the name Inner Healer for that power. It was the name chosen by Christina and Stan Grof at Esalen during the birth of Holotropic Breathwork.

Numinosity and the Power Within: Experience, Not Theory

Without an in-depth acceptance of the inner healing dynamic, and an oper-ating strategy, such as the breath, entheogens, or a dynamic, conscious-ness-shifting transpersonal therapy to mobilize this power experientially within seekers, a therapeutic endeavor is not actually holotropic. Simply a mental understanding of, or a superficial acquiescence to, the existence of something like an Inner Healer is not sufficient. Assisting seekers in accessing this healing power, and totally supporting the emergence of this vital inner dynamic, must be the core, unalterable operating strategy of every holotropic practitioner, or any therapy that may emerge from the holotropic perspective.

We proposed that Grof may be called a deep seeker and how his unveiling of the transpersonal paradigm required way more than a mere mental understanding of the power of numinosity. One of the few things that could initiate a multi-leveled, cellular absorption of a new paradigm is a deep personal experience of this numinous dimension. The basis for our present inquiry is exactly the same: A radical dispensation of numinosity—one that shatters our belief that we are "skin-encapsulated egos," or com-pels us to recognize an ongoing process of the dissolution of this false operating platform—is essential for us to truly operate with unreserved trust in the resources of the Inner Healer, or the power within the seeker in every interaction.

Through a slightly different lens, we may highlight two poises within this dynamic. One has to do with the role of the seeker, and the other has to do with the role of the facilitator. We have repeatedly observed that when seekers systematically engage in the holotropic work, they will inevitably confront the radical truth and therapeutic power of their inner healing resources.

However, it is imperative that support people in a holotropic milieu must also commit to systematic daily psycho-spiritual work. We must do this in order to maintain a conscious, ever-evolving relationship with our own Inner Healers, and to continue working with the issues underpinning the myriad, entrenched, almost incessantly recurring machinations of our false selves.

As holotropic practitioners, or as proponents of a holotropically based therapy, the radical re-ordering of our psyches, and the transformation we ourselves undergo, will always challenge us personally as well as professionally. Deep self-exploration consistently confronts us with the way in which we too have been disempowered in our own lives, or the way we have participated in disempowering others.

As we open to this disempowerment, we will also have an opportunity to embrace the deep healing resources within us. This confrontation with our own egoic powerlessness, accrued through a lifetime of external disempowerment, will then mobilize a crucial dynamic of our own journeys toward wholeness. These life-changing experiences are based on our profound realization of an unshakeable, innate inner power.

Without deep inner work on the part of prospective holotropic practitioners or therapists that train as holotropic practitioners, we would never be able to fulfill our responsibility as supporter—and not director—of another's process. We would continue to be part of the problem for seekers, instead of the solution. We would not fulfill our responsibility to be midwives for the inner-guided emergence of their own unique solutions to the challenges of their life paths.

An initial revelation of personal power for seekers almost always widens into a deep, supportive foundation for everyday life. It is natural that we "people-helpers" will periodically revisit our ever-diminishing dynamics of disempowerment and other core issues during our inner work. These multi-leveled inheritances from the past dissipate, as any deep-psyche adventurer regularly embraces her inner healing resources. As a result, this power within us can eventually be relied upon as an infallible guide of our evolution toward wholeness.

Furthermore, for facilitators, this discovery, plus a rigorous training in which we learn, at a core level of our consciousness to *support, not direct*, the breather—to "go down the stream with them," as we say, to be a *co-adventurer* with them and be neither nominally nor in fact the expert in any way for them—are some of the prerequisites for our becoming certified as Holotropic Breathwork practitioners.

These requirements can often prove to be formidable difficulties for any facilitator. A primary reason for this is the unfortunate tendency of many people helpers to take credit, consciously or unconsciously, for the work of their clients. In particular, we often observe how we as support people will embrace and internalize the positive projections coming from seekers. We will then often use these for our own self-aggrandizement. These disempowering practices require extremely rigorous, ongoing inner work on the part of therapists—practices akin to the embracing of an authentic, unflinching daily psycho-spiritual *sadhana*. We must also remain open to feedback from peers, instead of isolating ourselves in the ivory towers of what we may consider our sacrosanct personal authority to effectively support others.

But what about the wide array of transpersonal modalities? Any number of them might be principally based on similar dynamics as those that are required for Holotropic Breathwork practitioners. However, in almost none of these modalities is there a non-negotiable requirement for absolutely honoring a seeker's source of a power within, as it is required within the holotropic perspective.

In fact, if we explore the transpersonal strategies being practiced today, it is quite clear that many of these do *not* exclusively, or perhaps even marginally, rely on, or in some case even explicate or admit, the existence of the power of the client's inner healing resources as an inviolate wellspring of healing. In many cases, the therapist has been specifically trained to play a central, active role in guidance and directorship for their clients. This is true, even if they say that their clients possess the resources within themselves necessary for their own transformation and empowerment.

This inquiry is in no way an exercise in rating the efficacy of different transpersonal strategies. Nor is it a game of philosophical sophistry—nor do we have time or space to pinpoint the minutiae that highlight the differences between the many transpersonal perspectives. Yet it is essential to be straightforward concerning the ways these two paradigmatic approaches may perhaps diverge.

There will always be differences between the plethora of psycho-spiritual disciplines. However, both therapists and seekers deserve to be intimately acquainted with the glaring as well as subtle differences between the various schools. A seeker's chance and opportunity for authentic, in-depth transformation depend on it.

We wish to offer seekers the opportunity to explore for themselves two things: One, if in their life work they are moved to support others in their transformation, they must ask themselves with which modality would they feel most at home as they undertake their journey of service; and two, if they are considering delving more thoroughly into the mysteries of their own psyches, which strategy would they feel most naturally meshes with their own inspirations.

How will we each arrive at answers to these questions? The ideal recourse would be to go deeply within as best we can, and listen for the voice of our own authentic truth and being—what we call in holotropic work the Inner Healer, or as in this inquiry, a power within. This inner dynamic may be, of course, be referred to by a different name in other modalities, if it is a part of that modality's operating strategy. In this way, we can each discover the truest path for ourselves in this life adventure.

CHAPTER VIII

A New Definition of Psychology—A Radical Proposal

Thus far, in our discussion of psychology, psycho-spirituality, and paradigms, we have examined what has gone before, as well as where we are now: the current climate of paradigm conflict permeating so many scientific and psychological disciplines globally. We have explored nature of paradigms, plus an overview of the outdated, traditional worldview from which we are currently laboring to free ourselves; the new paradigm based on the best of the old, plus language, method, and structure for the numinous experience; and the collision between the two, in which we are all engaged at this time. A central purpose of this inquiry is to provide, in a sense, a baseline from which the holotropic perspective may be nurtured and ultimately recognized as a revolutionary upgrade for human and planetary evolution.

We mentioned a number of names this new paradigm has assumed: among them, holistic, integral, and the wellness model of the psyche. We settled on the term *transpersonal*, for a number of reasons. It was the first name applied to the worldview embodying this profound shift we have been exploring. It was also the name chosen by Stan Grof and his colleagues in the earliest days of this paradigm's gestation. The transpersonal perspective will probably be recognized historically as the blueprint for the profound wave of change, which has slowly begun to permeate most strata of philosophical and scientific disciplines on the planet at this time.

Our holotropic inquiry begins in the earliest days of Stan Grof's work, the clinic in Prague, and the mysterious package from the Sandoz Laboratory in Switzerland bearing its potent cargo, LSD. It seems that what we call truth, or the history of an event, is the result of looking through a particular lens at a certain aggregate of information teased from some much larger source of data, and then formulating a theory, or group of possibilities, derived from these observations. So we might propose shifting the lens slightly, so that we get "history" from another point of view. In doing so, we may again find ourselves in the presence of a mythic elephant—a Ganesha perhaps—in that Czech laboratory.

As a recovering addict for over thirty years, and a dedicated proponent of a transpersonal model of recovery, I am well aware of Bill Wilson's story and his pivotal role in the birth of the Twelve Step era, as well as the twentieth-century recovery and treatment movement. I cannot help but feel the astonishing parallels between his story and Stan Grof's journey.

Just as the transpersonal era began to really take shape with the numinous experience Stan Grof had in Prague in the late 1950s, the entire recovery movement began with one person. It also was catalyzed by a radical dispensation of numinosity that forever changed Bill Wilson's life. From this point forward, no matter how much resistance and ridicule Wilson had to face, his most heartfelt task was to facilitate, in his arena, what Grof later accomplished in his: *provide language, method, and structure for the numinous dimensions of the psyche.*

Just as Grof proposed an extended cartography of the psyche as an expanded framework for consciousness evolution, Wilson formulated the authentic modern Western yoga known as the Twelve Steps. Both teachers have written and spoken of a kind of isolation they experienced. This isolation was permeated with relentless personal attacks from colleagues ever seeking to discredit their work. They were both faced with a steadfast adherence to outmoded principles and practices that were the lifeblood of a powerfully insulated paradigm and status quo.

One can only imagine the questions ever-circulating in their consciousness as they prepared for their life work: How can I write and speak of an experience that, for all intents and purposes, is unspeakable? How can I shed some light on what has been called for millennia the Great Mystery? How can I provide some kind of palatable framework to assist those with entrenched, traditional mindsets begin to make their own evolutionary leaps in consciousness?

From this self-questioning point forward, Stan Grof's work seems to have been deeply grounded within what we may call the tradition of the *philosopher-seeker*. This puts him in the category of many of the world's most profound and influential teachers. We reiterate that this is how many of *us* feel, not how Stan sees himself. However, as he was to share later, some of the only historic references he could find to fundamentally validate his life-changing experience came from the world's most respected and timeless psycho-spiritual systems.

Like Bill Wilson, for Stan to share even a fraction of what he knew, or how he felt, might be to consign himself to the limbo of crackpots, misfits, and delusional dreamers whom scientists and psychologists would unequivocally ridicule and reject. Like Stan, within Bill Wilson's personal crisis were sown the seeds of his life work: as we have already stated, to reset what had become a dogma of addictions recovery by providing a new psycho-spiritual mind-set in a manner paralleling what Grof accomplished for psychology, science, and other disciplines. In so doing, his task was to re-envision a host of strategies, including science and psychology as well, by offering a broader lens through which to view these inquiries.

As with so many pioneers, the challenge for both Grof and Wilson was to manifest, in the external environment, the power of their inner convictions. These convictions were the psychological and scientific insights they had received, birthed by the overwhelming, reality-shattering experiences each had undergone through LSD, and in other ways. Their life work became the search for ways to make palatable, to scientists and proponents of many disciplines, the therapeutic and transformational power of their insights. This life goal and purpose ultimately became tangible and accessible through the birth and unfolding of both transpersonal psychology and the formulation of the Twelve Steps—in essence, a modern Western yoga.

Yet, once again, we flirt with heresy. It is absolutely true that transpersonal psychology, especially through the power of the world conferences of the International Transpersonal Association (ITA), has been a vital force for an upgrade of planetary evolution. By most accounts, it would seem that the transpersonal perspective is in some crucial way the centerpiece of Stan Grof's legacy. But let us take a closer look, and in so doing, propose something very rarely considered.

So far, no paradigm has ever been unassailable. That a paradigm should last forever goes against every insight gained from deep inner work. What if transpersonal psychology—or other uses of the term *transpersonal*—actually describe a *transitional* term, concept, and perspective? What if Stan saw it as having a certain temporarily expedient usefulness? Could it be that, at some point, the designation known as *transpersonal* might be a passing, perhaps even limited, description of scientific as well as psycho-spiritual structures and dynamics? Furthermore, at a time when existing institutions—however at the growing edge they may have once been—were prepared for new vistas of consciousness, might not an upgraded, more accurate terminology be some day called for to reflect new horizons of ever-evolving insight?

As radical as this sounds, Stan Grof has already often pointed to this possibility. We have just presented what we call the holotropic lineage. As we shared, a large portion of this lineage centers around Stan's coining of the word *holotropic* to name Christina's and his now well-known breathing practice. To reiterate, the term *holotropic* comes from Greek and Latin and means "moving toward wholeness." This idea of an evolution of consciousness toward some mystery of completion—or a kind of synergy that mystical systems call Becoming and Being—is well known throughout perennial philosophy. This is the case, even if the word holotropic is more modern, and perhaps less inflammatory for traditionalists.

But this is only part of the story. Another central principle of exploration into expanded states of awareness—either through the breath or any other means—requires us to take another look at and to re-evaluate what we mean by the term *psyche*. For the past several centuries, the term has come to mean the circumscribed, specifically human consciousness—itself a brain-based function which scientists are absolutely certain creates our experience of the self, world, and cosmos.

However, deep work reveals that the psyche, although operating at times within the expediency of individual consciousness, is in fact infinitely more expansive and comprehensive than traditional psychology and science have previously assured us is the truth. In fact, thousands of seekers, through their own self-exploration, using methods that access a broader spectrum of consciousness, have had the experience that the psyche is actually *equal to all that is*.

As such, the psyche is infinite—both beyond, as well as including, a personal individual focus—the cornerstone of accepted, traditional theory. Viewing the psyche in this expanded light is much more aligned with its original definition from the Greek, which means *soul*. And when we say "soul," we are not just referring to a dimension of the individual psyche, but with the fundamental nature of a universal field of consciousness available to all human beings—a world soul or anima mundi—an insight either spontaneously or evolutionarily acquired through various methods of self-exploration. With this understanding—of psyche as soul—we can once again revisit Christina's and Stan's use of the word *holotropic*—moving toward wholeness.

It seems inevitable that we point out the unmistakable similarity between the concept of "wholeness" and the expanded definition of "psyche," which is a cornerstone of the wisdom of the ages and an experience available to any seeker working in expanded states of awareness. From this perspective, as we said, consciousness is equal to all that is. In this light, the similarities between *psyche* and *wholeness* are difficult to overlook. They are, as we say, "of a piece," as, for example, ice and cold are nuances or characteristics of a unified phenomenon.

To suggest a radical proposal, we revisit Stan Grof's revolutionary extended cartography of the psyche, which, among its three components, includes a personal, individual domain of consciousness. It also encompasses what he calls the perinatal level—biological birth and/or psychospiritual death/rebirth. Seekers often find that the perinatal dimension is an interface, a dimension doorway, to the third level of consciousness, or the transpersonal realm. In short, transpersonal means "beyond the personal."

As Shakespeare might have said, herein lieth "the rub." If tradition-ally, the term *psychology* explicitly or implicitly refers to a study of the *individual*, brain-based human psyche, then a "*trans*-personal psychology" would encompass an inquiry into what is *beyond* the personal. This is inherent in the prefix *trans*, which means "across" or "beyond." So, could we not perhaps be in danger of falling into the same old trap of traditional psychology?

If traditional psychology explores a limited field, would not a psy-chology that calls itself "above or beyond" the personal also explore a kind of limited, or less than comprehensive domain? Or, even if transper-sonal psychology professes to encompass transformation throughout all three levels of the psyche, then wouldn't the name *trans*personal actually be a limited, inaccurate description of a comprehensive, all-inclusive psychology?

It is always a possible conceptual, as well as experiential, pitfall that we lapse into a type of linear thinking, where we cognize in terms of a step-by-step trajectory—in this case a movement from the biographical, or per-sonal, to the perinatal, and from there to the transpersonal. Or from the other way, we may again presume a linear logic, and envision evolution as always moving from the transpersonal through the perinatal and on into the biographical. We might find ourselves beginning to conceptualize in a kind of linear concreteness. Or we might subtly, unconsciously frame these dimensions as being in some way discrete. Ironically, the very use of the terms personal and transpersonal at least *implies* a dichotomy in definition. *Moreover, neither term implies wholeness.*

For example, it seems logical that a *personal* psychology deals with the biographical material of the psyche, and a *transpersonal* psychology would address the collective contents of the psyche, or issues common to humanity at large—that which is *beyond* the personal. Consequently, both of these terms—even if it is accidental—reflect, or at least imply, a *limited, circumscribed understanding of wholeness*, or what perennial philosophy espouses as the true nature of the term *psyche*.

Again, all of this depends very much on what any group of seekers or thinkers believes is the definition of the word *psyche*. If we mean the exclu-sive, individual, matter-based field of consciousness, then the term *psyche*, and therefore psychology, is limited. But, here is the immodest proposal: If we use, as our default mode, a totally comprehensive, expanded under-standing of the word *psyche*—in fact, taking it back to its original numi-nous roots as espoused by the wisdom of the ages as *equal to all that is*—then we would be confronted with a radical, altogether revitalized meaning of the term psychology. This revolutionary, yet simple insight—without having to add any prefix such as "trans"—would irrevocably reveal the true purpose of psychology itself as *the exploration of an unlimited, universal field of consciousness.*

When we do this, we will no longer need, in contradistinction with the *personal*, to refer to the term *transpersonal*, which on the surface *seems* to be a more comprehensive understanding of psychology, but, in fact, actually only describes one dimension of the totality of the psyche. We may realize that the term *transpersonal*, too, is actually, in certain ways, just as restrictive—and as equally non-comprehensive—as the original, but in fact inaccurate meaning of the term *psychology*, which it seeks to enlarge and complete. Nor would we need any longer to differentiate between, or defend, "this or that" definition of what psychology is.

At last, another dimension of the true nature of psychology may finally be revealed. Any schism or debate may become ultimately meaningless, as we open to the depth, breadth, and power of the individual and collective psyche, and the fluid interface between these two aspects of an inseparable unity and oneness—all under the aegis of the true meaning of the word *psyche*, as the inner dimensions of all that is. This may be the flower which has been unfolding and opening from the bud of psychology all along.

Now we bring this inquiry back to our discussion of a holotropic perspective. As we have said, holotropic means, "moving toward wholeness." Interestingly enough, *wholeness* seems to be an accurate characterization, if not, in fact, a precise definition describing an expanded understanding of what the psyche actually is: *wholeness* in the sense of *all that is*. Compare, for a moment, this new understanding of psychology with the individual and collective journey of moving toward wholeness, as described by Sri Aurobindo and many philosophers and teachers. If we do this, then we would confront a new definition of psychology itself—as a *philosophy of, and a means to facilitate, an individual's journey toward wholeness.*

With this new accurate definition of psychology, it would seem that the term *transpersonal* will have served its purpose as a valuable, transitional concept. Of course, it will still be valid for describing one aspect of psychology. Ultimately, the deep work individuals have been undertaking, which takes them into expanded states of awareness, will at the very least accomplish two things. First, through a radical experience on the nature of the psyche, it will finally reveal the true meaning of the word *psychology* itself, and open this discipline to facilitate the richest fulfillment of the human experiment possible. And second, as has already been stated by Stan Grof so beautifully, it will restore and expand the nature of the individual psyche to its original cosmic status.

PART III

Paths Beyond Personal Disempowerment

CHAPTER IX

Soul Killer: The Insidious Nature of Personal Disempowerment

As seekers in modern culture, almost all of us are programmed to expect therapists to have the answers. We trustingly offer up our power to those whom we consider to be outside experts—in any field. In regards to therapy, to our detriment, all too frequently, those among us who work with others will take the power that our clients innocently and freely give us, often to fulfill our own unmet needs.

Sometimes we may have an unconscious personal investment in being helpers—perhaps to see ourselves as worthwhile, important, someone worthy enough to be put on whatever pedestal looms like a beacon in our own fantasies. If this is the case, then, without them even realizing it—and even committed to this fact *not* being so—the seeker's cycle of personal disempowerment we have referred to earlier often continues. It is our hope that we can address these issues and other related subjects in some detail, here and now. In light of our inquiry into a holotropic perspective, our exploration into the nature of true empowerment is absolutely one of the most important premises of this book.

After doing systematic deep inner work, many of us share how, throughout our lives, we have unconsciously allowed ourselves to become mesmerized by the illusion of an imagined impotence, or, at the very least, the need for greater access to a wellspring of personal power. We recognize that for years we may have attempted to mitigate the feeling of disempowerment by a relentless, exhausting effort to manipulate our external environment. We almost universally look *outside* ourselves for fulfillment.

As seekers, we may also discover that human existence has been, at the same time, a diabolical and, for the most part, well-intentioned propaganda program that has consistently trained us to feel helpless and incomplete. In our incompleteness, we probably have often settled for a belief that the ideas, prescriptions, and opinions of others were the primary source of power or healing we could trust. And nowhere is this dynamic more soul killing that when it pertains to our personal psychological and spiritual growth.

Given all of this, it appears that pervasive personal and collective disempowerment is reaching a kind of zenith here in modern times. We see it most glaringly in two seemingly disparate institutions—modern medicine and psychiatry, on the one hand, and orthodox religion on the other. It is a tragic wonder how eager most of us are to place the wellbeing of both our physical constitution and our spirits in the hands of others, including so-called experts.

One of the pivotal characteristics in psychology that makes the Inner Healer so revelatory as well as controversial is that seekers' reliance on this inner radar eliminates what we might call *therapist bias*. It seems to be challenging for many of us people-helpers to accept the psycho-spiritual truth that clients know better than we do about what is good for them. How does this happen? Most schools are systems with a set of particular foundations, which include what each school believes comprises the nature of the psyche, or consciousness itself. A further part of the system presents a set of strategies that, as therapists, the followers of a particular school are trained to utilize when working with seekers.

Each of these strategies frequently depends on, not the seekers' own inner resources, but on the school itself and the practitioners of that school. It is often consciously or unconsciously assumed by both clients and therapists that therapists know what is best for seekers. The scientific/medical/psychological/religious system for the most part seems programmed this way. The competeveness of this bias is the inevitable outcome of the often polar differences between hundreds of traditional therapeutic procedures resulting in clients receiving a wide range of diagnoses—each based on the particular school in which the therapist has trained. Yet very few of us realize that this strategy has a much more profoundly insidious effect than even the presence of all these conflicting schools might suggest.

Very few of us were raised to irrevocably trust that we have an amazing power within us. Most of us never learned to rely on this perfect source of truth, healing, and wisdom that can be experienced as a kind of inherent default mode—a core, constitutional power within every person. For the most part, it appears that world societies have just not evolved sufficiently to support such a radical truth. But whatever we call this core attribute, it is impossible to overstate the importance of the Inner Healer as a catalyst for fundamental empowerment and transformation.

We are spending such concerted energy on this truth because the Inner Healer—this mysterious, provocative dynamic—is *the* golden thread holding all together through this book. It is also the therapeutic, healing soul of the holotropic perspective, exploration with entheogens, support for those in spiritual emergency, new frontiers in traditional psychotherapy, a holotropic addictions recovery strategy, and Holotropic Breathwork itself. To recognize this power within us, and to discover a means to jumpstart and nurture it in our lives, gives us the unlimited ability to free ourselves from one of the most soul-killing dynamics modern humanity faces. This soul-killer is *disempowerment*.

Disempowerment and the World Dream

Breathers often share a disconcerting insight of deep work, which shines a rather glaring spotlight on what many feel is a universal human predicament. Not surprisingly, I and many of my colleagues have arrived at similar conclusions. It is a rather bleak take on certain planetary conditions. Our purpose is not to sound an alarm of hopelessness—quite the opposite. Yet as troubling as these observations are, they are shared by millions all over the world. In our final chapter, we will highlight what is probably the greatest crisis of modern times—one with tremendous implications for us all.

This crisis is the immanent possibility that our actions as a human species may have already caused irreparable harm to the fragile biosphere we all share, and on which we depend for, literally, everything. However, no matter how dire the situation may be for the planet, as a result of our deep inner work, most of us still feel optimistic. We really believe that, collectively, we absolutely *can* find solutions for our world—and true empowerment and freedom for humanity.

Yet the heart-breaking, insidious dynamic of *disempowerment* is a horrendous malaise of our deepest selves. It is the overwhelmingly seductive tendency, in almost every area of our lives, to give ourselves away to experts who claim to know what is best for us. The result is a tragic, lifelong treadmill characterized by a systematic, maliciously insistent trajectory of negativity and powerlessness.

How might this happen? To trace its origins, we may discover through deep work that disempowerment can become focused by a download of relevant material from the transpersonal domain, or by a certain way of dealing with a challenging constellation of planetary archetypes operative at the time of our births. It can also be further imprinted during birth, particularly when we are subjected to unnecessary obstetric interventions.

Unless we have the luxury of a natural delivery—preferably in the hands of midwives, who are tradition holders of a very ancient lineage of the divine Feminine—we can sometimes begin our Earth incarnation without ready access to our birthright of positive inner resources of trust, connection, courage, empowerment, and self-esteem. With the possible exception of the enclaves of indigenous cultures remaining on our planet, for the most part, a modern medical paradigm shapes the birth process. In contrast with this indigenous poise, modern birth often seems to be a mere mechanical procedure, supported frequently by invasive, controlling sub-sets of the current scientific, medical system—and dominated historically by men.

Seekers report experiencing how, after being born, comes a well-meaning but often disempowering indoctrination by parents and relatives. They too seem to have been subjected to a similar acculturation when they were young—and even earlier, through their own births and legacies of generational trauma, as well as other transpersonal influences. This is fol-lowed by pre-school, where, with the exception of a growing number of conscious environments staffed by people who are themselves waking from their cultural dream, children often receive deeper levels of overt, as well as subliminal disempowering reinforcement.

This reinforcement can be daily applied by a misplaced encourage-ment that children, without any real, inherent trust in themselves, should look to others for their truths and self-validation. This often comes from teachers who have themselves become unconsciously acculturated by the prevailing multi-generational belief system, as their parents and teachers had before them, and who were also frequently subjected to a rather soul-less, medically orchestrated birth.

In the process, this paradigm—the one dominant in the world we are born into—becomes an ensnaring source of disempowerment for many children. We can discover that our lineages—through our frequently wounded mothers and fathers, and back through many generations—are all-too-often based on introjected, freedom-stifling customs, taboos, and religious beliefs. In addition, we are often the inheritors of a multi-genera-tional history of physical, emotional, mental, and sexual abuse. Further-more, we can hopefully make conscious and work through the fact that we are subjected daily to a worldview imbued with outmoded medical, psychi-atric, and scientific assumptions.

At some point, we may realize that we have paid unconscious homage to dysfunctional societies based on paradigm-weaving governments whose officials are themselves as morally, spiritually, physically, and psychologi-cally wounded as those they would govern. And if this is not enough, we recognize how we have become mesmerized by, as Bruce Springsteen has said, a virtual "devil's arcade" of economic and cultural systems fueled by an outrageously amoral global multi-media, advertising campaigns, and a hypnotically addictive cyberspace.

To take it even further, we can have the insight that we have often become the addicted pawns of a global financial apparatus, which virtually holds billions of people in poverty. Many of us have based our hopes and dreams on a cyberspace-driven marketing network headed by giant, absolutely soulless corporations, and overshadowed by a Madison Avenue archetype with mushrooming satellite bases permeating almost every country.

We uncover how our nightmares are often fueled by the possibility of global annihilation based on a power-inspired and fear-generating arms race, in league with an environment-destroying plague of economic expansion with absolutely no regard for the planet-killing implications of massive pollution. As some or all of this emerges for us, we may begin to deduce how it is grounded in a miasma of outdated scientific, ethical, religious, and moral systems that have been passed down in relentlessly deadening overlays of inherited trauma and shame. The good news is that all of these programs can be made conscious and then released through work in meta-ordinary states.

In the early 1970s I became fascinated with a teacher named Stephen Gaskin, an acquaintance of Zen master Suzuki Roshi, and in his own right a social and spiritual pioneer of the Sixties revolution. Gaskin had been an integral part of the early days of the psychedelic era in San Francisco, which was a "ground zero" for the great spiritual, sociological, and cultural awakening at that time. He had a dream of establishing an intentional community based on the revelations he and many of his friends had experienced through the use of psychedelics and other psycho-spiritual means during that convention-shattering era.

So he persuaded a group of San Francisco natives, women and men from many different disciplines—doctors, lawyers, philosophers, farmers, teachers, scientists, mothers, fathers, and more, whom he called "San Francisco's Finest"—to load up in old school buses and head out across America. Their collective dream was to travel around the country until they found the perfect place to start their new community. They ended up in Tennessee, and there, on an initial property of four-hundred acres, they started what came to be known as "The Farm." The Farm—based on the archetype of "communitas" and the way it had been manifested throughout history all across the world for millennia—became a blueprint for the communal living experiments which sprang up everywhere during that time.

Every Sunday, the tribe would gather on the land, and Stephen would do a teaching. His lectures were recorded in a number of books. This, along with my own inner psychedelic experiences, was how I became acquainted with, and then fascinated by, this dream of a new way of living on the earth. Now, in one of his lectures, he began to share his thoughts and feelings on the global crisis as he saw it at this time. Remember, this was the early 1970s. He was discussing the archetype of the demonic, and its role in the cosmic scheme. I will never forget one of the things he said. I bring it up because it was absolutely prescient of a pivotal dynamic of the current global crisis, and the issues we are exploring right now in this inquiry.

He said that the most striking example of a demonic presence in world culture at that time was the growing shadow of what he called "multi-national" corporations. He stated that these corporations were in essence soulless entities bereft of, and beyond, any human ownership and now imbued with a life all of their own. These soulless entities operated absolutely sociopathically, sucking the life from humanity and the earth, with no human compunction of morality or compassion at all.

Amazing! Multi-national corporations! He was the first person I ever heard put such a face and name on what has become both a ubiquitous title and a global nightmare. I am reminded of this story, because it reflects our current crisis of human disempowerment. When we begin to awaken, to become more conscious of ourselves and the world around us, we often feel powerless in the face of such global sociopathy.

In short, this anecdote shines a vivid spotlight on our crisis of disempowerment. The burning question before us is what, really, can we do to transform the plague-like presence of these poisoned fruits of greed and selfishness? Based on the reports of many who have done systematic deep work in meta-ordinary states of consciousness, there seems to be only one real thing.

Faced with this powerlessness, millions are now turning within, seeking that source of power within themselves. We do this because we seem to intuitively know that it is only through the mobilization of the infinite, untapped resources within ourselves will we be able to find, not only a freedom individually, but also solutions for a transformation of the global crisis externally that can actually make a difference. This is the promise of strategies such as a holotropic perspective. And this is what we hear from the thousands who have turned inward, and found the source of true power within themselves.

Despite this disheartening scenario, *No one of us is to blame*. The condition is historically, generationally systemic. Mystic or metaphysical traditions would suggest that it is a glamour, a *maya*—that we have become mesmerized. It is an experience we here in modern times can have, as well in our own deep work. But where are we in all of this illusion? How do we get free? In a sense, it appears that virtually every one of us is caught in some way.

This consciousness plague is so ubiquitous that it has assumed the status of a global hypnosis. From the time of birth, it seems that most of us embark on a journey of a paradigmatic acculturation akin to brainwashing. It is as though we have become sleepwalkers before we are ever truly awake. For all intents and purposes, we appear to be living in "Maya," the

"Dream of Brahma," the "Realm of the Hungry Ghosts," or the "Twilight of the Gods."

As Stan Grof would say, we often find ourselves on a *linear binge*. We see how we have frequently ignored the wisdom of the ages, which tells us that every kind of growth is cyclical in nature. From the cycles found in seasons, to the evolutionary spiral of human growth—through birth, childhood, maturity old age, death and rebirth—the great philosophical and spiritual traditions and the most ancient wisdom of indigenous cultures all point to this truth. Yet we have created a global cyber-culture with absolutely no place for the down-cycle, or ebb within the flow, for death *and* rebirth. Our surface consciousness seems to be hardwired into the addiction of "more is better," on and on, in a linear trajectory most see as lasting forever. This is what he means by the "linear binge."

So, once more, what can we do? The good news is that the signposts for the way out of this personal and global disempowerment, the beacons that can point us in new directions, have always been with us. They can readily be found in hundreds of texts, from every part of the world, from every culture of recorded time. The inheritance from these sources for any seeker is an array of methods for individual and collective transformation that can free us from this malaise.

We are excited to be sharing accounts—a summary of the inner journeys of thousands of seekers who are finding ways to awaken from this dream in which so many of us have become ensnared. What thickens the plot for us is that we are no longer looking only to the past—the wisdom of the elder ages. Yes, they have been valuable supports, validations, and comforts along the way. We have learned much from them.

Yet seekers today appear more restless than ever. This restlessness, fertilized by the use of powerful methods accessing deep states of consciousness, seems to be morphing into an even greater fiery, cosmos-exploring passion. In a sense, more than ever, all bets are off. Our far-reaching vista is like the glance from the second head of the cross-cultural two-headed deities, one looking back, the other gazing forward. So many are now looking forward: We are "point-omega-driven," to borrow a phrase from Teilhard de Chardin. At this point in our evolution, it is the mystery of what is unfolding and the far horizons of wholeness that are our modern culture's "juice." It is not just what *has been* long ago, but what *will be soon* that seems to be the passion of our time.

Waking from the Dream

We have explored already one way to see the powerful, mesmerizing, nature of the current paradigm. But there is another deeper octave to which we are opening. This broader lens sweeps us all the way back, and beyond the current manifestations of this plague of disempowerment. Gazing forward or back ultimately opens us with vivid clarity to perennial philosophy—the wisdom of the ages. We learn from the deep and lasting teachings passed down through ancient cultures from all over the world. And we dream of the revelations still to come; through any of these, we can discover a variation on two central, all-pervasive truths. The first shines a light on the dilemma of suffering for all human beings: and this is that many of us are lost and deeply confused about what will truly fulfill us in our life journeys. The second proclaims clearly, like a clarion call: *There is a way out.*

Joanna Macy has beautifully proposed a revolutionary binary definition of power. She wrote and spoke about the necessity of the profound shift from a *power-over* to a *power-with* mentality. This reflects our focus on the power of an ongoing death of the false, constricted self, into an ever more expanded dispensation of wholeness, interwoven with an awakening numinosity. We may envision that there is a further component, or simultaneously positive outcome of relinquishing a "power-over" mentality. It is likely that a fruit of the realization of a "power-with" consciousness might be an inspiring recognition of an infallible inner resource—our *power within.*

The first of the Buddha's Four Noble Truths states that all life is, or contains *suffering*. No kidding. Here is a principle on which we can all agree. The second truth says that that suffering is caused by *unfulfilled desire* or *craving*. Stated informally, the Taoist Lao Tzu offered that the Great Way is easy if we are not addicted to our preferences, to our personal desires. Almost all spiritual systems—as well as many modern psychotherapies—agree that one of our most basic and powerful human drives is the search for true happiness, freedom, and empowerment.

Most systems propose, in one metaphor or another, that one of the core causes of our suffering is that we are deeply mistaken about how to go about finding this lasting, authentic happiness. We all wish to confront this looming tragedy of disempowerment that has for millennia gripped planetary civilizations. As Morpheus told his disciple in the movie *The Matrix*, before he "unplugged" him from his imprisonment in the Matrix: "You've been living in a dream world, Neo." What seemed to make this movie series so wildly popular was that it struck a universal, or archetypal, chord.

It sounded a note that so many of us either consciously or unconsciously feel—most of us for our entire lives. This is that we have been misled by the current world dream. Because of this, we are unable to find our way to freedom. The glamour that binds us is daily rewoven. It is a spell of global magnitude. It is consciously or unconsciously reinforced by systems of thought, where the primary directive seems to be to prepare each new generation to be continually "slotted into" some subservient role in the global cultural dream experiment.

What fuels this so-called dream experiment? At least part of it seems to be the result of a wild, unchecked exercise in greed and power. This exercise is itself the result of a deep longing for happiness that has gone horribly awry. The dream experiment is what world teachers have been referring to in all spiritual systems in one way or the other. Some say that this world is nothing but an illusion—that it is false altogether—and that the purpose of life is to free ourselves from it completely. This proposes a great mystery for which, it seems, there can be no one answer. In our work, we might encourage a seeker to find out for herself, through her own authentic power within, the answer to this and other cosmic riddles.

Others say we need to awaken from the dream of Maya—to get free by recognizing that Maya is a great delusion or illusion. We also hear and read that this world as we see it is only an appearance of limitation and falsehood. We are assured that—perhaps freed from the bonds of linear time—we have the ability to experience it in a glorious perfection of which, at this point, we can only dream. And once having awakened, we can then be moved to serve others—to do what we can to help them be free of suffering as well.

Still others say that we live in a desire-fueled shadow play, a program, a matrix, a fixed, limited operating system, or a "dark city," as the modern film classic of this name suggests, fed by this addiction to power and greed. The result of this collective hypnosis is that we are blinded by the light of false promises that we are guaranteed can be fulfilled in our frantic pursuit of various addiction-dreams in the external world. Here is one of the most cruel of these false promises: If we just work hard enough, we can wrest from life, from the resources of the planet, and from other human beings, whatever we feel we want or need to bring us lasting happiness.

The main problem with this fantasy was addressed in a quote by Oscar Wilde, and most teachers of spirituality would agree. "There are only two tragedies in life: one is not getting what one wants, and the other is getting it." In the case of the former, if we don't get what we want, we will be unhappy because of the pain of our continued wanting, our grasping, and the emptiness we feel when we don't receive the fulfillment of our desires.

The other sorrow is getting what we want. And why would this cause us suffering? Because if we have it, we will always be afraid we will lose it—something which inevitably occurs in our pursuit of happiness. Or else we will become addicted to it and crave acquiring more and more. In either case, we suffer.

This is exactly the situation that we face on the planet today. There seems to be a great dream woven by the relentless pursuit of countless threads of egoic and material greed and obsession. As we said, there is a global culture now, more and more enmeshed and fueled by cyberspace—a formidable, shadow-generated experiment in electronic dream weaving. On the one hand, we have at our fingertips a whole array of information, knowledge, and opportunities to pursue the eventual reality of planetary transformation. So many of us would long to play a part in a drama which sees us each undertake what some Sufis call moving *"toward the One: the perfection of love, harmony, and beauty."*

Sufficient means for everyone to live in health and safety are gifts all humanity deserves. It seems to be all possible, here and now. Perhaps one day we will utilize world resources toward these goals. Yet instead, most of those in power seem driven to successfully manipulate other members of the world human community toward their own ends, so that power and wealth are increasingly acquired by fewer and fewer individuals and consortiums. And one of the ways they do this is through an insidious manipulation of the electronic dream machine.

We are taught to "go get it," to fight for it, to be radiantly healthy, cool, and beautiful. We are schooled to acquire more and more of whatever it is we think we need, even though what we think we need is changing almost hourly due to the cyber-fuelled advertising barrage promising the newest happiness craze. This fantasy is being beamed at us relentlessly through a thousand forms of an instantaneously available and ubiquitous multimedia. The message: that it is possible for us all to get it all. We become stultified and stupefied by cyberspace, even as we may walk through a grove of sacred trees.

Yet we are forever overlooking one major flaw in this trajectory. If we are pursuing our dreams in the external world—the ones we are promised that we deserve—we have to realize that so are the rest of the seven-billion people on the planet. Therefore, it is inevitable that we will be in constant competition with a number of these people throughout our lives. Sometimes we will succeed, and sometimes we will fail.

Then, at the end of our lives, as we look back on our earth adventures, if we have come anywhere close to experiencing the fulfillments of our desires half the time, then we can consider this to be about as successful as we could expect. A certain statistical percentage on a graph on some website: for all our struggles, do we really want to be satisfied with this return on the investment of our dreams and ambitions? Ought this be the final reward—the result of a lifetime of want, craving, and a pervasive sense of lack—of never enough?

As we bring this section of our inquiry to a close, the good news bears repeating: *Engaging in any systematic deep work over a period of time will almost certainly reveal to us a way to find a true lasting freedom, independent of outside circumstances.* This is one of the promises of perennial philosophy. It is something we have heard a thousand times from breathers who have systematically embraced the holotropic paradigm: *that within us all along has been a force more powerful than any the outside world can offer.* It is a source of inspiration many feel certain will always be available for the fulfillment of their dreams.

This unlimited power goes by such a diminutive, unassuming name that it is easy to overlook it in our frenzied search outside ourselves for happiness. But the search, though sometimes difficult, is just not that complicated. As you may have guessed by now, this unlimited power is none other than the Inner Healer, or what we also call, in our inquiry, the power within.

Many true spiritual paths in one way or the other lead us to our inner selves and the power latent there. Yet even though it is the promise of virtually every form of therapy, many of these psychotherapeutic and transformational systems can often be misguided as well. Instead of recognizing the Inner Healer and supporting us to discover the true resources of a power within, they often direct us, consciously or unconsciously, to rely instead on them—to look outward to the therapists who become their priests and priestesses.

Most of us, at some point in our lives, will recognize and confront the need for a download of some kind of true personal power. Without power, it is impossible to reach a level of worthwhile fulfillment, be it for any kind of outer or inner riches. In this search for power, and if we are fortunate, or some might say blessed, three things may happen. First, we may become disillusioned with the ability of any outside person, system, or circumstance to know what is best for us, or be able to provide whatever that panacea may be. Second, we may then arrive at a disconcerting existential crisis. In this crisis, we can have the experience, based on whatever operating system of the false self we are using, or constricted lens through which we see ourselves, that these limited tools of the ego, for all intents and purposes, are simply powerless to fix us.

The third event that may occur is a milestone, a true breakthrough. This one can happen either spontaneously, or through some deep experiential method like Holotropic Breathwork, meditation, psychedelics, shamanic practices, a spiritual emergency, and the like. The transformation seems, at least in part, to be a flowering of what philosopher Macy has called the culture-changing shift from "power over" to "power with."

Yet the dynamic of *power with* is still but an essential, important element on the trajectory toward the fulfillment of any exploration of true power. Of course, it is not far-fetched to propose that a cornerstone of any new transformational millennium will be the evolution from power over to power with. But might this still not be the final frontier of our experience of power? Perhaps, even at this point of great shift, there is a further, deeper horizon of power that must be embraced for there to be a culmination of the true human dream experiment. We have, in the manner of a mantra, referred to it already. This further horizon is what we are calling a radical—full-bodied, mental and emotional—turning inward, to the treasure of power always, already within.

Through this gift, we are able to get in touch with and to activate a previously untapped dimension deep within ourselves. This inner resource can then become a constant catalyzing agent for true empowerment, with the absolute potential to lead us to our evolutionary fulfillment as human beings in this planetary cycle. We now have very real means to embrace freedom, power, and wholeness in our lives, one moment at a time. This is the basis of a holotropic paradigm.

CHAPTER X

Flashbacks on Caring and Support

Intellectual knowledge—even on its own—has an important place is our lives, including our endeavors to serve others. In order to support seekers in their holotropically-oriented work, we are also required to develop other faculties—those that are centered in what we may call the intuition, a capacity to empathize, or, to be metaphorical, simply the Heart. Through a process known only to our deepest inner healing resources, what we learn through our minds must become "alchemicalized" within our capacity to love, to care, to serve. We cannot merely "put on" this alchemy between mind and heart, like a cloak—or "turn it on" like an exotic mechanism. It is an *experience*, almost a grace, wrought by the Inner Healer, from which we may derive a wonderful purpose, in service to those around us.

We often discover what we most need to truly support another human being when we are not even looking for it. This capacity is not something we can buy or read to make it real. We may find it in a classroom, in those moments when we look up from the notes on our computer and connect with a teacher whose heart is open in service to us. If we do find it in a classroom, we are fortunate indeed. But we do not get a diploma for meditating alone in a deep forest, walking open-hearted through a crowded thoroughfare, or sitting with a dying friend.

Mystics tell us that, ultimately, real education just does not seem to be about "accruing," but about "letting go." The truth of this is in the definition itself. The word, *education*, comes from the Latin, and means to "draw, or lead forth from within." It does not mean that we "came with" a program with a mental intake capacity alone, a band-width for downloading information from outside us. It is a sweet irony how many seekers feel that their most valuable education has ultimately been a process of *unlearning*. For most in this work, transformation has been a systematic relinquishing of our cluttered, concept-focused consciousness, and an opening into a mystery of what can only be called the heart—a space of caring, honoring, trusting, and holding space.

For people-helpers attracted to the holotropic perspective, we find that our awakening is usually the result of life experiences accrued while in the process of trying to learn some outside therapeutic technique. Being of service seems to be about experiencing a kind of "figure/ground reversal" within ourselves. What we *know* becomes the veil that separates us from what we have always/already *been*. We may be fortunate to discover what we have rarely found solely from the outside: a mystery that innately shines forth from within, ever tapping the power of presence and healing we always, already are.

This confusing, "upside-down" search eventually comes to an often initially painful, yet ultimately freeing ending. We uncover from within that our ability to be with others on the road to transformation has been about this *unlearning* instead of learning. All of this "Alice-through-the-looking-glass upside-down truth" brings us wide-eyed to where we have always been already—an innate, true, inherently natural ability to be of service with others. Even though we can learn much from many teachers, ultimately, we will not get it "out there." The process becomes one of allowing what comes "from without" to sink in and "alchemicalize" with the core of who we are. Thus, we can all open to it—within, right here, right now—where this truth has always been.

Even though some of us "get here" by un-learning, we must be open to those who never learned in the first place. We learn or un-learn when we work in the *heart space of presence*—that magic talisman that is the alchemical healer in any relationship between healer and the one healed. It is a dimension of transformation where the boundaries between these two seem to dissolve in the presence of a third: *the Mystery within*, the true source of healing.

As presence, it is the miracle of the moment that cannot be found here or there, in a classroom or outside of one. It can only be discovered through what many call *grace*—a deep experience that we did not necessarily pay for, or earn, but one with which we seem to have been blessed. This dynamic could reduce most of therapeutic endeavors to marveling at the miracle of healing, rather than being proud of anything one did for the person we imagine we have the power to "fix."

In the Twelve Step yoga, we say that the only thing we have to offer another person is our own *experience, strength, and hope*. I came to rely on certain basic principles of this revolutionary paradigm long before I became involved with Holotropic Breathwork at all. I have heard many tales similar to mine, from my friends and co-workers in the holotropic work around the world. We *all* are the beneficiaries of a numinous inheritance. These are our life adventures, which have been the real, true source of our ability to "be there" for other human beings on their journeys toward wholeness.

Two realizations will forever stand out as pearls beyond price for me. The first is how my holotropic work—both inner and outer—was the natural child of my psychedelic heritage. The second is that my first breathwork experience was as powerful for me as those psychedelic journeys that, years before, had radically upgraded and transformed my life. In some strange, yet experientially logical synergy, these two continue to imbue my personal journey, as well as to ever operate as beacons of support in my efforts to be of service to other seekers.

After a breathwork session, sometimes a seeker who has uncovered a pattern that she will be working with for some time, requests to be given something, anything, she can take home with her. So, I have asked myself frequently, "What did we do together during her inner journey, as we went 'down the stream' together? What is the essence of this practice? What actually happens?"

To answer these queries, I often recall—out of a host of blessings— several milestones from my own life that now seem to have been inextricably woven into a tapestry I am absolutely convinced I did not weave. However, they did become foundational truths for me, which, through some mechanism of the Inner Healer, I was able to draw upon later as the core essence of the holotropic dynamic when supporting other seekers. Here they are, in a rather non-linear but interrelated fashion, as insights from our past often seem to be.

Beginning in the Middle

I was working in addictions treatment in Macon, Georgia, in a nationally known corporate treatment system. This was around 1982. I was something of an apprentice ninja on my team. I had almost no formal training. Yet I was hired by the psychiatrist and program director who ran our unit for, I suppose, something indefinable that they felt I might be able to offer our clients. But they were not stupid. So when they got the opportunity for me to get some professional training, they took it.

Their strategy included a series of three adventures that, all these years later, I can only imagine as their desperate attempt for me to receive in a few months what takes years for most counselors to understand about working with others in addictions treatment. So it was a kind of crash course—actually, it was way more of a boot camp for extremely raw recruits. The first trial by fire occurred a few months before our center opened. They sent me to a growing-edge, sophisticated, and well-respected treatment facility in Jackson, Mississippi, to attend the month-long family program for codependence. I was basically "in the trenches," but not playing the role of the hotshot whiz-kid counselor. I was, in fact, in treatment myself.

We have been speaking about the power of the death/rebirth experience all through the adventure of this text. This is exactly what happened for me there. In case I have not made myself clear, *the ego death hurts.* I had already experienced earlier increments of this, but it never seems to get a whole lot easier, nor do I think I will ever become accustomed to it. I guess this is why they call it a death. When I headed back to Georgia after the month was up, I was not the same person who showed up at work as a counselor—as the one who strutted into treatment in Mississippi one month before, thinking he had all the answers and knew himself so well.

The second trial was a trip to the well-known Johnson Institute in the treatment mecca of Minneapolis, Minnesota, where I spent two more weeks really coming to understand—as if I did not already—how the ego death is not a one-shot deal, but an incremental trajectory of experience. After becoming recognized as one of the growing edge centers for addictions recovery, the Johnson Institute had, in addition, developed a reputation as ground zero for the budding codependence movement. Many of the codependence movement's pioneers had been initially based there, or lectured there regularly.

It was at the Johnson Institute that I experienced my first therapeutically based expanded state of awareness. It was a music-guided journey into my earliest present-life history, where I came face-to-face, as well as heart-to-heart, with my *wounded child* self. This episode inaugurated a whole new level of my personal recovery. Through this meta-ordinary experience, I began in earnest a vital stage of biographical and interpersonal healing that has proven to be as important as any inner work I have done in my life—all of which has been repeatedly validated and enriched by my inner exploration through Holotropic Breathwork.

While there, we also had the good fortune to be supported by some very well- trained and loving humanistic therapists. We spent several days in groups that lasted in some cases more than twelve hours. It was a marathon that was as difficult as it was life enhancing, both personally and professionally. Many "psychedelic yogis," who eventually come down to earth, have gone through what happened to me there.

A lot of us have had astounding spiritual experiences. Yet there is a way that we have also done what Hayat Ricki Schechter, a young Sufi teacher, first shared with me in 1991. She said that many on the spiritual path have experienced what in the Sufi tradition they were calling the "spiritual bypass," a term coined by John Welwood in 1984. That is, that we may have spent a lot of cosmic time in outer space. However, we have also just flown right by our biography. As many of us were to learn, it is the biography that is the "hotbed" of unconscious, multi-dimensional psycho-dynamics—but the foam on the surface of an ocean of inner causal issues.

I have since come to call our biography the playground of the transper-sonal and the perinatal dimensions. Spiritual teacher Ram Dass was known to have said that it is okay to "trip the light fantastic." But we ought never to get so high, or so supposedly spiritual, that we forget our own zip code. A lot of us from the earlier psychedelic era did not even have a zip code we could forget. But it was in this group setting that, for the first time, I deeply confronted, in a loving supportive place, the intense wounds of my bio-graphical life.

Three Words That Changed My Life

The third episode of my "walkabout"—as the indigenous people of Austra-lia call these kinds of soul adventures—was in some ways the most revela-tory, in terms of how I would eventually learn to be of support for seekers. The gift came in the form of a one-day workshop with the celebrated exis-tential psychiatrist and therapist Irvin Yalom. This workshop changed my life. This was also 1982. As I have alluded to, I was about three years clean, and a bit of a throwback. I went to the event with my long hair, big earring, t-shirt, and jeans. Everyone else was pretty much in his or her professional finery.

The subject of the day's seminar was group and individual therapy—not something I knew much about—at least from any traditional educa-tional standpoint. However, by the end of the workshop, it occurred to me that I actually already did have some experience supporting people in their search for wholeness. Moreover, it also dawned on me that I had not gar-nered the benefit of this experience from any traditional form of psycho-logical education.

Rather, this therapeutic gift I had already received appeared to have emerged, quite some time before this workshop, in a way I could not under-stand, from something within me that had nothing to do with my head, or my mind. It was not anything I had *learned*, or received through some hard-won victory on my part. Instead, it had just serendipitously, spontane-ously emerged in certain moments of intense interactions with individuals where we both were participants in dramas whose fundamental unfoldings relied on trust, safety, caring, and respect.

In these situations, without my orchestrating it in any way, I found myself to be a guide or a support for someone else who was in a crisis, and was in some way reaching out to me for help. Much later, what I had learned from the counter-culture—in deep forests, on riverbanks, at rock music festivals, in crash pads, and in the streets—turned out to represent the essential, priceless core of a very real education. This *learning from within* with which I had been graced would later seem to validate my being allowed to support individuals in their own deepest crises.

Each of these experiences was imbued with the inherent characteristics of a very natural, down-to-earth *human relationship*. In this relationship, I and my fellow journeyer seemed to discover ourselves to be co-adventurers on an odyssey where neither of us had any clue as to what would or should happen. Somehow, though, we were allowed to feel an inherent trust in an indefinable, yet natural force or presence within us that could guide us through the mystery of whatever the crisis was that we were involved in. In these adventures, *there was ultimately no arbitrary delineation between helper and the one who would be helped.*

There was merely an inherent opening based on what can only be described as, we have said, an *unknowing*. And from this space of not knowing, it was possible for a miracle to occur, which was ultimately beyond the ability of either the helper or the one helped to have orchestrated for themselves. To put it simply, we were both allowed to experience a sense of grace.

Before I share the marvelous outcome of this seminar with Yalom, I will flash back to a couple of these episodes pivotal to my rather befuddling ability to trust a healing dynamic beyond what I could have learned from any mental exercise alone. These experiences occurred, of course, after the ones to which I just referred during my counter-cultural years. The first is related to the fact that I was in Twelve Step recovery from a murderous addiction. I believed deeply, as I have shared before in my first book, *The Wide Open Door: The Twelve Steps, Spiritual Tradition, and the New Psychology*, that the Twelve-Step process is a true world yoga.

I also practiced the Twelve Steps for my own recovery. The last step says, in different words, that once we had undertaken the Twelve Step yoga and had been graced with a level of freedom from our condition, then it was our responsibility, in order to deepen our recovery, to work with others suffering from addiction too. The primary "modality," if you will, for this Twelfth Step service could be summed up like this: The only thing we ever have to offer another suffering addict is our own *experience, strength, and hope*. So, I suppose that this constituted at least a part of my so-called credentials to be of service to others.

The second indefinable gift seems to have emerged from an even earlier time—before addiction finally worked its dark alchemy within me. This chapter is related to my experiences with LSD and other psychedelic substances. For years, when I would be a speaker in an Alcoholics Anonymous or Narcotics Anonymous meeting, I was always straightforward about my psychedelic use and the hugely important role it played in my life.

When I was sharing "what it used to be like," as this part of the talk is called, here is a summary of what I would share: I always relate that I feel very blessed to have been involved in spirituality years before the fellowship found me—to have already been graced with the reality of the divine, or of the numinous, and its incomparable importance in my life since that time. I say something to the effect that I have to be honest in this talk, and then I add this: "My Higher Power fundamentally, irrevocably embraced me through a series of experiences with LSD and other forms of psychoactive substances." These experiences began in my late teens and continued periodically, yet rather intensely, I might add, for over ten years.

I had heard a number of people in the fellowship say that if I had the Higher Power experience while on "dope," then it was not real. But those experiences absolutely changed my life, and to this day represent a core level of the fundamental, lasting game-changers I have experienced. So, when I was sharing my recovery story, I always made the point that if the Higher Power was ever going to find me in those days, then She would have had to do it through a substance, because I was always high. And this is, apparently, exactly what She did. When else would She have found the time?

It is essential to share, once more, that my psychedelic use during this period is one of the four most powerful influences in my life journey—an odyssey which is, as much as possible, consciously dedicated to moving toward wholeness. The other three are, one, my practice of the world yoga—the Twelve Steps—two, my ongoing inner work with Holotropic Breathwork, and finally, the myriad strategies that constitute my own individual, ongoing *sadhana*, or yoga.

At that time in my early recovery, those life-changing experiences with entheogens became one of the two indefinable attributes—the other being the Twelve Step practice—to influence my being hired to work with addicts. It seems fairly obvious that a firm grounding in recovery principles would be essential to working with others. Yet what about the fact of my having ingested a rather large amount of psychoactive substances? The benefits from this endeavor for an aspiring recovery counselor seem a good bit more ambiguous.

However, looking back over the often hazy yet incomparably enchanting period of my psychedelic use, one thing comes into a slightly sharper focus. I seemed to have acquired a rather small, and possibly bogus, reputation for being able to support a few people through what we call "bad trips." My memories of that era are certainly suspect. There were a great many other substances I ingested besides psychedelics. Not only that, it is probable that I was supported by others way more times than I was able to be of service to anyone else. But I do remember a number of times doing exactly what I now call, in our holotropic facilitation, "flowing down stream" with someone who was in a rough psycho-spiritual space.

This support definitely was not like performing any kind of healing. It was more akin to meeting them where they were, finding the same "wave-link," and then taking the ride with them. It definitely was not about knowing what was best for them. It was way more about trusting them to tap the deepest possible resources of healing and wellbeing within themselves. When they came through, or resolved something, I was as surprised as they were, particularly given the fact that most of those times I was tripping too. I am not saying I wouldn't feel pretty special after that. As you can imagine, I was not nearly as spiritual as I would have liked people to think.

For a lot of that time, I was still an addict. And one of our defining characteristics as addicts has never in a million years been humility. The truth is, my deep spiritual work had only barely begun at this time. By far my most entrenched default mode for that time was a rampant self-seeking—hopefully mitigated somewhat by repeated painful experiences of death and rebirth over the past thirty years.

But back to my new job as an addictions "specialist" and group therapy leader. My dear friend and mentor, Al Stein, the program director of our unit, had actually found a wonderful way to train this ex-hippie whose modus operandum was the "lone outrider" with virtually no formal education. So he threw me into group and said something like "sink or swim; let me know how it goes."

After one or two excruciating episodes of getting absolutely "hooked" by a few "revolving door" treatment veterans, by dumb luck or amazing grace, an old habit kicked in. I found myself once more just "being with" the clients, meeting them fully where they were, and again flowing down stream with them. Although I had no language for it at that time, somehow I had "gotten out of the way" a little bit, and was accidently trusting the clients' Inner Healers. It was interesting that at some point during this work, my mentor let it be known to me that he always found my groups to be "in their feelings," as he called it. This was a good thing.

Not only did I not know what I was doing, but whatever it was, I certainly did not have a name for it. Even though I could see that something mysterious was at work, I had no idea what it was. Nor did I find any compelling reason at that time for this indefinable thing to be defined. It just worked. So later, this unlooked for, but somehow natural affinity for what I have learned to call the Inner Healer was one more reason that I was attracted to the holotropic perspective from the very first time I was exposed to it.

Another important mentor of mine, a sponsor, as we call these helpers, was a senior counselor trainer in the treatment center in Jackson, Mississippi, where I experienced one round of my several, most impactful ego deaths. He shared with me one time that he always knew whether an addictions counselor was "on track" in her group, even if he did not know who the counselor was or who the group members were when he first entered the setting. He said that all he had to do was walk in and sit for a moment. If he was having a hard time figuring out who the therapist was and who the group members were, then he knew the group was in good hands and doing great.

He knew, then, that the counselor was not separating herself from the participants by either her own greater recovery time, education, experience, or title—in short, her own ego, or sense of self-importance. Instead, she maintained her most fundamental connection with her group in a simple yet profound way. First and foremost, she was a human being, a seeker, just as the so-called "patients" were. She was "in the current" with them, "going down stream," supporting, learning, growing, feeling deep emotions, being first a real human being—just as they were.

She was demonstrating, by who she really was beneath any titles or trappings, what her group members were as well, always already, even if perhaps in a more potential than actual state. This basic humility, simplicity, and trust in the power of others to heal from within are the requirements of anyone who chooses a path of service toward others' wellbeing. It cannot be taught. It must be experienced from within through deep personal work. This is the holotropic path toward personal wellbeing and service toward others.

I must also mention one other indispensable helpmate that became available for me around the time I was beginning my work as a counselor on the addictions unit. Besides what I had experienced at the Johnson Institute; my work in the family program of the Mississippi center; my adventure with Yalom, which I will relate soon; my tutelage under my mentor, the program director of the hospital where I worked; and my accidental, yet core, cellular absorption of a holotropic perspective in the middle of my psychedelic era, there were not too many sources available for me to get more training outside of traditional psychological curricula. Yet I was blessed with one more gift of support that, to this day, has been an indispensable source of impeccable therapeutic strategy totally enhancing a holotropic perspective.

At some point fairly early on in my work at the treatment center, I had become disillusioned with most of the traditional psychotherapeutic practices used on our unit—especially those that were being employed in group therapy with the addicts. For some reason, I was having a really difficult time resonating with most of the interventions I saw being implemented with our clients. With the exception of the work of a few fellow soul-brother, soul-sister counselors, many of the strategies and interactions appeared "canned," or sterile.

These interventions seemed to overlook the power of "heart," or the authentic sharing of oneself with the client—that relationship that for years I have called "going down stream" with someone. Often, it felt as though there was a barrier between the "patients" and the therapist. I learned over time that this was no accident, but was, in fact, a nuance of many of the modalities that were being employed in treatment settings all over the country, during this so-called renaissance of addictions treatment.

The problem for me was two-fold: First, I had not been trained to interact that way with addicts; and second, even when I was coached in these types of interventions, they absolutely did not feel natural to me, or supportive in any way that would foster a meaningful, healing connection between client and helper. They seemed lifeless and even heartless.

It was clear to me that many of the addicts were just not responding to this kind of offered support. When the support team noticed this psycho-emotional wall between themselves and the clients, their strategy was to vigorously confront what they felt was the addicts' entrenched denial system which, as text books suggest, was bolstered by a host of biographically and addiction-generated egoic defenses.

It was a tough time for me—a trial of soul purpose, if you will. I felt confused by my own inability to grasp this particular therapeutic style—one where I would need to effect an operating motif derived from a set of textbook-learned directions. But more importantly, I felt compassion for the clients, whom I saw daily sinking deeper into their own individual strategies of defense. I witnessed them drifting further and further away, as opposed to moving closer, in heart and mind, to our offerings of support.

Looking back, I recognized this time as a crisis of trust for me. First, I found myself unable to champion the application of this kind of treatment itself and its ability to actually reach the clients in any meaningful way. The second part of the crisis was that, at some point, I began to doubt myself, and even begin to entertain the notion that I would never be qualified to do this type of work without a few college degrees, and a series of letters after my name.

However, an amazing event took place that, to this day, has proven to be pivotal, not only for me, but also for all of us who have come through the holotropic training for their own growth. This also includes the ones who have themselves become the guides for prospective practitioners and seekers in training. While I was working in the treatment center, I took the opportunity, offered to us by the administration, to attend a conference on addictions treatment. I was looking forward to hearing what leading-edge pioneers had to say that might help me in my own current malaise of doubt.

When I arrived there, I scanned the program and the list of speakers, and the topics they were going to share with us. For my part, most of the lectures felt lifeless and dry. They seemed to be presenting the same traditional strategies we had already been taught. Yet they would subtly dress their concepts in slightly different language. In a sense, they were merely re-packaging the status quo, so that it only appeared we would be receiving something radical and revolutionary.

Through a slightly different lens, I noticed another disquieting trend. Many speakers appeared to be championing strategies that were, in fact, merely finer and finer points of long-accepted doctrine—a parlor game reminding me of the philosophical koan, "How may angels can dance on the head of a pin?" Many of the presenters seemed eager to position themselves as experts on certain areas of trendy specialization. But, metaphorically, the problem was that all of these specialties were being unveiled within the same classroom we had been in for the past decade, and on the same blackboards, as well. Even though it was touted as the growing edge, for me it was an already outdated paradigm.

However, there was one person presenting who really stood out for me. Her name was Jacqueline Small, and she was the only one I knew who was proposing what, in relation to the traditional recovery field, seemed like a radical spirituality. In fact, it was by far the most exciting, heartening, and refreshing perspective I had experienced during the entire time I had been involved in the recovery movement. I have repeatedly shared in this inquiry my stance on this subject and its crucial importance to our current exploration: *language, method, and structure for spirituality.* And this is what she was offering. Finally, I was witnessing something "off the grid"!

What she shared gave me permission to trust myself as a counselor in an addictions treatment facility. At some point before I got clean, she had arrived at the very same conclusion I was facing at the time I went to this conference: That is, that in general, addicts did not seem to respond too well to what they felt was a sterile, non-supportive, de-humanized traditionally psychotherapeutic environment.

Small described the naturally supportive basics of interaction therapists should employ with their clients. Among these were the humanistic faculties of *empathy, warmth, immediacy,* and *concreteness.* She also advocated an effective, yet humane way of confrontation, one of the standard practices in traditional addictions treatment utilized to help break through what was called denial.

One of the issues that had most concerned me when I went to work in a treatment setting was that I had occasionally witnessed some counselors' use of aggressive confrontation under the guise of "helping" the client. Instead of support, they were often expressing an unconscious, powerful negativity that leaked or exploded out as aggression toward the addict. It seemed clear to me that these counselors were actually projecting their own unconscious motivations onto the so-called therapeutic interaction. Small's strategy was what she called "straight talk"—a brand of honesty with compassion—and an ever-present concurrent focus on helping the client to point out her own sources of inner strength.

What I had seen, and what she pointed out, was that clients often felt disconnected from techniques that had been derived from psychological manuals, where the heart and soul of the therapist took a back seat to the often impersonal, "by-the-book" strategies being implemented. Addicts appeared to crave a down-to-earth authenticity and *connection*. For the most part, they were not stupid, even if they were terribly confused, and frequently engaged in a lifestyle that would ultimately kill them if they could not find a way to make a profound psycho-spiritual shift.

What they were looking for, she said, was authenticity, a true caring, from the heart, where that needed sense of connection was implemented before any other technique learned in school. She was saying what we have often shared here, in this text—that the most important things in human interaction could not be taught, but were in fact inherent, natural components of honest, loving, straightforward human relationships. These components were qualities that could not come in from the outside—from teacher to student—but could only manifest from the *inside, out*. As she so aptly pointed out, nearly all human beings had the ability to become naturally therapeutic. For our purposes in this inquiry, *it is the cultivation of this naturally therapeutic poise that is so important in all holotropic interactions with seekers.*

This innate quality is exactly what we have been stressing in this section of our exploration. Her work is a verification of what we mean when we share how disempowering it is for seekers if we present ourselves to them as the expert. It can be a tragic, anti-therapeutic mistake, to entertain the notion that any kind of training we might receive in an institution would, in and of itself, qualify us to be a director for another human being's journey.

We have repeatedly seen that the most effective strategy for the practitioner-in-training is to engage in some ongoing experiential practice, to work with the issues in her own psyche. At some point, we might hope that an unmistakable essence of authenticity might emerge, and reset the default mode of our engagement with other human beings.

This poise is founded on the recognition that the best we can be for another person is to present ourselves with a truth-oriented transparency and attitude of non-judgmental support. These are the very same things we ourselves would wish for from those who would support our own deep seeking. The readily available good news is that we all have the ability to become naturally therapeutic.

I left that conference excited in ways I had not felt before in my work at the center. What I heard there was not new information. It was not radical, or difficult to understand at a profound level of my being. Nor did it represent a paradigm collision for me. The truth is, it was simply, utterly validating. From this point on, I absolutely knew I was on the right track. As they say in the Twelve Step movement, in thousands of daily meetings all over the world, the only thing we have to offer another human being is our own "experience, strength, and hope." It is this elegant simplicity that has become a cornerstone of our training of facilitators.

Of course, it is essential that we develop a sound, deep theoretical basis as an underpinning of the support we offer seekers. But how we maintain *presence* with them, on the mat, in the middle of their deep processes, has nothing to do with what we know intellectually. It has everything to do with who we are as human beings. And who we are is the result of the work we have done on ourselves. There will be much more about *presence* and these other qualities later.

This was the capstone of my schooling at the time that I had my first Holotropic Breathwork experience. And it was one of the main reasons why I became so enamored of the holotropic perspective. I recognized its inherent, absolutely profound, yet simple authenticity. These are the qualities we have endeavored to bring into the training, as the basis for a true, in-depth ability to be present for breathers in their deep experiences. In truth, this quality is available to all of us, if we embrace our innate ability to be naturally therapeutic.

Learning on the Front Lines

I was also graced with another field of experiences at the recovery center. These were episodes where I began to trust a healing power that had nothing to do with any school, therapy, strategy, or philosophy. Our addictions unit shared a floor of the hospital with the psychiatric ward. In fact, there were no doors between the two units—just open space occupied by a few desks for the staff. During our preparation weeks before we opened, we were told that everyone—from the addictions recovery hall as well as the mental health unit—would be responsible for answering the call of any emergency that may be occurring for a client on either unit.

These emergencies seemed almost entirely to originate in the psychiatric wing. I recall one or two of them that occurred in the early stages of my employment there. A certain signal would summon us to the area of the crisis. This usually involved situations where a mental health patient was "acting out," as we say, or who might be posing a threat of attempted flight or violence. Our goal at this point was to basically "contain" the person in some way, while the nurses prepared the appropriate medication, which would render the patient compliant and passive.

I remember a couple of times early-on where I was in the front lines of the circle which would have been drawn around this frightened, confused, or angry patient. I always thought that what we were doing was, in fact, "risky business"—both for the client and for ourselves. As we were circling this disoriented and possibly dangerous person, I could not help but put myself in his shoes. I would try to imagine how he was feeling, as he gazed about himself at the ring of us so-called support people. I wondered what we looked like to him. It seemed that we must be fairly ominous and threatening.

I could not help but laugh a little inside, as I embraced the gestalt, the scenario we all shared—the "stand-off," really, which, to my eyes, seemed for the most part to be primitive and counter-productive. In addition, it appeared to be as frightening and threatening as anything the client was experiencing within his own psyche, if not more so. In fact, in some diabolical way it actually appeared to mirror and amplify the crisis that must be emerging from within the patient to begin with.

I remember one early time, standing in the circle around one of these wounded people, where I found myself beside one of the chief hospital administrators. I was just doing what I did in the rock festivals when someone was on a bad trip with psychedelics. I am not sure I can explain it. But it has something to do with becoming empty, open, trusting, and heart-centered. It includes attempting to present myself as a being with no agenda—attempting to radiate that I was, in some sense, not there to *do* anything. I was there, just being a presence—hopefully one of caring and equanimity.

What surprised me on those occasions, as much or more than it did the directors of the unit and the hospital, was that for some reason, the client would seem to respond, and allow me to approach a little nearer. When this happened, he would gradually become calmer. Looking back on it, it seemed as though we must have been connected in a way that could not have been orchestrated externally—neither by protocols, regulations, or some kind of psychiatric orthodoxy.

By the time the nurse and orderlies got close enough with the hypodermic of medication, we would have been looking into each others eyes, almost with what I can only call a recognition of connectedness and respect. It seemed to me—and perhaps the client as well—that, at this point, the shot, the needle, was just an afterthought, and not really needed at all. But of course, protocol had to be followed. And it was really painful to see how, when utterly medicated in the prescribed manner, the light would go out of his being, and he would become devoid of nearly all that had made him human.

I am aware that this is tricky territory. I truly do not wish to criticize this system. I discovered these types of milieus to be filled with very dedicated, loving, caring people. Violence is a totally real component of mental and emotional crises. I witnessed this plenty of times, both in facilities, and in the front of towering stages among a hundred thousand young people and the pounding of the rock and roll wave.

What we were doing on the unit was necessary, particularly within the system in which we were working at this evolutionary stage of mental health service. I have experienced what it is like to be physically attacked by someone in deep crisis. The truth is, safety in the face of an ever-present threat of violence in a psychiatric ward is a very real issue, at least for now, within a majority of prevailing modalities.

As a result of these first few episodes, I must have come to the attention of the administrator. She knew I had very little formal university education. But from then on, I was sometimes called in to be with a client who was in a deep crisis, as the staff prepared the pharmacological support, which was always so prevalent in those systems—and still is. One episode really stands out for me, though. It was both revelatory and extremely painful for me.

One day I was summoned to the psychiatric side of the hospital to sit with a teenager who reportedly had ingested a large dose of some psychedelic and was having what they called a "bad trip"—or, to them, a psychotic episode. My job was to sit with him while the nurses prepared the paperwork and the hypodermic. We just sat down together in a little alcove. I became as present as I could be, opened myself, and prepared to listen to him—to *hear* him—as best I could. This listening, this hearing, was really fascinating, because at first it just seemed as if he was just randomly babbling. But I must have done that thing I actually did not really know how to do: I opened to him, and went down stream with him.

Gradually I began to understand what he was trying to communicate. Not only that, we also began to have quite an interesting conversation together—laughing, connecting, and feeling safe. He was not crazy. He was absolutely sane, within a rather state-specific framework that was just really different from the prevailing, consensus reality of the present world and, definitely, this particular hospital.

I am certain that anybody else who came by probably figured that the nurses actually needed to prepare two shots instead of one. I don't think either of us made much sense to anybody else. But between us, what was happening was extremely meaningful. He was communicating with me. And I was certain that he was not mentally ill. He was just way out—or way in—the cosmos somewhere, where there is simply very little verbal, rational, or practical way to express the intensity and beauty of what was happening inside his world. So I just settled in, and took the ride, and we became fellow travelers in that magical, cosmic moment. Basically, I was just not trying *to change, label, or fix him*. The truth is, I believed with all my heart that he was not really broken.

This was our shared universe until the nurses came with the medication. In a tragic sense, this was the last time I ever "saw" this young man. Oh, I saw him the next day on the unit—drooling, doing that horrible medicated, mindless shuffle that is so common on some psychiatric wards. I came up to him to say hello. Yet I knew what was going to happen, and, sure enough, it did. Of course he did not recognize me. That bright light of connection, respect, and innocence of the day before was replaced with the vacant, numb, deadness of non-recognition, of a vacuity beyond emptiness, beyond loneliness. Almost all that was truly human was gone.

It was a realm of nothing—of what I sometimes call the walking dead. This was his world and way of being for the six months he stayed there, as he shuffled up and down the halls. When he went home, it was with a psychiatric diagnosis that he would bear for the rest of his life, as well as an armamentarium of powerful suppressive medication to "cure" him, or to help him "cope" with his particular "psychosis."

To this day, I wonder how he is. I hope he has found a few others willing to take that journey down the stream with him, without trying to judge him, or change him in any way. It is a strategy thousands of us have experienced that holds great promise for millions in similar crises as the one this young, free spirit underwent.

Three Words That Changed My Life—Part Two

So, back to the hotel ballroom and the Yalom episode; in the beginning of the workshop, I felt somewhat disconnected, out of place—"less than." These feelings were very old traveling companions. I noticed myself resorting to a familiar posture, the Rebel Bad Boy archetype, doing my best to cover up a rather insidiously ingrained dose of low self-esteem. But some better angel of my nature intervened.

I sat in the back—of course—and resolved to listen. Yalom was a brilliant lecturer, as well as an amazing group leader. Every participant seemed mesmerized—totally on his wavelength. Some of the questions he received required answers that seemed extremely technical and overly specialized. At times he would be quite specific about therapeutic dynamics, types of interventions, and the right words to use. I was often baffled by what seemed occasionally pointless questions from the audience. In addition, they proved to me how little I knew. Yet, with certain technical questions, I felt, or imagined that I felt, that Yalom seemed just a bit exasperated, as though we were missing the point somehow.

Looking back, the group seemed to operate within a paradigm often framed by a jargon that for me perhaps, intellectually or experientially, was missing the point. Very little of it really resonated within my heart. But I kept listening. I liked this man, even if not everything he said felt relevant to me. He had presence, connection with the group, and intuitive alertness. But most of all, he had passion and heart.

I began to focus on one thing Yalom repeated all through the day, in nearly every subject he covered, and in practically every question from the group he answered. The words began to stand out for me as though both italicized and bold. They became a mantra. It began to dawn on me that they contained the absolutely vital essence of true therapy.

Here is that one thing he kept saying, all through the day, the mantra that transformed my life of service: *SUPPORT, SUPPORT, SUPPORT*. Really, he would say it three times. After a while, I became almost giddy. He always seemed to find a way to insert this rallying cry into the dialogue. He artfully made it a part of every answer to every question he was asked, no matter how technical, no matter how abstruse a point. I was mesmerized. Bells were ringing. I was hooked. I became a lasting fan. And of course, it was the one thing I took away from that seminar. *SUPPORT, SUPPORT, SUPPORT.*

It was also becoming clear to me that this was about way more than just therapy. He may not have meant it to be about anything else. But, for me, it was definitely about something more profound. It became a magnetic, pulsing beacon of truth that I was convinced was incisively relevant in virtually every form of human relationship. This was not just therapy. This was an art form. He was unfolding for us a therapeutic yoga.

In the dance of virtually every interaction and relationship I have experienced, this mantra has been among the most valuable gifts. If I can remember to summon it moment to moment, then I can also stay true to what my role is in the lives of others. I must try to be constantly attuned to the truth that the most powerful force for wellness we ever need comes, not from anyone else, but directly from within our own selves. Therefore, our role can almost be seen as that of a cosmic cheerleader for each seeker.

We only require two things. The first has three dimensions: a framework—an extended cartography of the psyche; a strategy powerful enough to access all these dimensions; and to make what is unconscious in us conscious. The second is that, through some deep change within us as support people, seekers can feel safe and willing to take the journey within—where they will *trust us* to go down that stream with them, and to "hold space" without judgment or any sense of being the expert. The only way a journeyer can benefit from this adventure is to know in her heart that she can totally rely on us to "be there" for her.

We commit to assisting a seeker to feel mentally, emotionally, physically, and spiritually safe. When we are working with practitioners-in-training—sharing our experience, strength, and hope with them—we may often sound a bit simple. When we say there are three things they need to know, they get their iPads ready. Then here it comes: ***Support Support Support***.

If each of us has all the power we need within to transform ourselves, to move us toward wholeness—an Inner Healer—then what is it that we need from others? It seems quite clear that what we do *not* need is an outside expert to direct us. As seekers, we should never give up the autonomy of our own sacredness and individuality, and hand these into the keeping of someone else who we may think has the magic wand perfectly chosen to use on us for our healing.

What we absolutely *do* need is a heart/mind set based on what we can only call "caring" or "love." We must be allowed to discover this power from within, midwifed through supporters' absolute respect for who we are in the world. Helpers must know that through deep work each seeker can access a perfect, cellular knowledge of her own inner healing ability. Each facilitator must express in word, deed, and personal atmosphere a total trust in each seeker—that they themselves can heal from within.

CHAPTER XI

The Holotropic Comes of Age

A Foreshadowing: Just to Rock the Boat

With a philosophical base of the holotropic inquiry, exploring the revolutionary *therapeutic octave* of a holotropic paradigm logically follows, especially for readers unfamiliar with Holotropic Breathwork, or even the term, *holotropic*. To present new applications to therapy based on the healing strategy of the holotropic paradigm, it might be valuable to provide a look at how Holotropic Breathwork unfolded in the early years.

It might also be helpful to re-emphasize our focus in this phase of our holotropic inquiry, and indeed the entire endeavor. We are hoping to demonstrate the innate applicability of the holotropic perspective and practice in a number of modern therapeutic settings. As we have shared, these would include the possibility of a holotropic therapy; an overhaul in many existing therapeutic milieus; creation of an effective, standardized therapeutic support for grounded entheogen work; and a viable strategy to reframe psychiatric labeling to include the power of what we call *spiritual emergency*, as well as addictions recovery treatment.

This next section provides a nucleus of the principles of facilitation for the holotropic paradigm. Consider this a brief recap—to refresh you if you know the perspective already—and to give you the basics, if this is your introduction to the material. A comprehensive description of holotropic focused release work is not within the scope of this inquiry. There are several valuable sources available, which highlight this aspect of holotropic practice. One of the latest books by Christina and Stan Grof, *Holotropic Breathwork: A New Approach to Self-Exploration and Therapy* addresses this component in detail, as do the much earlier, ground-breaking works by Kylea Taylor.

We begin with the critical philosophy behind holotropic techniques of release work. Our meta-purpose has always been to present that which so beautifully and irrevocably defines the special essence of the holotropic paradigm. We will use as a baseline the manual I wrote in 1988 called

Doing Not Doing: A Facilitators Guide to Holotropic Focused Release Work which has been a core teaching tool for decades in Grof Transpersonal Training. How this monograph came to be written is as important to our purposes as an explanation of the various strategies a holotropic practitioner may employ to support a breather during a holotropic session.

The Grofs, as well as those of us who have taught holotropic focused release work for decades, all over the world, have always stressed that the actual holotropic techniques themselves are really quite simple and straightforward, and can be explained and demonstrated in a relatively short period of time. However, we all agree that the primary difficulty for trainees is something else altogether. The problem lies not in the acquisition of a certain type of practical knowledge, such as one would expect from any number of *"How to ... "* manuals. The critical challenge centers on an absolutely essential *consciousness shift* that must occur, in order for practitioners to effectively support breathers in the nuances of the authentic holotropic manner.

By consciousness shift, we are not referring to a type of mental refocusing, nor is it a new, hands-on retraining of core techniques, or simply the relinquishing of an outmoded mindset and replacing it with an updated program. Any type of rote application usually results in a superficial charade, which at best only mimics the true power of the original strategy. No matter how effective any quasi-accurate employment of hands-on techniques may appear in the moment, in no way do they reflect the true essence of what is required to be a holotropic practitioner. Nor do they, in and of themselves, have anything to do with the essential consciousness shift to which we are referring. One could never truly "get it" just by observing a hands-on demonstration. "Getting it" is in the job description of the observer's own Inner Healer.

For holotropic practitioners, true understanding and effective practice require the emergence of both personal and transpersonal qualities and perspectives, which transcend traditional psychological learning and training. These qualities represent a radically new therapeutic baseline, which can only be acquired through our own systematic inner psycho-spiritual efforts. Furthermore, these efforts must ultimately result in a fundamental shift in our understanding of human nature, as well as a radically new universe-view in general.

This dramatic metamorphosis of perspective—beyond intellectual learning—becomes available through systematic personal episodes of a profound experiential nature. Our ongoing inner work becomes the catalyst for a radical re-evaluation of, and revelation on, the nature of the human psyche and the healing mechanisms required to effectuate the real psychological, and meta-psychological, transformation that seekers can undergo. It is the power of these personal inner experiences that result in an ability to revision completely almost every traditional therapeutic strategy, and, ultimately, radically reset the relationship foundation between helper and seeker.

This is a priceless principle to which we will refer often. The reason for this thorough, regular attention—beyond its critical importance theoretically–is that it is also the most difficult dynamic for seekers and practitioners-in-training to thoroughly absorb. Why this is so will become apparent in many contexts as we systematically explore the nuances of an impeccable holotropic approach to supporting seekers in a host of different contexts.

We begin our inquiry into the core teaching points outlined in *Doing Not Doing* with what has become a kind of essential mantra that we share repeatedly throughout prospective practitioners' certification process, as well as through our entire inquiry here: *The only thing we truly have to offer another person is the work we do on ourselves.* The companion lines to this mantra go something like this: "The breathers are doing fine. They have Inner Healers ..."

As practitioners, we are not experts, healers, or directors. Our task is to support seekers—to keep them mentally, emotionally, physically, and spiritually safe—while their Inner Healers do all the work. The only way we can truly allow and support breathers to discover their own power within themselves—and not to consciously or unconsciously operate as though we know what is best for them—is to commit daily, and moment-to-moment, to working on ourselves, in an ever-deepening experience of moving toward wholeness in the hands of our own Inner Healers. This is our mantra.

In-depth transformation is cellular, multi-leveled, and profound. It is a mind/body/emotional *experience,* or, as in most cases, a series of experiences. It creates for the seeker/facilitator a radically new, dynamic poise. It provides a totally fresh operating platform—to use another metaphor, a different classroom altogether—one with a crystal clean white board—no old adages, equations, and theories on the board, as in the old classroom. Transformation is, ultimately, an *art form* that emerges from a *tabula rasa*—a clear, clean slate of psychospiritual possibilities.

If we could *think* our way into truly *being* different—perhaps happier, smarter, more at peace—we would absolutely have done so already. But we have not done this, simply because it cannot be accomplished of our own egoic selves. If we are also therapists in other modalities, we must at the very least be open to the possibility that, through the lenses of our previous training alone, we have no sacrosanct authority—either earned or innate—to effectively know what is best for another human being.

Nor are we, based on our own life experiences, capable of formulating any accurate, fool-proof prospectus, goal, or outcome for seekers. This is true, even though we may sincerely believe that we have been empowered, initiated, or inherently blessed to provide such information for others. Moreover, many holotropic trainees report confronting the very painful, yet likely possibility that, in terms of being a readily applicable cross-over to holotropic practice, all the money, energy, and time we have spent in other schools may not ultimately be as valuable or as uncontestable as we once thought.

Even if, as prospective practitioners, we are willing to accept that we do not know what is best for another human being, it is still profoundly difficult to actually, irrevocably, operate from the new revolutionary platform we are proposing. In addition, underneath all of these challenges lurks the awareness that most of us have also experienced a lifetime of situations imbued with *our own* personal disempowerment. No matter how willing we may be to accept a radical reorientation of our professional worldview, we still must commit to the rigorous, life-time practice of clearing our own unconscious motivations that deeply color the lens through which we view our prospective clients, as well as the world around us.

At some point, we realize that this disempowerment has been carefully nurtured by a lifetime not knowing that many of what we call our personal truths have been transferred to us from sources outside ourselves. These cellular programs will not, as they say, "give up the ghost" without a fight. They just cannot be simply eradicated by the insertion into our consciousness of an alternative belief-set alone.

As people helpers, we must eventually embrace our own sacred adventure of cellularly accepting that all the power we need for our own fulfillment is always already latent within us as well. It is astounding how rigorous the developmental path can often be for us as holotropic practitioners, as we attempt to truly operate from the sacred trust that all seekers, including ourselves, have an infallible inner healing capacity already.

Doing Not Doing Not Doing Not …

In the late 1980s, about the time of the first certification of holotropic practitioners, some of us had been supporting breathers for a number of years, and had spent much valuable time being mentored by Christina and Stan. We were feeling the need for some kind of "hands-on," practical manual on the holotropic-focused release work.

So the Grofs agreed to meet with some of us in a hotel in Atlanta, Georgia, after one of our large weekend workshops. These weekend seminars were becoming our "go to" format for introducing Holotropic

Breathwork to the public—a forum that continues to this day. So, we began with a seemingly innocuous question for the Grofs, "When you move in to support a breather, what are you thinking, and what is it that you do?"

Those who know Stan experience how he is seldom, if ever, at a loss for words. A questioner should be prepared to settle in for, as we say in the cinematic universe, "the extended cut." If you ask for it, you are definitely going to get the unabridged version of the answer. This was probably the only time that I have ever—ever—witnessed Stan purposely modeling a rather Zen, "no mind" approach to an answer.

He thought about what we asked, was silent for a moment or two, shrugged, and said…well, actually not a whole lot. Basically, as near as we could figure out, in the conspicuous absence of an erudite response, Stan, as well as Christina, was implying that there really was not much point in a long-winded explanation. The reason for this was that holotropic release work is just not that complicated.

What became clearer and clearer was that the practice of Holotropic Breathwork does not seem to require an encyclopedic, theoretical explanation or basis. It occurred to me that to engage in such an intellectual exercise reflects the antithesis of holotropic strategy. It also highlights what can be, for prospective practitioners—particularly those of us with any type of traditional psychological training—a therapeutic "blind spot," or inability to grasp the minimalist elegance of holotropic support.

For the Grofs, all this was really quite simple. Many times over the past decades I have seen Stan shake his head, smile, and wonder why most of us just seem to want to complicate what they truly have felt is profoundly simple and obvious. Nevertheless, they both patiently repeat the truths they have espoused since the beginning, in unique metaphors for each particular audience. Yet in this early time, their silence was the most rigorous truth they could have shared.

For me, what they did *not* say spoke volumes. Over the years, we have each found that, as we share this perspective in the training, even though the principles are simple to understand intellectually, to *operate* from this perspective is definitely not easy. Holotropic support has nothing to do with being "in the head"—with thinking our way through a therapeutic process. In fact, Stan actually said something like this: "Well, we don't actually *do* anything." He suggested that what we do is more akin to just "holding the space"—allowing the breather to show us what she needs. The strategy is never to lead—to direct—but always to follow the spoken or unspoken promptings of the breather's own inner healing power.

Most of the time, we do not need to intervene with a breather at all, except to wish her *bon voyage*, and greet her on her return into ordinary consciousness. During the session, we pay attention to whatever is going on in the breather's body, or in her emotional expression, or to what she is saying. The strategy is to be as mindful as possible of whatever is emerging—from whatever level. If she asks for help, we encourage her to intensify, or to do more of whatever it is that is manifesting in the moment. We do this, in full faith that she is in the absolutely skillful hands of the most perfect support she will ever need—her own power within.

We are *not* required to understand what is actually happening for the breather. She will either tell us what she needs, or her body will show us. The Grofs made a point to emphasize that holotropic support is so naturally straightforward that the main obstacle is nearly always in the over-zealous mind of the practitioner. Here, in the mind, is the natural propensity to complicate a situation already full of healing potential, and one which actually contains an infallible, inner, or *experiential logic* already.

Part of the confusion among more traditional schools of psychotherapy involves a fundamental difference in strategy on how the seeker experiences emotional, physical, or psychological relief. In prevailing psychological and medical modalities, the standard strategy centers on a battery of interventions in an attempt to *lessen*, or *alleviate altogether*, presenting symptoms.

We love Stan Grof's metaphor for this approach. He likens this situation to what happens when one is driving an automobile, and the oil light comes on. The obvious solution is to pull into a service station and report this problem to the mechanic. The mechanic says, "Sure, no problem." Then he lifts the hood and disconnects the oil light. This solution to the oil light problem is truly ludicrous. Just because the light is no longer flashing in no way means that the malfunction has been repaired. The reason the oil light was on in the first place was to indicate that something is wrong. Removing the indicator is not fixing the problem.

This is exactly what happens within many traditional modalities, where the accepted strategy is the alleviation of symptoms. What's more, the standard approach to symptom suppression is frequently the use of psychotropic medication. There are a number of reasons how and why this strategy permeates the mental health arena. But perhaps the most glaring is the standard practice of understanding psychiatric issues as having a primarily medical, or physical, basis—particularly in the brain—as well as originating from a place of illness, or disease.

Traditional science has made a critical "leap of logic"—a strategy that now amounts to nothing less than a religious pronouncement. As we have pointed out in other contexts, this is the virtually unassailable truth that consciousness is an epiphenomenon of the brain. This so-called scientifically proven pronouncement is the baseline for most psychological and medical interventions today. The prevalent "truth" is that most psychological problems stem from a physical abnormality of brain function.

The inevitable result of this metaphysical assumption is the overwhelmingly prevalent practice of administering psychotropic medication designed solely to alleviate symptoms by altering brain chemistry. This approach is unfortunately eerily similar to our metaphor of the automobile with the oil light flashing. This practice seems to be a truly profound error, which defies even a most rudimentary form of logic. The fact that the symptom is not present has nothing to do with the fact that the underlying condition can often still be there—unconscious and untreated.

For true psychological health, we may envision an altogether different strategy—again using our metaphor of the automobile. As we shared, would it not seem immanently more logical and effective if, instead of creating a situation where the symptom—the oil light—is the only thing that is in fact changed, helpers could create a situation where the oil light *would not need* to appear in the first place? The good news is that there already is such a strategy, which has proven to be an effective medical practice. This is the discipline known as homeopathy.

Homeopathic medicine is based on—not the suppression of a symptom—but the *intensification* of that symptom. The strategy is to provide a situation—not where the symptom does not occur, leaving the underlying causes of the symptom to remain operative in the system—but to create a situation where the symptom will no longer need to manifest at all. The basis for this is that the underlying causes of the symptoms have been addressed directly, so that actual in-depth healing can occur.

In homeopathy, healing takes place through a remedy, which actually intensifies the symptoms, thereby creating what is known as a healing crisis. This crisis results in freedom from the underlying causes and the condition itself. *This is precisely the holotropic strategy.* As practitioners, our task is to observe what is happening—take our clues from what the breather shares or shows. Then—with no attempt to diagnose or to imagine that we actually know what is happening—we encourage the breather to intensify that symptom. The "symptom" is merely whatever it is that is manifesting at that time. *Simply stated, we ask them to do more of whatever it is that they are already doing—be it mental, emotional, or physical.*

By following this straightforward approach with breathers in Holotropic Breathwork, we have regularly witnessed thousands of transformative experiences. In the vast majority of situations, by the systematic intensification of whatever expression is manifesting from within the breather's body or psyche, the support, either rapidly or eventually, leads to a positive physical, psychological, emotional, and spiritual up-grade.

Through another lens, we get a useful look at three core holotropic dynamics. The initial observation is theoretical, and the next two are experiential. The first principle presents an extended cartography of the psyche from which the various types of healing experiences emerge for breathers. This experiential domain, as we have said, includes the biographical, perinatal, and transpersonal bands of consciousness. The second tenet reaffirms what we have already addressed as the focus of our entire inquiry. This is, that the power to heal always—*always*—resides within the breather, as the Inner Healer, or as a *power within*.

The facilitator is present for physical, emotional, and psychological support and safety only. The facilitator should never bring what he believes or feels is the appropriate intervention, based on some preconceived notions he may have. Nor should he rely on so-called intuitions, or learned strategies that he may have acquired through his previous training in another school of psychotherapy. What's more, it is also a trap to rely on his own previous holotropic experiences supporting breathers; in this situation he wrongly "intuits," or "deduces" that the psycho-physical-spiritual issues this new breather is presenting must be the same as what he has already experienced before.

In addition, he must be aware that many of his assumptions about the psyche of another human being are colored by his own unconscious motivations. This is what we call "getting hooked." It is a pitfall characterized by his own internal, intra-psychic reaction to what is currently happening on the mat with the breather. This personal re-activation is all based on a previous internalization of past events in his own biographical life, his perinatal, and whatever transpersonal material and archetypes are operative within his psyche at that time.

Finally, the third component of effective holotropic intervention involves, as we have said, encouraging the breather to intensify whatever is already happening within her—be it physical, emotional, or even mental. This support takes place, always within the over-arching imperative of keeping the breather physically, mentally, and emotionally safe. This is obviously an extremely brief summary of the basic tenants of holotropic facilitation. Yet, as brief as they are, and as straightforward as they may seem intellectually, we are always amazed at how much inner work we practitioners must undergo, in order to truly, cellularly, operate from these essential poises.

Christina and Stan were pointing out to us in that meeting that most of the problems we practitioners have can be traced to issues within our own psyches. This would of course include any unconscious material that we have not yet brought into our awareness. The good news for practitioners is that through our own systematic inner work, we can free ourselves of the emotional charge with which this material is imbued and which always colors our interaction with breathers in some way.

We must always be conscious of the fact that, driven by our own unconscious motivations, and the acculturation of previous training we have undergone, we run the risk of resorting to—either consciously or unconsciously—a kind of ego-centered directive analysis and diagnosis. This, then, is punctuated by attempts to "pigeon-hole" what we are observing within the breather into some preconceived notions of therapy or healing in which we may have been trained, or have been influenced by at some point in our own psycho-spiritual development.

To add a personal therapeutic predicament, we too may also experience an unconscious or conscious "self-contraction," or personal reaction to the breather's process. It may be one that, as we say, "rocks our boat," to the point where we ourselves are activated, thereby compromising our ability to be as clean or clear a mirror as possible for the breather. As we shared, we call this self-contraction "getting hooked" by our own unconscious inner material.

On the other hand, the foundational clarity resulting from our own systematic self-exploration is an essential ingredient for our ability to be of maximum support in holding the space for the breathers. Our goal is for there to be as little contamination as possible from our own unconscious issues, as breathers embrace the emerging contents of their own psyches, guided by their own powers within.

Once we are hooked, however, we can no longer cleanly hold space. At this point, we become a part of the problem rather than the solution. What should be an entirely inner-focused adventure on the part of the breather becomes, at least in some part, just another horizontal interaction imbued with interpersonal material. This interaction can only serve to provide "fuel to a fire" that has been smoldering, or blazing, throughout the breather's life—one which will need to be fanned by her deep breathing and ultimately extinguished by in-depth work at some future point in the unfolding of the breather's evolution.

All of these above situations represent serious obstacles ultimately antithetical to effective holotropic work. In light of these possible contaminants of the healing potential engendered by deep holotropic breathing, it becomes increasingly clear that the process of holotropic support—as we must repeat as our mantra in each new scenario—is much more about *unlearning* on the part of the facilitator than it is about learning. Hence, as we will continue to stress, as also a kind of holotropic sutra, the primary strategy any holotropic practitioner can bring to the interaction with a breather is always the inner work she has done on herself.

But back to our meeting: After this enlightening, yet minimalist discussion, Christina and Stan felt it would be a good idea for me to write a manual outlining the bodywork. So, this is what happened. As I stated in the monograph I subsequently wrote, the text is probably more of a *How Not to . . .* than a *How to . . .* When it was finished, I offered it to Stan and Christina for feedback, and they were pleased with it. So, along with their books, and the works of Kylea Taylor, *Doing Not Doing* has been for over twenty-five years required reading for those in training to become holotropic practitioners.

Notes from the Early Front Lines

I experienced Holotropic Breathwork for the first time in 1984, when I was working in addictions treatment. This was an interesting epoch of the holotropic movement. There was no training at the time. Christina and Stan were primarily working out of their home base at the Esalen Institute in Big Sur, California. This work was liberally interspersed with trips all over the world, doing Holotropic Breathwork intensives with pioneering groups, and paving the way for future trainings.

This was sort of the "Wild West" of the holotropic paradigm. To begin with, the breathwork did not actually have any official name. When *Beyond the Brain*—the book by Stan that changed my life—came out in about 1986, Stan still had not settled on a moniker for the practice. He was flirting with *"holonomic integration."* But it was not until a few years later, with the release of *The Adventure of Self-Discovery,* that he settled on the name *holotropic* for his and Christina's work.

My first breathing experience was in Texas with Jacquelyn Small, whom I have already mentioned in another important context. She had been doing the breathing practice at Esalen with Christina and Stan. The Grofs had given her permission to share this work with others, and we had somehow received a brochure of this event at the treatment center in Macon, Georgia, where I was working. As I pointed out, I had met Jacquie at an addictions conference where she was presenting, and was really excited about her radical, growing-edge ideas on the spiritual frontiers of recovery and treatment.

When I saw the brochure, I signed up, and off I went. I have shared in a number of settings about the importance of that first breathwork experience. This was true, both in my own life, in my personal growth, but also for the possibilities that I believed Holotropic Breathwork offered for the radical upgrade I felt was essential in the addictions recovery movement at that time. I embraced the holotropic work from the start, doing the breathing as much as I could, and experiencing my version of what almost all systematic holotropic adventurers undergo—intense, multi-leveled, inner transformation.

I also stayed in touch with Jacquie, who was beginning to do breathing workshops all over the country. Very soon, she asked me to work with her. She had been given permission by Stan and Christina to provide necessary breathing sessions for those who would attend the upcoming month long certification intensive in Holotropic Breathwork.

I was thrilled. Breathwork support for others—as long as we continued to put our own deep work first—has a way of putting the experiencer on a fast track, and this is certainly what happened for me. I will be forever grateful to Jacquie for trusting me and giving me an opportunity to embrace what had already become my life passion, and which continues to be until this day.

Many of us who were working with others years before the first certifications have often reminisced about that time—with a heady mix of nostalgia, laced with a bit of embarrassment and relief. How did we not harm our breathers? How did we not contribute to others' suffering, as opposed to supporting them to transform? After all the soul searching, the one conclusion we all arrive at is a metaphor as completely irrational as it is wishful thinking: There were greater forces at work than our own failings. In those cases then, as it still is now, the power of the breathers' own Inner Healers was the saving grace and protector force.

I have absolutely no doubt that at this point in my life—thirty years later—after working with thousands of breathers; after the profound gift of a decades-long mentorship with Stan, working side by side with him all over the world; after being intimately involved with the training of holotropic practitioners since 1990; that there is one observation from the entire odyssey that, to this day, continues to confound and amaze me. This is, that breathers had experienced just as profound life-changing transformation all those years ago, when I had almost no experience and very little idea of what was transpiring, or why, as they do today, after all my so-called invaluable experience working on the mat.

I am aware that, in one way, this pronouncement is not a scintillating endorsement of the value of holotropic practitioners, or the training. Yet there is more to this observation than at first glance. I have described some of my psychedelic history, my accidental "sitting" for journeyers in trouble. I have shared my in-patient group therapy strategy while working in treatment: to basically "be there" for the clients, and to take the journey downstream with them in group. I have alluded to my Yalom workshop episode, and the lightning-strike of "support, support, support" that has indelibly defined all my work with others since that time.

So it is likely that, if nothing else, I must have somehow—almost accidentally—found a way to stay out of the breather's way, and allow the Inner Healer to do Her work. In the absence of any rational explanation for how we were able to be present for breathers in a manner resembling sound holotropic practice, at this point we can only resort to conjecture. We can only fantasize that these breathers had what amounts to *good angels*. In this case, their guardian angels just happened to be a *power within* them— the power of their own deepest inner healing resources—what we call the Inner Healer.

On Doing Doing Not Doing

Before moving to California to begin in earnest our life adventures with Stan and Christina, Cary and I spent a few months in Highlands, North Carolina, on the side of Satulah, a haunting, windy mountain in the Blue Ridge. This was where I wrote the focused release work manual. And it was here that I struggled with what to name the document. I had hoped that some title would emerge which might reflect the heart of the inquiry, and could actually highlight what seemed to me to be an unavoidable dilemma inherent in the basic idea of *doing* holotropic bodywork.

At first glance, it becomes glaringly obvious that practitioners are caught in both a conceptual, as well as practical, therapeutic double-bind. On the surface, at the most obvious level, all practitioners are trained to be proficient at "doing" holotropic focused release, or bodywork. We are required to "be with" breathers, to psychologically and emotionally engage with them—to be present, as we say. This act of "being with" them, or "holding space," often requires that we engage with them physically, in the repertoire of interventions that particularly characterize holotropic support.

Here is a drastically simplified description of the principles of our physical intervention with breathers. Actually, this is *not* a drastically simplified version of what we do. *The truth is, holotropic release work is, by its very nature, drastically simple.* The primary difficulty faced by all practitioners-in-training is our virtual obsession with the conscious or unconscious need to complicate and exaggerate the therapeutic importance of our interactions and interventions with breathers.

The bottom line is, this practice is just not "rocket science." As breathers, in opening to our own inner healing resources, we heal, as we have emphasized, homeopathically. We are transformed by intensification of our "symptoms" of which we become aware during a session. By "symptom," we mean whatever is emerging into our consciousness, or awareness. This would include any physical sensations from the body complex; emotions; and whatever psychological or mental states that may emerge during the session, particularly those that seem to have a strong emotional charge. It would also include the emergence of any content that feels as though it has a numinous, or spiritual origin.

Our task is, first and foremost, to be the clearest possible observers of their process, and to keep breathers safe. We are not responsible for knowing what is happening for them. We are not required to be intuitive, or psychic. In fact, these gifts can often just get in the way, preventing us from actually "seeing" the breather for who she is, as opposed to some impression we may have that we might rely on before trusting the breather herself.

First, we must do our utmost to protect breathers physically, mentally, emotionally, and spiritually. Each of these areas requires a different nuance of what constitutes safety. Physical protection is an obvious responsibility. We must prevent breathers from injuring themselves during their often-dramatic release of muscular tensions and other psychosomatic energies.

Emotional and mental safety often seems to require even more nuanced offerings of support. This would include the usual utmost respect and trust for the sacrosanct nature of breathers' own power within, and this power's ability to unerringly mobilize the breather's healing resources, and to make conscious exactly what she needs for her healing. Basically, this means "staying out of the way" as much as possible—psychologically, physically, emotionally, and spiritually. The strategy is to refrain from imposing *any* of our own ideas, beliefs, or prescriptions about what we feel is best for the seeker.

Secondly, this type of spiritual support would also encompass all that we have just outlined. Yet it envelops these within principles providing a kind of rarified atmosphere—a matrix—of, if it is in fact possible, even more rigorous sensitivity and absolute respect. It requires a commitment on the part of the support person to honor and preserve the indispensible autonomy and sacredness of the individual's journey toward wholeness. We must never forget that, when a breather lies down, closes her eyes, and begins to breathe, she is not only offering herself to her own Inner Healer. She is also placing herself totally into the care of the facilitator or sitter, or both. These are the persons with whom she has entered into a pact of profound trust, as deep as any relationship of which we can ever be a part.

A natural response to these observations is that there are many things practitioners have to learn in order to support breathers, and to *do* effective holotropic release work. But here is our timely mantra once more—the paradigm-shattering paradox: This type of support is not about learning—about having to *know* more. It is about *un-learning*, if there is such a word. It is about *letting go* of what we know, of simplifying, of freeing ourselves from the burden of a lifetime of preconceptions about healing, psychology, and support. It also requires us to reassess our understanding of authentic individual power itself, including, the very basis of what it means to be a human being.

For those who imagine that these strategies cannot possibly be more contrary to traditional therapeutic understanding, here is the final indignity: There is nothing about true holotropic support that we actually *do*—unless it falls under the aegis of what has come to be recognized as a unique holotropic *koan.* This koan can be stated like this: As holotropic practitioners, we are only effective if we are *doing not doing.* Like so many sutras and aphorisms from various mystical traditions, this is one of mind-bending perplexity, if not infuriating contradiction.

Here is the problem: Of course, we must *do* things as holotropic support people. For a small example, we must do what some of us call "pillow yoga"—making sure breathers do not hurt themselves. We often refer to the pillow as a practitioner's best friend. In addition, we must sometimes engage them verbally—particularly at the end of a session, when we are supporting them in the all-important integration stage of the holotropic process. We teach that there are three stages of deep work done in the holotropic manner: *preparation, session, and integration.* Of course, during these three stages, there are many other practices we must engage in, or *do.*

But there is a great mystery, a confounding truth that has the potential to wreck our personal or even transpersonal status quo. It is a maddening paradox which, if we are to consider doing this holotropic work, we must each confront. Yet, at a higher octave, it proposes what can best be described as a universal human dilemma.

This dilemma compels us to re-evaluate what it means to be an individual in a world of individuals, all of whom are toiling, as Teilhard de Chardin might say, toward some preconceived or unimagined evolutionary apotheosis, or mysterious *point omega*—or as we say in this work, *moving toward wholeness.* To state it in a manner reminiscent of many world mystical traditions: In order to *do* what it takes to find fulfillment, we must, along the way, give up being the actual *doer* of our yoga, or our works.

This line of inquiry requires further elucidation. First, it proposes a possible deal-breaker for seekers and practitioners: As separate individuals in the earth adventure, almost all of us primarily see ourselves as being the actor, the focus, or causal impetus of "doing" in our lives. It is almost impossible to imagine a world where we stop being doers, or the one who acts, or the essential initiators of individual effectuation. But if we are not doers—or were to become "not doers"—would we not then cease to exist as individuals? In addition, if we are not the doers, is anything actually, ever, going to get done?

The answer to this question is a "yes" and a "no." Yes, we would cease to exist—at least in the habitual form, or state of consciousness, in which we have previously always lived: that is, as the sole, individual, circum-scribed executor, or doer of our works. However, mystics for all time and cultures have proposed an individual operating platform that is radically different. It is one that also happens to encompass a realization available to anyone in modern times who may choose to undertake deep self-explora-tion in meta-ordinary states of consciousness. This inner experience reveals that, for individuals, there is an optimal, greatly expanded, more fulfilling way to negotiate life on planet earth. These revelations suggest that we could live in a poise from which, for all intents and purposes, we are no longer the individual creator, initiator, or doer of our actions.

Whether by a sudden dispensation of a power within, or by a realization of a shift in consciousness that, although guided by our inner healing resources, has taken place over a gradual stretch of time—we cease to experience ourselves as "skin-encapsulated egos"—separate, isolated, totally self-oriented entities. Instead, who we are as human beings becomes a much more expanded field of consciousness—more all-encompassing—and capable of an almost unlimited horizon of interconnection. This consciousness is possessed of a tremendous power of creative will. Yet this power also is capable of transcending exclusive domination by the isolated entity we call the "false self." In a sense, we can come to recog-nize that "being" is commensurate with oneness, unitive consciousness, or "all that is."

At this crucial point, our current inquiry irrevocably thrusts us into the domain of yogas, of timeless spiritual systems. As we are hoping to dem-onstrate, it is also the province of Holotropic Breathwork, and the modern practices that have the power to take us into expanded states of awareness. In the states available through the use of these practices, we are guided by the inner healing power, which can free us from this kind of exclusive identification with the body and the ego, or false self.

These life-changing realizations will then require us to ask the fol-lowing question: If I myself—that is, my *individual* personhood—am not the doer of what I do, then who or what is? The answer, stated in hundreds of ways in just as many world traditions—goes something like this: There is ultimately only *one* doer in all of existence. This Doer goes by many names: the soul, the One, the Higher Power, the Higher Self, God, Goddess, the Force, the Tao—and on and on …. As we identify with this unlimited state of consciousness, we can also recognize that our previous identification with a limited individual self is but an interesting expediency. It becomes a fascinating, if temporary, way to negotiate relational existence with other human, temporarily individual, units within the planetary or cosmic domain.

When we experience this freedom from exclusive identification with a limited unit of consciousness, this becomes, in a sense, a cosmic revelation. We realize that the new poise from which we now "operate" in the world—both interpersonally, and with the world at large all around us—is absolutely different from anything we have known before. We recognize how we have become accustomed to a kind of supreme isolation, as well as the existential dilemma of defending at all costs our own circumscribed, exclusively separate, individual, egoic kingdom. For all intents and purposes, we enter a brave new world with seemingly limitless parameters.

We begin to see that previously we were little more than auto-focused, isolated entities with what Sufi teacher Pir Vilayat Khan calls a "worm's-eye" view of life. This was a view that encompassed an extremely limited sphere of influence over either ourselves, other people, or the unlimited universe enveloping us. However, now we experience ourselves as something altogether different.

We can sense that, even though we may temporarily operate as an atom, if you will, we are not exclusively bound by this identification. As this atom, we recognize that we are now connected with the whole—yet in some way *are also the whole itself.* Even more fulfilling, we can not only see ourselves as an atom connected to other atoms, we can feel that we are the wave itself, the all-encompassing stream in which all atoms move. We can open to what Pir Vilayat calls the "eagle's-eye" view of existence.

When this realization occurs, and we pursue our daily lives, interacting with people and the world around us, we are no longer the isolated king, queen, or slave of our lonely and disconnected fiefdom. We can experience ourselves as an infinitely creative channel of an indescribably larger field of consciousness, encompassing both oneness and connectedness. From this often-limitless experiential platform, it seems inaccurate and self-defeating, if not dishonest, to profess any longer that we—our egoic selves alone—are the sole doers of the work in which we are engaged.

In addition, it becomes almost impossible to intellectually explain exactly what has transpired that is the impetus for us to feel so radically re-oriented. In the manner of poets and mystics, we find ourselves having to resort to lyrical metaphors to explain what is essentially unexplainable. We in this holotropic work have attempted to address this fundamental inability to put words to this new way of being in the world that becomes possible for us—even if we are far, far, from anything close to much more than a partial realization of the full implications of such a state of being.

However, we are convinced that, even though we ourselves are power-less to explain it—and must look to the poetic metaphors of world teachers to help us—something altogether wonderful has happened within us. These realizations, and the perspective generated from them, may, if we work on ourselves wholeheartedly, ultimately translate themselves for us into a pro-found, revolutionary way of interacting with other human beings and the cosmos of which we now feel intimately a part.

In this light, we refer once more to the almost unacceptable koan we have stated a few paragraphs above: that even though we have to *do* focused release work and be a support for breathers, the only way we can effec-tively and wholeheartedly accomplish this support is to operate from a poise in which we are actually, factually, not the "doers" of the work. This is what we call "*doing not doing*." This is the somewhat Taoist philosophi-cal underpinning for the title I gave to our manual, in an attempt to express this fundamental, and virtually impossible-to-describe, contradiction.

Many would-be practitioners ask, "How do we learn to operate from this holotropic perspective?" The stone-cold truth is, we cannot *learn* it. We cannot *think* our way into not being the doers of the work. It cannot be accomplished by any prescription of systematic behavioral shifts and machinations. Nor can we hypnotize ourselves into not being the doers, or attempt to "act as if."

Failing in all these ways, we must also share that there is absolutely no way we can *fake* not being the doer. In short, from out current life perspec-tive and operating system, it is literally impossible to orchestrate the true poise of having at last given up being the doer of our works. This does not even include the companion realization that we hope will at some point follow: the recognition that the only doer is in fact what can best be char-acterized as the Great Mystery.

At this stage, some trainees report feeling that the holotropic inquiry seems to be more obtuse, ungrounded, unscientific, or event ludicrous with every revelation. Many of us who have at one time or another been at simi-lar confounding crossroads, begin to intuit that we could actually be part-ing the veil on a paramount mystery. It could be that what feels like an unassailable double-bind might be a prelude to a lightning bolt of realiza-tion. After all, isn't this how transformation often works?

We have already referred to the old joke about the person who was lost, and upon asking directions, was told by a person who was equally confused, "Come to think of it, you just can't get there from here." This is precisely where many of us may be in this inquiry. As long as we oper-ate from the platform of being the exclusively individual doer, there is no way we can actually create for ourselves a reality where we are not *being* the doer.

But as hopeless and as confounding as all this sounds, there actually *is* something vitally creative within our current universe that can free us from the limiting prison of exclusive doership. This catalyst is the commitment we can make to systematic work powerful enough to open us to the deepest, most expanded dimensions of the psyche. The beacon, the lighthouse that is our goal of wholeness, would at all times be under the aegis of an unlimited power within—our Inner Healer.

This is what we mean by psycho-spiritual death/rebirth. It is what we mean by the death of our individual false self, which imagines itself as the doer of our works on planet earth. At this level—as the exclusive doer—we are in fact totally powerless to transform either ourselves or another person. The diamond-like truth of the first step of the Twelve Step yoga from Alcoholics Anonymous says that only a "power greater than ourselves" can heal us.

This higher, or deeper power—available through Holotropic Breathwork, entheogens, and any method rigorous enough to access expanded states of awareness, or even through the grace of what we may call serendipity—can effectively shift us from the exclusive focus of personal ego. Having accomplished this, it can open us to an essential psycho-spiritual freedom. This freedom encompasses the wide-open, expansive domain of connectedness, as well as oneness—what the mystics call Becoming and Being. It is a domain, a state of consciousness, dominated by an abiding trust in a universally accessible and unlimited power with which we may be blessed to find deep within ourselves the Inner Healer. This is what we mean by *doing not doing*.

But back to our current inquiry: In order to be an effective holotropic practitioner, we are often required to undertake a "journey of the ages"—one that will at some point take us through systematic episodes of death and rebirth. These episodes are almost never a "one-shot deal," a once-in-a-lifetime experience. As we have stressed, they are more often the ongoing results of life practices to which we devote ourselves daily. Without a commitment to this life-long work of transformation—one day at a time—it is much more difficult for us to effectively free ourselves.

But more importantly, if we fail to undertake this journey of transformation toward connectedness and wholeness, we betray all those seekers who open their hearts and souls to us for support on their own life journeys. In short, we must consistently recommit to inner work, in order to truly support those with whom we journey down the streams of their own healing. If we cannot face the systematic ongoing death of our own false selves, our interaction with seekers, as we have said, can become just one more "bead on the rosary" of their disempowerment. To quote one of our mantras once again, the only effective work we can do for others is the work we continue to do on ourselves.

A Cosmic Validation

Years later, we moved our, by then, quite nomadic training for a short while to a beautiful center outside of Sedona, Arizona, often considered to be one of the world power spots, and sacred to a number of tribes, both ancient and modern. The facility was run by a group from Korea. I was given a lovely room as home base. And though quite enigmatic in a number of fascinating ways, our Korean support people were a fascinating group with which to share this gorgeous space.

One evening, I happened to open the drawer to the side-table of my bed. I was half-way consciously, and at the same time, unknowingly, expecting the drawer to contain what lies in the bedside table of virtually every hotel room in North America, as well as many other countries in the world. This is, of course, a copy of the King James version of the Bible. On the cover of every one of these Bibles I have ever seen, or ever heard of from the countless friends from around the world who have opened a similar drawer, was the inscription: *Placed by the Gideons.* To this day, I have never met one person who knows who the Gideons are. I had come to believe, quite comfortably, that they were an elusive race of alien beings fulfilling some kind of cosmic mission.

But, lo and behold, there was no such Bible in this drawer. Instead, would you believe it, there was a copy of the *Tao Te Ching*. Well, of course there was! This was a facility run by Koreans—at least from the same hemisphere as Lao Tse, the author of this world-famous text. So, I was quite happy to have some late-night reading material so pertinent and readily accessible.

Late one evening during the workshop, while I was randomly perusing the pages, I realized that this was a different translation from the ubiquitous popular one with which I was familiar. The original version of the sutra I knew so well read, *"Practice Non-Action."* To my surprise, as well as my great awe and wonder, the sutra in this version read—and I am not kidding—*"**Do Not Doing**."*

I rarely have felt so grateful. In a way, it seemed that we were being validated for our passion for the true holotropic perspective. We were on track. What a delight! These kinds of synchronicities seem to emerge into this dimension—like Athena from the head of Zeus—with equal parts of awe, mystery, and even humor. It was humbling and exhilarating to imagine that the work in which we were engaged might have such a pedigree. If anything, it deepened what was already a great passion—that our endeavor to honor a power within—the Inner Healer—might somehow be sanctioned by the wisdom of the ages.

Other serendipitous validations have appeared over the years as well. For example, in the *Bhagavad-Gita*, Krishna shares at some point with Arjuna—who is one fortunate warrior to have the Lord of the Universe as his charioteer—that in terms of transformation, it really does not matter so much whether we do bad deeds or good. Whichever we choose, we will of course reap our appropriate measure of karma. However, the bottom line is that, as long as we feel that we are the *doer* of our works—good or evil—we will always—*always*—remain caught. The yoga is to give up being the "doer," and to recognize that there is truly only one "doer" of the work. And this is Krishna, or the Divinity itself.

I have also always been drawn to the work of Ramana Maharshi—who seems to be one of the true teachers from India—who advocated a practice of *self inquiry*. In this work, the mantra was to continually enquire of oneself, "Who am I?" By the succession of realizations that *I am not that, I am not that,* one arrives ultimately at the conclusion of who one, in fact, is. At this point it is no longer, "I am not that." It is now *I am That*—the *Self*—the One and only, who has many names.

In the process of this self-inquiry, Ramana Maharshi says: *"Give up also the attachment to the subtle body and its nature and sense of being the doer."* And at another point he declares, *"I am perfect stillness; I am neither the doer or the enjoyer . . ."*

For Those of Us Not Yet Enlightened . . .

In the past few paragraphs, we may seem to have proposed a daunting requirement: achieving a kind of penultimate spiritual "success"—whatever that is. When we refer to relinquishing our addiction to being the *doer of the works*, we imply that the only way we are to be successful at holotropic support is to be adept at one of the most universally recognized accomplishments of yogic and meditative discipline. As we shared, this accomplishment is the experience that there is only one Doer of work—the "Divine"—whatever that mystery actually is.

The truth is, if any of us had to accomplish anything more than a mere beginning on this kind of arduous spiritual journey, there would not be one single holotropic practitioner on the planet to support people in this wonderful work. How, then, do we reconcile the need for a powerful numinous realization, in order to be a successful practitioner, with the fact that we are all, more or less, beginners on whatever we conceive of as a spiritual journey?

Once again, we can turn to Socrates, whose belief about the nature of knowledge, as well as our *ability to know*, underscores the realizations breathers and other cosmic adventurers discover in their systematic deep work. The foundation of these realizations is an experience, or series of experiences, that break apart the hard shells of the false self. We realize that we have been living in a self-contraction caused by what seems to be an age-long accruing of multi-leveled challenging episodes of a physical, emotional, mental, or spiritual nature. If our journey is one of moving toward wholeness, then this adventure becomes one of embracing—gradually yet whole-heartedly—"all that is"—which of course includes the experiences we see as painful or difficult.

Among the self-defeating, painful results of this cosmic predicament is the cementing of an erroneous belief, or dream, that our circumscribed worldview is *the truth*—that we in fact *know* the real from the unreal—the world from the not-world—and the universe from what cannot possibly exist. Fortunately, one of the most liberating realizations with which we can be graced is that we *can* awaken, if only a little, from this paltry dream, even if this awakening occurs rudely or painfully. No matter how it feels when it happens, we are approaching the foundational truth that Plato's Socrates supposedly thought powerful enough to record for future civilizations—another of our holotropic mantras: *The first thing we have to know is that we do not know.*

From this fundamental realization—this ego-death—arise the rudimentary beginnings of what it means to be authentically human. The *first beginnings*—not the final realization—this is what puts us on the path. This is a journey with at least two tracks. The first—the highest octave—is the unfolding of what it means to be a human being in the evolutionary journey toward wholeness. This is our "moving toward wholeness," or our Becoming. The second—a companion octave—is the initiatory requirement for us to undertake a path of *service* for other human beings on their journeys toward wholeness. Indeed, one of these countless paths of service is the adventure of becoming a Holotropic Breathwork practitioner.

In order to embark on either of these octaves of the journey toward wholeness, we are each required to have experienced at least the barest beginnings of what we call *humility*. It is humility that teaches us at least one certain thing: that *we know that we do not truly, irrevocably, definitively know.* To paraphrase a wonderful Alcoholics Anonymous koan: the one thing we know about the Higher Power is that, in our ego self, *we are not It.*

Another of our holotropic koans is that we cannot *think* our way into this realization. It is not something we *decide* to be, and then we *are* just that thing. Most of us experience that realization is a gift from our power within. When the gift comes, many seekers are certain of one truth—that we, of our own false selves, did not create it. There seems to be no way we could have made it happen. We cannot lift ourselves into the air by trying to pull ourselves up by the bottom of our feet. The gift is not something that we *do*. It is something that *happens to us*.

This experience, no matter how much of a small beginning, is the game-changer. From this point on, everything is different, even if everything often feels the same. It is the foundational experience. As such, this realization must be nourished, cherished, and held sacred. Like the first two, tiny, unfolding leaves of some unknown mighty tree, it must be watered, supported, protected—remembered and reaffirmed in a ritual, experiential manner. This experience can feel so heady; can be such a blast of freedom, that we often believe we have arrived, that this is all there is, that there is nothing else we will ever need. Its appearance can produce such elation, even ecstasy, that it consumes any thought and experience of self-contraction—at least for the moment.

But every practice on the planet, every text of every teacher, will share that this is only the first step—that the ecstasy will fade, and leave in its place the upsurging and re-unfolding of the great streams of patterns we have cultivated for what seems like lifetimes. The metaphor I have used before is that our egoic, self-centered patterns have the overwhelming power of a locomotive engine roaring down the track. And it is we who are feeding the fire in the boiler.

Just because we stop stoking the fire for a moment does not mean that this train is about too screech to a sudden halt. It is fueled by the almost limitless power of our self-oriented desires, actions, and thoughts—incessantly for eons. The accumulation of all this egoic energy—with us feeding coal into the furnace—has created this awesome, yet all-consuming fire. There is only rarely a way that the locomotive of our false self will come to this sudden stop, just because we have one powerful experience, where we throw down the shovel of our self-motivated desires for a few moments and stop feeding the boiler on this train.

Instead, what looms before us is the beginning of a new and altogether magnificent adventure—one that we will be embarking upon, for who knows how long. This is what seems to happen for nearly every seeker, including each of us who would become a holotropic practitioner. We may feel that we have experienced a flash of freedom, a call to service. We may unequivocally recognize that this is our work—that our Inner Healer has chosen this for us. It can be an inexplicably reverent feeling. It may feel like a *calling*, or that it has been sanctioned by the power of truth—that Spirit has blessed our embarkation on a sacred adventure.

Yet, it is only the beginning. The real work is still in front of us. If we are steadfast, or fortunate, we may come to ever cherish and maintain the original grace of humility and wonder of that first realization. We may learn to hold sacred the recognition born from that first, powerful time—that we are not the doers of our life and work. We remember as a mantra that there is a radically potent mystery informing us. We realize that we must nurture this delicate flower of humility—that we must strive to stay as a little child, as the mystics have taught.

Once again, these musings return us to another mantra of this text. What we can offer others is the result of our own inner work. This "work" is the ongoing, daily practice we undertake—no matter what it is—no matter what our Inner Healer reveals to us is the appropriate method. Most of us have discovered that the yoga, the practice, the search we seem required to embrace, and the paths we are to navigate, change often. No matter what we attempt, it all seems to be under the guidance of our deepest source. As the old saying goes: "Just do something, even if it's wrong." The difference, in our case, is that as long as we try to follow the guidance of our Inner Healers, we cannot really mess it up.

This is the way that we can stay clean, clear, and fresh for the journey down the stream with breathers, those who trust us and place the care of their deepest selves into our hands. Do we make mistakes? Does our ego get in the way? You bet. This is because we all have lessons to learn. Do we have to be great at this learning? Fortunately for all of us, we absolutely do not. The majority of us are just a flicker of an instant on the journey toward wholeness.

But there is more good news in the repeating of yet another holotropic verse: Breathers heal, not *because of* who we are, but *in spite of* who we are. *The best we can hope for in any session is to minimize as much as possible how we contaminate the therapeutic interaction with the breather.* It is inevitable that we interject elements of our own unconscious issues into our relationship with seekers. We will always "muddy the pure spring," at least a little bit. It is a powerful lesson in our own search for humility to recognize this.

But here is more good news: Lest we forget, breathers have Inner Healers—an all-encompassing power within. This unerring "ever-presence" truly keeps them safe. We just do not have to be perfect. We are only required to know that we do not know. We strive to stay on track: to remember that the breather has one main problem with her support—our own level of disconnection from our Source. We strive to remember that we are just not in charge of healing them. And it is a good thing for them that we are not!

We are responsible for one healing mechanism: the grace to be allowed to *witness* another seeker's transformation—to be a midwife, a cheerleader—someone who puts the pillows in just the right space, so that breathers will not bump their heads. That's it—this is what we mean by *doing not doing*. We accomplish this only through our personal systematic work that continues to cradle us in this level of "unknowing."

CHAPTER XII

One More Long, Hard Look at What's in It for Us

We are now deep in the middle of our holotropic learning curve, as we view our task through yet another lens. This inherent problem of the false self, and the need for ongoing inner work, contains multiple octaves. One of these brings us back to where we began—to Prague, and the power of Stan's first LSD experience. This overwhelming numinous dispensation transformed Stan's worldview as a psychiatrist. Even more, it radically up-graded his experience of what it means to be human in a cosmic order.

Even as the transpersonal perspective addresses a revolutionary shift in science and philosophy, we must also include its similar re-envisioning of psychology—both theory and practice. This is where Holotropic Breathwork may take a center stage. As far-reaching as Stan's scientific and philosophical contribution has been, the iconoclastic strategy inherent in his and Christina's breathing practice has already sparked a tradition-shattering perspective whose full implications for world transformation have only begun to be felt. As we have stated, the elephant in this particular living room is the Inner Healer, or a power within. It is the golden thread weaving its way through the fabric of a therapeutic reality shift that may come to be known as a holotropic paradigm.

We have briefly covered the game-changing nature of Holotropic Breathwork. Among its centerpieces are the extended cartography of the psyche and the paradigmatic re-orientation required to accept the psyche's cosmic status. To highlight the essence of a holotropic paradigm, we must emphasize the inherent dilemma practitioners of this approach must rigorously address. This is the same dilemma that all practitioners of any school must eventually acknowledge, if they are to truly embrace the power of this new, or any, philosophical and psycho-spiritual/therapeutic paradigm.

By offering a spectrum of lenses through which to view the dilemma, we have stressed the requirements practitioners must accept in order to support seekers with maximum clarity, and with a minimum of personal contamination of the therapeutic process. However, we must "thicken the plot" once more—to face clearly the cosmic elephant in this living room of Holotropic Breathwork.

Facilitators who have been "in the trenches" for any length of time have a number of interesting stories they can share. If we are ruthlessly honest, most of these would involve the unessential interventions we have instigated with breathers. These are the ones that served no purpose but to assuage our crafty, rampantly active egos, and in the process sabotage the breathers' experience of the Inner Healer. These embarrassing episodes definitely belong in the manual on *How Not To . . .*

In our evolution as practitioners, we all admit having fallen prey to the most insidious yet common posture known to almost all people helpers. This is, that we, either consciously or unconsciously, all too often take credit for the healing of others. We do this, no matter what the underpinnings are of the therapeutic strategy we employ. We do this whether it is a principle of that practice that the seeker is her own healer, or whether the philosophical basis is that the helper plays the principle role. Even if we do not take full credit, then we at least feel that there must have been something special within us that has made it possible for them to heal.

Within the holotropic perspective, this tendency is a tragic deal-breaker in the development of the optimal, synergistic relationship between breather and practitioner. It is tragic because, through our egoic clinging to self-importance, we often participate in, if not in fact sometimes create, the setting of disempowerment from which the breather looks to the practitioner for validation and guidance. When this happens, the true power of the holotropic work ceases to exist.

As part of our growth as practitioners, we must face the uncomfortable proposition that we frequently serve and nourish, not the breathers, but *ourselves*. We egoically capitalize on the natural tendency of seekers to give us credit and the power for their own transformation. It is astounding to awaken to how avidly we drink in the positive projections of others, as though we ourselves are dying of a thirst for external validation.

The mantra we repeat here is a spiritual truth: *The most effective strategy we ever have to offer breathers is the inner work we do on ourselves.* Breathers are already well supported and taken care of. They have always possessed an infallible, all-knowing power within.

There was a scene in an early eighties film that really highlights this ubiquitous therapeutic error of believing we people-helpers are all-powerful. It also shines a spotlight on a universal human dilemma: the tendency for human beings to attribute a personal, meaningful, causal connection between themselves and other people or external events, when in fact there is no such de facto correlation at all.

The film was *Cannery Row*, a rather whimsical take on the John Steinbeck novel. One of the characters was a gentle, homeless man, who walked that fine line between psychological profundity and irrational, even psychotic befuddlement. At one moment he shared that he never missed a sunrise from the beach. Then he said that, after watching the phenomenon for so many years every morning, he almost believed that the sun would not rise at all without him.

I wonder how many of us unconsciously operate from a similar belief in our interactions with those around us, as though we must at least play *some* major, vital role in determining their fate. Or have we felt that if it were not for us, they could not possibly initiate certain meaningful changes in their own lives? What a heavy, yet in most cases, completely pointless burden we assume we must carry.

Unfortunately, this belief in our power to effect change in others is a ubiquitous dynamic, a posture that consciously or unconsciously pervades nearly every therapeutic method. Of course, we are not saying our being with a seeker might not be supportive in some way. Without a doubt, the presence of another human being can be tremendously valuable in countless therapeutic interactions. This dynamic that we call *presence* is vital, but not in any kind of causal way. We will have much more to say about "presence" soon in our inquiry.

But we must ask ourselves, even as part of our central mantra: "In what way do we, as people helpers, compromise or contaminate the cleanest, richest potential inherent in a therapeutic interaction between ourselves and seekers?" Those of us who have done this work for a number of years agree that the deepest healing power, the greatest potential latent in any therapeutic interaction, cannot be realized if we do not address the unconscious, ever-present dynamic that *seekers inherently and naturally tend to give their power away to the one whom they see as the designated support source outside themselves.*

This truth of our inquiry into personal healing is the inestimable transformational potential in the seeker's *personal empowerment. All* of our strategies must be directed toward the effectuation of this healing mechanism within seekers. There is absolutely nothing we can add from the outside to the fullness of this power. In fact, as support people, our primary problem is to limit the ways that we consciously or unconsciously contribute toward clients' inability to fully recognize and embrace this power within themselves.

Just how do we address this therapeutic requirement? To echo a mantra once more, we cannot merely *resolve* not to disempower them any more. We cannot do this with our minds alone. Our inability stems from an overwhelmingly tenacious egoic tendency of nearly every human being to either consciously or unconsciously assume directorship, or, as we say, *doership* of our therapeutic interactions with others.

The truest strategy for the effective relinquishing of this core, insidious belief system and its resulting operating platform, which says that we have the power to effectuate change in another, is a rigorous, moment-to-moment effort toward our own transformation. The basic therapeutic problem is *not* within the seeker. The problem is within *ourselves*. The mantra again: *Breathers have Inner Healers! They are fine.* We must face the fact that we are operating from an inherently false posture of imagined personal power over the lives and wellbeing of others.

The illusion of egoic power is a fundamental pitfall, not just for therapists, but for anyone who has at least an imagined that he can control or shape another person. This group includes many parents, teachers, physicians, educators, therapists, politicians, world leaders, scientists, religious leaders, and many others. We honor in others, through Holotropic Breathwork, the common occurrence we call the *ego death*. Nowhere is an embracing of the ego death more essential than in our *own* psyches, where we identify ourselves as "people helpers."

We should each undertake a little self-inquiry: When we support others, what are *we* getting out of this? How is our support of others actually benefiting *us*? We humans are "quick studies." Once we know that something is effective—that it feels exciting to *us*—we will of course strive to repeat it. Yet, there are so many more nuances of this opportunity for us to enjoy the way breathers give us their power! Among these are feeling needed, loved, special, gifted, important, powerful, essential, valuable, validated, worthy, spiritual, indispensible, loving, wise, sexy, mysterious, knowledgeable, or kind.

To thicken the plot, facilitators face a critical, almost diabolical irony: Holotropic Breathwork is *so* powerful and works *so* well, that the only real downside of the method is the problem it poses for practitioners who really wish to support breathers effectively. It is practically impossible not to feel irrationally ecstatic about ourselves in the face of the regular, quite miraculous-seeming experiences breathers have, and for which they often worshipfully wish to give us fantastic kudos and credit. Ironically, when we practitioners are the breathers, we frequently have as much difficulty as our breather clients do. It is often equally challenging for us to truly accept that *our own* healing is also totally generated by a power deep within *our own selves*.

As we pointed out much earlier, most of us—including facilitators—have become acculturated to a ubiquitous yet insidious social program. From our earliest memories, this program indoctrinates us to look to a whole range of experts outside ourselves for our validation and fulfillment. We have covered this in a number of ways already. The plague of disempowerment also seems to be embedded in a hypnotically pervasive belief system singled out by world philosophies as being a primary cause of individual and global human suffering.

This core problem poses two dilemmas. First, as we said, breathers—indeed, most human beings—are acculturated to give their power away. The second—and this is by far the most insidious—is that practitioners receive a barrage of overwhelming positive projections from those whom we would support. The problem for us is that we ourselves have often not done sufficiently deep work within *ourselves*. We have only begun to clear a host of issues dealing with our own unmet needs.

These needs take many forms. Among them are those programs where we ourselves did not receive the nurturing in our family of origin that all children should have received. In more challenging circumstances, this lack of nurturing is amplified by its mirror opposite, which would include a whole range of the covert and overt abuses we ourselves have experienced—those that were perpetrated by the adults in our own specific life situations. The issues are further complicated by the unconscious urges many of us carry, including those for the recognition and self-worth to combat *our own* ever-present human dilemma of low self-esteem.

In many cases, our own need can be so strong that we are therapeutically crippled by it. This blind spot then unwittingly channels us to greater and greater machinations to enhance our own self-worth at the expense of others. In addition, we cannot overlook the addiction so many of us have for the approval of others, in order to shore up, even if in some false and precarious manner, a kind of validation we may believe, or at least hope, we actually feel for ourselves.

This is just a quick glance at the range and nuance of unmet needs we ourselves have, which we may have never seen, or perhaps merely glimpsed—or, having glimpsed, never actually come to real terms with. The travesty is that we may often consciously or unconsciously maneuver ourselves into situations where we can orchestrate getting these needs met from those around us. Nowhere is this a more likely or insidiously harmful scenario than when it occurs in therapeutic relationships where others, who are themselves wounded, and who place themselves unreservedly and trustingly into our care.

It is shocking and heart-rending how many exposés have been written over the years that have brought to light this perniciously creative malaise. These dark-hearted revelations show how the voracious desire for self-aggrandizement by leaders and support people has fueled the prevalent toxicity of so many healing schools, therapies, personal growth centers, ashrams, and various experiments in intentional community.

No amount of mental preparation, or schooling from any psychological textbook, can free us from the power of our own unmet needs, which so often leach from seekers their personal power. Nor can a few sessions with a therapist clear the slate. This limitation and inability is particularly true where the primary strategy is to receive some insight into our self-defeating motivations through a superficial foray into our blocked emotions generated by our early post-natal history alone.

This truth is validated by thousands who have done Holotropic Breathwork and other powerful strategies, where they have accessed the biographical, as well as the perinatal and transpersonal, domains of the psyche. These seekers almost always discover that the post-natal environment is but the tip of the iceberg of the dynamics motivating their present behaviors and emotional needs.

The essential requirement for those of us working with others in these deep states would be that we have systematically made conscious a sufficient degree of our own motivations latent within the deeper dimensions of our own psyches. This is the only ethical and effective way that we would be able to, as we say, "sit" for breathers—or "go down the stream with them," in a manner that is not harmful, but truly supportive.

The over-arching goal—the intended nature, purpose, and atmosphere of the training environment—is based on one central necessity. This ultimate requirement is to support facilitators, so that they will be able—not just intellectually, or theoretically, but *actually*: physically, mentally, emotionally, and spiritually—to hold the space for the breathers who have placed their deepest trust in us to keep them safe in their journey of transformation. We must remember that nothing prepares us for this arduous task more elegantly than a series of ego-deaths as a result of our own inner exploration.

Only in this way are we able to consistently give back to seekers what is theirs already, but which they will repeatedly, through no fault of their own, attempt to relinquish to us, from their trusting hearts. This is their sacred power within. Only then will we truly be able to allow them to own and integrate the positive aspects, as well as challenging dimensions, of their own psyches. This is the inviolate, sacred task every practitioner must commit to, in the service of seekers who choose Holotropic Breathwork as part of their journeys toward wholeness.

The Challenge of the Inner Healer for Already Trained Therapists

There are even deeper challenges that therapists who *do* actually commit to systematic breathwork may face—both in terms of their own growth, but also if they wish to become certified Holotropic Breathwork practitioners. The knowledge that students of many schools acquire involves the use of a particular strategy or philosophy. These can easily lapse into cellular imprints, and the fluidity of the original insights becomes hardened dogma.

This dogma—now almost a religion—can become focused in circumscribed lenses through which helpers will routinely evaluate and support a seeker. This therapeutic "creativity-become-orthodoxy" is a real problem for all of us in the helping professions. We, including holotropic practitioners, mesmerize ourselves into believing that we actually know "how it all is."

But what are the implications of this theory-become-law? We have often observed that this may falsely empower therapists to believe that they actually "know" what, in truth, can probably never really be known to any outside helper. We have to ask ourselves: "What does it truly mean to be a human being?" And more specifically, "What is the perfect, truest, most effective strategy and path, both therapeutically and spiritually, for individual seekers?" Can any of us answer these questions for *even one* journeyer?

It becomes clear that each system, with its related therapeutic strategy, is a particular, circumscribed *lens* through which to view, and intervene in, the processes of seekers. Those interventions that will be initiated are directly related to the training we as therapists have received, and what we have been taught to see as psychologically relevant within the client. It is as though we throw a kind of focused spotlight on seekers' issues. This spotlight ultimately specifically defines within a limited framework who this unique voyager is as a human being, and what is either *right* or *broken* her psyche.

Metaphorically, a flashlight is only as useful as the power of the beam and the wielder of the light. No beam can do more than illuminate a limited portion of what is in a person's "basement or attic" at any one time. The rest—particularly the crucial connections and relationships between what we see and what is a mystery—remains unknown. This limited beam, directed this way and that by therapists, ultimately stifles the limitlessly stimulating possibilities of multiple levels of causality, as well as the deepest, still-latent healing potential. The only unlimited beam capable of opening to the entirety of a breather's—all at once or incrementally—is the breather's own power within.

As people helpers, we often overlook altogether the one thing that might constitute a much broader field of inquiry and the possibility of a more profound resolution. Through the lens of any one school, or even a group of schools, for that matter, it seems nearly impossible for us to truly understand anything like the true nature of another being. We are simply deluded if we believe we see anything close to the entire field of possible interrelations between behavior, motivation, and the mysteries of a person's true life purposes.

Limited, directed, and virtually controlled by the particular lens through which we gaze, we people-helpers make what is, in essence, an unprovable assumption. In good faith, we will provide so-called expert advice about what particular pathology is manifesting, and what the correct healing dynamic and intervention for that issue should be. This strategy begins to look eerily like another people-helping dynamic with which we are all familiar. In short, psycho-spiritual support seems to be a child of the traditional Western, medical profession. This is what many call a disease model of the psyche, in which the process so often involves the responsibility of *diagnosing a so-called pathology and, as a result, providing a prescription* for the client.

But we are not just talking about one diagnosis or prescription. If seekers were to present the same set of symptoms to any number of different schools, they would almost definitely receive entirely different diagnoses, treatment strategies, or even pharmacological support. Each, of course, would be based on the particular lens or spotlight through which the practitioner has been trained to look. Hundreds of breathers have reported just how confusing the procession of therapists and their well-meaning but contradictory diagnoses and healing strategies have been for them.

These lenses can be very narrowly focused, or in some cases even quite expansive. But the sheer variety and volume of the diagnostic and treatment possibilities render any one external strategy incomplete and ultimately unsuccessful. The irreducible truth seems to be that our lenses may or may not have anything at all to do with who the seeker truly is, or to be of any lasting value whatsoever for her transformation. Having had even a glimpse of how vast and rich the mystery of the psyche is, as well as how powerful our clients' own inner healing capabilities can be, we almost inevitably have to ask a different set of questions altogether.

How can any other person or system outside ourselves really *know* what the authentic, personally relevant motivating dynamics within our psyches are? Who can fathom those mysteries within us that constitute our core life purposes, or the truest needs of our most veiled and precious selves? Who else but ourselves, through our own deepest sources of truth and wisdom, should guide us on our journeys toward wholeness in this lifetime? And if we become helpers of others, how could any of us, as we peer through the lens provided by *any* school, believe that we might have anything more than a fleeting snapshot of what constitutes the deepest, optimum trajectory for the transformation of another human being?

If we recognize that our observations of another will always be relative, suspect, changeable, and limited to certain pre-ordained principles, not to mention colored by the lenses of our own life experiences, we must ask ourselves some more questions: What, then, would a modality entail that could offer seekers the opportunity to truly know and fully heal themselves? Or, based on our previous training, how would we even know what such a practice would look like?

From the recognition of our own *unknowing*, it seems sensible that we should be providing them with a method that would, in the truest sense, afford them the opportunity to undertake this journey *for themselves*, and to come to the relevant truths and conclusions *about* themselves *by* themselves. It ought never to be our goal to direct seekers to see themselves through some lens provided by a school that professes to know what is optimal for them. This individual, sacred adventure of transformation, of psychological and spiritual wholeness, can only be undertaken using strategies that mobilize the unerring power always already within seekers—what we call a power within, or the Inner Healer.

The Ultimate Lens

We must begin this section by honoring the fact that, as people helpers, most of us are motivated by a very real desire to be of service. Yet, in spite of this, many of us have somehow become indoctrinated by myriad misunderstandings of what constitutes this true nature of healing. With the deepest sense of impeccability we can summon, we do the best we can to put into practice what we have been taught.

We have often been trained to be a certain kind of expert—one that is expected by clients and family members to have many, if not all, the relevant answers. This is a long-accepted tradition, and even doctrine—and by the power of its entrenchment, one very rarely challenged. Metaphorically, we seem to be irrevocably empowered to be the knight or goddess on the winged horse who swoops in with a magic talisman to heal the wounded.

Many discover this to be a seductive, mesmerizing archetype under which to operate. It puts a heavy, often overwhelming, and eventually unfulfilled sense of responsibility on people-helpers everywhere. This dynamic may exist throughout the medical spectrum, from physical health practitioners to mental health providers. It is one that is very difficult to change, once we have become transfixed by its attractive, self-rewarding enticements. Nor is it easy to relinquish the heady sense of power and egoic wellbeing when we are lauded for having all the answers, and for being looked up to as experts.

We have also experienced some interesting complications with therapists from all over the world who wish to be certified as Holotropic Breathwork practitioners. Many of them are already working within some transpersonal strategy. When they join us for deep inner work and a rigorous educational program, they immediately become exposed to the critical Inner Healer factor, and its central role in the holotropic milieu. For some attendees, this principle so deeply contradicts many core tenets in which they have been trained that they have difficulty accepting the deepest implications of a sacrosanct, personal, healing power within.

We hear a number of reasons for this. One is that they almost "cellularly" believe in the central role they play with clients. Of course, we all play an influential role in our relationships with seekers. But it depends on what exactly this role *is* that will determine whether we are in fact allowing seekers to empower themselves by *our* recognition of the supremacy of *their* own Inner Healers. Or whether their role, in fact, merely prolongs the charade of disempowerment for their clients.

Often therapists who do the holotropic work share how they have become accustomed to seeing themselves as expert guides or catalysts. They actually believe that they intuitively know what the best intervention is for their clients. At other times, they feel so immersed in their particular school's system that to free themselves from this deep imprint feels just too difficult.

With all the investment—both financial and emotional—we may have in our previous training, it can be a real shock to face the possibility that we are not as indispensable or as "needed" as we had previously believed. The truth is, we *are* indispensable and needed, but just not in the manner we thought. We are absolutely essential as support persons who keep the breathers safe in every way. We are just not needed to be the director, or to have all the right answers about what is optimum for each individual seeker.

It is immensely productive, yet also painful, to ultimately recognize how trapped we have been by our own self-aggrandizing "false self," or ego. The truth is that, if we are fortunate enough to "die a lot"—psychospiritually—most of us eventually see ourselves as, simply, seekers, no matter what type of "helping" role we play. When we ourselves experience an ego death, many people helpers also report how freeing it is to admit how much personal investment we have had in being important, or looked up to, as the expert; or how special it felt to be praised by our clients for our well-honed skills. Many of us also share how difficult it has been to "change horses in mid-stream"—to accept that we had invested so much time, money, and hard work in a strategy we may have to give up, or at least fundamentally re-envision.

In addition, we often work with proponents of other schools of breathwork. Many of these seekers have been trained to trust their own inner selves to orchestrate the proper strategy for their clients. They report how, in their own breathwork sessions, they struggled with the need to rigorously defend their previous training and worldview. They then find themselves in the very same paradigm collision we addressed earlier in relation to ourselves—that is, a disconcerting confrontation with deep attachments to being the helper, healer, or director.

In one holotropic training there was a well-known, respected practitioner of a different school of breathwork. She was an amazing person and deeply dedicated to her own growth. She had years of experience working with breathers in a context in which the practitioner was definitely the director. We developed a warm, respectful relationship while she was in the program. We always honored each other, for who we were as persons, as well as for the differences we had when it came to supporting seekers in our groups. She would frequently challenge me. And it often amazed us how far apart we were philosophically, while at the same time liking and respecting each other so much.

One day the team was demonstrating some release-work techniques we used to support breathers in freeing themselves from energetic blockages. I always share that, for us, the optimum strategy is to clear our own mental slate—to have absolutely no clue as to what is best for a breather. We should operate from the poise that there is no way for us to definitively know how to assist people in freeing up blocked energy using the breath.

I reported that we always defer to the breather to show us or tell us what they need. Incredulous, she asked, "Do you mean you don't know where the block is?" I said that I did not, nor how could I ever truly know? I added that I would let the breather, through her Inner Healer, tell me what she wished for and where in her body she might need it. She responded, "Because I teach my trainees that if you don't know where the block is, *you are the block*."

It is just fascinating how different the two of us saw the nature of the healing process. For us in the holotropic milieu, we would say the opposite: If we act as though, or in fact believe, that we know where the block is, then this is when we are in danger of being that block ourselves. However, as far apart as we were philosophically in this situation, she and I never felt a need to argue about who was right. In the first place, since she was a participant in our seminar, my job as a practitioner was to support her in the same manner we would all attendees.

Our task was to honor her to feel as free as possible for her to be exactly who she felt she should be. So, I just took the poise that I believed in—that her Inner Healer was perfectly guiding her to trust her own healing abilities. This was totally fine for me, and she later shared that this was exactly what she needed as well. Even though we worked so differently, I was certain that, by her presence, she was really helping people on their inner journeys.

Sometimes breathers who are therapists state early on that the Inner Healer perspective will not be an issue for them. They share that the methods they have been trained in are exactly the same, or very similar, to what we do in the holotropic work. Yet after undergoing some very profound inner exploration, they often discover something they did not expect. Even though they have espoused belief in the inner healing power of seekers, they recognize how they, through the nuances, tenets and practices of there own milieu, still accidentally sabotage the true depth of this inner healing principle in their work with others. They also often discover that they have been unconsciously controlling in some way the seekers who have sought them out for support.

Sometimes we hear statements like this: "Oh, I *know* I am not the healer. I am just a guide who assists the client to see herself." Occasionally therapists will report that they see themselves as channels through which a Higher Source or Inner Healer operates, flowing from them to the client. After a number of breathing sessions, they often come to see that, in truth, if there is any healing power coming through any one person when doing deep inner work, it is being channeled through the *breather*, not the support person. In most instances, they recognize how they have been subtly, unconsciously clinging to directorship of another's process.

It is important to emphasize that we are in no way denigrating the millennia-long global tradition in which gifted individuals from virtually every culture have actually become healers within their particular settings. This profound gift has occurred either spontaneously, or it has developed as the result of systematic training under the tutelage of elder guides or shamans. It is also true that there are many today in every culture—even in the more secular global environments—who carry this sacred gift of healing power and who see it as their life's work to help other human beings.

Moreover, many of these healers will be drawn to the holotropic training as an adjunct to, or enrichener of, their own healing work. Or, they may be attracted, not because of the healing work they have been doing, but because they wish to immerse themselves in a whole new tradition altogether. For any number of reasons, they may feel particularly drawn to the holotropic milieu. However, both these situations can pose a problem for these gifted individuals.

Let us consider the difficulty that those blessed with healing abilities may encounter as they begin to immerse themselves in the holotropic strategy, particularly in relation to the Inner Healer. We have heard from a number of psychics that it is really hard to ignore their inner guides, the sources within them or above them from which they feel their therapeutic, healing authority and power comes. Many of these practitioners truly feel that they *know* what is best for the breather—that they are infallibly in touch with deep, irrefutable sources of wisdom and insight.

From the holotropic perspective, the issue is not whether these healers' wisdom is sacrosanct or infallible. Nor is it that they may in fact actually have an expanded sense of what is happening within the breather, or be in touch with any number of potentially valuable and perhaps correct heal-ing interventions. The most relevant question—in terms of the basic holo-tropic strategy—is whether their interventions would *in any way deprive the breather of an opportunity for invaluable self-discovery.*

Or might their external interventions overshadow seekers' sense of personal empowerment derived from the priceless experience inherent in the discovery of the healing source within them. The true gift they *could* offer should be an honoring of the vital, living essence of power always already a part of seekers' own psyches, and not something that is transmit-ted from another person.

The bottom line is that as therapists or healers, no matter how well intentioned we are, we cannot help but be invested in the strategies that we believe are optimum for health. Yet what gives us the right to recommend that any seeker surrender the mystery of her unfathomable uniqueness to us, as outside experts? As we have pointed out, when we continue to work on ourselves, we recognize that our prescriptions and diagnoses are fre-quently projections based upon our own unconscious dynamics and needs.

To thicken the plot, our "treatment plan" for others may even be based on the practices that have been psychologically beneficial for us. But this does not mean—definitively, or even in any way whatsoever—that our own prescription for wellness is the perfect one for someone else. Nor can we overlook the question that, with all the ongoing, deeply-rooted issues we ourselves still have—and believe me, we always have a lot more work to do—how can we ethically take responsibility for another's truth at any stage of their growth?

Over and over, if we are fierce about our own inner work, we uncover layers of belief systems and patterns by which we have been blindly moti-vated. Any one of these prohibits us from truly being present for seekers, much less knowing what is best for them. We repeat our holotropic mantras in this inquiry for a reason. This is because it is we practitioners who need to hear them over and over.

The power of our false selves demands that we stay rigorous with the truths these particular mantras impart. So, here we "re-chant" another: *The breathers are fine. They have Inner Healers to guide them. It is we our-selves who must get clearer and clearer, always relinquishing or trans-forming more and more of our limited and unconscious selves.* By doing this, we can more and more become, in a sense, a clearer lens through which to observe and support the deep process of another.

It has been painful for many of us to realize, in our own intellectual arrogance, how superficially we actually have plumbed the truest deeps of either our own or another's psyche. No matter how clear we may feel we are, no matter how much of a *tabula rasa*—a blank, clear slate—we may feel we are operating from, we still can know only what we know. No matter what we actually may know, there is always an infinity beyond us of that which we, in fact, do *not* know at all. All these realizations are certainly humbling for us. But in the long run, we are always amazed at how much lighter we feel when we recognize that we need not, or cannot, carry the weight of another's wellbeing.

The concluding portion of this part of our inquiry reflects a different dynamic, one that entails a slightly more conscious level of dishonesty in ourselves. Regardless of whether, in the past, we worked solely through verbal communication, or whether we employed any other type of intervention with our clients, if we use deep breathing with clients *even once*, we will often be absolutely astounded by the rapid breakthroughs they can report. What usually happens at this point is that the breather will project some extremely positive attributes onto how great we are as therapists or even healers. Here is a holotropic news flash: *Breath works!*

From the "front lines," we hear over and over how, at this critical therapeutic juncture, many of us "lose it on the last curve." No matter how diligent we are, no matter how much work we have done on ourselves, we succumb to the siren-call of ego. Self-aggrandizement is a subtle but powerful addiction. Like all other addictions, we must appeal to a deeper, truer source within our nature—a higher self, empowered not by any fleeting, ephemeral external source, but wholly and completely by a power within— the Inner Healer.

To repeat: The truth is, *breathwork makes all of us people helpers look really good*. It becomes so easy to be seduced by these positive projections from our clients. From here, it is equally easy to imagine somehow that "we have done it"—that we really *are* the wonderful healers they think we are. We often revel in that fact that it was through us that they experienced their breakthroughs. For us support people, this is often just too good a feeling to give up. Subsequently, it is also too painful to give back to the breathers the power they have so innocently and trustingly bestowed upon us.

What is the antidote to this pervasive manifestation—how our own false selves manifest as pride and arrogance? Those of us who have been through this seductive sense of power have one particular thing to share as a sure-fire cure for this theft of a breather's inner power. We have found through systematic deep inner work that *nothing succeeds like a series of uncomfortable, yet cleansing, ego deaths*. These deaths will awaken us to the truth that we have actually done *absolutely nothing* to heal another person. In fact, every bit of healing anyone receives through deep work has truly come from his or her own inner healing power. This is the heart and essence of a holotropic paradigm.

CHAPTER XIII

Through the Looking Glass: Darkly, Brightly

A Meta-Lens

There are at least two octaves within which the holotropic paradigm seems to be making a cutting-edge contribution during this current era. First, its philosophy and practice demand an expanded, rigorous commitment to service through its challenge to therapists and people helpers to "walk their talk" by committing to their own systematic inner work.

Second, it also offers a meta-perspective proposing the vital role a holotropic paradigm might assume in human evolution, particularly in terms of the part radical personal empowerment plays in the individual and collective human adventure toward wholeness. With these perspectives in mind, we should offer another metaphor for the way unconscious dynamics shape what we commonly, and perhaps falsely, call either *an individual, or a universally recognizable, external reality—or both.*

Lenses: Through the Looking Glass of Transformation

We have often used the term, *"through the lens of,"* in describing how we view, or evaluate, the roles other people play in our lives and in the surrounding world environment—their personalities, psychological makeup, or way of being or functioning. But there is a more basic, and perhaps more profound way to understand this metaphor of "the lens." As we have alluded to already, at its most influential level, the lens through which we see the world, for all intents and purposes, actually shapes, or even creates, our universe experience for us.

A number of factors may "color" the lens through which an individual gazes. These would encompass any mental or emotional characteristic that comprises her belief system, psychological or spiritual attitude, or way of presenting herself interpersonally in life situations. They would also include whatever philosophy, mindset, religious or spiritual orientation, opinions, predilections, type of training, or emotional habits she may have. In addition, we should add the power of psycho-spiritual patterns, prejudices, complexes, attitudes, desires, fears, attractions, or repulsions that commingle to constitute what we might call her individual personality.

We could even envision that we *are* a tabula rasa—a clear, or blank, slate—as Freud suggested, but just not in the way he imagined it. The tabula rasa of which we speak is something entirely more expansive. We are referring to an extraordinary level of awareness that often emerges for seekers, spontaneously or gradually, during their work in expanded states of consciousness.

This level includes a personal focus, but is ultimately *meta*-transpersonal. This "clean slate" is what we may envision as a *clear light of conscious awareness* that, in some way, always already exists prior to its coloration by any type of collective or personal experience. This clear light would also include the existence of a witness consciousness, a powerful transformational strategy known in many schools.

We are referring to a state of consciousness described in different metaphors by philosophers and mystics through many world cultures and cycles of history. In other systems, it has been called the soul, higher self, or atman, among other designations. These are not just abstract principles. They are experiential realities, or states of consciousness, available to anyone who engages in inner exploration into expanded states of awareness.

Based on a core tenet of many philosophies, we might propose that the record of what it is to be an individual human being is the sum total of physical, emotional, mental, and numinous impressions that superimpose themselves on the lens of this primary clear light of awareness. In one way, this is not really that different from Freud's belief in his conception of a tabula rasa. However, the major departure stems from the vastly more comprehensive possibilities inherent in the recognition that the human psyche is not merely a post-natal affair, but is in fact equal to all that is.

We can imagine that this pristine light of awareness at the core of consciousness itself acts like a lens. In this scenario, before experience takes place, the lens is perfectly clear, bright, and clean. Then, we could suggest that the beginning of individual consciousness is a "down-stepping" of the clear light of awareness, generated by the accruing of those impressions of individuality, in the form of experiences, as they begin to color the bright clear lens. This becomes our individual psycho-spiritual history, the inner record of our psyche—what we call impressions and imprints, or, if we use psychological terms, our issues, complexes, patterns, gestalts, chief features, or, as in Holotropic Breathwork: COEXs.

As we continue to explore the foundational possibility of a holotropic therapy, we will emphasize the therapeutic power of the healing mechanism we call COEXs, or *systems of condensed experiences*. You may recall that COEXs are deeply ingrained patterns that are the result of unconscious experiences and associated behaviors and attitudes that periodically recur in a seeker's life and are linked by a common theme.

These gestalts, or psycho-energetic clusters, have causal roots throughout the various dimensions of the psyche—the biographical, perinatal, and transpersonal domains. As we work systematically with every stage of this multi-leveled inner structure, it is the Inner Healer that is the golden thread connecting all strata of the psyche. It is the beacon shining a spotlight on our myriad inner psycho-spiritual dynamics. It is the Inner Healer that, brought on-line through the workings of whatever modality is employed to access expanded states of awareness, orchestrates, crystallizes, and serves to focus powerful insights for our healing. All of this takes place under the aegis of consciousness itself.

The Inner Healer "midwifes" this healing quite elegantly. Imagine that our psycho/physical/spiritual issues are like beads within the psyche. Each bead will contain the psycho-emotional essence of a certain pattern, the full meaning of which is still not fully disclosed to us. Before our healing begins, these beads appear to be randomly scattered throughout the psyche—in the biographical, perinatal, as well as transpersonal domain.

Before work in non-ordinary states, we are sure we have dozens of things wrong with us. Traditional work will help us make conscious the beads uncovered within our biography, but that is about as far as it goes. The rest are out of reach, yet still operative within the psyche. As such they continue to cause us a sense of dis-ease, incompletion, or outright suffering.

Through the power of the Inner Healer in our deep work, however, our healing journey now opens us to the far reaches of the psyche. We may uncover, from the various deeper dimensions of our being, first one bead of an issue, and then another of the same nature or problem, and then perhaps another. Or we can have the transformational epiphany of unveiling the *entire* gestalt or pattern at one time, in a glorious "aha!" moment of far-reaching, incisive inner consciousness.

At this point, all relevant, related beads of an issue will, almost miraculously, line up together, like beads on a string. Lo and behold, we have made conscious an elegant "necklace of beads," a COEX, or a *system of condensed experience*. This is one of the most profound healing mechanisms available to us through Holotropic Breathwork, and by contact with the Inner Healer and its dynamis, the power within. These mechanisms can also, of course, be brought on line by other methods capable of accessing expanded states of awareness and the deeper dimensions of the psyche.

To continue our inquiry, through another metaphor based on COEXs, imagine that, as an individual unit of consciousness, we are continuously looking outward, at the world around us, through a *lens* colored by an end-less variety of experiential material latent within us. This material has roots, as we discover through deep work, in the transpersonal, perinatal, as well as the biographical domains of the psyche. We could say that the light of consciousness shines through a lens, on which is projected the tremen-dously varied contents of our psyches. The best metaphor we have found for this phenomenon is that the lens through which we look becomes a many-faceted, multi-colored *kaleidoscope*.

We are now at ground zero of the issue. It would appear that seeing the world or existence through the kaleidoscopic view, for all intents and pur-poses, orchestrates our own personal reality. In light of this, it seems quite doubtful that there is anything approaching what we call an actual, unified, universal reality at all, or a common external manifestation that we all agree on is exactly, objectively, the same for everyone.

Paul of Tarsus, a follower of Jesus of Nazareth, allegedly said, "We see through a glass darkly." It is highly likely that at least a part of his pur-pose in making this statement was to demonstrate this particular perennial dilemma to which human beings are subject. This is that we live in a reality of our own making, one that is significantly limited, in comparison to what the total realm of possibilities actually are. Or some might say that we live in a prison "forged by the chains of our own artifice."

We may eventually come face-to-face with these disconcerting possi-bilities, even as we ever strive to convince ourselves that we are the mas-ters of our fate. William Blake also expressed this universal human dilemma in a similar fashion. He spoke of the necessity of "cleansing the doors of perception" in order to experience the truth and be free.

This phrase was, of course, borrowed by Aldous Huxley, the famous consciousness pioneer, for the title of his book *The Doors of Perception*. Again, he was referring to the importance of breaking free from a kind of *maya*, or even a realm of fantasy, created by what we have experienced—biographical, perinatal, and transpersonal—as well as how we think and feel about these experiences. This amalgam of impressions, coloring the lens through which we look, becomes, as we said, a kind of prison that limits our ability to feel the deep sense of fulfillment promised by many traditions.

This prison is made up of the same kinds of inner unconscious mate-rial we have been describing. Huxley advocated the use of entheogens as a tool to help us to become psycho-spiritually free. He does this in the same way that, in this inquiry, we also attest to the value of Holotropic Breath-work, along with psychedelics and, indeed, any method that can help us gain access to the deeper dimensions of the psyche.

It is challenging enough that we see the world colored through the lens of our inner dynamics. But what are the global implications of the possible absence of one sacrosanct objective reality? What thickens the plot is that all other human beings on the planet are also looking through their own lenses, through the light of their own more-or-less conscious awareness. As a result, they too are seeing the world through their own special kaleidoscopes. Their inner experiences, patterns, belief systems, and conscious or unconscious emotional and psychological material are, in essence, creating their own individual reality. This is true for others, just as our own inner world—previously unconscious and now thrown onto the screen of our consciousness and viewed through the lens of our conscious awareness—is creating our unique world experience.

Now, if we *were,* in fact, a tabula rasa at the time of birth, then our particular kaleidoscope would be initially colored by our earliest post-natal experience. The kaleidoscope would then become more complex, multicolored, and faceted as we gather experiences through our interactions with our parents, siblings, teachers, friends, enemies, including what kind of education we may have had, and so on. This ever-accruing complexity of our own kaleidoscopic view would become more intricate as we get older and experience more and more of life. To be sure, if this is all that we humans are—the post-natal history alone—then exploring cleansing the "dross" from this kaleidoscope, in order to be more fulfilled, would definitely be a daunting task.

However, in what can initially seem to be a diabolical manner, we find out that we are anything but a tabula rasa at the time of birth. We learn that our birth process and our collective, transpersonal history, including what we call karma, are tremendously influential in how we negotiate life. Or, to use our current metaphor, we can often be overwhelmed by how the lens through which we view our ever-shifting present has been kaleidoscopically enhanced with so much unconscious, multivalent material.

Consequently, we can now suggest metaphorically that *the process of healing, of transformation, of maximum personal empowerment, is characterized by the gradual and systematic cleansing of the lens through which we view the world.* In order to cleanse the lens, we are required to undertake systematic, deep self-exploration. As we do this, we may begin to characterize our transformational endeavors with a new metaphor. We each may experience that the kaleidoscope of inner patterns that color how we experience this elusive dream of a uniform external reality might gradually clear itself through deep work. As it does this, there may finally be revealed a graceful, creative harmony between our inner and outer lives.

The implications that every being is looking at the external world through a fantastically painted kaleidoscope of inner impressions has tremendous implications in our pursuit of a holotropic evolutionary reality—or a personal and collective *moving toward wholeness.* Perhaps the most fascinating implication of this metaphor entails the psychological mechanisms whereby we unconsciously create our own individual experience of that reality, when it results in a profound sense of personal disempowerment or disconnection from self, others, and the cosmos at large.

COEXs: Through the Lens of the Lens

In our training, we spend a lot of time working with COEX systems. As we do this, presenting the metaphor of the *lenses* through which we look at the world has proven to be a prelude to our work with this structure. By, in a sense, "alchemicalizing" the dance between COEXs and the lenses through which we experience external reality, we engage another wonderfully simplified yet powerful way for trainees to understand how the inner dimensions orchestrate our perception and experience of outer reality.

Here is a closer look out how a COEX operates in our lives, and how we can work with it. Remember, COEX stands for *System of Condensed Experience.* It is like a string of beads, where the string is a multivalent pattern spanning all dimension of the psyche—the biographical, perinatal, and the transpersonal.

Each bead represents a currently unconscious experience or quality whose essence is of the same nature and charge as that of the string. However, it is essential to point out that, before a seeker makes a COEX conscious, the beads are often experienced singly, as randomly distributed throughout each level of the psyche, yet unconnected by any thread, or for the seeker, any valuable conscious insight. This "scatter-shot" healing process is arduous and daunting, at best.

Now, in order to make this dynamic clear to participants, we offer a simplified presentation on our lens metaphor, as well as the operation of COEXs in our lives, along with the consequent transformation available to us. I might ask the group to imagine that, when a person is born, she comes into her life with only *one* previous inner experience—one color—which paints the kaleidoscope of her lens though which she views the world.

Of course, in reality, our kaleidoscope is a phantasmagoria of color and design, as one can imagine, given the vast spectrum of perinatal and transpersonal, as well as unconscious biographical, material latent within the unconscious and which individuals uncover through their deep work. We also point out that, on the far end of this continuum of inner experiences, the seeker ultimately may open to "all that is."

I usually give, as an example, the ubiquitous trauma of *abandonment*— a hot-button issue for many seekers. I ask them to imagine a situation where the only pattern that comes from the perinatal and transpersonal domain with effects in the biographical dimension is this one trauma of abandonment. We may propose a scenario whereby the seeker has had a compromised intrauterine relationship with her mother throughout the pregnancy.

Perhaps the mother was not supported during her own intrauterine episode and birth. This would be a basis for her to be unconsciously motivated by the disconnection in her own birth to experience more of this aloneness and separation in her life experience. All of this can be communicated to the fetus in her own womb, thereby setting up what we call an episode of generational trauma. Therefore, when the contractions begin, and she is propelled into the birth canal, the fetus' sense of separation is even further compounded, setting the stage for additional beads of trauma on this "rosary of abandonment."

So, the walls of the uterus have contracted. The oxygen and blood supply—a physical connection with the mother—have been cut off. Perhaps the mother is in pain, or experiencing waves of panic, fear, separation, or aloneness. Any or all of these situations might cause her to contract, to withdraw emotionally from her closeness with the fetus. This is through no fault of her own. Nevertheless, the fetus is not privy to this insight.

But the story is more complex: There are other reasons for the fetus in the intrauterine environment to interpret the mother's own delivery crisis as abandonment. It would be experientially logical if the fetus had *already* had some previous contact with the issue of abandonment emerging from her own history preceding this birth. As we know, this prehistory is available in the collective dimension, the transpersonal domain, and which includes the astrological record of our birth, or the archetype of Birth itself.

If we use our metaphor of the lens, we could say that the fetus's lens has been colored by a transpersonal experience of abandonment. Perhaps this is a past life, or series of lives, in which she experienced abandonment. Or it could be an archetypal overlay, as we pointed out, a pattern of generational trauma, or some other motif, including personal or collective astrological configurations.

Whatever it may be, the relevant issue is that she entered the womb experience for this particular life, not as a tabula rasa, nor with a clear lens. In this situation, the fact that the lens of her awareness was already colored by a transpersonal experience of abandonment selectively ordered, or helped create or interpret, what her mother was going through as a further validation of her abandonment in the womb.

Now, we scroll forward, bringing this scenario into its next important stage—the birth process and immediate post-natal environment. First, there is the almost universally reported anxiety and sense of separation and aloneness created by the experience of expulsion from the womb and the constriction of the second matrix while the cervix is closed and there is "no way out" yet of the birth process itself.

Next comes the often violent and wounding episodes of the third matrix—the struggle through the canal following the opening of the cervix. Then comes the birth itself. It may be that through an orchestration of prevalent medically dominated birth practices, or through some kind of physical emergency involving either the mother or the new-born child, or both, the infant was immediately separated from her mother. Perhaps she was placed in an incubator or in a hospital crib for special care. In any event, once again, the newborn will find herself looking at the outside world through a strikingly concentrated lens of abandonment.

Remember, we are only focusing on the quite unlikely scenario in which this person, this experience of singular consciousness, has but *one issue* with which she has been imprinted in previous dimensions of her life experience. We have purposely chosen the tableau of highlighting just one dynamic, one color, to paint the lens through which she gazes at the world, thereby ordering her external reality. In this way, we can keep simple what in reality is quite a complex, multi-colored phantasmagoria of patterns that paints the lens through which she gazes and which orchestrates her external existence.

So far, in this example, we have been focusing on the metaphor of the *lens* through which we look. However, with equal value and facility, we could be framing our explication of healing in terms of what we call *COEXs*. In this case, of course, the COEX can be easily identified as one of *abandonment*. And every event that the seeker has made conscious—from the transpersonal, into the perinatal, and ultimately manifesting in the biographical domain—represent the beads which the Inner Healer has deftly strung on the rosary of the seeker's consciousness through work in non-ordinary states of consciousness.

The psyche's remarkable ability, through the Inner Healer, to organize our transformation through easily identifiable and nameable patterns, such as *abandonment*—even after a seemingly random amalgam or display of confusingly separate issues—is of tremendous value to us. This gift is that *viewing transformation through the lens of COEXs greatly simplifies the process of transformation.* Instead of believing that she has dozens of random issues wrong with her, through the work of her Inner Healer and the COEX process, a seeker ultimately realizes that there are probably just two or three central patterns with which she seems to be working in this incarnation.

It appears that, in addition to being an inner healer, this power within has a heart as well. This heart quality manifests as the psyche's power, and apparent inclination, to ultimately free us from suffering. In this and almost every scenario, however challenging they may yet be, we frequently receive the validation and sense of peace that our inner work is just not as arduous as we once thought. Once again, we are deeply supported by our proposal of the power in a *wellness model* of the psyche and transformation itself.

Implications of the COEX Lens

With these insights in mind, there are some interesting meta-questions before us: First, "Is the external world which any individual experiences truly the same world that every other person experiences?"; and, second, "If there is no such thing as consensual reality, what, then, is the mechanism whereby individuals create their own external experience?"; and, third—the most vitally relevant question of all—"Can we empower ourselves to recreate our own reality in a way that is absolutely fulfilling, and ultimately moves us toward optimum wellness and wholeness?"

Any seeker who undertakes a systematic exploration of the multiple levels of her own psyche can answer these questions. Through our own inner experiences and our support for others over the years, this is what we see: The kaleidoscope through which we look—the COEXs, or unconscious patterns of emotional, mental, and psychosomatic issues—all create a unique universe of which each of us alone is at least the co-creator.

Of course, we share much of the external world: be it a tree, a fire, the sun, the moon, the turn of the seasons, or the reality of physical birth and death. All these and countless other phenomena seem to be part of an objective reality more or less common to all. Yet even this so-called common reality is still unique in many ways for each person. Still, it is as though existence provides a kind of collective meta-canvas on which we may paint our own distinctly individual brushstrokes and interpretations.

The nuances of our responses to these and all things external: our embracing or rejecting of them—those things we fear and those things we crave—these and a thousand reactions seem to create our own unique life experience. We are like cosmic explorers as we navigate the consensual as well as separate universes created by billions of others with whom we sometimes share a common world space and experience. We each observe what is external to us through the kaleidoscope of our own unique lens. In perpetually doing this, we each, then, create and inhabit this so-called reality for ourselves.

How often have we heard others, or ourselves, use the phrase "out of reality"? Based on what we learn from our own inner work, it seems as though each of us—all of us—are in truth "out of reality" in relation to almost every other human being on the planet. But it is not our intention to focus on the philosophical implications of this *Plato's Cave* of the human conundrum, even though this ancient philosopher seemed to have it absolutely right. At a certain stage of our own individual evolution toward wholeness, we are all in some way deluded and blind, groping through a darkness, grasping a piece of the whole, and claiming this piece to be *The One Whole Reality*.

But there is a way out of this darkness and into the light. To continue our metaphor, we can choose to embrace any of the myriad practices that help us to cleanse the lens through which we view the external universe. We do this, as we have pointed out regularly, by *making conscious that which is unconscious* to us. We do this, in full knowledge that *consciousness itself is the Inner Healer—our power within*.

The result of this ongoing life endeavor is that we often find ourselves approaching and ultimately embracing the truths espoused by some of the great teachers of our evolution. We learn "to be with what is"; "to be here now"; to practice the "Great Way"; to rest in the "Clear Light" or the "Tao"; or to live in the spirit of *kanyini*, as the indigenous people of Australia call "inter-connectedness."

Lenses and COEXs: Through Another Lens

However, let us return once more to this scenario of *abandonment*—the one issue with which we propose to color our lens. Perhaps we may simplify this issue yet again. This time we will explore abandonment within the biographical domain—in the same way we explicated it in each of the other two dimensions of the psyche—the perinatal and the transpersonal. After all, it is within the biographical domain that we live, move, and breathe, alone and in various connections with those around us.

So, with this in mind, we will describe an example of a scenario we use when we are having a discussion in our training on how COEXs shape our everyday reality. The scenario this time is that abandonment will be a *presenter's* issue, in teaching the principle of COEXs during a group discussion. This is an imaginary tableau I regularly share with the group: In this scenario, I play the role of a presenter who has only one issue—abandonment—coloring the lens through which I am interacting with and experiencing the group, or any other life situation.

So, imagine that there is a facilitator, a true friend, with whom I, the imaginary presenter, have developed a good relationship, based on mutual respect, trust, and shared values. I am in the front of the room presenting this material on COEXs to our group of trainees. And as I gaze around the room, I notice that this close friend seems preoccupied, uncomfortable, and distracted.

As I continue to steal glances at her, I get what we call being "activated." I become uncomfortable myself, perhaps imagining that I must have said something to upset her, or that I am not making any sense in my presentation. Basically, I am taking personally and internalizing something that in fact has nothing to do with me at all.

The truth is, unbeknownst to me, she wants to go to the lavatory to wash her face and hands. So, at some point, she gets up and leaves the room, right in the middle of my lecture. When I see her leaving the room, I feel a kick in the gut, a kind of panic, as though part of my personal power has left me.

Even while I am lecturing, however, I feebly try to "go somewhat vertical" within myself. I recognize that I have a horizontal attachment to this person. It is clear to me that I must be unconsciously trying to get some need met. I figure it out, or at least I think I do. All this is occurring while I am "multi-tasking"—sharing with the group, and yet, at the same time, bringing the light of consciousness to my own, unique inner landscape.

However, I intuit at some half-conscious level that I have, as we say, "lost it on the curve." My stream of consciousness goes something like this: "She truly has done something harmful *to* me. I have been *abandoned*! She knows how important her presence is to me! She has *made* me lose my center." I forget what I was lecturing about. Now, I am certainly not vertical, but horizontal once more, allowing myself to be a slave to outside circumstance.

My spirit—the majority of my *willed focus of attention*—has followed her from the room: I *am* hurt—not I *feel* hurt. She betrayed me! I long to confront her—to blame her for *making me* lose my center in front of the group. I may even experience a kind of perverse pleasure on being hurt, relishing how satisfying it will be to see her forced to accept the responsibility for my pain. I may even look forward to the gratification of observing how she will attempt to assuage me—*make* me feel better. And on and on …

The truth is, when she gets up and walks out of the room, it really has absolutely nothing to do with me. Yet, because I am projecting onto her an unconscious need for her to alleviate my sense of abandonment, I make the following assumption: *She has abandoned me! I must have done some-thing wrong. I am worthless, unloved, rejected. It's all my fault!* I have allowed an unconscious dynamic within myself—my trauma of abandon-ment—to absolutely control and orchestrate—actually *create* my current reality. My reality now is, simply, that I have been abandoned.

Remember, in this scenario, only one issue—just one—has thoroughly created my reality. The truth is, my friend's getting up, walking out, and going to the lavatory to wash up is an essentially neutral act. The only thing it has to do with me is what I make of it—what I create. I can even become quite paranoid about it. Perhaps I conclude that my friend really "had it in for me." I can make all kinds of assumptions about her motives in relation to me. Maybe she was very angry. What if she knew about my COEX of abandonment, and orchestrated this scenario to really hurt me? As ludi-crous as this storyline sounds, it is likely that most of us know what it is to feel at least a little paranoid.

But, in the so-called real world, most of us humans have a fantastically complex kaleidoscope of unconscious motivations that are triggered daily, or moment-to-moment—not just one thing. The major question is, "How do we become free?" How do we cleanse the lens of this shimmering, mes-merizing rainbow of unconscious issues which limits our deepest fulfill-ment in life?

Once again: We can never *think* our way out of this dilemma. We can-not *intellectualize* our patterns into non-existence. Attempting this, we unconsciously create barriers of denial and dissociation, which are no more than "fuel to the fire" of our dysfunction, and triggers of an ever deeper sense of personal and planetary isolation and separation. We cannot get truly free through any doomed quixotic attempt to forever manipulate external reality. The only way we can be free is to engage in systematic deep work powerful enough to reach, not just the biographical level of the psyche, but the perinatal and the transpersonal as well.

Now, imagine how a day might feel when we are looking through—not just one coloration of our lens—but an impossibly complex kaleidoscope of unconscious material. This phantasmagoria ranges from biographical issues, back though the traumas of our birth, and even further and wider into a transpersonal dimension connecting us with the collective dynamics, in essence, of all that exists. No wonder we feel disempowered by the world around us!

By some seemingly diabolical internal psychological mechanism, we have lost right-relationship with ourselves and the external universe. The practical truth, the pearl of wisdom that will emerge when we really come to grips with this, is the realization that it is *we ourselves* who are the pri-mary orchestrators of our own realities.

This core error is debilitating because we are, for the most part, unconscious of the dynamics, whereby we imagine ourselves to be the puppets of fate, and helpless victims of world machinations. It takes a nuclear blast of realization to accept authorship of our own personal stories, and to break free from the hopelessness of an imagined personal disempowerment. It is a challenge to once-and-for-all recognize that we are truly the creators of our reality.

Yet within this seemingly overwhelming, hopeless scenario, there is miraculous good news. If we have created our reality, then we can un-create it, or *re*-create it. We can all discover that we are not slaves to what we feel is an external reality. We recognize that it is most often our *inner reality*, or experience of what we *feel* is reality, that is causing us our suffering. We see that we can transcend the hopelessness of disempowerment by embracing the infallible resources of healing power that are always already at the inner core of our consciousness.

This healing power works through *consciousness* itself—what we call the Inner Healer, or a power within—by bringing into our awareness those issues from within that color the lens through which we look. This internal stream of intra-psychic material is set free, in a manner metaphorically resembling the act of casting into a fire of purification that of which we wish to be cleansed. This is the promise of the wisdom of the ages, and one of this remarkable lineage's most powerful, creative progeny, the holotropic paradigm.

CHAPTER XIV

Presence—The Art Work of the *Power Within*

In holotropic work, what we call *presence* is a critical force in establishing the optimal therapeutic relationship with seekers. Yet it is not that easy to define presence in the context of this, or, for that matter, any inquiry. As we explore this critical psycho-spiritual dynamic, keep in mind that presence is a vital component of every type of therapeutic interaction.

As such, this section directly addresses how the therapeutic power inherent in a holotropic practice has tremendous implications for all therapists of any school. Moreover, *presence* must also be a central component for those who are supporting seekers in their exploration via entheogens and those who are working with the psycho-spiritual crisis known as *spiritual emergency*, with addictions recovery, or with any future-focused efforts toward a holotropic therapy.

A Meta-Perspective

How many times in our lives have we been impressed, or even mystified, by an experience we have had with some individual? If we examine the context of this interaction, we often find that it was not so much about something this person said or did that was impressive. It had more to do with something about her that was quite elusive. We realize we have been deeply moved by an attitude she exuded—by her way of being—by a subtlety of personality, or a quality of magnetism she seemed to radiate that was independent of her words or actions.

When we relate these experiences to others, we find ourselves at a loss as to how we have been so moved. We often resort to metaphors yet remain mystified. In the final analysis, we often give up and admit that there was "just something about her," or we say something like, "I don't know. It just felt *good* to be around her. She had charisma."

The very act of recalling our interlude with this person often moves us once more. We find ourselves again bringing to consciousness the special atmosphere of the original encounter. Without knowing how this could be so, we re-experience that special feeling emerging from our own psyches, and are uplifted by its mysterious ability to have this kind of recurring effect upon us. Most of us will simply "chalk it up"—shrug, shake our heads, and just live with the mystery. Rarely will we recognize that we have had an encounter with what in the holotropic work we call *presence*.

In the same fashion, we can find ourselves contracting, withholding, or guarding ourselves around some individuals. Again, upon reflection, we realize that our cautious attitude had little to do with their words or actions. Yet, something about them we cannot name or adequately express has led us to feel ill at ease, perhaps mistrusting, or even fearful. Of course, rigorous self-inquiry may show us if there is a relevant issue within us that has been triggered by this interaction—in which case we have more "grist for the mill" of our own unfolding.

But sometimes what we feel seems to be generated more by an actual "unpleasantness" in another person. In this case—regardless of what we can work on within ourselves to free us from our distrust—we are still disinclined to trust this person outside us. No doubt, in virtually every type of therapy, *trust* is touted as one of the primary dynamics necessary for a positive therapeutic outcome.

Even if trust is not immediately present in the initial phase of inner work, every person-helper recognizes the need for this power to be established, if therapy or support is to have any kind of success. Nowhere is this need for trust more critical than during work in expanded states of consciousness. And *presence* is one of the most critical components of the psyche likely to be a creator of trust for any person with whom we may come in contact throughout our lives.

Meta-Definitions

Through the most panoramic lens, "presence" seems to be an amalgam, a snapshot in time and space, or, in any given moment, a multi-leveled manifestation of who we are as human beings. Presence reflects and radiates our current evolutionary development to individuals, the world outside us, as well as to ourselves. In holotropic circles, we often refer to presence as our *being level*. Through systematic inner work, many of us experience that presence also represents a function or attribute of consciousness itself.

Through another lens, presence appears to be the "dynamic ground," or the essential nature of our being, manifested to those with whom we are in relationship. Its essence, its character, can be experienced—for ourselves, and by others—as an atmosphere. This atmosphere is the result of our psycho-spiritual evolution—what we call our Becoming—as we move toward wholeness. This wholeness, as we have addressed already in a number of contexts, is also what we call Being.

Presence may also be intuited and experienced as a *state of consciousness*. We can discover through introspection and deep work that presence radiates a type of power in our lives, based on the stable achievement of certain levels of expanded awareness. We can also recognize a magnetic quality in presence, which many consider to be its impetus for consciousness evolution in the first place. We will delve deeper into this healing dynamic in our discussion of the *Awareness Positioning System*, or the *Yoga of the Cross*—a powerful strategy based on holotropic dynamics used in *Movie Yoga* and for working with any holotropic therapy, or a moment-to-moment holotropic life practice.

As we stated, we often interchange presence with what we call our "being level." It reflects a synergy between the two basic levels of existence to which we have been referring throughout this inquiry. These levels are Becoming and Being. Through another lens, our Becoming seems to be the multivalent, ever-shifting, millisecond-to-millisecond manifestation of where we are in our own psycho-spiritual evolution toward Being. In other words, to view this dynamic holotropically, we could suggest that our presence, in any given moment or interpersonal encounter, represents an energetic "way-station" in our daily evolutionary trajectory of *moving toward wholeness*.

We might also suggest that presence is a power of Self, or what in metaphysical language is sometimes called the "true self." This power of Self appears to inform the coloring of personality and *pattern* the way we present ourselves in relationship to self, others, and the universe around us. Through another lens, presence might also be the temporary, ever-morphing manifestation of an evolutionary enlightening process. These perspectives continue to validate the core holotropic dynamic of moving toward wholeness.

We have heard all kinds of interesting stories from breathers on this issue of presence. From a metaphysical trajectory, many report that presence represents the power of the clear light, or being, as it shines through our separate self, or ego. The dynamis of presence is often experienced as creating the "prism" of our personality self in our Becoming, as individual entities or souls evolving toward source, or Being.

Whatever gifts of power, truth, sincerity, or authenticity we radiate—or, for that matter, of any of these attributes' mirror opposites that we may embody—reflects, absolutely accurately, our presence—where we are in our individual, personal development. The individual effort toward this development is what we often call the "work we have done on ourselves." It would be congruent, then, to refer to this ever-changing snapshot of our being level as none other than the evolution of presence itself.

The Power of Presence

Presence is also recognized in how these personal operating systems of which we spoke—our being level—color or shape our interactions through the energetic, physical, or psycho-spiritual stances we constantly assume in our relationships. Many of us have arrived at a rather stark conclusion: We just cannot escape, or hide from, the truth-telling, soul-baring manifestation of our presence with others. Nor can we fake for long the glaringly obvious effect our presence actually has on those with whom we share our lives.

We have no idea how powerful, how influential, our presence, or being level, can be for another person. This appears to hold true throughout the entire spectrum of human interaction. Whether we pass someone on the street; hug a friend, lover, or child; shake hands in a business transaction; or hold space for a friend in distress, the fullness of the mystery of who we are as unique, individual entities radiates tremendous power—for good or ill—in the lives of the countless beings with whom we interact on a day-to-day basis.

It seems a nearly universal truth that we cannot maintain for long the facade of an inauthentic *being level*. *Being level* can be accurately described by the international koan we can hear or read almost any day, streaming through world media: "It is what it is." "What it is"—or presence—simply cannot be created by any machination engendered by the false self. We may actually succeed in consciously or unconsciously misguiding or fooling others some of the time. However, who we are—where we function in our evolution toward wholeness—ultimately, irrevocably shines forth with scathing clarity—through our eyes, our words, our body language, and our actions. This is what we call *presence*.

For the most part, our influence on others is unintentional, or unconscious. Yet there are those times when we are not merely reacting, but *acting* with a purpose. In these situations, we have a greater awareness of who we are, and how we operate in any given scenario. We bring a conscious intention, perhaps a force of love or will, or a combination of both these attributes, for either good or ill, to our relationships with those around us. When we do this—again for good or ill—our actions have a vastly enriched, enlivened power to influence the wellbeing of those in whose presence our own personal presence operates.

In holotropic practice, it is essential that we take presence, or *being level*, seriously. As we have said, these dynamics—of Becoming and Being—seem to be two inherently possible poises of the way we function as consciousness in the world. However, by speaking of a "being level," we may be accused of presenting a metaphysical conundrum. Whether or not this occurs depends on our arriving at a psycho-therapeutically functional definition of the term *being*. For our inquiry, at the most expanded level, being seems to connote an all-encompassing, indissolvable reality that is the primary baseline of consciousness behind all other more localized foci of awareness.

Yet as we flirt with the term *being*, we are also speaking of it to denote a certain *modification* of this all-encompassing beingness—a downstepped, separate, perhaps limited focus of what may otherwise be a universal field of consciousness. This is what we term *a being*—a unit within an unlimited field of other *beings* and within the unity of *Being* itself. It is in this context of individual beings within the most expanded field of beingness, or pure being, that we derive our holotropically relevant definition of presence, or *being level*.

Now, if we use a psycho-spiritual lens through which to explore this metaphor, we might say that "being level" represents a particular investiture of attributes teased from the field of unlimited *being* in any one moment of existence. We could say that, from a human standpoint, the universe manifestation consists of a host of beings, operating with a certain limited dispensation of the unlimited, all encompassing field of pure being. Once again, this is where the term *holotropic* emerges as a core dynamic and principle of our inquiry: *moving toward, or Becoming*; and *wholeness, or Being.*

Presence in Everyday Life

Many of us have reached a conclusion of vital importance in our support of others. Every facet of the systematic inner work that we do—in this case with the intention of becoming effective holotropic facilitators—has always upgraded, or radically enhanced, our *presence, or being level*. It is absolutely impossible to over-emphasize how critical a practitioner's "being level" is in the essential holotropic role of "sitting for," or supporting any seeker, or, in our current case, a breather in any particular breathwork.

As practitioners, we must systematically address our own psycho-spiritual evolution. Our hoped-for outcome would be an incremental upgrade in our level of consciousness, our "being level," or our presence.

Our own willingness—or *willed focus of attention*—in regularly addressing our moving toward wholeness seems to play as important a role as our being level in how effective we may be as Holotropic Breathwork practitioners. We must always—*always*—be *willing* to work on ourselves.

There are pivotal, definable, experiential dynamics that characterize a discomfort in our frequent human interactions. In many instances, they take place almost entirely within what in the holotropic work we call the *horizontal*, or external interpersonal dimension. That is, we are frequently accustomed to feeling that all our interpersonal dynamics are generated from the *outside.* We have a tendency to disown our part in what is occurring. We believe—often quite vehemently—that the trouble is being generated by the person with whom we are conversing.

Unfortunately, as we have stressed so often in this inquiry, many are unaware of what we call the *vertical dimension* of communication. By the term "vertical', we are referring to the domain of our own inner consciousness, as unconscious as we often are of either its power or existence. It is in this intra-psychic dimension that we can uncover all the past events of our biographical life, plus, as we have often pointed out, the dimension of biological birth and the experience of psycho-spiritual death/rebirth. Nor can we overlook the powerful influence of the transpersonal or archetypal domain of the psyche has in our moment-to-moment everyday life, as well. All of these nuances will be explored more deeply in our discussion of the *Awareness Positioning System.*

In these inner dimensions reside a high percentage of the motivations for our reactions in current interpersonal relationships—or, as we say, with someone *outside* us, on the *horizontal.* Yet, it is considered absolutely normal by most people that "the other" is the source of our own emotional and psychological trouble. We are just barely touching on an issue, here, that is so essential to our inquiry.

We have promised to address more fully how powerful these two levels of dynamics are in the holotropic work. In this case, we are referring to the synthesis between the *horizontal* and the *vertical* dimensions of who we are. In the GTT training, we commonly refer to the practice of embracing both the vertical and horizontal vectors of who we are as the *Yoga of the Cross,* or the *Awareness Positioning System.* Much more on this pivotal strategy later.

Presence and Emotional Clarity

There is a critical component of communication in countless situations that, when absent, only serves to sabotage, marginalize, or trivialize the true power in relationships. This component often results in a deep dissatisfaction and sense of incompletion within either or both of the participants in the interaction. This component is, of course, the *emotional* level—the realm of feelings.

As we pointed out, in this kind of deep inner work—and a host of other disciplines as well—feelings, or emotions, are often the "royal road" to transformation. These forces—for this is truly what they seem to be—are the human elements that are often the most highly charged with transformational power. This is true whether these emotions had a physical base, such as birth and other body trauma or pain. Or they may be generated strictly through biographical emotional interaction. Often they arise from unprocessed perinatal or transpersonal material. Or, as we often discover in deep work, our reactions may be the product of unprocessed material from across all dimensions of the psyche intermingled—in what we call a COEX, or *system of condensed experience*.

A person can be absolutely, physically present in relationship. He can also even be mentally present. By this, we mean that he clearly *understands* what is attempting to be communicated. But if there is no emotional component involved, it is for many people almost impossible for there to be an in-depth, enriching, magnetically authentic experience at the interpersonal level.

This stratum of arid, sterile, and to a certain extent inauthentic form of communication can stifle the transformational potential latent in so many interactions. In countless more like them, seekers who have done systematic inner work relate that they have been consciously or unconsciously looking for a vital sense of *connection*. What most people report they need seems to emerge, not just through the mind, but also through the *heart*.

As we pointed out, we may have hundreds of interactions every day in which we intuit there is no need to invest ourselves emotionally to anything more than a superficial extent. In fact, these types of interaction occur so normally that we are for the most part unconscious of any impulse toward anything else. Yet, even in these types of interactions, we hear from many people that, when presence includes an atmosphere of positive emotion, it is more likely to be creative of a refreshing, respectful set of impressions and results. We can often point to these particular encounters as having been imbued with a fuller sense of open-heartedness and an enhanced sense of wellbeing.

On the other hand, we also have countless interactions with family, friends, and co-workers where an atmosphere imbued with positive emotion or just that sense of *heart-felt* listening was entirely absent. Here again, deep inner work reveals what we call, not just a trauma of commission, but a trauma of *omission*. In these kinds of situations, it is not that we received something traumatic from the outside. Instead, our sense of psycho-emotional discomfort comes from the *absence* of the positive benefits possible in so many relationships.

Presence for Holotropic Facilitators

The above scenarios prepare us for the unveiling of our deepest inquiry at this point: the *power of presence* in the practice of Holotropic Breathwork facilitation. We have touched on physical, mental, and emotional presence in everyday human interaction. Of course, all of these are essential in holotropic work with breathers.

Physical presence is totally obvious—a "no-brainer," as we say. Our bodies must *be there* for the breather. We must also on occasion support the breathers with focused release work. The mental level is more nuanced. We as practitioners must also have acquired a thorough theoretical base of holotropic and transpersonal theory. In addition, we must receive and subsequently "own"—or thoroughly absorb—a rigorous theoretical and practical basis for specific holotropic strategy.

These bases include an in-depth explanation of all types of holotropic support and intervention for breathers' physical safety, as well the type of direct work that may be appropriate during the course of an inner session. Trainees also receive in-depth information on the all-important dynamics of what we call "working for closure," or integration at the end of the holotropic session. It also includes a cognitive facility for, as much as possible, impeccable interactions with breathers during the many challenging situations that may arise during the support of a breather.

These components of holotropic practice are taught to all trainees in modules devoted specifically toward this purpose. Of course, all trainees participate in specific, thorough demonstrations of, and practice engaging in, every nuance of physical, mental, and emotional contact with breathers. This includes the interventions themselves as well as other supportive strategies. It also includes an intense foray into the ethics of appropriate verbal interaction arising in the course of breathers' work in the expanded state of awareness.

This challenging training format takes place in intensives over a minimum of two years, and includes two major components. One is the process we have just outlined—an intellectual exercise in the nature of a "how-to" type format. However, the second is in almost every way the most important. This is the ongoing deep work every trainee is personally engaged in over the minimum of these two years. This includes a commitment to pursue regularly the adventure of self-discovery beyond the time of the training itself, by whatever means feel appropriate to the individual practitioner.

Those of us who teach this work have repeatedly shared with trainees the importance of our own individual practice and ongoing personal and transpersonal development. In lectures, I sometimes say that that one can learn the names of every muscle one uses in how to tread water, or float, or engage in specific types of strokes designed to propel one through that medium. We can also memorize the various molecular structures of the aquatic environment, the nature of breathing and holding the breath while under water, closing and opening the eyes, etc. Yet none of this will teach us how to swim. To do that we must actually get into the water and do it.

The nature of facilitator presence in holotropic support is similar to this particular metaphor on the nature of swimming. In this case we do not mean that the only way to be good at this type of facilitation is to actually practice a great deal working with breathers. Yes, of course, this is important. This is how we gain experience and at least a certain needed level of trust in the process.

Perhaps we imagine that if we can read most of the books ever written about presence, then we will be able to support breathers. The truth is there just are not that many sources in psychological literature to specifically address this dynamic. But there are a great many references to this among the texts of ancient wisdom and perennial philosophy.

If we believe that by doing this we will get some idea of presence, then we are absolutely correct. But all we will receive from reading and studying is just this: some *idea* of the reality and actual functioning of holotropic support. We will have gained some knowledge in our heads, in the same way that we would if we read a book about swimming in order to learn how to swim.

But even if we were to read every text on the nature of *presence*—both for our own growth and in our relationships with others—none of this would ever, ever prepare us to be truly present for breathers in the manner that would support them most impeccably in the holotropic relationship. To return to one of our central mantras of a power within: Our ability to support others in the sacred work of in-depth transformation is absolutely, entirely based on *the work we do on ourselves,*

As we have stated in various contexts, presence is essentially our *individual atmosphere*. It is the portion of Being that we as individuals radiate in the world, in all our interpersonal relations. As we said, we cannot fake it for very long. Regardless of how we *think* we are presenting ourselves to others, at some point—and often immediately—the reality, the truth of who we are, is either recognized or felt by those within the radius of our influence. *Presence never lies.*

Metaphorically, presence seems to be a constantly beaming output signal of the truth-telling power of our individual consciousness, or as some say, the soul. It is composed of all that we are aware or conscious of, and all that we are unaware of, or not in touch with yet about ourselves. Presence always reveals an ever-morphing dance between the various faculties of our being—those to which we have already alluded: our physical, emotional, and mental presentations of our selves in the world.

Yet these three characteristics are but a portion of presence. There is a meta-characteristic which encompasses these forces, and a whole lot more. Once again, our inquiry must take us beyond the domain of psychological orthodoxy. In so doing, it is essential—once again—that we acknowledge the Ganesha in the living room of presence. There is a womb, a matrix, in which these three modes of *humanness* are but instruments of operation in the planetary field. This womb is *numinosity* itself.

As we stated, this numinosity has become known and subsequently taught by virtually every spiritual system known to humankind. It is a vast realm of psycho-spiritual experience—in fact, unlimited in scope—that can be verified by anyone doing deep work in expanded states of consciousness. With this in mind, we can reiterate that presence is a manifestation of our Becoming—the ever-evolving outpouring of Being. Being, then, can be said to be none other than the ground of presence.

Yet we must still address the specific issue of holotropic support. In what way does presence actually affect the therapeutic unfolding and subsequent outcome of any holotropic experience? In an ideal universe, a facilitator in a holotropic experience would operate entirely from the domain of pure being itself.

In other words, she would be a pristinely clear representative of spirit, not down-stepped in any way by any of the multiple domains of the Becoming—what we colloquially call "our stuff." To sum up, these modifications of Being in its manifestation as a Becoming would include any and all conscious or unconscious psychological and/or physical material emerging from the biographical, perinatal, or transpersonal domains.

Any manifestation of this conscious or unconscious material can inform, influence, direct, and sometimes even control energetically the "operating vehicle" of the facilitator, including her mental, emotional, and physical domains and responses in the world around her. We may employ our "lens" metaphor again to describe the way presence influences, and even co-creates, how we perceive or experience other persons in a direct or indirect interaction. We might also say, then, that the clear light of being becomes a prism of manifestation as it shines through the conscious and unconscious material operating within the facilitator at any given time.

As we suggested, in an ideal universe, of course, we as facilitators and support people would be perfectly clear, having cleansed ourselves through systematic inner work—by the grace or the fiat of our own inner healing resources—of all patterns and influences from all dimensions of our consciousness. So far, we can safely say that none of us have been anywhere close to this crystal clear mirror through which the light of being can shine unsullied. In view of this admission, the good news is two-fold: First, there is an entire array of human psycho-physical characteristics that, for the most part, are not therapeutically toxic and would not in the majority of cases have any negative influence that we know of for the breather.

Secondly, we should never forget the seemingly miraculous, grace-bestowing inner, often unconscious presence of the breather—what we call the Inner Healer, or a power within. As we have mentioned, a well-known mantra throughout the world holotropic community states that breathers heal, not *because* of who we facilitators are, but *in spite* of who we are. As we say, the breathers are fine. They have Inner Healers, a healing resource always readily available for true self-empowerment and optimal psycho-spiritual healing.

Still, several issues thicken the plot as to what type of influence a facilitator's presence has—for good or ill—in a seeker's process. We often witness what we call a "cosmic setup" taking place as the result of a fateful interaction between a particular breather and facilitator. The following tale is a classic example of how this can happen.

A Holotropic Scenario on Presence

Imagine a seeker at her first training module who, in her childhood, was the victim of possessive, smothering, aggressively over-protective parents. Who knows what her parents' childhoods were like? It is clear that they never had the opportunity to work on themselves psychologically. Or if they did, they were not successful. They did not make their own traumas conscious, which, from our holotropic standpoint, is a primary goal. Driven by their own need for love, they projected this onto their child, overwhelming her with a diabolically twisted form of auto-focused infatuation that was little more than a passive-aggressive, self-centered possessiveness.

The result of this for the child—now a young woman—was that she internalized a reservoir of resentment, which deepened over the years and overflowed into a powerful hotbed of rage. As a side-effect, this anger left her fiercely mistrusting of any show of affection toward herself from others. For her, love was suspect at best, and likely dangerous, or else nothing but total selfishness. Needless to say, this situation makes healthy interpersonal relationships almost an impossibility.

Her smoldering rage had two dimensions. First was the anger toward her parents for stifling her throughout her childhood. Second, there was a kind of double-bind, in which she forcefully rejected from others the very thing she needed: a love unadulterated with selfish motives. She always felt an inexplicable need to lash out in self-protection at what she systematically interpreted as attempts by others to control her for the fulfillment of their own needs.

For simplicity in our inquiry here, we are not even mentioning the deeper roots of her frustration and anger beneath her biography. In virtually every situation, a seeker will have perinatal as well as archetypal underpinnings, which provide more complex implications and roots to her surface situation. Suffice it to say, one of the most important things she would probably need, at least at some point, would be support to release her pent-up rage in a very safe place.

Now, we turn to an apprentice facilitator at her first module as a helper. In her breathing experiences while in the training, she has begun to get in touch with a trauma both similar and different from that of the young woman who has come to the workshop. For her, the principal trauma centered around abandonment and neglect—what we call a *trauma of omission.*

As in the case of the seeker, this would also mean that she did not receive from her parents the one thing she needed the most: a foundation of real love. The main difference, here, is that she, the apprentice facilitator, was simply neglected, whereas the seeker was overwhelmed with a false, aggressive, and selfishly focused attempt at love by her parents. This actually makes the seeker's trauma not just one of omission, but one of commission as well.

The need to be loved and supported unconditionally is everyone's inalienable right. In this case, the trauma of neglect for the apprentice is not something to be expunged or gotten rid of by abreaction. What she needs for healing centers around something that is missing. As we pointed out, healing traumas of omission requires the *receiving* of the missing thing— in this case the nurturing support from someone in her training, which is an effective therapeutic surrogate for the love the parents could not provide. We have all seen how creating a nurturing environment of holding—as for the breather who welcomes this while in her expanded state of awareness— "on the mat," as we say—has tremendous therapeutic power in Holotropic Breathwork.

Often our traumas are just below the surface of our conscious awareness—reflecting the natural tendency for that which is unconscious to move toward consciousness. These traumas are ready to burst forth into our everyday lives, activated by the countless stimuli to which we are subjected within our surroundings. Diabolically, these external stimuli often exactly match whatever trauma may be prevalent within our own psyches.

This accounts for the scenario where one would feel activated by a certain gestalt of stimuli in the first place, while another, in the exact same setting, would feel triggered by an entirely different set of factors. In any event, the emergence into consciousness of this kind of material represents, not a sign of pathology, but an appropriate function of the psyche and consciousness toward wellbeing—that is to bring into conscious currently relevant material from the unconscious. This function is, of course, what we call the Inner Healer, a power within.

To continue this example, all the stimuli in the breathwork room—and in particular that of this breather of whom we have spoken and upon whom she is correctly focused—bring the apprentice's trauma surging into consciousness. It is important to note that just because a pattern emerges into our awareness in no way ensures that we will have immediate insight into its origin. In most cases, we are just experiencing the introjected, intrapsychic material which is the result of the trauma as the various scenarios pour into our awareness. This is what is now happening in this facilitator apprentice's case. Consequently, she reacts in the way that she does in her everyday life when her own pattern is triggered by some kind of magnetically charged action/reaction in her own interpersonal dynamics with others.

She responds by acting out with her breather her own unmet need for love. She projects what *she herself* needs, as the facilitator, onto her breather, assuming that this is what the breather herself needs. She impetuously rushes in, grabs the breather, and attempts to hold her, or rock her, perhaps muttering, or at least imagining, "There, there, mommy's here." However, what she is offering her breather happens to be exactly the thing she did not receive *herself*, but what she desperately needs for her *own* healing.

However, again diabolically, the breather is experiencing the *exact opposite* of what the sitter thinks she is going through. What the breather actually needs is to express her anger and frustration at being smothered by her parents, while perhaps simultaneously, if not subsequently, experiencing a physical, emotional, and psychological rebirth of her own independence. Instead of being "smothered" by the facilitator, she needs space, as well as physical protection, to really surrender to the up-surging volcano of her own unexpressed rage and frustration. She does *not* need another person, like her parents, who was supposed to support her, actually use her once more to get her own needs met.

In this tableau, the facilitator's presence has been over-shadowed and contaminated by her own unconscious trauma. Her presence is irrevocably compromised. There is absolutely no way she can be a clear, therapeutic support for the breather. Instead of being "breather-focused," most of her attempts to support the breather will be reactive and *self-focused*. She is, for all intents and purposes, no longer part of the therapeutic solution. She has instead become unconsciously part of the problem. She is, as we have pointed out before in other contexts, another bead on the rosary of the breather's original trauma.

To amplify this critical issue of the facilitator's presence, we might add that, as a clear, conscious force of safety, support, and a love unclouded by personal need or co-dependence, the facilitator has essentially disqualified herself. She has become "hooked," as we say. From this point on through the remainder of the interaction, most of what will happen in this tableau will be, as teacher Ram Dass says, just more "grist for the mill" of both the breather and the facilitator's future efforts at transformation.

Keep in mind that we have explicated, here, only one inner unconscious issue or interpersonal dynamic that the facilitator and the breather are carrying. In fact, they each have quite a few patterns unconsciously motivating them and coloring, in kaleidoscopic ways, the lens through which they view their external environments, thereby creating what they think is a "real reality."

A Final Word on Presence

Perhaps the most effective way to impress upon ourselves the power of presence would be to focus on some time when we ourselves truly felt the power of this human and cosmic dynamic in our own lives. This could have been when we were very young, or at any point in our life journeys. In order to mobilize the forces of our consciousness toward this end, we might practice a moment of self-inquiry.

What was the scenario when the magic of presence occurred for us? Looking back, might we be able to recognize it, now that we have focused on it for a little while? Where were we, or with whom? By this self-inquiry, we can more easily bring online the critical importance of this presence in our work with others, as well as our own psycho-spiritual development.

From a meta-perspective, many feel that presence is ultimately a force of "Mother Nature" herself—that overwhelming silence which is alive and pregnant with creativity and power. This dynamic of presence does not feel personal, but somehow meta-personally omnipresent. It can feel as though the cosmos has the ability to focus its unlimited, multi-dimensional expansiveness into an almost overwhelming creative immediacy—all within a human context.

We have the gift of this type of presence in a deep forest, on the mountaintop, at the core of a subterranean cavern, on a placid lake, in the swell of a surging ocean tide, in the ruins of a magnificent temple, in the pregnant silence of a majestic cathedral, or in the arms of a lover. In truth, it is in this manifestation that countless inner adventurers recognize the face of the Beloved, or the spirit of the Divine that radiates from the presence of certain people whom we have been blessed to encounter on our life journeys.

Presence can also transform us while we are in the company of great poets, teachers, athletes, artists, children, infants of all species, and countless other sources. It is that profound depth of silence, of guilelessness, of consciousness, that within its apparent formlessness and untouchability there seems to dwell the unspeakable intensity of love and the sacred—all pinnacles of the power of presence.

Presence is the clear, unseen, untouchable mystery that we can truly feel but never name. It is one of the aspects that we remember about every special encounter we have ever had, yet can rarely articulate to ourselves or to others. In short, it is the footprint, the touch, the breath of the Great Mystery informing all that is.

When we find ourselves in musings of this sort—in attempting to formulate our confrontations with the miraculous—it tends to put our somewhat paltry discussion of *presence* for a holotropic facilitator into a more humble focus. So, is it to this far horizon of presence we are aspiring, in our heart-felt attempts to be present for breathers? Indeed, it is.

Does it matter that we will always fall pathetically short of such a perfect manifestation of this holotropic essentiality? No, it does not. Lest we despair, we must always—always—remind ourselves of one central truth. It is one of our mantras we have been reciting throughout this inquiry into a power within: We are all heir to the experience that, of our own false, limited selves, *we ourselves are not the doers of our work*—of our facilitation of others.

Breathers are already blessed with a perfect power within to heal themselves. Our job, as breathers go about this sacred business of healing themselves, is to be as clear as we can, based on a second-to-second commitment to do our own inner work. Why should we worry by taking on the impossible task of knowing what is best for another human being and then attempting to implement this in their lives? Our task is much more simple. It is to do the very best we can—to commit as wholeheartedly as possible to our own inner work. In doing this, we make the job of the breathers' Inner Healers a whole lot easier.

Our own presence is what emerges for us when we are not looking for the glory. It is what sneaks up on us, or peaks out from behind our masks, when we forget to pay attention to our own wants or how others may feel we are doing in the game of life. In its lower stage, we feel it is *our* presence. Later, after a few ego deaths, we come to understand that it is *just presence*—independent of us, impersonal, a force in which we live and breathe and move—in fact, consciousness itself. We know presence, but we do not know it. Breathers know it, because it is what helps them to feel trusting and safe. Presence is a paradox—at the same time an unknowable mystery, yet a mystery whose dynamis is the transformation of ourselves—an upgrade in our Becoming as we move toward wholeness and the mystery of Being itself.

Finally, we part the veil on the numinous once more, as we have done throughout our journey. In this instance, we invoke an experience that is reported in many metaphors by hundreds of breathers and seekers: Every aspect of presence we have mentioned here is but a flavor of an un-nameable mystery permeating the realm of humanity and existence itself.

Behind each of these characteristics, and beneath, as wings which support all that we have attempted to explore—and from within, as the living essence of a seed as it bursts forth into manifestation—exists the power mystics and scientists alike have attempted to describe. Each seeker before us has done this in her own metaphor and from the heart of her own passion. It is Presence itself—the thought, power, feeling, and mystery of the Great Mystery itself gazing through every particle of creation.

This is the power that permeates every sacred spot, and every hotel ballroom floor where Holotropic Breathwork is taking place. Do we actually think we have presence "pinned down" now? Whether we do or don't, we can always *hope* that we manifest it, at least in part, as we do our best to support breathers on the mat. No doubt, we must, at least in part. Every mystical system, in its own way, is a testament to this power, this presence, this essence of who we are and what is always larger than this. As we have said, in a host of different metaphors, our task is to be as open as we can, to allow whatever vestige of this mystery to inform us as our own inner work affords.

This task ultimately leads us—not to be healers ourselves—but to trust the most perfect presence of all—the power within each breather— the only true doer of the work. The good news is that we are not required to be super-efficient at this allowing. After all, we are each only manifesting a certain vestige of what we call the Becoming. Being is, for most of us, still the lighthouse somewhere far beyond us, or deeper within us than we have yet fathomed. However, we *are* required to recognize where true greatness lies: always, already in the hearts of every breather we have the blessing to support.

[handwritten margin note:] Alignment — Unhindered those Let Her Flow through

[handwritten note at bottom:] Healer vs Witness

CHAPTER XV

The Underpinnings of a Holotropic Therapy

Our next inquiry into the power within introduces us to an exciting epoch of our holotropic adventure—the unveiling of a holotropically-oriented psychotherapy. We hope we have communicated our great respect for the, so far, barely tapped power of Holotropic Breathwork and the implications of a holotropic perspective for individual and collective psycho-spiritual transformation.

We would hope, as well, that we have at least flirted with the possibility a holotropic paradigm holds as an ancient, yet at the same time revolutionarily modern, recreated matrix of personal power for individual and planetary evolution. We have also steadfastly maintained that this holotropic worldview may play a vital role in rechanneling humanity's outer-directed addiction to power toward the infinite resources of healing power always already latent within every individual.

We begin with a recap of the core holotropic strategy with which facilitators are intimately familiar. Each of these components is also a cornerstone of any therapeutic endeavor derived from the core holotropic perspective:

First, the Inner Healer is the sole, infallible source of healing for breathers.

Second, facilitators are always supporters and never directors of a seeker's process. Their job is to function as co-adventurer or even midwife, as well as to keep seekers safe—physically, emotionally, mentally, and spiritually.

Third, there are three essential parts to every holotropic session: *preparation, session, integration.* We have emphasized that integration is the most important for positive therapeutic and psycho-spiritual outcome.

Fourth, Holotropic Breathwork functions homeopathically: that is, breathers heal by intensification of whatever is emerging into consciousness during a session—physically, emotionally, mentally.

In imagining the implementation of holotropic dynamics into what we may call a holotropic therapy, or holotropic support for self-exploration

via entheogens, or a holotropic structure for spiritual emergency or addic-
tions recovery work, these requirements, outlined above, must also be the
indisputable bases for any such therapeutic endeavors.

The following is a more detailed description of the origins of, and
bases for, any currently emerging holotropic strategy providing the revolutionary potential as a foundation for a holotropic therapy.

The Holotropic Sharing Group: Blueprint for the Adventure of a Holotropic Therapy

We are closing in on a multi-tiered application of holotropic dynamics
toward which we have been moving this entire adventure: a holotropic therapy, entheogen work, a rethinking of mental illness as spiritual emergency, a
revolutionary approach to addiction recovery, and a wellness model of psycho-spiritual health. Toward that end, a rigorous study of an authentic holotropic sharing group is critical. It is within the dynamics of this unique style
of group strategy and interaction that we find the "keys to the kingdom"—a
blueprint for the true power inherent in this revolutionary perspective.

In Holotropic Breathwork, the sharing group is the primary setting for
the integration phase of any holotropic enterprise. Yet it is toward the end
of a breather's experience on the mat where the first stages of actual integration begin. In particular, this occurs when she opens her eyes and gazes
around her, thereby beginning a transition into what we call the *hylotropic*,
or a matter-oriented, or ordinary state of consciousness. At this point, a
facilitator should always approach the breather to initiate an episode of
verbal, and, if necessary, experiential interaction that may help her feel
more whole. By more whole, we mean that she feels as physically, emotionally, mentally, and spiritually complete as she can be for that day.

However, integration almost always reaches its culmination during the
sharing group episode, which follows soon after the end of the breathing
session. In reality, when we speak of integration, we are referring to what
we call a "completion, within the larger field of incompletion," which
seems to be the general nature of an evolutionary healing process. Integration often continues quite beyond the end of all phases of the workshop,
always with the ongoing support of the facilitator team when necessary.

Most seekers report that, no matter how powerful and valuable an
episode of deep breathing can be, at some point they will once again hear
the "piper calling" from beyond. This seems to be the general nature of
psycho-spiritual evolution—this completion within the larger field of
incompletion—manifesting as the continued episode of Becoming, within
the arms of the meta-framework of Being.

This kind of further support—beyond the actual sharing group session—includes verbal and online communication, referrals to supportive professional and non-professional milieus, as well as access to further experiential work by facilitators in what we call a "clearing session." However, along with successful completion of the experiential work on the mat, the sharing group—the final episode of the holotropic experience—is the most efficacious element of the integration process.

The sharing group holds tremendous potential for optimum fulfillment, integration, and the most effective resolution of the breather's experience. In addition, it is here that the breather often experiences cognitive and emotional clarifications, as well garnering the most enlightening insights into the power of what has transpired on the mat and how these may be implemented in her everyday life.

Most importantly, it is here that she is unequivocally validated for the work she has done, and the insights she has derived from the experience, as well as being supported for whatever the plan may be for her future, as she moves on into the next phase of her life. All this occurs as the Inner Healer, through a power within, continues to orchestrate a cellular, multi-leveled integration of which the seeker may not even be aware. Yet this orchestration is always given deference by facilitators in their interaction with breathers.

The principles which characterize and shape the holotropic sharing group will represent a vital component of any holotropic therapy that has already, or will in the future, emerge from a Holotropic Paradigm. The psychotherapeutic elements that comprise this integrative strategy center around the principles of interaction between breather and facilitator, as well as breather with breather. What happens within these relationships reflect the potential inherent in the holotropic perspective to be of dynamic applicability in the host of other therapeutic settings we have mentioned, some of the most exciting of which we will soon explore.

Traditional therapy involves, first and foremost, a *relationship* between a person seeking support, and the one—the therapist—who provides such support. Historically, for many people, within the broad ranges of possible therapeutic support, therapy may bring to mind a setting, such as an office with a sofa, a desk, or two chairs—one occupied by the therapist and the other—across the desk—the client.

What happens between these two? For one, they often talk. The nature of these conversations will follow the strategy and pathways espoused by the particular therapy in which the support person has been trained. We should mention that almost all of what is true for the initiation of a holotropic individual therapy would also be true for a holotropically-oriented group therapy—of course accounting for a holotropic negotiation of additional group dynamics.

Sadly, a great many traditional "therapeutic" interactions today end with the support person scribbling a few words on a pad, tearing off the piece of paper, passing it to the client across the desk; or typing a few words into a computer or a cell phone. The seeker will then go to her pharmacy for her prescription, the primary function of which is the alleviating of a set of symptoms she previously discussed with the person on the other side of the desk. Knowing what we know about the current mental heath paradigm, we seem to be revealing an almost unbridgeable gulf between what we have come to see as a therapeutic norm and what we are proposing as we unveil a holotropic therapy.

Throughout this inquiry, we have been exploring a therapeutic, or, at another octave, psycho-spiritual strategy, where the client may lie on a mat with a support person by her side—often with many more seekers in a darkened room around her—each with a sitter/support person and a number of facilitators walking among them.

When the "therapy" begins, quite loud, powerful, evocative music fills the room. The client's role is to close her eyes, and breathe rhythmically—a little faster, a little deeper, and a little more continually than she ordinarily breathes. Or this may be an inviting setting where the seeker does her inner work individually, with a sitter and holotropic practitioner present solely for her support.

Along with the didactic introduction, in preparation for this phase, she has been encouraged to pay attention, as she breathes, to whatever emerges within her mind, her body, or her emotional self. The therapist's—or facilitator as she is called—as well as the sitter's role, is to keep the breather mentally, emotionally, physically, and spiritually safe.

She, the facilitator, only intervenes to offer support if the breather asks for help, or if she becomes quite active and needs supportive contact for her safety, or if she directly makes a request for nurturing. The final episode of intervention is a non-negotiable requirement, and takes place at the end of the session when a breather opens her eyes and signals she is finished. This is a very special part of the session, which we will cover in great detail soon.

During the contact occurring after the breather has asked for support, the facilitator would encourage her to express as fully as possible whatever it is she may be experiencing. This can be either physical, emotional, or intra-psychic, or any combination of these, of which she has become aware as the result of the systematic deeper breathing. This is in keeping with the holotropic dictum, that a seeker heals by intensification of whatever her manifesting so-called "symptoms" are—or the physical, mental or emotional signposts indicating the continued work of the breather's power within.

Facilitators are not at all required to know what is happening for the breather. Nor is it their role to control, guide, or direct her in any particular way, or to offer any kind of diagnosis or opinion about what she may be going through. Their role is, as Irvin Yalom has said, to **support, support, support.**

With these images in mind, think back to the original therapeutic strategy we mentioned before—the one in the office, the desk, and the prescription pad. The differences in these two formats—office, on the one hand, and breathwork room floor, on the other—represent what might well be called "quite a stretch"! It is not so much that the settings and methodologies are antithetical to each other. Something even deeper and more revolutionary than these dynamics is actually in play.

The really interesting question before us—and the goal of our explication in this section is, *"Could the Holotropic Breathwork strategy in the hotel ballroom be in any way translatable to a traditional therapist's environment?"* Even more to the point, *"Are there viable components of the holotropic perspective—even if they appear antithetical to traditional therapy—which, in fact, while still absolutely holotropic—represent a powerful alternative to the traditional office milieu, even while still taking place within that very same office?"*

To answer these questions, we refer again to the principles of the holotropic sharing group. For a support person, among the obvious tenets are total reliance on the seeker's inner healing resources, and to never see herself as the director of the inner work. These elements are the core of the breathwork experience itself. *They are also the underpinnings of the sharing group experience as well.* The facilitator "holds space" while the breather shares her experience in a non-directive atmosphere imbued with total support, trust, and safety.

In addition to verbal interaction with the facilitator and the rest of the group, the seeker may also share what we call her *mandala*—a drawing or painting of her experience—or a written story, or her experience of any one of a number of supportive creative practices in which she may have engaged at the end of the breathwork experience itself.

These sharings—along with her verbal account of what happened for her in the session—represent a further emergence and flowering of integrative, healing possibilities from her inner work on the mat. In the exact same manner as the final stage of her work in the breathing room—and the rest of the breathwork, for that matter—the facilitator is there totally as a support person. She is always as non-directive as possible through the whole of this critical phase.

To further clarify this crucial difference between the holotropic perspective and most traditional modalities, we should juxtapose a pair of therapeutic poises representing two ends of a therapeutic continuum. As we pointed out in other contexts, these are based on what we call *reduction* and *amplification*. Reduction refers to a nearly universal strategy of therapists to channel, or reduce, what they hear from the client into whatever framework on which they have been taught to rely. But of course we do this! Why else would we be trained in a particular method, if not to trust, and then implement, this method as a lens through which we see, and subsequently hope to understand, diagnose, prescribe, and otherwise be of support for, our clients' dilemmas?

For a holotropic inquiry, the problem with this strategy is easy to ascertain. Diagnosis is arrived at through *reducing* the contents of the experience, and their implications, to whatever the specific coloration of the lens through which the therapist is gazing. As we have recently explored, by coloration, we mean the psycho-therapeutic paradigm taught by the therapist's school, which has now become the worldview coloring the lens of the specific therapist.

We also must include, as a powerfully influential factor, the consciousness at which the therapist is operating—what we call her *being level*, or *presence*. This would, of course, include the amount of inner work she herself has done. In the holotropic universe, this would also involve experientially—not just intellectually—familiarizing herself with the realms of the extended cartography of the psyche.

The critical problem with the above traditional approach is that such a predominant, multi-faceted reduction is often, in essence, a case of well-intentioned ignorance. Well-intentioned or not, this reduced lens can still be a framework quite limited in transformational power and possibilities. Such a strategy explicitly sabotages the basically unlimited potential, as well as profound mystery, of unexpected healing opportunities, inherent in the deepest therapeutic processes, guided by the insightful power of the Inner Healer. These are multi-leveled processes—ones that so frequently bring into awareness relevant material from not just the biographical level of the psyche, but the perinatal and the transpersonal as well. It is highly unlikely that any foray into the exotic depth of the infinite psyche can be directed through the lens of most traditional therapies—even a substantial percentage of those few which see the psyche as larger than the biographical dimension alone.

This essential ignorance of the deeper dimensions of the psyche—an "unknowing," masquerading as *de facto* truth—thereby often straight-jackets the therapist's evaluation of who the client truly is in the full expression of her current life manifestation, as well as her unlimited potentiality. Even more disheartening, at this point the "lens-specific" treatment strategy is in many cases designed to *suppress* whatever spectrum of symptoms has been highlighted through that modality's particular worldview.

In addition, most therapists will be operating from a baseline view of dysfunction, or sickness, thereby ignoring the unlimited possibilities in a wellness perspective. And—lest we forget the obvious cogent point—the therapeutic potential is, for the most part, greatly reduced by the primary use of a "talking strategy" to ascertain relevant issues. This strategy can often be a limiting distraction, when compared with the potential of the deep breathing to quite easily bring into the seeker's awareness a treasure-house of relevant material from previously unavailable deeper strata of the seeker's psyche.

The above scenario is frequently the case, even if therapists may offer a tangential, or even overt, nod to reliance on the inner resources of the client. In this scenario, what we frequently hear from new breathers who come to us after some therapy is that this half-hearted focus on self-empowerment has only manifested as a more or less superficial, ultimately impotent level of "lip service." Instead of providing an atmosphere imbued with potential for radical self-empowerment, it can actually create an additional element of doubt, sometimes resulting in an even deeper experience of trauma.

If the therapist—of course, in attempting to do the opposite—unconsciously displays an inauthentic, half-hearted show of support for the client's trust in her own self-empowerment, a kind of therapeutic double-bind can be communicated to the seeker. In this situation, the additional trauma of the double-bind may result in a greater level of either conscious or unconscious distrust in herself, the therapist, or both. This, then, can lead the client to perhaps question her own ability to heal, thereby cementing her belief that the therapist knows best and has a power to heal that she herself does not. This is exactly what we mean by the perpetuation of radical disempowerment.

The good news is that after the holotropic work, clients often recognize that in many previous situations, true empowerment has only been peripherally implemented, if not dismissed outright in the therapeutic dynamic. They gain the insight that empowerment of their true selves is a fundamental healing mechanism they themselves have discovered and embraced from within their own psyches in the holotropic work. The seeker frequently reports that she has been able to move beyond the entanglements of her self-doubt, as well as many other negative influences of her own previous low self-esteem.

We have highlighted the controlling power that our lenses hold through which we evaluate another person, or the nature of reality itself. We have pointed out that the more expansive the lens through which we view a seeker, the more personally empowering and effective will be the work of the seeker herself. In short, ideally, a universally expansive lens would hold maximum potential for the self-empowerment of any seeker. This is what we call *amplification,* as an antidote or alternative for the nearly global tendency among therapists toward *reduction* to their own circumscribed strategy.

We should perhaps face the fact that very few traditional modalities come anywhere close to honoring the panoramic lens through which Stan was able to view existence during the peak of his LSD experience in the Prague clinic. In expanded states of consciousness, the traditional "truth" that we are biographical entities alone is, in fact, often unmasked as no more than a metaphysical assumption.

Nor do many of these biographically oriented methods provide strategies powerful enough for the seeker to access the full spectrum of intrapsychic material. There are two foundations of the wide lens to which we are referring: First is a method powerful enough—such as entheogens or Holotropic Breathwork—to access the deeper dimensions of who we are. The second is the comprehensive worldview, or extended cartography of the psyche, that develops and becomes available through the deep experience.

However, even if we as practitioners have not fully viewed reality and the healing adventure through this ultimately expansive type of lens, the *greater possibilities* of what can be experienced through this lens must become the lighthouse beacon toward which we aspire in the holotropic work we do to support others. Anything less than a willingness to embrace at least the *potential* of this wide open perspective is a therapeutic disservice.

As we have shared, we as support persons do not have to be perfect at this endeavor of a lifetime. What we really need is commitment to a daily *sadhana* of some kind of rigorous psycho-spiritual growth. The humility to trust in seekers, accrued through this systematic inner work we ourselves do, will be the foundation of the essential presence we must exhibit in order to fully "go downstream" with breathers in their own inner adventures.

For us to be personally impeccable and to operate from a broad perspective of transformational possibilities—through as wide a lens as we are able to envision—we must at least aspire to the archetype of the infinitely wide-open vista. In addition, we must have no illusions as to the actual depth of the particular lens through which we are in fact viewing the journeys of the seekers we attempt to support.

Any facilitator who has been "going down stream" with inner voyagers for quite a while in Holotropic Breathwork has a number of exciting stories to share about those times she was faced with something brand new, wild, and free, emerging within a breather's process. It is here that we are really required to "walk our talk"!

As always, we rely on a dictum sometimes attributed to Plato's Socratic, yet now holotropic mantra: that we are certain of the one thing we know—*that we do not know.* How could we ever, ever know what is truly best for another human being? This lens of unknowing is in many ways a powerful foundation of what we may intuit to actually be a vast and mighty knowing. With anything less than a heart-felt commitment to either of these poises—to the most expanded sense of existence, as well as the unlimited possibilities of self-empowerment—we fail to reach the full potential of holotropic support that seekers truly deserve.

What, then, is the best way to communicate to the seeker this so-called therapeutic limitation we all possess—that we do not have the power to heal them? Through our interactions with the breather—in the preparation talk, on the mat during the breathwork, and in the sharing group after-wards—our *presence* should communicate to her that transformation is a great mystery—that we know that we do not know.

However, there is one thing we definitely *do* know: We are absolutely certain that the breather—through opening to her own deepest inner heal-ing resources—most assuredly *does* know, or *can* know, at some deep level of her own self. It is a bedrock truth for us that she can fully heal herself, in her own Inner Healer's time. The truth is, we just cannot fake this level of trust.

Our presence—for good or ill—will always be a testimony of where we truly are in our own journey toward wholeness, as well as our ability to support others. From the moment we meet a participant, or have any other contact with her, it is our task to communicate through whatever presence we have—our words, actions, and attitude—that we honor her seeking and are committed to supporting her intellectually, emotionally, physically, and spiritually.

Further, it is our sacred responsibility to attempt to instill in every word, gesture, and action that we take on her behalf that we absolutely trust her to heal herself. When the accolades are heaped upon us, as they so often are through seekers' tremendous gratitude, we must be impeccable in therapeutically reframing such praise so that they may learn to honor them-selves and their own inner healing resources.

Within the holotropic share-group setting, when a breather is "report-ing in," there are two levels to the necessary reliance on the inner resources of the breather. The first is quite straightforward and comparatively easy to implement. This involves a situation where the breather shares that she is doing well—is in a good place—and that she feels complete. By this we mean that she feels open, and that a resolution of her process has occurred—physically, emotionally, mentally, and spiritually. It would also mean that she may already have some valuable insight into her experiences in her session. As we shared, we refer to these resolutions as "completion, within the larger field of incompletion."

The seeker's revelations tend to shed light on either her current life situations; her past, including any experience of the perinatal and transpersonal domains; or where she feels she is to journey from here, into her future. In these situations, the facilitator's role is often one of a caring co-journeyer—one who is a witness and supporter of the breather's adventure. The support person becomes one who applauds the efforts of the seeker without judgment, direction, or sense of ownership. In every case, the atmosphere should be a celebration and honoring of a job well done.

In some cases, however, even though she felt integrated when she first got up from the mat, a breather may now feel somewhat incomplete. Her sense of incompletion can include some physical discomfort; unfamiliar, seemingly random thought processes; or perhaps emotional states with which she may be previously familiar, yet may be more glaringly intense than she has felt before.

Or she may share emotional material or physical sensations that are currently emerging into her awareness, and which are quite new. In addition, a breather often has a sense that her previous "mode of operation" in the earth life sphere has been rearranged. She may feel that new, somewhat disconcerting insights, vistas, and possibilities are now at the forefront of her consciousness. For these reasons, she may feel fearful to some degree—and of what she may not be so certain.

Once again, our job as support persons is to "hold space" and to honor the breathers exactly where they are. This honoring should reflect our willingness to once again go downstream with them—in this case not in the expanded state, but in the everyday mode of consciousness. One of the most effective healing gifts we can give breathers in these situations comes from the psycho-spiritually powerful Twelve Step traditions. For example, in Alcoholics Anonymous, seekers are taught that the only thing we really have to offer another person is our own "experience, strength, and hope." We do not tell seekers what they should feel or think, or how they should conduct themselves in every-day circumstances. Instead, we offer what *we ourselves* have experienced.

This type of support is truly unsurpassed. It affords us, as support people, to once again, model that of which we speak. That is, that we have no idea what is best for them. However, we are totally willing to go all the way with them, so that they can feel from within themselves what paths they might negotiate. It is this co-adventure—with the breather and ourselves—where we are not the expert or the guide, that has such an alchemically powerful transformational potential.

We may seek permission to ask them a question or two. We must definitely not resort to a prescribed mode of traditional therapy. It should simply be a demonstration of true caring, courage, support, and a desire to learn more about the breather's situation, simply to serve her better. It is, as well, a willingness to help the seeker move toward a satisfactory completion of her inner, and now, *outer* experience.

We must learn to "draw her out"—that is, to gently encourage her to share a little more, and then a little more. We must learn to be conscious of that for which she is asking. This help may include a new angle, or another amplified psychological or psycho-spiritual lens through which to view and ultimately understand what has occurred. Or it can be just good, old-fashioned emotional support.

This support may include inquiring of her how she is feeling in her body or her emotional level, or how comfortable she may be cognitively. Remember, this is not therapy—calling up a litany of enquiries we have learned through a certain school. Our job is to carefully gather whatever information we may need from what she shares, and what she shows us by her physical, mental, and emotional presence. All of these goals serve the one purpose of assisting her to frame for herself her experience. Often, as she feels our presence and willingness to be there, the integration proceeds beautifully—always under the auspices of her own Inner Healer.

If uncomfortable physical sensations have emerged since she got up from the mat, we share with her ways to support herself through this very normal phase of the integration phase. Or we can ascertain if she perhaps wishes to do a little intensification clearing work at the end of the sharing session. Often our task is simply to allow her to feel that she is doing beautifully, and to hold open-hearted and supportive space while she proceeds to experience as much trust in herself as she can. In the meantime, she now has the time to become acquainted with the new emotional, physical, or psychological states in which she finds herself.

Again, we are trusting that she will feel "complete, within the larger field of incompletion." Often, her fellow group members will wish to offer support. Our job at this point is to be sure that this occurs, not as some lecture or type of traditional therapeutic grandstanding, but again in the mode of being a caring "cheerleader" or trusted support person.

Attempts by fellow group members to "therapize" her, or to "show off" in some way, rarely occurs, especially if we ourselves have been modeling an approach that puts the helper in the role of a co-adventurer, not the healer or the therapist. However, when it does occur, we immediately reframe the dialogue in some way that protects the breather who is sharing, as well as gently but firmly redirecting the feedback from the other group member who is probably, for the most part, just good-heartedly attempting to be of some help.

Periodically, we may ask the seeker how she is feeling in this current moment. In almost all cases, a breather will report feeling much better, and ultimately having a sense of understanding and closure for the journey. Anyone who reports that she may still feel incomplete, or whom we ourselves may see as possibly not quite finished, we either engage in this moment, or let them know that we will spend time with them when the sharing group is over. Or we return to them later, after other group members have shared.

The final piece of the support group is devoted to the facilitator's sharing of what we have seen and heard from breathers, as well as our own adventures post-session, and about what they might expect upon the return home. This includes our own "experience, strength, and hope" about how to be with loved ones and friends, how to stay in touch with others from the community, what our dreams may be like, the most effective diet within their own framework that most supports deep work, spending time in nature, and the need to stay open to what their Inner Healers are attempting to share with them that they may need.

We also provide guidelines about where they can continue this type of deep exploration, or other milieus complementary to holotropic work. In addition, we share other supportive hints about how to readjust to this "new self" they have become as the result of their deep work.

One important concluding suggestion is that breathers should be encouraged to re-ground themselves in whatever therapy, support group, or spiritual discipline in which they were involved before the breathwork. Or, if these now feel incompatible with what they have learned about themselves, our task may be to offer suggestions on new possibilities. Our suggestions should always be framed within the strategy of encouraging seekers to trust their own inner healing power in choosing with whom to work.

CHAPTER XVI

Interlude: An Amplification of Amplification

Those of us who worked with Stan and Christina from the beginning of the current training format—from around 1990 onward—were blessed in countless ways. One of the most precious gifts involved the hours we spent with Stan in the sharing groups after every breathwork session. During that early era, the share groups started rather late—after all but the final few breathers' volcanic sessions were complete for the day, up off the mat, and having had a good, grounding dinner.

These groups were marathons. Sometimes we did not get to bed until 1:00 am. Then we would be up and at work—holding consultations with participants an hour before breakfast, then through breakfast, up until we began the group at 9:00 am.

As exhausted as we were, we would not have missed these late-night/into-the-early-morning sessions for anything. It was here that Stan might go "off script"—if there ever really was a script during the daily lectures and teachings. It was here that we truly had the chance to see what he meant by *amplification*, as well as countless other valuable holotropic strategies. We were clear about *reduction*—an attempt by the guide or therapist to force the breadth and power of a holotropic experience into a narrow, traditional framework, resulting in adding just one more bead on participants' rosaries of disempowerment. But amplification was an art form at which we would learn to marvel.

Here is a typical snapshot of these marathons: By 10:00 pm, nearly everybody in the sharing circle gave up sitting in their chairs, and more or less slid to the floor on the mats and cushions that covered everything. This included Stan, who needed no podium to "hold forth." Breathers would share their sessions—on the continuum somewhere between either a kind of *fait accompli*, or a searching, wandering attempt to find meaning amid a kaleidoscope of inner, often confusing experiences. Probably one of the few attributes of Stan's that matched his encyclopedic knowledge was his unlimited curiosity about—well, everything.

To keep it simple, imagine that a breather reports that she had a powerful inner experience of a snake. This experience had catalyzed vivid imagery and intense emotions, with which she worked on the mat. This took place in the homeopathic manner of which we spoke, where she was supported by a facilitator to intensify whatever was emerging in her body, her emotional being, or by some vocal means if this felt right. However, even after all this deep work, she finished the session still somewhat in wonder, and a little confused by what had happened.

In other words, her Inner Healer had not yet finished assisting her in fitting all the puzzle pieces of her journey together in a way that might provide the in-depth insight for which she was searching. However, since she was tired, and her body felt relaxed, she reported that she was willing to "be with it" for a while. Breathers sometimes refer to this "don't know" place as "surrendering to the mystery."

At about 11:30 pm, it was her turn to share. By then, we "beat-up" facilitators were secretly dreaming of our beds. But Stan was just getting started. The participant shared what happened, and, of course, spoke of the experience with the snake. She reported that the only psychological references she had previously seen came from some forms of biblical Christianity and a Freudian interpretation in which the snake was a symbol of male sexuality—of course, having something to do with the penis. Or else it was the Devil himself. She admitted that she just could not, in any way, relate to either of these interpretations, other than to feel insulted, irritated, and dismissive of them when these musings arose while she was in the experience on the mat.

When she shared this, she became silent. Then, she and the rest of the group slowly turned, all eyes on Stan. Their expressions revealed what they expected—that Stan would now *diagnose* her, pointing out the true meaning of the snake in her session. First, however, he asked her a few questions, checking on how she was feeling physically and emotionally—basically encouraging her to continue to share as much as she wished. Then he asked her to say a little more about her experience with the snake, which for her was still clouded in mystery.

Now, here is archetypal Stan—in an interaction with a breather and the rest of the group. What he shared reflected a revolutionary, psychotherapeutic way of being, like hundreds that we witnessed over the years, which became the blueprint of how we ourselves would learn to interact with breathers in our own groups. This was also the archetype of how we would be working with facilitator-trainees later, who may have been looking at us in a similar, yet mitigated, way as we were when looking at our mentor that night. Stretched out on one elbow on the mat as he was, we knew we were in for the "long haul." And, like so many sharings before and since, it was magical delight to witness.

Many of his questions and points would begin with, "Well, I don't pretend to know, but in the (fill in the blank) culture, there is this ritual..." Or teaching, myth, whatever. Then he would hold forth, while we all woke right up once again and began to absorb another dose of priceless information. But more precious than the information was the style of his support. Yes, it was a sharing, not a therapeutic interaction—at least not in the form that anyone of us had known before. He was simply "casting bread upon the lake"—allowing whatever "being from the depths" would rise, bearing a diamond of insight for the breather.

He proceeded with *no agenda*, no pre-conceived sense of knowing what she may have experienced, or what might be the implications for her in her healing and life-unfolding. He was just providing a broader, wider field of inquiry for her inspiration—always holding mental and emotional space for her, waiting to see what her Inner Healer might seize upon in a flurry of revelation and excitement—or not.

He believed with all his heart, and ultimately we did too, that her Inner Healer would reveal her truth to her in its own perfect time. She would know it—right then, six months later, or whenever. But no matter how long it took, no matter how much breathwork, or study, or therapy, she had already received the most priceless gift of all. She would continue to benefit from this treasure for as long as she continued her inner odyssey, and even after. This diamond was the emergence of a power within—her Inner Healer. The underpinning of her entire search would always be the priceless gift she gave herself of personal empowerment.

So, what did she discover in this situation? I really do not remember. We witnessed this with Stan and Christina hundreds of times. And we have witnessed it with seekers in our groups for as many times, and more. This is what we mean by *amplification*—merely providing a broader, more creative and expansive universe of possibilities. An insight arrived at in these situations may or may not be what the breather ultimately realizes about herself.

Yet, the most precious value of the process lies in the power of her Inner Healer—allowed to manifest unrestrictedly, in our willingness to be holotropic. We have been saying this throughout our inquiry: that is, to go down stream with the breathers, and to keep them from bumping their heads. When we do this, and stay out of the way as much as we can, miracles will happen.

Each of us has experienced our own versions of doubt countless times—not about the Inner Healer, but about our ability to hold that much knowledge of world myth, culture, and mystical systems. But we needn't have worried. We remember Stan saying on a number of occasions, when he himself just simply had no idea of how to most helpfully provide an effective amplified lens for a breather, "Oh, I wish Joseph were here; he would know ..." Of course, he was referring to his dear friend Joseph Campbell, one of the world's most famous mythologists.

In lieu of our not being good friends with Joseph Campbell, we all learned quite quickly the value of a good dictionary of symbols to have in the share group. This was not so that we would know what was occurring for a breather, who was in the dark about what had happened for her. It was simply a wonderful feeling for us to be able to hand *her* the volume—ask her to take a look over the next few days, and see if something struck *her* fancy, if some light came on—often providing what we sometimes call the "a-ha" experience.

But this issue of "acting the expert" can be a complex, tricky thing. In one evening sharing group during my own certification, I was very fortunate to have Stan *and* Christina in my group as mentors. One of the group members, who had "worked the floor" during the breathwork session, led the group. This gentleman was a Jungian therapist in his day job, so he already had an expanded worldview, or lens through which to view what may be happening for the breathers. Now, in this case, he actually addressed *every* breather who shared by employing the Jungian standpoint—framing his questions and feedback by pointing out archetypal and alchemical imagery and theory from the Jungian perspective.

I was a little concerned, and kept watching Christina and Stan, wondering when and if they would intervene. I was worried because, even though his lens provided a more expanded territory of the psyche than the biographical framework alone, still, the way he was interacting with breathers seemed controlled and directive in some way. Well, Christina and Stan never said a word—until the session was over. Then Stan looked up and smiled at him, and said "And thank you so much for your *Jungian* interpretation."

This was all he offered. It was crystal clear—in truth, absolutely all he needed to say. This was one of the most impeccable, powerful, and non-directive teachings I have ever heard. I took it to heart, and have been trying—in every setting through the years—to emulate this form of incisive, yet non-confrontational way he shared with the facilitator/trainee. No form of teaching could have been more effective. He *trusted* the gentleman to get it. And he did!

CHAPTER XVII

A Hard Look at a Holotropic Travesty

As revolutionary and transformational as the sharing group can be at its best, at the same time, the episode can be the occasion for an utter violation of non-negotiable holotropic principles. Specifically, what's even worse is that, if it is not conducted in the true holotropic manner, it can be quite wounding for a seeker. It is always a possibility that in any stage of the holotropic process—preparation, session, or integration—our core, foundational focus on the breather's maximum self-empowerment can be sabotaged. Yet, no other component of the process than the share group harbors such potential—for good or ill—to shape, and in fact concretize, the ultimate value of a hopefully realized holotropic experience for the evolution of the seeker toward her optimum level of empowerment and wholeness.

As a cautionary tale, we must highlight one such possibility of this holotropic travesty. In this case, we will use as an example something we have seen, if only rarely, in the third phase of the three-part process—the integration, or sharing group episode. Imagine a scenario in the preparation phase of the holotropic journey, where the extended cartography was appropriately spelled out; the breathing was modeled correctly; the initial group dynamics were honored; and the primary power of the Inner Healer was thoroughly stressed.

In addition, the actual breathwork process was skillfully negotiated—including a well-done three-hour music set, and inner sessions skillfully supported and made safe throughout. In addition, the entire breathing episode was brought to a caring close through thoughtful, supportive interactions between breathers and facilitators, and appropriate focused release work engaged in for optimum closure and resolution.

Now we arrive at the sharing group. To put it simply, the basic holotropic strategy within this group amounts to "show and tell." In essence, the breathers tell their stories, which in a majority of episodes are found to be wonderfully integrative experiences. As we mentioned, appropriate verbal support is given in the manner of amplification, validation, and honoring of the breather's efforts.

However, in this scenario, these particular facilitators have another agenda in mind entirely. At this point, they set the stage for the breathers by outlining the parameters and strategy of the sharing group. They share with the breathers that they—the facilitators—may make comments at certain times during the sharing process. What then happens is one of the most devastating perversions of the holotropic process possible. Depending on the nature of the therapeutic school in which the facilitators trained before they became holotropic practitioners, they proceed to analyze, interpret, and frame the breathers' stories within that particular milieu.

The panoramic holotropic lens through which the group operated throughout the preparation stage and the breathing process itself is now *reduced* to the particular limited lens through which the therapist has been originally trained. For all intents and purposes, this is *absolutely, effectively the end* of the Holotropic Breathwork session. We are now merely engaging in some form of traditional circumscribed therapy—as we said, using whatever modality, or combination of modalities, the facilitators think the situation calls for, and in which they have been trained.

For the facilitator-turned-therapist, this type of therapy will be rich indeed! But it is rich, not because of what she, the therapist, has added to the setting. It is rich from the very beginning, because of the power of the Holotropic Breathwork itself to bring into awareness such a broad spectrum of previously unconscious dynamics.

Through Holotropic Breathwork, therapists will have at their disposal *way more* uncovered material than they could ever have coaxed from the breathers in a traditional one-on-one, or regular group, process session in the office. To be blunt, therapists will have what we call a "field day"—an opportunity to appear really important and skillful. For some therapists, this scenario is ridiculously seductive, and just too good to pass up!

However, all this self-aggrandizement—flaunting their previous training—comes at the expense of the breathers, who may, in their session, have contacted their deepest inner resources for the first time ever. Yet now, in what can be a truly bewildering turnaround, breathers find themselves once again being directed by the structure and guidance of the outside expert, and waiting to be told by someone else what has *happened to* them, instead of what has *emerged from within* them, *by their own deep work*. It is painful to witness how easy it is for seekers to revert to looking to the "expert" for their power. This is habit is almost automatic—something most of us already know so well, in so many settings throughout our lives, and for so many years.

The tragedy is that their short-lived foray into radical self-empowerment—through preparation and session—transmogrifies, or regresses, to traditional therapeutic "business as usual" in the final sharing group episode. In this case, breathers find themselves once again, as always before, *in therapy*—looking to the leader for direction and, ultimately, interpretation of who they are. All of this transpires, while, simultaneously, their expanded state of consciousness shrinks from the wonderful new connection they have made with some greater mystery, right back into the all-too-familiar territory of their designated, disempowering pathologies.

In an early workshop—over thirty years ago now—I was rudely confronted with just such a tragic perversion of a holotropic session absolutely dishonoring the sanctity of a seeker's Inner Healer. I was invited to do a workshop in a midwestern U.S. city by one of the most respected therapists in that particular state. She had experienced one or two holotropic workshops herself, and had undergone powerful experiences. We had spent much time together after her inner work. She was so excited about the breathwork and wanted to know if I would like to conduct a workshop in her city.

I agreed, and a few months later I went there for the workshop. Now, this was in the early stages of the holotropic work—actually when the certification process was not yet firmly established by Christina and Stan. But they, as my mentors, had given permission for me to conduct workshops—for individual participants' transformation, of course, but also to provide required breathing hours for any who were thinking of coming to the certification training that would soon take place.

I had a dilemma when I arrived for the workshop. There were no other experienced facilitators in her area, but I did not ever want to do a workshop singlehandedly. So, I invited a well-known therapist and a couple of more of her friends who had experienced breathwork to help "cover the floor"—that is, to keep the breathers safe. I reviewed with them the basics as thoroughly as possible. And since they had been to breathwork, and reported a level of comfort with the process, I felt fairly confident that they were sufficiently familiar with the principal of the Inner Healer and other holotropic dynamics to keep the breathers safe for their adventure.

So, we conducted the two breathwork sessions—each breather from the first session switching roles with their sitters, and then sitting for those who supported them in the morning session. I remember spending a great deal of time with one young man—a client of the therapist who had arranged the workshop—whose process was very deep and powerful. He was in terror some of the time, and cringing and weeping for much of the session. I lay near him, to make sure he felt safe, or in case he needed other support of some kind.

After he had wept for quite a while, he reached out his hand toward me. I gently extended my own hand, and he, sensing my presence, I suppose, softly made contact with me. At this point, he grabbed my arm and pulled me to him. For the next hour, I held him while he wept and shuddered deeply. Toward the end of the session, the music had become the meditative, gentle pieces that characterized the third hour—to give the breathers something to ease their transition back into hylotropic consciousness when they felt ready. I continued to hold the breather, waiting for some clue from him as to what he may want from my presence.

At some point, the young man opened his eyes, his face bright—almost filled with light—peaceful and smiling. I held him this way for a while, waiting for him to make whatever overture he wished. At some point, he sat up—and I with him—and he began to share with me a little of what had happened in his session. In essence, he reported that he had had a life of abandonment, and emotional, as well as physical, abuse. During this session, he had relived some of these painful episodes, and experienced, at first, a magnification of the shattering disempowerment he had undergone for most of his life.

But then he said that a glorious woman in light had come to him, and had carried him to a meadow on a mountaintop. There she held him in the most authentic embrace of safety he had ever known. He added that it was the most exquisite feeling of healing, connection, and love he had ever experienced in his life. These kinds of outcomes to a session—actually quite common—are always a special blessing to behold. So, after checking in with each breather for their appropriate, optimum closure, and after a beverage and snack break, we all came together for the sharing group.

I have to confess that I was just a bit concerned about how the expert therapist—who, by the way, was this young man's support person—would handle a holotropically-oriented sharing session. She had been on TV, and had written a book about her therapeutic style. Even though I had shared with her how crucial her honoring of the seeker's Inner Healer was, to be honest, I really was not totally sure how she would react in the integration session.

The sharing group began, and we "held the space" for each breather in the recounting of their adventures. Our task, as I have said, was to be a truly caring ally—a cheerleader, in fact—and to ask a few questions as to how their bodies were doing; how did they feel emotionally after the sharing; were they feeling complete for the day—all of these enquiries as a way of supporting the all-important integration phase of the breathwork.

The last breather to share was the breather with whom I spent so much time. I should mention that, after he got up from the mat, and all the way into the sharing group, and up until the time he was to speak, he looked absolutely radiant—smiling, bright, and full of wonder. So, we all sat back and proceeded to listen to one of the most beautiful breathwork stories I had ever heard.

He was so moved, as he wept for joy and gratitude in the recounting of the whole adventure: from the hell of abuse and aloneness; then the white light experience with the woman-angel who held him on the mountain top; and the perfect connection and love he had felt for the first time in his life. It was one of those sessions where the only response the group could offer was sit back, smile, marvel, and be connected to the rebirth—the miracle that the young seeker had experienced.

Then the tragedy of a lifetime occurred. The prominent leader, who was his therapist, spoke up to her "patient." As near as I can remember, here is what she said: "Robert, I notice that you have been weeping for quite a while now, even though you are smiling. There seems to be a sort of ambivalence, a kind of confusion. Perhaps we should stop for a minute, so you can focus on what's really going on—probably one of your usual disconnects or avoidance games. Let your mind wander back and see if you can get in touch with where these tears are truly coming from—where you have gone off-track."

To this day, what happened next breaks my heart. I watched this newly free, bright young man, slide down the mountain of his freedom right back into his previous lifetime of pain. His countenance morphed slowly, from light and brightness, to ever-increasing shades of reds and darkness. By the time he spoke again, he was once more, exactly, in the horror he knew so well, doing that so-called good work in the therapist's office, like a "good boy" should.

He proceeded to recite the litany that was his tragic mantra, episode by episode, while his therapist nodded approvingly. After a while, as he tried desperately to regain his therapist's approval, he talked himself right back into the state of consciousness whence he started—once more drowning in the miasma of his trauma. He was totally disconnected again from the goodness and the brightness of the new world he had briefly visited, and which had the potential to reset a healing blueprint for his upcoming life adventures.

I was horrified, and longed to immediately attempt to restructure this tableau. But, for the sake of group dynamics, I let him share, and just held him while he trembled in his old pain. Of course, after the sharing group, I immediately spoke with him, held him, and spent some very powerful time with him—once again doing whatever I could to allow him to recount the experience. However, this time, my only task was to encourage him to really trust the beauty he had experienced in the session. I allowed him to once again re-experience that fragile state of healing that would, of course, take many more sessions to anchor and complete.

I did not try to lift him up emotionally—that would have been another external power directing him still. Instead, we sat in the corner, and I asked him to please close his eyes and see if he could recall, if he wished, the way he felt during the session. Gradually, his light began to return, and his body relaxed into the softness that dissolves wrinkles and pain almost miraculously—something we see so often in sessions, that we may forget just how special it can be.

Following this, when he had come back into the everyday consciousness of the room, we spent a good bit of time discussing a "going home plan," and ways that he might continue this wonderful beginning as a powerful healing trajectory. All the while, I was doing the necessary dance of honoring his therapist, yet encouraging him to really continue to trust himself.

This is a true holotropic tragedy. This is what happens when the amplification of the light of the Inner Healing power is reduced by a certainly well-meaning, yet much more narrowly prescribed, ultimately directive, and disempowering therapeutic strategy. It was likely that this lad would need many more hours of deep inner work, along with a great deal of non-invasive yet supportive human contact. He would still benefit from a loving, honoring therapy of some sort, of course. However, he had, beyond a doubt, responded to the holotropic framework. So, we encouraged him to find a way to continue this kind of self-exploration.

Now and then I muse upon an episode in my own unfolding. This absolutely healing event occurred after I had been doing Holotropic Breathwork for some time, while still was working in addictions treatment. I had sought out a well-respected local therapist for some intense biographical work that I felt I needed to do. The person with whom I chose to work turned out to be the most skillful, loving, honorable therapist I ever had the good fortune to be supported by.

And she knew *absolutely nothing* about working in expanded states of awareness. Yet, in every respect, she herself was the epitome of the holotropic. I have never felt so heard, so supported and in such good hands as I was with this woman. The work I was able to do, with her holding space for me, were some of the most important milestones in my healing and transformation. She always met me where I was, and, from there, took the road with me, side-by-side, into the unknown. She was the epitome of a creative, respectful, and powerful love. Her presence was impeccable. To this day, I feel that presence, as a therapeutic archetype toward which I strive, in every holotropic encounter in which I have the grace to participate.

We in the holotropic ranks are not anti-therapy! There are dozens of modalities that can be of tremendous supportive value—either before, or after a holotropic session—but *not* in the breathwork milieu itself. There are many, many therapists from every therapeutic school who impeccably serve their clients through love, non-directive support, and an honoring of the clients to truly, deeply know what is best for them. Many of their strategies—as well as their presence—could be a valuable precursor to holotropic work, as well as providing a supportive integrating modality following sessions in expanded states of awareness.

In returning to our current tragic example of a breathwork gone horribly wrong, we must reiterate that the psycho-therapeutic unfolding of a Holotropic Breathwork session is a *three-part process*—not one, or two. These are preparation, session, and integration. *If, in the integration phase, a specific therapy is employed to support breathers, then this is absolutely **not** Holotropic Breathwork.*

If we as therapists "do our thing," and take over from the Inner Healer at the sharing session, or even before, or during the breathing itself, we profoundly violate the spirit of rigorous self-empowerment, not to mention the authentic holotropic strategy itself. This is true even if the therapeutic strategy seems to be similar to breathwork in some of its means and aims.

Although an extremely powerful and effective modality, we have occasionally seen this dynamic with Gestalt work—Fritz Perl's powerful method, also established at the Esalen Institute in Big Sur, where the holotropic work was birthed. We have heard from a number of Gestalt practitioners that the seduction is often present for them to assume that Holotropic Breathwork and Gestalt therapy are exactly one and the same, and can be employed interchangeably.

The client-centered Gestalt practice of intensification—itself a "relative" of the holotropic strategy—might seem—"on paper"—to be marginally effective in a breathwork session, if the breather is working within some aspects of the biographical domain. Yet in a holotropic session, it still, for the most part, can be an intrusive, therapist-centered overlay, particularly if the breather's process had deepened beyond the biographical domain.

The reason for this is that there are many powerful processes available through deep breathing, such as biological birth, or the intra-uterine episode, which are, of course, primarily or definitely non-verbal, or even preverbal episodes. Any directive verbal intervention can actually take the breathers partially or completely out of the intensity of the original episode.

Gestalt or other practices with a strong verbal component can also be quite invasive when the breathers have accessed the realm of the transpersonal, where experiences often transcend identification with any human species-specific characteristics, such as language. Verbal therapy at this point would totally short-circuit, or simply derail that process altogether.

There is undoubtedly a valuable place for all kinds of therapy in seekers' lives. However, these should not occur within the holotropic milieu.

The holotropic perspective is quite simple and specific in this regard. The overarching strategy is the total focus on allowing seekers to fully experience the self-empowering benefits of a radical connection with their innermost selves. Through a different lens, how would a therapist in any modality feel if, in the middle of their session with a client, another therapist walked in and took over, adding to, or contaminating the strategic elements of his own method?

Transposing any modality into the Holotropic Breathwork process—preparation, session, or integration—might appear to be an interesting exercise for some therapists. Yet we must understand that, if a therapist wishes to make these changes, then the resulting product, although perhaps effective in its own specific way, is simply no longer Holotropic Breathwork. Stan and Christina have always been absolutely clear on this issue. It is the task of every practitioner to rigorously honor the tenets that are sacrosanct within the holotropic milieu. If a practitioner wished to insert some modifications, well and good. But, as Stan and Christina have said over and over again, in this case, *just don't call it Holotropic Breathwork.*

It deserves recounting here that the most basic, core intention of the holotropic practitioner is to hold sacred space for the breather's experience. This focus also includes a sense of fierce protection, so that the breather's inner healing resources may be unquestionably supported, safeguarded, and honored. Without this commitment on our part, the true therapeutic, as well as numinous power of Holotropic Breathwork fades away, resulting in a merely transitory, ephemeral foray into the possibilities of healing.

The episode will then no longer be able to fulfill its truest, far-reaching potential to provide the priceless gift of authentic, in-depth self-empowerment. This gift offers the seeker an opportunity to explore her self in the safest, most effective inner sanctum of her being; to profoundly embrace her Inner Healer; and to own her most authentic power within. This power within is a birthright of all human beings in our adventure of Becoming, as we consciously embark on our journeys toward wholeness, or, as some may say, toward the unfathomable realm of Being itself.

CHAPTER XVIII

The Yoga of the Cross

Historic Underpinnings of the Yoga of the Cross

Throughout the text, we have sometimes italicized two words: the *vertical* and the *horizontal*. They represent the two essential therapeutic and philosophical vectors of a holotropic paradigm, therapy, and moment-to-moment yoga, or spiritual practice. In this case, they are the two arms of the cross to which we refer in the process known as the *Yoga of the Cross*, and later, the *Awareness Positioning System*. For many, this system has greatly simplified, as well as amplified, the transformational possibilities within a much broader implementation of a holotropic milieu.

The Yoga of the Cross and it's more "agnostic" name, the Awareness Positioning System, represent the same transformational structure. They are both totally derived from holotropic roots. In fact, the practice that these two names represent is a simplified, easy-to-implement mechanism and application of authentic, core holotropic elements into broader psycho-therapeutic and transformational settings. Many report that the use of this structure deserves its founding pedigree in our celebration of a truly effective power within.

Holotropic Breathwork stands completely on its own, as a powerful psycho-spiritual method. Yet, as we have seen, like many modern practices, it inherently reveals certain time-honored similarities to a number of ancient practices, including mystical traditions of all kinds, rites of passage, shamanism, mystery schools, and many more. In this century, the holotropic perspective seems to elegantly reflect many cultures of deep seeking known throughout the ages. It is a modern biographical, perinatal, and transpersonal strategy, which for thousands of years has taken many other forms.

We are not saying Holotropic Breathwork is directly derived from any of these ancient practices. Nevertheless, the stages of transformation we negotiate as we experience a Holotropic Breathwork weekend; a peyote, ayahuasca, or LSD session; certain renditions of the "rave"; a meditation retreat; and many other forms of seeking, each reflect various elements of practices that we can study throughout perennial philosophy. Most of these modern strategies, if presented in a safe and sacred manner, contain the three essential parts of any deep work: *preparation, session,* and *integration.*

However, there are other similarities that Holotropic Breathwork has with ancient, as well as modern, rituals of transformation. Within the holotropic ritual itself, there are particular guidelines to ensure maximum possibility for a successful experience based on a framework of honoring and safety. It is critical that there be a willingness for the seeker to turn deeply inward—what we call *going vertical*—letting go of the ever-magnetic pull, at least for the time being, of external relationships, phenomena, and circumstances—what we call the *horizontal.*

In the holotropic work, in addition to facilitators, we have "sitters," or support people who protect the individual's space. Just as important is a teaching on the safest, most effective way to maximize the emergence of our innate inner healing power via the power of the breath. There must also be a willingness to open to the inherent core possibility that *neither transformation, nor distraction from that transformation, are directly, or mainly caused by circumstances "outside ourselves," or, as we say, on the "horizontal."*

Instead, these horizontal, or external phenomena are seen as *triggers* that bring on-line internal healing mechanisms from within journeyers. In order to truly heal, we must recognize that the transformative power of our healing adventure can only be garnered from *within* our own psyches, or as we say, on the *vertical.* The companion piece to this directive is that the outside environment—the *horizontal*—ceases to be the *cause* of our problems, but, when viewed through a different lens by the breather, rather as an unsurpassed *opportunity to heal.*

Through a more current therapeutic lens, what we are proposing refers to the requirement of seeing *projection,* or focusing externally to define the causal roots of our suffering, as a powerful source of the malaise of modern existence. We are also certain that focusing *on the horizontal* to somehow "fix" ourselves is ultimately a doomed attempt at transformation. In addition, it sabotages any subsequent positive redefinition of our everyday life episodes, including any hopeful prospectus for our life adventure in the future. Ultimately this misplaced direction of the *willed focus of attention* dooms any lasting benefit from radical self-empowerment.

There are a few non-negotiable requirements for optimum outcome of the holotropic experience. To borrow a phrase from Ram Dass—an important teacher for many of us—it is important to frame every experience we have in the breathwork hall as *grist for the mill* of our own awakening.

External, or horizontal, phenomena are neither the cause nor the reason we transform. The role of these everyday, external phenomena is to spur us to turn inward, to the *vertical* dimension of who we are.

It is *within*—via the power of our Inner Healer—that we investigate, and find the link, as to how any such external phenomena are not the cause or source of our problems, but represent an ideal occasion for us to use these phenomena as a starting place for deep inner work. By far the most simple, effective way to demonstrate what we mean by this, and learning to use our life experiences as extremely effective *opportunities to heal*, seems to be through what we have been calling in the holotropic milieu the Yoga of the Cross, or the Awareness Positioning System.

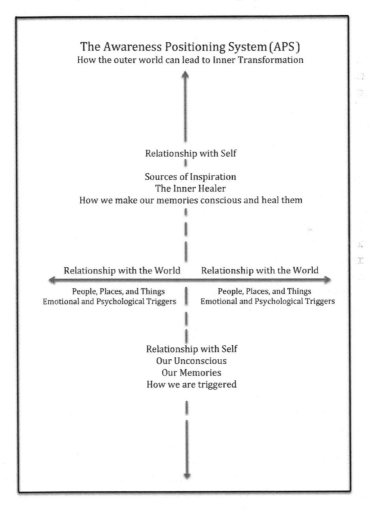

Figure 1. The Awareness Positioning System

We share with you the diagram in this early stage of our inquiry into the Yoga of the Cross, so that, as we begin to speak of it—and the various therapeutic possibilities of it to unfold in our exposition—the visual will make it much easier to grasp this strategy. It is our firm belief that, as this structure has done for us, it may become a wonderful support for all inner seekers by truly simplifying the process of transformation.

As the text enfolds, and if it helps to visualize what we are demonstrating, please use the diagram. Incidentally, the metaphor of the cross we share here is exactly the one we employ in nearly every seminar of our training, as well as the many "sister" holotropic formats we are bringing to various countries around the world.

A non-negotiable holotropic truth reveals that we cannot heal if we believe that what happens *outside* of us, on the horizontal arm of the cross—that is, "people, places and things"—*causes* us to feel or be the way we are. We must reframe this statement to say that what happens externally, or, as we share, on the *horizontal*, is not the cause of our pain, but rather a wonderful *opportunity to heal*. The *horizontal* becomes the playing field, if you will—a *trigger* of internal, or, as we say, *vertical* material that is either unconscious, or becoming conscious, from within our own psyches.

In order to truly heal, and break the cycle of projection, blame, and dis-empowerment with which most of us are burdened, it is absolutely essential for us to focus internally, on the *vertical* arm of the cross, the source of our intra-psychic material. It is here that the alchemical fire of our inner healing resources frees us from the hypnotic trance of being slaves to outside, or *horizontal* circumstances.

Looking at it through a slightly more simplified lens, Holotropic Breathwork is essentially a *vertical* method. By this, we mean that it is a completely internal process. By internal, we do not mean that breathers cannot be outwardly expressive during inner work—energetically, physically or vocally. We mean that our consciousness must be inner-directed toward what we may term the true source, or causal level, of our reactions. Simply stated, everything that appears to be *outside* the breather is what we call *horizontal*—the sitter, the facilitator, other breathers and the noise they may make, the music, the temperature in the room, and so on. Everything that we experience as *within* our own psyches is what we call the *vertical*.

Here are some directions crucial for true, in-depth transformation: What we feel and experience *horizontally* depends on our reactions to the activation and emergence, from a kind of stasis, of our own *vertical*, intra-psychic material. What is *horizontal* becomes *fuel for the fire of our awakening*. The holotropic healing strategy proposes that external triggers can be reframed within us on the *vertical* arm of the cross. This reframing sets the stage for bringing on-line the operative healing mechanisms of our unlimited inner healing resources—our power within.

Through yet another lens, by the impetus of what occurs on the *horizontal*—the power of the breathing, the music, and what is happening in the breathwork room—it seems that the contents of our inner psyches are somehow converted into a stream of experience. This stream of experience then emerges into our awareness, where, as we say, *consciousness* itself becomes the mechanism of our Inner Healers for our transformation. In other words, we heal by making fully conscious what arises from within our psyches, from the *vertical* dimensions of who we are—the heretofore unconscious material from the biographical, perinatal, and transpersonal bands of consciousness.

From the dynamics of the Yoga of the Cross, there emerges an imperative, holotropic truth. If we are unwilling or unable to relinquish the fantasy that we are somehow the playthings of these outside circumstances, we perpetuate a great human tragedy. This truly avoidable tragedy is that we believe we are, in essence, slaves to forces we cannot control. As slaves, whatever power we think we have will be subject to, and dictated by, outside, external, or *horizontal* circumstances.

This renders us nothing more than the *victims* of life and the world around us. As an antidote to this seeming tragedy, we are proposing a radical self-empowerment that each of us may bring quite quickly on-line. The true purpose of our acquisition of this uncompromising self-empowerment is a profoundly enriching sense of a wide, expansive freedom inherent in our everyday life experience.

None of us would wish to be playthings to the ever-swirling winds of an external, horizontal, and thereby dubiously fickle fortune. This truly *would* be a tragedy. The sad fact is that a great many people live their whole lives disempowered by this focus on what seems to be the relentless, nearly iron-clad whim of the *horizontal* axis of our existence. With this perspective, we are effectively severed from the true source of our freedom and happiness—that which exists inside us, on the *vertical* axis of who we are—what we have called the power within.

What are the signposts that awaken us to this condition of disempowerment? An absolute "red flag" flutters within our consciousness any time we make statements like these: "You *made* me angry, sad, happy, upset ...";"You hurt my feelings, freaked me out, broke my heart. ..." Most of us have heard the term, *giving our power away*. These statements are prime examples of this insidious human dynamic. This perverted perspective is the real source of our unhappiness, our disempowerment. If these things are true, then we might likely be led to wonder whether this life is actually worth living.

It may be difficult for some of us to imagine the full implications of these pronouncements. If we must depend on a certain configuration of horizontal circumstances for us to be happy or fulfilled, then we are, quite frankly, doomed. We would be not much better than powerless automatons. We would be reduced to a Sisyphusian labor of failure—often acting like an ever-disappointed yet inveterate "control-freak," as we attempt desperately and in vain to shape the outside world—our *horizontal* existence—to our own satisfaction and fulfillment. But no matter how much energy we invest in trying to rearrange horizontal reality to our benefit and liking, it is an almost iron-clad impossibility for any human to control for very long anything more than a tiny portion of the universal, horizontal dimension.

But what about the myriad episodes of our lives where we have been abused in some way externally, either by people or by a host of what we consider to be the personally antagonistic machinations of society or world forces at large? We often make the critical mistake of professing, "Why should I work on *my*self? I am not the one who caused my suffering. I am the victim here. He did it to me. I am not going to blame myself!"

This is often a bitter medicine for many of us. The fact is, it makes no difference if we are totally innocent and have definitely been abused by someone or something outside ourselves. *Blame is not the relevant issue. Assigning blame is an egoic sideshow to true transformation.* The bottom line is, it is infinitely more valuable to us to get free than it is to win an ego struggle about who is right or who is to blame. *It is a spiritual truth that as long as we stay focused on this outside person or event—expecting that we will heal if they change, or apologize, or make reparations in some way – we ourselves will never heal.* As we often hear in Twelve-Step meetings, "I don't want to be the one left holding the bag!"

Healing is just not about playing mere ego games—establishing who is right and who is wrong. It is not about winning egoic, horizontal battles. In our lives we will always lose at least as many of these struggles as we will win. It is about transformation—a dramatic shift that results in *our feeling better* in a lasting, authentic way. And the only way we can be free of this type of pain of victimhood is to turn inward—*go vertical*—not blaming ourselves at all—but *empowering ourselves*—taking over responsibility for our own selves and our own healing.

This is the freedom and empowerment promised by a very exacting yet rewarding personal yoga or practice—easily brought on line by what we call the Yoga of the Cross, and later, the Awareness Positioning System. It is an issue we have addressed in different contexts many times so far. The overwhelming affirmation that emerges from the experience of any seeker who turns inward—vertically, as we say—and embraces there the possibility of an unlimited healing source within, is that we absolutely *do* have the power within us to change, to move toward wholeness.

We are capable of wholly freeing ourselves of that which has always caused us such emotional and psychological suffering. Most authentic healing modalities—ancient or modern—attempt to liberate us from this imagined powerlessness, so that we may effectively transform our lives. Most of them direct us *within*—to the fertile, creative *vertical* dimension of human existence.

For thousands of us who have utilized the holotropic perspective—not just in the breathwork room, but as a framework for a revolutionary therapy, effective entheogen work, support for those in spiritual crisis, and as practical principles and bases for living a moment-to-moment life grounded in true psycho-spiritual freedom—we know, or at least have faith, that fulfillment is possible. We trust this, even if we have only tasted the fruits of this holotropic perspective. We also realize that Holotropic Breathwork has no "corner on the market" of healing. Every method worth its pedigree presents strategies, in their own metaphors, for turning inward—going vertical, for effective transformation—many as powerful as in the perspective we have been exploring here.

Each of us can verify for ourselves the observation that, in one way or another, if we examine any deep, authentic practice, we will uncover strategies that benefit from, or rely on, some nuance of this internal foundational truth—what we are calling the Yoga of the Cross. Without any hesitation, we are certain that Holotropic Breathwork, and the great traditions from which it seems to have emerged, all are founded upon the unquestioned reality of an internal, *vertical power within* each of us capable of directing us toward wholeness and the mysteries of fulfillment beyond—in the vast universe playing field we call the *horizontal dimension* of who we are.

Applications of the Yoga of the Cross

From a therapeutic standpoint, then, "going vertical" connotes, simply, looking within, focusing on the contents of our own inner psychological environment. "Going horizontal" implies directing our consciousness outward, toward the world we envision as being outside ourselves—including, but not limited to what in Twelve Step parlance is termed "people, places, and things."

This seemingly simple act of what I call the *willed focus of attention*—either outward or inward—leads us to one of the most profound, creative benefits of the holotropic paradigm. For a holotropic paradigm, it represents an effective, elegant bridge between traditional Holotropic Breathwork and a number of this method's foundational offspring: *Movie Yoga*, a holotropic *therapy*, a moment-to-moment holotropic *yoga*, or practice, effective exploration via entheogens, a dynamic method to support those during psycho-spiritual crises, as well as a holotropically-oriented addiction recovery model.

This holotropically-centered structure and strategy, the *Yoga of the Cross*, in addition to being an "instruction manual" for effective holotropic inner work, has also proven to be a simple way to transfer core, unalterable holotropic principles from the breathwork room to many still-more-traditional therapeutic settings. In addition, it has already been reported by hundreds of seekers all over the world as an extremely effective way to bring holotropic practice into their everyday lives.

A Little Backstory: How We Got Here

We began to use this strategy in holotropic work a number of years before we actually codified and gave these names to what we were doing. Through the early years, Holotropic Breathwork's pioneering practitioners reported a troublesome, yet not unexpected, therapeutic phenomenon in their sharing groups. It was also a recurring dynamic—but not as prominent—throughout the other phases of the holotropic workshop, including the opening preparatory circle, the "down-time" between planned events, and, of course, in the breathwork itself.

Almost every therapist will be well-acquainted with this occurrence. As we have shared, in common therapeutic parlance, it is known as *projection*. Another well-related nuance of projection is a centerpiece in Freudian approaches—where it is employed as a basic structure of the therapeutic process. This is known as *transference*. In most settings, projection represents a type of defense mechanism. Within the holotropic milieu, we also see it as, in fact, a "deal breaker"—a true obstacle to authentic change. For successful, ongoing, in-depth psycho-spiritual transformation, the holotropic strategy requires a re-direction of the seeker's willed focus of attention—from the *horizontal* to the *vertical* axis of consciousness, manifestation, and human interaction.

In the early days of the training, projection was well-covered as we presented directions on how participants should appropriately engage with each other and the facilitators within the breathwork settings. In a session, breathers were always encouraged to allow the music and the sounds in the room to be experienced, not as the *cause* of the problem, but as *horizontal "triggers,"* which would then become the impetus for them to "internalize," or *go vertical*.

Simply stated, what occurs externally is not ultimately to blame for how we feel. To put it another way, focusing vertically, within one's psyche, results in the realization that occurrences on a seemingly external axis are neither a *cause* nor a *distraction* from the breather's healing process. However, they are an essential *part of* that process—what we call *triggers*, or an *opportunity to heal*.

As such, they should be embraced and worked with in the same manner as any other phenomenon emerging from within the breather's psyche. This absolute requirement for seekers to turn inward is so crucial for deep healing that the inability of some seekers to do this, for whatever reasons, is a definite contraindication for a client to be able to benefit from the holotropic process at all.

The actual breathwork session itself was not the only place projection occurred. It would sporadically take place between sessions and planned events as well. This made sense here where the normal interactions of a group of seekers, in the sometimes stressful position of doing deep inner work, would occasionally precipitate what is commonly known in many circles as an "ego struggle." Yet the part of the schedule most prone to this issue of problematic human interaction—where horizontal projections might be the most disruptive and glaring—was the sharing group, or integrative part of the holotropic process.

However, projection in the integrative sharing group was not a common occurrence. By far, most of the interactions that took place during the sharing were attentive, caring, and supportive interchanges between seekers and facilitators. This prevalent attitude can be attributed primarily to the thorough inner work and integration that take place on the mat, as an effective closure of the process before the breather moved on to the integrative sharing phase.

It was not unusual, as well, that sharing groups were recognized by breathers as the most important experience they would have in their inner adventure. They often reported that it was here that the healing at last truly "came together." Amid an atmosphere of total support, breathers seemed to thrive. And they often reported a sense of great relief in attending a group session that was such a "non-therapy" as well as self-empowering type of environment.

As we shared, sometimes breathers were what we call "unfinished," or incomplete—mentally, emotionally, physically, or spiritually. This, of course, is common in holotropic work. By complete, we do not mean enlightened, or, as teacher Ram Dass used to say, a "cooked goose," with no more need for inner work. In honoring the incremental or evolutionary nature of many breakthrough experiences and periods of sustained growth, we mean, as we have said, "complete, within the *larger field of incompletion.*"

Being "unfinished" might occur in a couple of ways. Having thoroughly discussed with a facilitator where they were in their process, or how they felt, they would leave the mat feeling good for the day's work. However, it is not uncommon that some time later, some nagging psychophysical material may re-emerge as they move deeper into the integration phase. Or they may become "triggered" by something or someone at the mandala drawing, the dinner, or during the sharing group itself.

In most cases, this poses no real problem. The breather would just share with a support person what she was feeling. With this caring, nondirective support, she would most often be able to go vertical. From this therapeutic poise, she could reaffirm that what was happening was not generated by anything outside herself, but that she had been triggered by something. She would easily recognize that it was just, as we say, "part of the process."

In these situations, we would continue to go "down the stream" with her, either verbally or, later, perhaps with a little extra clearing work. This might include supporting her through some holotropically focused release work, or, in the cases of what we call traumas of omission, just holding her in supportive contact while back on the mat. With these types of support and interactions, the outcome was almost always positive and healing, and the breather well prepared to begin her journey back into her every-day life.

However, it could be more challenging for facilitators when, in a rare occurrence, a breather experiencing an emergence of anger or frustration became emotionally entangled—on the horizontal, as we say—with someone else in the sharing circle. It might unfold that these two people would trigger each other, and engage in some level of charged interaction. This is a challenge in any group setting, and definitely so in a breathwork sharing circle. Many breathers are still feeling quite new, raw, and tender, or open and extra-sensitized by their inner work. An outburst of "horizontal" anger or sarcasm can be experienced by other breathers not directly involved as a trigger—or unsafe or threatening.

Facilitators report that this represents one of their least favorite challenges. We can be triggered ourselves, and feel worry or fear that, as the saying goes, "the wheels are about to come off," or the group is close to imploding, or "losing it on the final curve." But we are required to mobilize, and address head-on—with grace, skill, and equanimity—whatever is emerging, individually or collectively. This is the time when we must inject ourselves into the group process and become a positive center or focus—a skillful therapeutic player.

We have frequently observed that, if facilitators are therapists in their everyday profession, they are likely to respond by going directly to "default mode"—that is, to employ whatever brand of therapy they are accustomed to using in their own groups. Yet, as we have pointed out, the employment of any type of traditional therapy can backfire, if not explained, translated into, and executed within the full holotropic perspective.

As an accidental side effect, using other non-holotropic strategies can sabotage the fragile beginning seekers have made with the group in the previously unknown holotropic process of totally trusting themselves and their own Inner Healers. As we have pointed out, if the last thing the group members experience and remember about their breathwork day is a stress-ful traditional therapy session, it is always possible that they will fail to internalize the miracle of maximum self-empowerment garnered in their breathwork experiences.

If we use a conventional or traditional modality in working with uncomfortable group dynamics, another problem may arise. Many individuals, or the whole group, may not ever have experienced this type of therapy before. Then, in order to avoid confusion among the participant/ witnesses of her attempt to resolve the confrontation between the two who are engaged in the "horizontalization," the facilitator may have to do quite a bit of teaching and explaining. Once again, there is the likelihood that the fledgling, still unfamiliar holotropic spirit may be subsumed beneath an overlay of the traditional, non-holotropic modality being currently brought on line.

At this point, through no one's fault, the entire breathwork atmosphere can become compromised, perhaps even spelling the end to the holotropic adventure. What if, in this case, seekers returned home, and were asked by family or friends what the Holotropic Breathwork was like? They might say something horrendous like this: "Oh, it's a place where we all go inside ourselves and do deep breathing, and have these powerful experiences of how we all have a deep inner wisdom. Then we go to a therapy group where the therapist directs each of us to…"

And then you name it: do gestalt, transactional analysis, or a Freudian, Jungian, existential, or a cognitive behavioral session. This would be tragic! This is clearly *no holotropic process* at all. We are not saying that these other methods are not effective and powerful. However, as we have already discussed, if they are implemented in any of the three components of the holotropic milieu, then this effectively spells the end of the holo-tropic adventure.

If we do not use a traditional modality, how, then, would we work holotropically in the group setting? Through my own experiences of this "externalizing of processes" in the sharing group through the years, I managed to come up with a rather simple, straightforward, "bare bones" strategy. This easy-to-implement practice, while containing the essence of many modalities, actually just does not sound like any particular recognized therapy.

For that matter, it just seems more like an interesting game than any therapy at all. What I propose to the group is framed in a simple, nontherapeutic sounding terminology. However, it is actually quite a *precise therapeutic enactment* of the true holotropic perspective. And, as you may imagine, it became the core basis and essence of the Yoga of the Cross.

In the case of confrontational interactions between breathers, or the individual episodes of acting out, it is essential that we, the holotropic facilitators, must intervene. We do this not as some psychology expert, but more in the spirit of an exhilarating game. Bear in mind, we have seen a few situations where a participant was really angry at someone, and expressing this quite aggressively.

Part of our strategy is to pay rigorous attention to this interaction, while at the same time our consciousness is spread throughout the rest of the group. We are aware that others may be self-contracting with fear or other emotions. All of them are staring at the facilitator, seeming to express a silent cry of "Help!" or "What the hell is going to happen now?" or something of this nature.

So, the facilitator brightens up, moves forward a little bit, smiles, and says something light-hearted, like, "Oookay ... now this is pretty intense, right?" Other group members stare at her, relieved. Here is one version of a standard holotropic opening line: "You guys are doing really well. Want to try something? You can always say stop if it does not feel right."

Almost always, one can feel the previous level of tension dissipate. Our words of this sort allow those engaged in the challenging interaction—and everyone else—to know that they are okay—that as far as the facilitator is concerned, everything is just "business as usual." The unspoken metaphor for this type of facilitator response is to "stay wide open; embrace, hold softly; gently uplift, uplift..." something like this.

Now that we have their attention—and all seem to be engaged in this next phase of the adventure—we re-enact a mini-version of the holotropic, three-part process: preparation, session, integration. All of this is occurring in quick-time—simply, and in very everyday language. For the preparation phase, it helps to have a white board. I usually make a joke, like, "Look at this symbol I invented. It's really complicated." Then I draw a cross, with a little heart right where the two lines intersect.

This gets some chuckles from some of the group not directly involved in the unsettling interaction. The atmosphere already seems to be getting lighter, the tension defusing. Then I might say, "This'll be like a mini-breathwork—real simple. *Remember, you can always say stop, and we'll stop.*" This reminder is an important self-empowerment safeguard that we have already shared with the whole group at the beginning of the holotropic session.

Next, I present, in simple fashion, what I have been calling the *Yoga of the Cross.* Here is the short form: "Imagine that you are like this cross, standing with your arms spread. Now, the horizontal arms of the cross—out through each arm—represent everything that is going on outside, or external to you—people, places objects, what the rest of the world is doing, etc. Okay, the vertical arm of the cross—below the intersection—going down—represents your personal history: your biographical life and your biological birth—everything that you have experienced in your personal history…"

Then I point out that "everything on the vertical line *above* the horizontal intersection represents your longings for moving toward wholeness, toward an expansive archetypal connection, or to the Great Mystery, as well as your experience or belief in any source of inspiration—god, goddess, higher self, inner healer, Buddha, whatever. If you do not have any source of inspiration, feel free to have fun, and just make something up—just imagine that you do." Once again, we are providing seekers an opportunity to widen their trust in their own deepest inner healing resources.

Once we have explained the cross, we proceed: "What we're going to do is a simple, light, mini-breathwork, while you two are still sitting in the chair—except without the deep breathing. Willing to give it a try? Just say 'stop', if it doesn't feel right." Then we ask the one who first expressed himself to try to name what he is feeling—usually, in this case, something like frustration, anger, or perhaps fear.

Once he has done this—perhaps with a little help from us—we ask him to attempt a form of self-inquiry, using what has become almost a holotropic mantra: "Is this feeling familiar? Have you ever felt it before?" Why the self-inquiry? Because, with it, he has now ceased to be focusing *horizontally*—outside himself, on the other person. Instead, he has turned inward—on the *vertical.* Now he has the very real opportunity to heal himself.

It is absolutely fascinating how, in virtually *every* situation, the breathers answer quickly and quite emphatically in the affirmative—that they absolutely know this feeling, for what seems like their whole lives. Next, we ask him when or how. And almost immediately he will pinpoint the time, or pattern of times, he has experienced this in his life. He will say something like, "This is exactly like what my mother used to do." Then he proceeds to go deeper vertically, to amplify the situation, to spell it out in more detail.

Now is the time for really powerful support and validation on the part of the facilitators. We are the cheerleaders. We let him know that this is courageous work—that it is not easy—and that what he is experiencing is extremely powerful, and can initiate a life-changing healing process. What he has done is to bring the unconscious material *from the horizontal to the vertical*—make it conscious, and then bring it upward *to the heart at the center of the cross*. This is what we mean by fully embracing our process.

Perhaps before facilitators ask the other person in the dynamic—the recipient of his emotional outburst sitting across the room—we may frame, for the group, what has just happened for the breather. We applaud him for doing a powerful piece of holotropic work. In truth, he has followed the breathwork strategy, just by sitting in a group. He has "turned inward," gone vertical—"down the line" as we say—allowing his inner healing radar to take him deep into his own psyche. By doing this, he sheds a powerful light of healing consciousness directly on some event or pattern that was previously unconscious and unavailable to him.

He and the group are often amazed when we share that what is taking place here is exactly what happens in the breathwork session. In both cases—on the mat and here in the sharing circle—the participant has surrendered to his deepest inner wisdom, and uncovered something that has caused him problems, perhaps throughout his life. The holotropic mechanism is fully operative at this point. Remember, *consciousness itself is the healing power.* What was unconscious has come to consciousness. This truly initiates the healing dynamic. It will unfold at various rates, depending on how powerful the pattern is, and how much attention the breather will give it in the coming days, or in the continuation of deep inner work.

Now comes the final piece: The group member has, as we say, "gone vertical"—down the lower arm of the cross. He has removed his focus from the horizontal—the woman in the group—out there on the horizontal arm of the cross. The only thing left is to complete the healing ritual. Now that he has made this issue conscious, what should he do with it? The strategy is to send it, as we say, "up the line"—into the *upper* arm of the vertical dimension. We have shared that this is where our inspiration lies. It could be some form of higher power—goddess or god. It could be Higher Mind or anything he chooses it to be.

If the breather has trouble with this, and cannot think of what this power may be, or if he does not believe in anything at all, we ask him to *imagine* that he believes. Even to just invent, or make something up, is extremely potent. It does not matter what it is. We assure him that whatever he chooses, it will have been directed and guided by his Inner Healer. We share with him what has worked for us. It may be that for a facilitator, her higher source is often the Divine Mother. So she shares that she envisions—at the top end of her cross—Ma Kali, there, within an awesome, raging fire of purification.

The facilitator shares that she brings whatever she has made conscious, from her heart, "up the line," and throws it in this purifying fire. Then she lets the participant know that almost always she feels much freer and more whole after she has completed the process. And of course, if he is still having trouble with this, invite him to just imagine his source of inspiration as his Inner Healer—keeping it really simple and appropriate to the current workshop itself.

We are still and quiet while the participant does whatever he needs to do. When he returns to outer awareness—or opens his eyes—we ask him how he feels now. In almost every situation, he shares that he feels different somehow—better, lighter. Breathers often report a sense of excitement at the possibility of a simple-to-use strategy to bring the power of holotropic dynamics on line and into their every-day lives.

Then we go through the same process with the one whom he confronted. After she goes vertical—through whatever healing process her Inner Healer reveals—I ask the group participants how they are feeling, and does anyone else need some guidance for what may have come up for them during this episode. Often, they smile and say they already practiced it while I was sharing with their fellow group members.

And it works! The shift of energy in the group is always palpable. Where before there was a contracted aura of tension, now there is an openhearted sense of relief and peace, and at the same time an inner validation and excitement. What had the potential to be a colossal side-tracking and sabotaging of the sharing group, as well as the Holotropic Breathwork session itself, has achieved an amazing individual and collective catharsis.

At this point, there remains one final piece of work for the facilitator to do before we move on to another breather's sharing. This part involves some explanation and feedback on our part about the origin of healing dynamics involved in what just happened. The group is almost always amazed and excited to learn that what has occurred, as they sat in a circle, in chairs or on the floor, was to engage a dimension of the same holotropic process and power in which they were engaged during their breathing sessions.

For one, they allowed themselves to be motivated and guided by their own inner healing wisdom. Just as in a breathwork session, that healing power took them within—along the vertical arm of the cross—to the place that was activated. Through the healing power of consciousness itself—the Inner Healer, their power within—they now have more trust in the natural healing dynamics that are so readily accessible to them in their everyday lives.

We call this inner turning *self-inquiry*. As we have shared, it is a derivative of an ancient, powerful Indian yoga made famous by Ramana Maharshi and other teachers. In the case of Ramana Maharshi, his self-inquiry was, "Who am I? Who am I?" Breathers ask themselves the questions, "Is this feeling familiar? Have I ever felt it before?"

They get the powerful insight that what happened outside them, on the horizontal—no matter what it was—did not *make* them feel anything. Instead of feeling victimized by some outside person or event, each person chooses to take ownership of her feelings and goes vertical. In other words, they followed the guidance of a power within. Thus, the cross turns out to be one of the simplest mechanisms and structures for this healing process.

Group members recognize the power in refusing to react externally—*at* someone else, blaming those around them, as we so often do in our lives. Instead, they have allowed their Inner Healer to work for them, and bring them to a healing awareness of an issue previously unconscious within their own psyches. From that point—at the moment of conscious recognition—they can then utilize whatever form their source of inspiration may take—knowing that they can even invent a functional power source. They understand that whatever they imagine their healing source to be, this too will have been guided by their new inner-found healing resources.

At this moment, they often reach an unforgettable turning point. Perhaps unbeknownst to them, they have enacted and completed the crowning piece of an ancient ritual—offering up what they have uncovered to whatever their own healing source is. Now is the time for us as facilitators to validate them! And for them to validate each other! What could have been a "deal-breaker"—or at the least, a temporary destroyer of the good work they have accomplished on the mat—has instead has become the occasion to "test their new-found wings," and to bring on-line the healing dynamic inherent in Holotropic Breathwork.

This celebrative juncture is the occasion for the final piece of support in our tableau. We encourage them to appreciate that they have just engaged in an amazing process that they can take home—one which that they may practice any time, in other challenging situations in their lives. Ultimately, through the Yoga of the Cross, we are explicating a *moment-to-moment holotropic yoga, or practice*—all based absolutely directly on the holotropic perspective.

We are also indelibly highlighting the powerful, ground-breaking possibilities of a holotropic *therapy*—a modality that can be experienced both in a group setting as well as one-on-one counseling. Many of us believe whole-heartedly that what we have experienced in these groups may be a significant factor in the dawn of a new therapeutic era—one that, among many designations, could aptly be termed a holotropic *paradigm*. But more on this possibility later in our inquiry.

What we have outlined seems to document a revolutionary possibility where the heretofore "breathing room-bound" practice crosses a previously considered insurmountable barrier. Now we may be opening a vista on a radical, new holotropic therapy, truly honoring the innate power of the Inner Healer absolutely present within every individual—where the therapist must play the role, not as director, but as co-adventurer. The new therapeutic responsibility will become exactly the same as that of a facilitator in the breathwork room. It will also be identical to the role of the sitter, whose primary job is to "hold space," keep a seeker safe, and be a cheerleader, as the client empowers herself right before our eyes.

An Interlude: Tales from the Breathwork Floor

The Holotropic Breathwork setting often casts a profound, sharp spotlight on the healing mechanisms inherent in the Yoga of the Cross. For example, a young man is breathing on his mat, his watchful sitter nearby. A facilitator, who is walking through the room, holding space, stops near him. Suddenly, a couple of mats beyond, another breather quickly becomes very active—something we see regularly. The facilitator "hurries slowly" over to this breather to be of support, and on the way his foot just barely touches the end of the man's mat that he passes on the way.

That breather springs upright, looking horrified, and appears to be either seething mad, frightened, or both. He opens his eyes, stands up—a little wobbly—and moves as if to leave the room. His sitter rises with him, puts his hand on the breather's shoulder. The breather cringes and shakes it off. By this time, another facilitator moves in to be of support. The breather reports that he has just been abused—his boundaries violated—that this setting is no longer safe, and that he wants to leave.

The three of them—breather, sitter, and facilitator—walk out of the room, where the facilitator asks the breather to sit for a while, and to share further about what has happened, perhaps over a cup of tea. The breather says that he was doing fine and feeling safe, and all of a sudden, someone viciously invaded his space. He says he feels violated and attacked.

The facilitator encourages him to share a little more about what was going on internally at the time. In short, he asks the breather to go vertical. The breather reveals that he had been seriously physically abused by his drunken father all through his childhood. He chose this workshop because he heard that it was a really safe place to heal such violations. But now he sees that the place is just as abusive as his life growing up.

Unbeknownst to the breather—and a situation for which neither he nor anyone else is to blame—he has externalized his process, from the *vertical* into the *horizontal*. From the therapeutic standpoint, he has been powerfully *triggered*—on the horizontal—by the facilitator's barest touching of his mat. In his expanded state of consciousness, this external touch felt horribly magnified as he relived the abuse of his past—that which is vertical, within his psyche. For him, it felt like just one more bead on the rosary of his childhood pain.

We spend much time in our training supporting would-be facilitators on how to respond to such a situation. Obviously, it would have been a whole lot better if the facilitator had *not* stepped accidentally on the breather's mat. However, these things will happen, no matter how careful and respectful we are. They are what we sometimes call a *cosmic setup*. This term connotes a process—seemingly orchestrated by the breather's Inner Healer—that, even though it may have an initial negative impetus, often contains the very real possibility of becoming a powerful healing experience. Nevertheless, in every situation such as this, quite a bit of dialogue between the facilitator and the breather is required.

This, of course, begins with very sincere apologies on the part of the facilitator. We, as facilitators, *feel awful* when this happens. We take extremely seriously the total safety of the breathers. In almost every case, however, the breather eventually understands why he has experienced such a powerful reaction. There are always meaningful personal historic underpinnings—down the internal, or vertical arm of the cross. As ever, these underpinnings continually send out a homing beacon, chanting "opportunity to heal—opportunity to heal"—based on the horizontal experiences triggered via what seems to be a kind of orchestration from our inner healing resources.

The breather, in discussion with the facilitator, often arrives at the insight that he has two choices he can make. On the one hand, he can get his money back and leave the workshop, forever believing that the event was an abusive setting. Or he can feel the possibility that what has happened may be the beginning of a very positive healing experience for him. His Inner Healer can reframe the episode as a case of his being triggered to go deep into his pattern. He can begin to trust that this is a tremendous opportunity to heal, if he can find the courage to lie back down and return to the breathing.

When he does this, he, of course, finds that the gestalt is just below his level of consciousness. Consequently, he has quick access to it. This time he proceeds to do a very courageous piece of abreaction and clearing work. All during this episode he is gently supported and encouraged to "stay with it," as we say, and to amplify it—that is, to always do more of whatever it is he is already doing. Of course, he is also regularly reminded during his deep work that he can always say stop if he feels he has done enough for that day.

Now, we can examine this kind of rather common occurrence in our work from the standpoint of the Yoga of the Cross. The breather's first reaction was to feel abused. In essence, he feels attacked—on the *horizontal*. However, his powerful reaction can hardly be attributed to a mere touching of his mat. There must be a powerful *vertical* pattern, within which his extreme reaction makes total sense. He says to the facilitator, "You hurt me; you abused me. You *made* me freak out."

Obviously, what happened was an unfortunate mistake—or, as we say, a cosmic set-up. But, as an occasion for abuse, it was hardly intentional. Yet this does not make it any less painful for the breather, whose vertical reaction is coming from a very real biographical, perinatal, or transpersonal episode of abuse—or all three, for that matter. But it is definitely emerging from within the now-vertical dimension of who he is.

In addition, in the case of this kind of trauma, it is often difficult for the breather to cellularly understand that what has happened can be logically construed as a "wake-up call" on the horizontal—or an *opportunity to heal* presented by his Inner Healer. The wordless injunction from his own healing power is for him to "take it internal"—to go vertical with it—and do a powerful piece of work.

In the case of serious, relentlessly recurring abuse, it is sometimes almost impossible for the abused person to have the sense in his life that he is just being triggered, or motivated by something other than the current episode. The main reason for this is that the old trauma that has become unconscious—gone vertical—is often perceived and judged by the psyche as being too just painful to face. This is the case of many who continue to feel abused by the unintentional, but nevertheless perceived, slights occurring daily, in our plethora of outside, or horizontal, interactions.

In these painful situations, a seeker's entire life can become a constant opportunity for projection—for relentlessly reframing what is vertical into a horizontal picture of so-called "real reality." This can seem to be, and actually become for a while, what he envisions as a continual experience of abuse on the horizontal, even if he is in fact not being treated abusively. A painfully ironic outcome of this scenario would frequently be that without ever actually being abused again, he would have no setting or recourse to go vertical to the healing source of his pain.

It poses a fascinating mystery, however, that those who have been seriously abused and are still unconscious of its power find themselves continuing to feel abused on the horizontal at various times in their lives. This is absolutely through no fault of their own. It's just that the trauma within is so deep and painful that it is almost impossible to face. The boundaries between inner and outer reality are often blurred for those who know intimately any type of powerful past abuse.

We should emphasize that, as a part of a rigorous screening process, we always strive to ascertain whether someone may, through really powerful, systematic abuse, react this way in a holotropic setting. In these cases, the holotropic strategy, at least within the day-long or weekend format, might not be an appropriate milieu. What would probably be needed—the most safe and effective—is an in-residence, around-the-clock, holotropic center. We are really looking forward to the advent of this phase of holotropic support, hopefully in the very near future.

However, in this case we are explicating, the good news is that this breather was able to feel that precious thing: a deep trust in his facilitators. What we have consistently seen is that, with trust, there is virtually no limit to the power of holotropic work in the expanded state of consciousness via the power of the breathing process.

One last nuance on this scenario seems to be in order. What about some other breather nearby the one we have been discussing? This breather may also have a facilitator accidentally brush her mat. Yet when this happens, if she registers it at all, she might have a passing sense of, "Oh, someone stepped on my mat." Then, without "missing a beat," she returns seamlessly to her inner world, following the guidance of her power within.

It is clear in this situation that this type of abuse we have been discussing is just not her main issue, or perhaps not even any type of issue for her at all. She will, of course, have her own particular set of triggering possibilities along the horizontal, based on what exists within the vertical dimension of her psyche. But having her mat barely touched is just not one of them. This particular episode—where *her* mat gets brushed against—does not seem to register on her inner healing radar. She gets no negative reaction at all from it.

To bring home the point, let us once more sum up these scenarios in terms of the Yoga of the Cross. The truth is, it is absolutely impossible to heal in the holotropic work if a breather cannot, for the most part, recognize that her reactions are coming from her own internal, *vertical*, recording of past history. By this we mean that she must be able to take whatever *horizontal* stimuli with which she is presented, and work with them *vertically* as "grist for the mill" of her own awakening.

This holds true even if something happens on the mat, *horizontally*, that triggers whatever pattern or process she may have *vertically*, within her own psyche. As we stated, the most important issue is not about who is to blame, and staying focused on this one point. By far the most important question is, "how can we get truly free?" The only true way we know is to turn inward first, and follow the trail presented to us by our own Inner Healers.

It is certainly possible for sitters and facilitators to do something unintentionally abusive. Or they may instigate something plainly unskillful, or even unconsciously aggressive, which is in fact wounding to the breather. In these cases, we have a responsibility to own our errors and to do everything in our power to rectify the horizontal abuse we have caused. In these cases, the breather's reaction is quite congruent, and they must be supported and honored for their reactions.

So, let us continue to clarify this dance between what is *within* or *without*. It is frequently the case, as well, that breathers who have been seriously wounded—and consequently virtually unable yet to go vertical to the source of such pain—will find other deep triggers in the breathwork room. One of the most powerful of these will always be the music itself. Breathers often will say something like, "That piece of music *made me* so sad, or so frightened!"

Music: The Glorious Trigger

Within the holotropic milieu, becoming triggered on the horizontal is something that is always occurring throughout the breathwork setting. It does not have to be anything like someone brushing the breather's mat. Perhaps the two biggest possible triggering mechanisms for *every* breather are, first, the sounds throughout the room—what sounds like wailing, laughter, screaming, cursing, babies crying, singing, and a veritable cacophony of human vocal expressions. All of these ultimately reflect deep healing work on the part of the breathers.

The second, and probably the most profound trigger, can be, as we said, the music itself. Let's look at it from a slightly different angle than the one we just covered. Concerning this dance between the vertical and the horizontal arms of our therapeutic cross, something that happened about twenty years ago—a great lesson for me—really drives home the point.

But first, a preface note on our use of music for Holotropic Breathwork. Based on what we have been exploring here, it becomes clear that the music is truly one of the most powerful *triggers*, or *opportunities to heal*, for all breathers in our work. We should point out, here, as an aside, that we absolutely *do not, ever*—*ever*—play any piece of music that is in any way designed to be frightening. The psyche has enough of its own scary tales to tell without us adding to the list, from the outside.

Here is a fascinating story on the creative influence of music for our transformation within the holotropic milieu. Years ago, I played a particular three hour music set during a breathwork—one of which I was particularly fond. Later that afternoon, two people came to me—one-at-a-time. In addition, one more approached me the next morning. They each asked me a question about a certain piece of music that I played in the set that had impacted them in some way.

We are frequently asked about pieces of music—sometimes because the breathers love what we use, and sometimes because they hate it. From a therapeutic standpoint, as long as we are following the appropriate structure and playing what we feel are really powerful, good pieces, it does not matter so much whether a breather loves the music or hates it. If they are willing to "go vertical" with their reaction, as we say, they can do some really good work, one way or the other. The reason they love it or hate it almost always can be found within.

But this was different. In the first instance, the breather asked me what the piece of music was, in which the "angels were singing." Well, this was news to me. To my knowledge, there was no piece with angels singing. Nevertheless, to be sure, we went through the set, piece by piece, until we found the piece she was talking about. However, now she realized that, quite surprisingly to her, there was nothing like angels singing in that music at all. She had what we call an "aha" moment on the power of our own inner vertical process to shape our external, horizontal experience.

Later that day, another breather approached me, and asked which piece of music was it that had the "train running through it." So, once more I found myself sharing that there was no piece like that. But, as before, I was happy to go through the set with him to so see if we could ascertain to which piece he was referring.

Lo and behold, as you might suspect, it was the *same* piece as the one where the woman thought she heard angels singing. However, there were no angels singing, but there was also no train running through the music. Now the therapeutic dynamic we have been highlighting is becoming even clearer. This is the issue relating to the power of our internal psyches—on the vertical—to create our horizontal experiences throughout our lives.

But the story is not finished. The next morning, *another* breather asked me about the set. You are probably guessing what's coming next. She related that she heard a piece of music where there were *wolves* howling. Wolves now! Well, there you have it—there were no wolves in any piece I played. You are also probably guessing correctly that—once again—it was the same piece as the one where the train was running through it, and the one where the angels were singing. If ever I needed convincing about the power of our internal *vertical* experience to provide a colored lens for us to look through and thereby shape our external, *horizontal* reality, I needed it no more.

How the Yoga of the Cross Became the Awareness Positioning System

We have one more demonstration to share of the remarkable applicability of this Yoga of the Cross for work in expanded states of awareness. Keep in mind that the meta-purpose of this section, and a major part of our entire inquiry, is the efficacy of this holotropic perspective within a broad array of therapeutic settings—or simply for a holotropic therapy.

How and why the Yoga of the Cross became the Awareness Positioning System is well documented in my last book, *Movie Yoga: How Every Film Can Change Your Life*. For one, I was attempting to popularize the holotropic perspective by demonstrating how using the structure and practice therein could add a powerful therapeutic component to film-going—one of the most popular forms of entertainment in the world.

In so doing, it was clear, given the powerful influence of a certain base of Christianity that might possibly take exception to my secular use of the term "cross," it seemed expedient to change the name. I also wished for the method to have as wide a chance as possible to reach a large segment of the population. If people could have fun while transforming at the same time, well, all the better.

However, the meta-reason I wished to call it the *Awareness Positioning System*, or APS, was to more accurately reflect a central characteristic of the process. I wrote about its similarity to the ubiquitous navigation tool in automobiles and most mobile phones called the Global Positioning System, or the GPS. With the GPS, drivers who were disoriented, lost, or confused could tap into a satellite system that within a few seconds could orient them to where they were, and then give them exact verbal directions on how to arrive at their desired destination.

The driver's need for a GPS seemed to have an almost uncanny resemblance, or at least a very close parallel, with certain difficulties seekers often face on their journeys toward wholeness. It appears to be perennially common for us to become what we call "stuck," "traveling blind into unknown territory," "lost in the second matrix of the birth canal," "feeling at a dead-in" in our inner work, or a host of other metaphors for what Jack Kornfield might say are just a few of the "promises and pitfalls of the spiritual path."

In any of these states, the seeker ultimately comes to a sojourn, a rest, a stop, and takes stock of where she has been, where she is now, and where she might be headed. The *Awareness Positioning System* represents a powerful talisman, ally, or homing beacon on this stage of the journey. We can become much clearer about what challenges exist for us in life circumstances and those with whom we are in relationship "on the horizontal."

Just as important, if not more so, we can "go vertical," and help ourselves get clear and clean through holotropic dynamics by working with, and making conscious, the horizontal, unconscious material that always holds us back, both relationally as well as individually. In addition, by learning to bring on line the upper arm of the vertical dimension of the cross, we can also continue to deepen our relationship with a more expanded sense of the Great Mystery, or higher sources within us. This includes, as well, discovering various configurations of psycho-spiritual practices that help ensure our ability to get clear, and stay clear in our every-day lives, as well as on our chosen path toward wholeness.

Here is the story of the GPS beginning. In the early nineties, Stan and Christina put Diane Haug and me "on the road" to bring the training into countries asking for it. Stan let me know that I was to teach a number of the modules. I felt honored, excited, and scared to death. We had been with Stan for years, and heard him teach. I easily recognized that I would never be a Stan or a Christina, and in fact was encouraged by Stan to present the material in my own way. My inner task was "to *own* that I *owned* it."

It made sense for me to rely on something close to my heart. I was passionate about film, and had seen many movies that quite beautifully and accurately demonstrated the principles of a number of the modules I had to present. So, in addition to teaching verbally, I would show films on the subject, and we facilitators and the group would discuss them afterward.

These were often not documentaries. They were fictionally-based films. Fortunately, the groups responded quite positively to this type of communication. We heard from many participants that the emotional narrative, coupled with powerful imagery and a compelling story, seemed to bring the teachings alive, and to provide a certain explanatory, or even revelatory nuance that lectures alone sometimes could not.

They would report that the depth of the emotional content truly enriched the conceptual bases of the particular module topics. In this way, the power of the films' subject matter added, in a sense, "expanded bandwidth" that an intellectual exercise alone may not always have. So this became an integral part of our modules, and we have carried on this practice ever since. It has definitely become part of the world holotropic mythos.

In one particular United States module—Spiritual Emergency—we put on a powerful film we had shown a number of times in different countries. Now, the films would be aired after dinner. So, once the movie started, the team—minus a team member or two and a couple of apprentices, who would stay with the group in case anything was needed—would retire to a back room to process how we were doing and how the module was unfolding.

The next morning I came into the group about twenty minutes ahead of starting time, ready to discuss spiritual emergency, in light of the didactic material from the day before, as well as to hear from the group about the film. However, there was one woman standing by the sound board who appeared quite disturbed. Before I was even able to put down my notes and outline, she approached me, clearly agitated, and, as we say in our work, very much "in process."

Before I could ask her how she was doing, she proceeded to berate me. In no uncertain terms, she accused me of seriously abusing her. Needless to say, I felt what we in this kind of work call being "blind-sided." But, my main feeling was deep concern for this breather who did not feel safe in our setting.

It so happens that there was a rape scene in the film we showed the night before. When she saw this, she felt abused, just as she actually had been years before in her own life. I was a bit in shock, and did my best to apologize quite profusely. She was very disturbed the rest of the day until her breathing journey, where she did some very powerful work on her history of repeated sexual abuse. However, during this time, I still represented a bead on her string of life abuses.

It actually took this courageous woman quite a number of years to let go of what she perceived had happened through my showing of the film. This is totally understandable, based on the power of deep abuse in the lives of seekers. On one level, it seemed accurate that I participated in creating what was probably an avoidable situation, setting up a scenario prohibiting her from really feeling safe in the module. I felt quite awful about this. As I shared, we facilitators take creating a safe container for the breathwork extremely seriously. For many years, we had often been praised for just such a safe atmosphere. The team processed this in detail, and I thought about the situation for a number of months.

Of course, I knew that, in general, movies can be extremely powerful. Moreover, it is almost impossible to find very many films showing deep emotional and psychological subjects that will not contain at least some material that is objectionable to somebody. The truth is, I recognized that the very power of most films stemmed from their portrayals of various challenging episodes of the archetypal human adventure.

I have shared already about the publication of my book *Movie Yoga: How Every Film Can Change Your Life*. In addition, I pointed out the emergence of the *Awareness Positioning System* from the original name for this process, the *Yoga of the Cross*. This was in order to instill the text with a more secular, popular feel, as well as an easily accessible and "catchy" title. My purpose was to bring the self-empowering nature of the holotropic into a more accessible forum for a larger segment of the world population.

The truth is, besides just to be entertained, this is one of the main reasons people go to the movies—that is, to be "moved" in some way. I wrote a number of screenplays over the years, and, in the process, studied a few books on the subject. Unanimously, these teachers shared that the premise of almost any film is that, "Someone wants something really badly, and is having trouble getting it."

One author pointed out that if there were a movie called *The Village of the Happy Nice People*, most people would not be interested. For the majority of film-goers, it would seem just too boring to bother with. We see movies *to be moved*—to have some kind of powerful experience.

But back to our current inquiry. Most people in our groups found our films to be powerful emotionally, but also felt that they were exceptional teaching tools, and integral to the training, as well. I did not want to give them up. But I definitely did not wish to participate in fostering any kind of situation that would be an occasion for re-abuse for anyone in our groups.

However, this was a formative period for our teaching and the unfolding of supportive structures for the holotropic experience, and many things were becoming clear. I have already shared in depth how I found the explication of the "vertical/horizontal" dynamic to be a valuable way to simplify and clarify conflict in the sharing group. Quite suddenly, it dawned on me that we were looking at the mere tip of an iceberg of deep opportunity to enrich the structure of the training in even more profound ways.

So, this was the birth of what later became *Movie Yoga*, or the psycho-spiritual practice of film watching. No longer were we only interested in the intellectual, *educational* capacity of film. We had become aware that there was a previously untapped treasure chest of psycho-spiritual healing possibilities inherent in the showing of these movies for the groups.

However, we were going to have to provide the identical "yoga of the cross" structure for psycho-therapeutic processing that we had brought on-line in the sharing groups and for the breathers during their sessions a few years before. By now, you probably know this structure well: Whatever comes up emotionally for breathers as they view an educational movie in the training should be treated as "grist for the mill" of transformation. The strategy is that the film is *horizontal* to the viewer, who may, if the Inner Healer so chooses, also have a powerful *transformative* experience *on the vertical*, along with an *educational* upgrade.

Watching the movie may be the impetus for a powerful healing situation in which the viewer "goes internal"—"down the arm" of the cross, on the *vertical* arm of the symbol—and makes conscious the emotional power latent within past experiences that have become unconscious within the psyche. Having then embraced the experience—made it conscious—she sends it "up the line," as we say, to the upper arm of the cross, to whatever source of inspiration she has, with the power of grace to transform, "burn up," or otherwise remove the trauma from her psyche.

In addition, through the practice of staying open and embracing whatever comes into her awareness, the breather treats the movie situation *almost exactly like a breathwork*. She works with the uncovered material, first through an inner practice with the Yoga of the Cross, the Awareness Positioning System, and then through the subsequent sharing groups we make available.

In addition, since she is in the middle of a Holotropic Breathwork seminar, she has the perfect opportunity to "take it to the mat," as we say, in her breathwork sessions. Through this multi-faceted process, the Inner Healer is provided ample opportunity to facilitate the emergence of unconscious, or newly conscious, material into the breather's awareness, where the charge can be released, and healing take place.

Since then, groups everywhere have responded in a tremendously positive way to this enrichment of their healing possibilities in the training. Quite quickly, the Movie Yoga episodes became almost "benevolently notorious," but very well thought of, and even looked forward to. We even regularly schedule a Movie Yoga module, where films take the place of most extended lectures and where the whole group just experiences movies and does the breathing—then experiences more movies and does the breathing.

After each film, we spend deep sharing time working with what has been brought into consciousness for the breathers during the films. They love it, and report that it is an extremely powerful healing modality—almost exactly like a Holotropic Breathwork session itself. The whole week is one beautiful, powerful, conscious opportunity to heal.

The most essential dynamic of all was that the breathers were able, through the embracing of their own inner healing resources, to feel *even more* personal empowerment from their work with Movie Yoga dynamics. As the core principal of the entire process, the Yoga of the Cross, or the Awareness Positioning System, became standard language throughout the world training.

It was common to hear breathers saying to each other, "Just take it vertical," or "You, know, you stay horizontal with it and you will never heal." The group, and the movies, did the work for us facilitators. This is one of the ways seekers are able to more intensely trust their own Inner Healer resources. They recognize that healing is coming from within themselves, and not any outside source.

Ultimately, especially after *Movie Yoga, How Every Film Can Change Your Life*, was released, we were able to discuss the deeper implications of the Yoga of the Cross. We began to reframe much of the therapeutic interaction over issues that seemed to regularly emerge in the groups. For example, we would use such language as "relationship yoga." As you can imagine, this ubiquitous issue of relationship is, world-wide, an incredibly hot topic!

Applications of the cross—and later the APS, the Awareness Positioning System—expanded to include a multitude of aspects of the everyday human experience. No longer were seekers seeing themselves as powerless victims of outside circumstances of all kinds. Instead they recognized that *every* life experience, every emotion related to *any* life experience, could be the occasion for something powerfully transformational—and, as we say, an *Opportunity to Heal*.

CHAPTER XIX

Creative Modifications of the Holotropic Milieu

If we maintain that the holotropic format is unique—extremely effective yet unalterable in its foundation—then we may actually be adhering to nothing more than the "letter of the law." Through a different lens, we could propose that we might in fact be limiting the transformational essence of the strategy. We may also deprive thousands who might not be able to practice the method in its original form, but who are craving something deeper and more effective in the therapies currently available to them.

Let's review again, succinctly, the basics of the holotropic perspective, to see how the method may hold an, as of yet, unlooked-at therapeutic potential within more traditional settings. To sum up:

1. Healing happens in expanded states of awareness, and within an expanded framework of the psyche, including the biographical, perinatal, and transpersonal dimensions.
2. The unalterable director of the process is the Inner Healer each seeker—a power within. This power can be experienced as none other than consciousness itself.
3. The facilitator's sole task is to be a non-directive support person and to keep the seeker mentally, emotionally, physically, and spiritually safe.
4. Healing happens homeopathically, by intensification of whatever is emerging from within the seeker's psyche.
5. There are three essential components of the therapeutic process: preparation, session, and integration.

If we examine these requirements, no component seems to represent a "deal-breaker"—or a reason not to pursue an inquiry into modifications necessary for the unfolding of a holotropic therapy within the sacrosanct tenants of a Holotropic Paradigm.

My exploration of this exciting frontier began in the early nineties, when I was invited to bring Holotropic Breathwork to a conference called Common Boundary. The founder of the group that organized these events had experienced the breathwork with us, had become excited by it, and therefore wanted to expose more people to the power of the method.

For a number of years during that period, Common Boundary was *the* conference to attend, or at which to present. The organizers successfully brought together the leading voices and practitioners in nearly every popular, growing-edge therapy or spiritual practice. It was an honor to be invited to introduce Holotropic Breathwork to a possibly new and larger audience. However, there was, as usual, a catch—a real deal-breaker—as we are calling these issues that we just do not seem to be able to get past, or "live with" within the true holotropic framework. In this case, he gave me about six hours to do the work—by his or any criteria, quite a generous offer.

However, for me, it effectively put an end to the adventure. From our experience, it was psychotherapeutically unsound—in fact impossible—to do Holotropic Breathwork in less than one, quite full day. Since each breather has a sitter, who is also a participant herself, it requires *two* actual holotropic sessions for everyone to experience the breathing, and for each person to be a sitter. Each session would be, at the minimum, approximately two hours long, while most of them lasted for approximately three hours. Of course, it was likely that some breathers might require more time, as well as an extended period of supportive release work, and a quite focused verbal integration session to become as complete as they could be for that day. As we said, we take completion, and the integration phase, quite seriously.

Under no circumstances would we create a milieu in which breathers were forced to get up from the mat before they felt "complete, within the larger field of incompletion," as we say. The process of Becoming, of moving toward wholeness, or Being, by its very nature implies "incompletion," or an evolutionary trajectory toward completion, "Point Omega," or whatever metaphor we may use to imply Being itself.

It is essential that there be sufficient time to assist people to reach their Inner Healer-guided integration. Nor could we not use sitters, as the sitter/breather dynamic is critical for a host of reasons, including maximum breather safety, integration, and a number of other dynamics less easily defined in this short framework here. Suffice it to say that "sitting" has almost always been an additional transformative experience for participants.

For a day or two, I despaired of the opportunity. But then I began to think about it more deeply. More accurately, I just let go of the current dilemma, and allowed my consciousness to wander. During these rather expanded musings, a basic inquiry seemed to wind its way through my consciousness: "Just what *could* we do in half a day, and keep the setting totally holotropic?"

I suppose I managed to get "outside the box." And, for all intents and purposes, the Inner Healer came up with something. The main question in front of us is, "In what way can we offer a practice not officially Holotropic Breathwork, but one that is a creative as well as effective modification, and yet *always totally grounded in unassailable holotropic principles*?" So, I had an inspiration.

We could call it something like *A Journey of Life Celebration.* We would employ almost every holotropic requirement—within a modified practice and time frame. All of the following would be honored: preparation/session/integration; an expanded state of awareness; session Inner Healer-guided; facilitators for support only; healing by embracing and intensifying whatever emerges into awareness. As strange as this may sound, the breathing practice itself would be the *one* thing we would not do. Instead, the *power of music* would be the catalyst for seekers to open to the meta-ordinary state of consciousness.

We came together with a warm welcoming, and a brief inner focusing—utilizing a short, mellow, heartfelt piece of music. Following the opening came cultivation of group dynamics and support: going around the room, everyone introducing themselves, including my small two-person team of close friends and holotropic practitioners. Of course, in honoring the full range of *preparation*, there was an opening discussion on what we would be doing.

As a meta-framework, we shared how seekers have come together in circles like this for thousands of years. I painted a picture of how, right at that moment, people all over the world were gathering in hundreds of different kinds of circles—to turn inward, to search, to transform, and to grow. I presented an easy-going, simplified explanation of the universal death/rebirth process—an extended map of the psyche, including the biographical, perinatal, transpersonal domains. I did all this simply, briefly, translating the language from heady theory into easy-to-understand concepts—to "keep it simple," as we say in Alcoholics Anonymous.

We unveiled the method for our journey; what I have been calling ever since, in settings like this all over the world, our *Life Dance*. We shared that dance and music have been used for thousands of years—and today in raves and trance dance—as a powerful way to open to our deepest selves—the expanded state of awareness. All morning we were just taking it easy, playing with a simplified, yet clear and accurate version of transformational principles—laughing, offering our enthusiasm, letting them ask a lot of questions, and do a lot of sharing. It was *Support, Support, Support.*

All of this was part of the preparation phase for the Life Dance to take place in the afternoon. This was the second phase of the three-part process; the *session* itself. And the Life Dance? It would be no big deal—just an easy, unstructured moving around the room, or sitting in a chair or on the floor, or lying down—whatever they chose.

The team would be circulating—basically just wandering through the room—making ourselves unobtrusively available for any support at all that anyone might need. We encouraged participants to expect that something might happen in their bodies; or some emotion might emerge. We also asked them to be open to whatever the Inner Healer might bring into their awareness, including an experience of numinosity.

We shared that if their eyes were closed at any point—or if they were turned inward—images, scenes, or patterns might emerge into their awareness. We encouraged them to trust as fully as possible that whatever emerges is coming from within their psyches, guided by their own inner healing power. Every part of their experience would be personally designed by that power for their healing, and not at all by any directing from the support team. All they would have to do is "be with it," or "embrace it" as best they could.

We orchestrated the music to last about forty-five minutes. It followed the basic holotropic music style, but would be quite less "driving," and in general, with more mellow, or easy rhythms to get started; some emotionally powerful movie sound track themes for what we call "breakthrough" in the middle, all followed by beautiful, heartfelt and meditative music afterwards. We emphasized that they would not be required to *do* anything at all—just be as open as they could be—with as little expectation as possible.

They can stop at any time—sit, lie down, or whatever. And when the music was finished, we would ring the chimes. If they felt like it, this would be the signal to sit, take a piece of art paper, and draw, if they wished, whatever felt right for them. Or, they might write something down, almost like a journal entry for their experience. This would be the initial phase of the *integration* time.

Then we would gather together in a sharing circle—on the floor or in chairs. We really emphasized beforehand that *this is not therapy*—or definitely no traditional form of therapy. It had way more kinship with an archetypal healing circle as enacted by tribes around the world for millennia. We *absolutely do not know what is best for them*. But *they* do, because they have a perfect power within themselves. We say that sharing is a lot like kindergarten: Basically a sweet "show-and-tell." This would be the heart of the *integration* phase.

Following the sharing, when everyone feels as complete as they can be—"within the larger field of incompletion"—we offer what it is like to go home—what they can expect. We encourage them to eat grounded food, and to reconnect with what support they may already have: therapists, counselors, body workers, Twelve Step groups, whomever. We suggest they can call us if they wish to share anything.

If the integration feels a little uncomfortable, or they are confused about anything, we encourage them to trust themselves and their Inner Healers. We remind them to journal, dance, and meditate—to not isolate—in that long ago time, to use *phone yoga*—whereas today it would be something like *text, email,* or *Facebook yoga.* And to remember that, no matter what, they are on the right track and are doing it right.

So, this was the set-up, and everyone seemed "on board." After lunch, we guided them with a few words and a ring of the chimes, into the music. They began to move around the room. Some whirled; others just swayed in one place. Others lay down, and some sat in chairs. Many smiled; some wept; some seemed sad for a while. But when the music was done, we checked with each seeker, and all was well. Next, they spent some time working with their "mandalas," as we call them, or writing in a journal they may have brought, or using the notebook we provided for them. And then, we shared.

The team was, for want of any more expressive a phrase, absolutely "blown away." The strategy worked! Everybody "went deep," as we say. Each person had a powerful experience. We witnessed surprise after surprise. The sharing group, well, it all sounded just like a Holotropic Breathwork sharing group. We could hardly believe it when two participants reported that they actually experienced a level of the *perinatal* dimension—the first they had ever had—just by dancing.

So, what had happened? The holotropic *structure and perspective worked*—preparation, session, integration; and music to support an expanded state of consciousness. We all felt that we had accidently, unintentionally opened wide the door on what might well contain tremendous holotropic possibilities and opportunities, including a holotropic therapy, support for those seekers using entheogens, and for those in spiritual emergency. We had witnessed how the holotropic structure could be, in the sense of a koan, "modified in a *sacredly unmodified* manner"—*where every sacrosanct holotropic principle could be honored.*

It seemed to us that the Inner Healer will always be available to come on line, within just a few basic non-negotiable structures: safety always, support always, a wonderful catalyst like breath, music, or films—and, of course, seekers in the modern world really ready to open. We all felt certain that this was the inauguration of an adventure in the holotropic unfolding that, to this day, is still expanding and blossoming—reaching more and more people around the world—all without sacrificing *any* of the non-negotiable, core holotropic principles.

Refining Our Appropriate Modifications

It was clear that we were "onto" something, and Australia became the testing ground of this next phase. We learned quickly that the one-day, or eight-hour, framework was an accommodating blueprint, applicable with any number of themes. Our first forays beyond Common Boundary centered around our work in a wellness model of addictions recovery, and we have continued to use this 9:00—5:00 framework in recovery settings in many places in the world.

So we "took it on the road" and brought it successfully into a number of cities. Marianne Wobke, Dave and Donna Misso, Nigel Denning, Lila Pesa, and Vicky Nicholson—all dear friends and co-workers there—organized and worked in the seminars, and really believed in the model. From the feedback we received, the work was something special and brand new for most. It really seemed to inspire a lot of seekers. With extremely few modifications, it was clear that we had stumbled onto an elegant, powerful vehicle for an authentic holotropic experience accessible to thousands of seekers who may not have the time, money, or inclination to attend a traditional Holotropic Breathwork seminar.

As an aside, I ventured into territory where even my angels feared to tread. Lest I ever call down the wrath of the spirits, I had vowed years before never to conduct a seminar whose main topic was one-on-one relationship. It has always been my experience that whatever subject we might choose for a workshop mobilizes the forces of that particular archetype—for the facilitator, as well as the group. These forces will then frequently pour in—seeming to demand that we really "do our homework" in order to be able to receive and become an authentic voice of the topic being explored.

From what I have heard from many workshop presenters, we each seem to have our special growing edges. Relationship has definitely been one of mine. But I offered myself before the gods and goddesses, and took the plunge. And I am pleased to report that at no time did I have to dodge a bolt of cosmic fire, and that all of us seemed to learn quite a bit.

However, one application stands alone for those of us who participated in this particular adventure. Over the years in our Australian holotropic training, we had had the blessing to spend deep intimate time with, and to get to know, an indigenous Australian—an aboriginal person—Marianne Wobke, who became a close friend, a fellow holotropic practitioner, and very important teacher for me. In addition, Vicky Nicholson—who organizes our training in Australia—and another dear friend and Holotropic Breathwork practitioner, Ruth Langford, an aboriginal person herself, were also closely connected with certain groups within the aboriginal community.

So, at one point we had the opportunity to travel to central Australia—Marianne, Vicky, Dave and Donna Misso, Ashley Wain and Nigel Denning—for two purposes close to all the team member's hearts. One was to spend sacred time at Uluru—the stone power center and sacred spring that were a spiritual dynamo there, and one of my most favorite locations on the earth. The second was to conduct one of our day-long holotropically-oriented workshops in Alice Springs, and to invite without charge any aboriginal person who wanted to be there.

We had heard that a number of aboriginal seekers from the local community might be attending. This was a cause of much excitement among us. But, for me, it was also a source of worry and stress. We knew that, traditionally, when white people offered to psychologically support aboriginal people, we tended to "colonize" them in a manner often containing the same ignorance of aboriginal culture and psyche as the original white colonizers. This is tantamount to heaping abuse onto abuse. What if we did the same thing? How would we know better? Could we find a way to authentically radiate an innate, truth-revealing presence that could reach anyone in a language of the heart that totally honors the universal, core human spirit?

In the end, we relied on our method. We consciously re-invoked our commitment to honor every seeker's inner healing power. We trusted that all we had to do was offer ourselves in service, as open-heartedly as possible. We felt that these people always already responded to an innate presence of a deep inner healing power—something which had been an undiluted part of their culture for thousands of years. What could we really offer, other than our trust in their ability to heal themselves?

To thicken the plot, Vicky was able to get in touch with a world-renowned aboriginal elder who's "mob" were the sacred owners of Uluru, and to invite him to come to the workshop as our guest. His name was Uncle Bob Randall. To all of our surprise, he agreed. The possibility of his presence was an opportunity for me to quickly bring on-line my own Awareness Positioning System.

I must admit that my Inner Healer allowed me a chance to do quite a piece of work, exploring some rather core, entrenched emotions and patterns. Among them were awe, nervousness, self-doubt, fear of failure, and being exposed as a fraud. So, I began the workshop in the knowledge that this process was already working for at least one person, and that person was, of course, myself. Well, of course, this is always true in the holotropic work. There is only one person we are ever really "working on" in a seminar, and that person is oneself.

There is a wonderful metaphor from certain Taoist or Zen traditions, which I paraphrase and recite regularly as a mantra in the emotionally fluid and unpredictable settings of our work. This is, *"to be like water."* If we show up with a will to order, control, and predictability—and this goes for any holotropic environment—we are setting ourselves up for quite an ego-death. This central Australian workshop, which we actually managed to go back and conduct once again after this—was a wonderful, relentless teacher in this regard. To our surprise, the *Aunties*—the women healers and elders—showed up with their grandchildren. The grandchildren were primarily interested in the snacks and some of the art supplies we use for the integration phase. And of course, the renowned elder came too.

As Sam told Frodo in Mordor before they marched down the hill into ten thousand orcs on their way to Mount Doom, "There's nothing for it." And this is how I felt. So, we dove in with only a wisp of a sense of holotropic order—preparation, session, and integration. All of this unfolded within aboriginal time, space, and consciousness. Amid the children playing and laughing, and the Aunties pretty much ignoring any of the usual protocols of "pay attention to the group leader," we forged ahead.

For the opening, we invited the group to spend a few moments looking for a tree on the property, as a source of connection—a centering axis and "lightning rod"—to which they could return for centering and grounding at any point during the day. One of my cohorts overheard an Auntie whisper to another something like, "Hey, he's talking about trees!" I believe this may have been a surprise, and not the usual way a white boy would open one of these *"let's help the poor aboriginals find the light"* kind of seminars.

All went well throughout the morning—except that the famous elder just leaned up against the wall in his chair, with his cowboy hat down over his eyes. This was occurring as I held forth in all my wisdom, which, by the minute, seemed to disperse like "a candle in the wind," as the song goes. It was definitely a perfect occasion for me to practice the art of dying. Even if nobody else in the group was enjoying or learning anything, I, for one, was doing a serious piece of work. It was the golden opportunity to practice what I had been preaching for years: *"The only person we are ever working with in any group is ourselves."*

After lunch—a raucous, playful celebration in which the children were quite clearly the seminar leaders—we returned for the *session* phase—the music journey. We invited participants to get comfortable, either lying down with mats, pillows, and a sheet, in a chair, or standing, ready to move a bit. We had prepared everyone for what to expect and how to "be with" their journeys.

So we played the music set. I must admit that, as I circled the room, holding space, as we say, I paid close attention to Uncle Bob. But he was enigmatic. He revealed nothing. He just leaned his chair back against the wall, put his hat over his face, and for all intents and purposes, and as far as anyone could tell, was having a nice after-lunch nap.

When the music was done and everyone—except Uncle Bob—opened their eyes and came back into the everyday consciousness of the room, they spent some time journaling or drawing, and had a cup of tea. Then it was time for the sharing. I was in a state—masking it, of course, with my best therapeutic visage. Here was my fear: We were just minutes away from our entire dream and effort in Australia becoming unceremoniously unmasked as one more fraudulent, insolent attempt by white people to indoctrinate the original custodians in what the Rainbow Serpent had already given them eons before any white person existed on the planet.

Some facilitators wryly report how often the *one participant* with whom they may have some kind of personal connection, for whatever reason—be it fear, doubt, need to please, or longing—will just about always, always, be the *last person* to share. It seemed ruthlessly fitting that Uncle Bob was also the final person in this group to share. He slowly let his chair come back to rest on the floor. Then he raised the brow of his hat so that we could all see his face. Taking his time, he opened his eyes, looked around the room, and then said quietly, matter-of-factly, "Well, I reckon this will work for everybody."

There are many certified holotropic practitioners globally who are just now coming to agree with him. We are seeing that the archetype of the holotropic model is a powerful method, with the potential to be implemented in an ever-widening number of therapeutic settings. But, what about the opening scenario of this section—where we painted a picture of darkened hotel ballrooms in which groups of one-hundred-and-fifty seekers breathe and transform? This happens while loud rock'n roll music booms through huge speakers, and facilitators move elegantly through the room, keeping everyone safe. Could there actually be ...?

Once Again: Pushing the Edge of the Therapeutic Envelope

You may recall how we suggested that it seemed "quite a stretch" to imagine a holotropic modality in any way translating itself into an office milieu. Here, in the civilized calm of an official setting, the roles often being enacted are that of a seeker, or small group of seekers, and a therapist often sitting in an easy chair or behind a desk, or as part of a sitting circle.

Toward this possibility, we have thus far presented a number of settings—modifications of the basic holotropic strategy—all as a gradually unfolding conceptual approach to perhaps augment the traditional therapeutic paradigm. Now is the time to attempt to finish what we started—to see if we can "make that stretch," in a safe, practical, as well as effective manner. But we do not begin blindly.

This issue of an actual holotropic therapy—that is, a modality in the vein of most traditional formats—has been discussed for decades in our training. The question most often asked is, "Can I effectively and safely use holotropic principles in talk therapy with my clients?" To answer this, we should spell out these principles again, so that we do not have to spend time searching back through the text to refresh ourselves:

1. Healing happens in expanded states of consciousness.
2. The Inner Healer, or consciousness itself, is the sole healing mechanism. The therapist is a support person only.
3. Healing occurs within the three bands of consciousness: biographical, perinatal, and transpersonal.
4. The therapeutic structure is in three parts: preparation, session, and integration.
5. Clients heal by an intensification of their symptoms, or what has emerged into their awareness.

To the first principle, there are already a number of therapies whose practitioners guide seekers into expanded states of awareness. Various forms of hypnosis and work with guided imagery belong in this category. We should point out that each of these very effective modalities relies on a more or less rigorous guidance-ship from the therapist, at the very least in certain stages of the process, including the integrative portion. At some point, a thorough, in-depth comparison of these methods with holotropic work would be a valuable contribution to the therapeutic field. But it is beyond both the purpose and scope of our inquiry here.

But before we delve into the possibility of any type of holotropically oriented therapy, we must point out another specific *elephant in the living room* of this current stage of our inquiry. If we use even a modification of methods that are commonly used to open seekers to expanded states of awareness—breath—however gentle; music, movement, guided imagery, a modified element of hypnosis, or some other practice, there is always one distinct, challenging possibility.

This is, that even if we are attempting to "tread lightly" with our client, there is always the possibility that her Inner Healer may guide her into a full-blown episode of an expanded state of awareness. This episode may contain all the physical, emotional, mental, or spiritual drama of the intense episodes to which we have been referring throughout this inquiry—including emergences from all bands of the extended cartography of the psyche.

Here is the elephant: If the therapist has not done a quite considerable amount of inner exploration herself, in which she has become acquainted with her own experiences of powerful inner work, she is quite likely, then, to re-enact the archetype of the *Sorcerer's Apprentice*. This could happen if the seeker has full-blown episodes from her own deeper dimensions. There may be no way that the therapist is prepared to support a seeker who has engaged her deepest self, without herself being intimately, personally familiar with what this terrain feels like. In this case, the session might well be traumatic for the seeker—as we say, another bead on the rosary of her dysfunction, or disempowerment.

Nor would it be advisable—even if the therapist could support her client– because the traditional one hour framework may be way too short a period for integration of a full-blown holotropic episode to be supported all the way through completion and integration. It would be absolutely much better for the therapist to have *never begun* to support her client, than to have opened her to a process in which there is no adequate recourse to help her to a "completion within the larger field of incompletion."

So, this takes us to the crux of the issue right away. On the surface, it would seem, then, that "all has been for nothing"—that there is no way to translate holotropic principles into traditional therapy. However, there is good news: There are two ways we imagine such a shift occurring. One would be that the therapist has done enough work on herself where she experientially—not just mentally—trusts in the power of her client's Inner Healer—her power within herself that absolutely knows what is best for her. Thus she "stays with" the seeker *all the way*—always trusting that seeker's power within to bring her to a successful completion, in that seeker's own time.

The second way would be that the therapist has previously undertaken a journey through a holotropic training—along with a lot of work in non-ordinary states of consciousness. The preparation portion is perhaps specifically modified to relate directly the needs and requirements of one-on-one or group therapy—all the while, at the same time, effectively cohering to core holotropic principals, as we have presented them throughout this text.

If the therapist herself has truly done rigorous deep work—to the point of at least beginning the journey of incremental psycho-spiritual death/rebirth, and she herself cellularly believes in an inner healing power, something wonderful can still take place. We can imagine a therapy session—based on *preparation, session, integration*—in which some mitigated, simple form of guided imagery, relaxation, coupled with a short period of focused, slightly deeper breathing—particularly with the use of non-invasive, soft, but evocative music—could be extremely effective in opening seekers into a form of expanded state of consciousness. At this point of opening, a process may unfold, guided always by the inner healing resources of the seeker. The therapist could then begin to ask general questions such as, "What is happening now?"

When responses come, the therapist may then gently encourage the seeker to "stay with it," and to report, if she wishes to, about what is unfolding. Or they may begin the internal journey to find an answer to a therapeutic dilemma posed by the seeker. If this is the case, then the therapist should share with the seeker to trust whatever response the Inner Healer reveals— verbally, emotionally, or physically—even if it offers answers to questions not even proposed by the seeker.

In this scenario, if the seeker really "lets go," then the therapist will have had enough of her own multi-leveled exploration that she will be able to, without fear, "stay with" the seeker through whatever her process may be. After all, we have shared repeatedly that we do not have to understand what the client is experiencing, as long as we keep her safe on all levels. We can be sure that the client—under the aegis of her own Inner Healer— will tell the therapist what has happened and what it means for her.

On the other hand, a full-blown "blast" from the deep psyche may not be what the power within intends. It may be quite powerful, yet much less outwardly dramatic. In this case, the responses of the seeker's Inner Healer should still, of course, always be honored and explored in as rich a manner as the seeker feels important. The therapist may also ask an "information-gathering" question, such as, "How is your body feeling?" If the seeker begins to emote, she can be gently encouraged to stay with it. The therapist may also ask her to gently tighten whatever part of her body feels tension—all this while the seeker's eyes may be shut, and she is sitting in her chair.

From our previous discussion of the three stages of the holotropic process, you may be able to ascertain that this holotropic strategy resembles fairly closely an "on the mat" stage of the integration process of the breathwork session. To continue, let us imagine that the seeker has reported uncovering various episodes of a pattern, and at some point she says she feels like "enough for today." Thus we would commence a gentle process of inviting the seeker back into the room, culminating in her opening her eyes.

As we enter the integration phase of the journey, it would be important for the therapist to provide an assortment of integrative media, such as paints, colored pencils, the amazing process known as SoulCollage®— developed by Seena Frost and nurtured world-wide by Kylea Taylor and Jim Schofield—or a notebook for journaling. Still, at this stage, some non-intrusive, up-lifting music—often centered in the heart—can be employed, with the strict purpose of allowing the seeker to become gently, but fully present.

Following this integrative phase, a culminating strategy would be a supportive dialogue between the seeker and the therapist, as in the sharing group of a regular holotropic breathing episode. As we said, this is basically what we call a "show and tell," in much the same fashion as it is done in pre-school with children. It is essential that every effort by the therapist should be directed toward a gentle *drawing out* from the seeker—or amplification—where she may now be in her consciousness, and how she feels. All of this should unfold *absolutely without any interpretation from any lens whatsoever that may be a product of the therapist's previous traditional training.* The therapist herself may imagine that she herself is a therapeutic *tabula rasa*—a clear, clean slate, unsullied by any of her past training.

The session would be considered concluded when this integration phase is reported by the seeker to be complete. This is the case unless it is clear that the seeker is unconscious of some physical, emotional, or mental unease or agitation that would, of course, signal that something is unfinished. If this is the case, it is essential that the therapist *not* conclude the session because of previous commitments. But she would then continue in the gentle process of helping the seeker to gradually intensify, either through sharing verbally, or of gentle further tightening of still-tense muscles or other specific areas of pain or tension.

Now, if you are a traditional therapist and wish to explore the holotropic possibilities, we are certain that already you will have some questions about strategies and interventions that are on the continuum from being "doable," all the way out on the continuum and becoming a deal-breaker. First of all, most therapists adhere to a daily schedule of clients, usually one after the other, with some—often not much—time in between.

In the case of most forms of traditional verbal therapy, the therapist is trained in how to bring these sessions to a satisfactory conclusion. In addition, most clients engaged in this type of therapy are "trained" by the parameters of talk therapy itself to expect their sessions to end at a pre-agreed time—a fifty-minute hour, or something like this. They are also taught that even if the issue on which they were working in the session is incomplete, they will "pick up where they left off" next time.

However, we can already see that this might well be an abusive travesty, in the case of working holotropically. The problem is that the therapist has often guided a seeker into an expanded state of awareness. Even if this expanded state is not as intense or powerful as a full Holotropic Breathwork session—which, of course, it may well be—nevertheless the seeker can often still be wide open and vulnerable. Her sensory apparatus may be compromised. She may still be immersed in a consciously operative emotional pattern. Or she may still be quite confused, ungrounded, and not oriented to three-dimensional space-time.

Any of these would render an attempt at culminating the session prematurely as unethical and perhaps dangerous. The therapist must then stay with the breather, employing any number of integrative strategies common within the holotropic milieu. This integrative work—even with a seemingly unrelated dialogue about any of a host of issues—including even such weighty discussions as the weather—should continue until the seeker feels that she is truly sufficiently returned to this external reality. These kinds of friendly, everyday, on the surface non-therapeutic interactions can be very healing. They can provide just what the seeker needs—time and human support until her Inner Healer lets her, the seeker, know she is complete for the day.

Signposts for this clear return would be based on her ability to negotiate the everyday demands of life in a so-called ordinary state of consciousness—driving an automobile, going back to work in a functional mode, and negotiating personal relationships with comparative ease. Lest we overlook the obvious, she must also have received a "game plan" from the therapist as to how to "be with" what has emerged, as well as to support herself in the coming days.

It should be clear what may happen to the therapist's traditional schedule—the usual practice of client following client within a *hylotropically* oriented, established time-frame set up by the therapist. As far as time scheduling is concerned, "all bets are off," as they say, when a holotropic modality is employed. This type of holotropic strategy, by its very nature, must follow its own internal unfolding over an appropriate time frame commiserate with the dictates of the seeker's inner healing requirements.

There is no room for compromise of physical or psychological safety—emotionally, cognitively, or spiritually—when a holotropically-oriented modality is employed within a traditional setting. In fact, we can effectively conclude that when such a method is employed, then the setting can no longer even be termed traditional. It has entered another transformational universe altogether. It takes on the gravitas of an ages-old archetype—the hero's or heroine's journey.

We are not saying such a methodology cannot be used in a previously conventional milieu. However, it *must not be used* unless the non-negotiable requirements of such holotropic practices are *all* rigorously, sacredly honored, in the manner we just prescribed above. If a therapist decides that she might like to try "a little of this" or "a little of that" holotropic component, just to see if it may enhance what she is already doing, this is unethical to the point of malpractice and even enters the domain of possible abuse.

There are quite well-known modern horror stories where deep, powerful practices that take seekers into expanded states of awareness are conducted in large groups without any properly trained facilitators. Within these cases is re-enacted, as we have pointed out, the archetype of the "sorcerer's apprentice" from Walt Disney's classic film *Fantasia.* Except, in this case, there is nothing whimsical about it. What happened there, and what has happened in modern times—even in the last few years—is that ambitious, unscrupulous so-called therapists or pseudo-shamans conduct truly dangerous, and, for the most part, unsupervised ceremonies using powerful techniques in which they have no true training.

These charlatans conduct these rituals for money and fame. They also do it for the aggrandizement of their own egos. Even for novices in these practices, it is so easy for powerful experiences on the part of the seeker to take place. But these often occur in a totally unsafe setting, which can be the cause of serious physical, psychological, and spiritual trauma—or re-traumatization—for duped seekers, from which it is difficult to recover. To ensure that this does not happen in our work, the best strategy for therapists, in employing a method with a holotropic underpinning, would be for them to regularly experience the holotropic practice first.

Even this is more than likely not enough for the client to be really safe, cared for, and supported. We should stress that, for the therapist, it seems that it ought to be almost a "deal-breaking" requirement that she be at least close to certification as a Holotropic Breathwork practitioner. In fact, the term *holotropic* is trademarked in most places in the world and cannot be used without permission. But the lure of witnessing—and being a part of, and given credit for—powerful healing is a truly seductive attractor to many people who harbor unmet power and self-esteem needs, and who can seem to become addicted to the glamour of fame and notoriety.

The truth is, it seems almost impossible to be *half or somewhat* holotropic. Nor can anyone, by reading a book alone, those by Stan, Christina, or any other holotropic practitioner, really acquire the skills or "being level" required to support people in expanded states of awareness. As we have stated over and over in various metaphors throughout this text, the only thing we have to offer another person is the work we do on ourselves. We cannot possibly read a book and think we "have it." For all intents and purposes, we have to die to ourselves. We must fundamentally, not just intellectually, reset our baseline of, not just a therapeutic, but our *universe or basic reality* orientation.

To be involved in supporting people through this kind of deep work can be an overwhelming, sometimes subtle, and initially and ultimately undetectable ego-enhancer. This often begins when we find ourselves taking credit for the work of the seeker's Inner Healer. Remember, we cannot support seekers in this kind of work by listening to some on-line "how-to" programs or by taking our current psycho-therapeutic baseline and adding a few of what we assume may be holotropic nuances or touches. A profound experience of ongoing ego-death is required for us to have the respect, awe, and humility necessary to even begin to support seekers in their inner journeys, without disempowering them and taking the power they will most often give us for ourselves.

However, none of these possible horror stories should prohibit us from exploring every means possible for the implementation of a holotropic therapy. Dave and Donna Misso and Nigel Denning, whom I have already mentioned—three close friends and excellent holotropic practitioners from Australia—are implementing a pioneering program for therapists based on holotropic principles. They are at the growing edge of making the holotropic paradigm a viable reality in many disciplines.

This is one of the most exciting frontiers that could have emerged. But it could only have taken place after decades of the dedicated work by hundreds of ethical practitioners from all over the world who have courageously, and fiercely, held space for seekers, that the greater possibilities inherent within the holotropic paradigm may soon become a global reality. It is our dream that one of the most powerful and important of these "offspring" of the Holotropic Paradigm will be the emergence of a safe, powerful holotropic therapy.

This can surely be accomplished by the impeccable work of therapists who have deeply experienced Holotropic Breathwork and are dedicated to successfully negotiating the borders between traditional milieus and practices in expanded states of awareness. And *only* by the personal commitment to, in sense, be willing to "die the ego-death many times" as holotropic practitioners have, all over the world for decades, can we truly "walk our holotropic talk."

Final Thoughts on the Dawn of a Holotropic Therapy

All of the modalities we have just discussed—including the crowning possibility of an authentic holotropic therapy—seem to demonstrate the efficacy of a philosophy and seeker-safety approach preserving only those modifications of Holotropic Breathwork that ruthlessly continue to adhere to the core principles which are the essence of the approach.

Yet, even though they may be time-shortened and setting-shifting practices, they have only pointed to, or paved the way for, the holotropic paradigm's applicability within modern one-on-one or group therapy. However, our most recent previous inquiry gives us a strong foundation from which to take one more clear-eyed, no-nonsense look at the very real, viable future of holotropic possibilities within these traditional settings.

As we move toward closure of this brief preface on a holotropic therapy, it should be no surprise that we revisit a core principle of the paradigm, the Inner Healer, or a power within. However, let us disregard, for a moment, the various permutations of an unfolding holotropic approach to therapy. Instead, here are a couple of "what if?" scenarios worth noting.

First, what if therapists—from no matter what school, philosophy, or technique—really internally understood, and had experienced at a core level, a radical dispensation of numinosity—including multiple dimensions of the human psyche beyond its traditional, limited biographical focus, as well as at least the rudimentary beginnings of an ongoing, incremental ego death in which they must commit to for a lifetime? Second, what if they absolutely recognize that this experience is fueled by the power of the Inner Healer? Or, third, what if—at least at a mental or intellectual level—they were intrigued, or even quite moved by a strategy which highlights total trust in the client, and reliance on the wellsprings of her inner truth? In short, what if they saw that their clients were always already blessed with infinite inner healing power and knowledge?

Again, what if, upon just hearing or reading about a Holotropic Paradigm, traditional therapists' own Inner Healers "came on line," giving them an "a-ha" moment of deep revelation? Or, what if there are strictly traditional therapists engaged in powerful death/rebirth practices for themselves, and have clearly undergone stages of in-depth transformation? This is, of course, already the case throughout the world—particular with entheogen exploration in safe, supported sessions, midwifed by experienced support people.

Might it be possible for these therapists to experiment with, in their own traditional settings, how it would feel to let go a little, expanding somewhat the lens through which they view the psycho-therapeutic adventure of their clients? It is already quite clear how fierce we are in the holotropic work to safeguard the inner healing principle. Our stance is also well-documented concerning how much deep, ongoing inner work on the part of therapists is required, in order for them to truly operate from a holotropic perspective.

What if it were possible for them to "try the holotropic perspective on for size" in their own offices, both in terms of their own reactions, as well as how a client might respond therapeutically? The answer seems to be, somewhat facetiously, a resounding "yes, no, and maybe."

We have heard from many seekers who are therapists how, when they first tried Holotropic Breathwork, they had two complementary revelations. First, even though they were not conscious of this previously, they realized how much they were really searching for deeper levels of transformation in their own lives. This was true, even though they could not consciously recognize it until after they did some core work in meta-ordinary states of consciousness. Second, they also recognized that, for quite some time, they had been feeling restless and dissatisfied with the real therapeutic depth of the work they were doing with their clients. They had the insight that they were unconsciously looking for something deeper and more authentic, in ways they could not yet ascertain. Often this longing was characterized by an intuitive revelation that what was missing in traditional therapy was a crucial component of *numinosity.*

These therapist/seekers comprise a part of a seemingly large segment of the therapeutic population who are, to use a couple of metaphors, "on the evolutionary fence," or a "ripe fruit just now ready to fall from the tree." By this, we mean that many have consciously or unconsciously arrived at a stage of their own personal evolution toward wholeness, where all it might take for them to awaken to their barely unconscious need for deep change would be a powerful inner experience, either spontaneously, or through some medium like Holotropic Breathwork.

We have seen many occasions—and experienced quite a few within our own ranks—where these types of seekers were totally transformed by their inner experience, with the result that they could no longer either live or support others in the same way they had previously. A high percentage of them would then embrace wholeheartedly a regimen of deep inner self-exploration in expanded states of awareness. This would often, at the same time, signal a radical transformation in how they supported their clients. We hear from these seekers that the principles of the holotropic perspective—and in particular the resonance they have now found with the Inner Healer—seemed to be exactly where they were headed all along in their work with others.

Next came a soul-searching period, in which they would examine the methods in which they had been trained. They often arrive at the insight that their previous training and work were "up for grabs"—that they were wondering whether they could continue within their current therapeutic setting. Or, they saw that they would be required to totally re-invent themselves as therapists—either wishing to become a holotropic practitioner, or shifting their modality to one in which the reliance on an inner healing power could be wholeheartedly embraced, and not just given an "energetic nod" as to its efficacy. In answer to our queries above, this group of therapist/seekers falls in to the category of the "yeses," or at least the "maybe's."

However, there is still one iron-clad deal-breaker: Holotropic Breathwork is trademarked nearly all over the world. Unless these therapists have become certified Holotropic Breathwork practitioners, they cannot call the work they do Holotropic Breathwork. Of course, they may use the principles of the method and philosophical underpinnings—within the ethical limits of their skills and understanding. But in no way can they say that what they are doing is Holotropic Breathwork or based on Holotropic Breathwork.

The "no's" are perhaps easier to recognize. These therapists may or may not have done some work in expanded states of awareness. They have learned of the holotropic perspective, either in a book or from the opening lecture of the Holotropic Breathwork seminars they may have attended. For them, the existence of an inner healing power seems, at least, intriguing. In this case, they essentially weigh this breathwork motif on a scale balanced by the practices they have already learned.

Curious, and somewhat interested, they may read what they can find on the subject, all the while weighing the pros and cons of both the holotropic perspective and the methods in which they themselves have been trained. The lens through which they look is, though therapeutic of a sort, often a mental, or intellectual one, as they juxtapose what they *think* they know with the principle of the Inner Healer, which they do not really in fact understand—or have even actually experienced at any deep level. They are attracted to it, but in fact have not yet experienced it to any meaningful degree. Of course, it is entirely possible for someone to have tried Holotropic Breathwork, or read about it, and then to decide it is not for them. This could be for many reasons, all quite valid.

Others may resolve to "play with" the Inner Healer concept—use it in a therapeutic setting, just to see what happens, or to test whether it may be interesting or worth exploring any deeper. This is where the "maybe" becomes the "no." Imagine, for a moment, the consciousness and particular needs of the client. In probably all therapeutic milieus, it will be important that she feels respected, heard, or "seen," as we say. In addition, it should be non-negotiable for her to be able to develop a sense of trust that her therapist is adept, authentically supportive, and has her best interests at heart.

If we really go to the core of the matter, it is difficult to imagine that a practitioner from a variety of methods—for example, from psychoanalysis to cognitive/behavioral approaches—would be able to find use for anything more than a fleeting superficial foray into the holotropic realm. There are a number of reasons for this: Of course, in the holotropic milieu, the client's inner self is the best source of healing power. The psyche is composed of multiple dimensions beyond the biographical domain. These principals merely scratch the surface of "deal-breaking" differences.

It just seems close to impossible to graft a holotropic perspective onto such traditional frameworks without significantly reframing many core teachings of these strategies, and at the same time destroying the power of the holotropic perspective through deal-breaking modifications in the core holotropic method. The truth is, there is a wide spectrum of methods which were never created for these holotropic modifications—even if a travesty—to be anywhere "in the picture" at all. This is particularly true of those which without question rely on the pivotal, active role therapists play in any therapeutic relationship—and all within the biographical domain, which, to them, is the only one that actually exists.

Consequently, it is possible to imagine a scenario where a merely occasional nod toward trusting the Inner Healer on the part of the therapist could do nothing more than confuse a seeker. In a worst-case scenario, one could envision that a temporary, intellectual exercise in the interjection of a mental interaction or concept based on the power of the Inner Healer—followed by the abrupt return of the "therapist as director" approach—could actually be quite psychologically wounding for a seeker.

As we have alluded to previously, this kind of periodic interjection of an inner healing lens through which the therapist could, in effect, "play with" something different, may trigger the seeker to respond—quite appropriately, we might add—to a kind of "double message" or a "double-bind." This would occur—again, in paraphrase—as a "therapist knows what's best/client knows what's best" parody of support.

It is quite likely that such a "schizophrenic" inconsistency in supportive intention could add another bead on the rosary of a number of patterns with which seekers may be working in the so-called therapeutic setting. It is also likely that a haphazard injection of the dynamics of a power within could actually do way more harm than good. The reason for this is that so many clients are working on the well-known, often malign trauma of having received an almost diabolical dose of mixed messages when they were young.

In short, as we have stated all along, a mere intellectual understanding of the true inner healing dynamic, where the client's deepest self is her one true healer, is an insufficient, if not antithetical, dimension to true, in depth, multi-leveled comprehension of this absolutely critical dynamic of any holotropic therapy. Therefore, it seems virtually impossible to recommend wholeheartedly that any therapist who has not done extensive inner work—experiencing some authentic episode of either a gradual or sudden sense of the ego death—attempt to incorporate such a radical, self-empowering dynamic into the existing framework of their therapeutic strategy.

On the other hand, we would welcome with open hearts any therapist/seeker who, in her deepest self, feels that her work with others must also be founded upon the principle of the Inner Healer, no matter what she herself may name such a dynamic. Without reservation, we would invite her to undertake, in her own way, the journey of a life-time—in-depth exploration of her own psyche, no matter what the means she may choose. We hope that she, like so many throughout the world, would commit to some kind of powerful therapeutic unfolding whose outer boundaries seem to always disappear into a true psycho-spiritual adventure toward wholeness. This is, after all, the best and truest gift we have to offer any seeker who trusts us to journey down that stream with her.

In closing this section, we should briefly revisit something we shared early on, as we outlined the holotropic lineage. We mentioned the research that had been done to ascertain which therapy was more powerful than any other. It is intriguing that the findings could not verify much statistical difference between methods. However, a host of personal intangibles were what seemed to make the difference.

The results pointed to the possibility that efficacy was not so much about the therapy or the method. It was more about the *therapist*. What was important was *who* she seemed to be—to paraphrase the findings, her "being level"—which would reflect how much work she had done on herself, or perhaps her evolutionary development toward such an approach as we have outlined. As we pointed out, there seems to be a direct link between deep inner work and *presence*—the almost indefinable component of expanded consciousness and client-focus on the part of therapists which can translate into a deep trust on the part of the client—a powerful baseline for all true transformation.

This observation appears valid, no matter what training these therapists may have undergone. This expanded consciousness supports the therapist's realistic evaluation of her own power in the relationship—her humility—by her recognition that she can never really know what is best for her clients. Even if this insight is not framed in our holotropic language, such as the Inner Healer principle, it seems experientially logical that the therapist may quite likely, at least unconsciously, be interacting with her clients on a level of trust hardly possible without her having done systematic, deep inner work.

Across the spectrum of therapeutic possibilities where the holotropic model may actually thrive, there are probably already thousands of therapists operating consciously or unconsciously with the knowledge that transformation and therapy are mysteries none of us can ever fully understand. They may already have the insight that, within this level of *unknowing*, the best we can do is, as we say, travel down stream with seekers on their journeys, and do whatever we can to keep them safe as they themselves turn inward to discover the "diamond mine" of authentic, in-depth personal and transpersonal power.

We know that many skilled, open-hearted therapists exist in a vast array of methods and milieus. In addition, we can always hope and trust that all of us may experience the grace of the ego death and the gifts of core transformation. We can also trust leaders in other modalities to truly empower themselves. The gift is available for everyone to discover their own answers from within the deep, authentic sources of self-empowerment always already within *all* of us.

From the Ballroom to the Office: A Holotropic Fantasy of Therapy at the Edge of Reality?

Before we close, we might play a little game—throw out all the "what-ifs" and "maybe's" and be, well, literal. If a proponent—a true believer in the strategies we are proposing—was doing one-on-one therapy, here is one way it might unfold. This is what we could perhaps term "staying with the literal essence" of our holotropic strategy, while at the same time revolutionizing the potential of a Holotropic Paradigm.

First of all, as an initial therapeutic effort for an individual, ***this may not be not for every client***. There are some seekers who have been so wounded that it is impossible for them to connect at all to any internal or vertical dimension of their being. This situation—of a default mode of entrenched projection as a defense strategy by some seekers—is quite well known to therapists within many different milieus. Here, there may be an initial period lasting quite some time, where the primary focus is a gently deepening establishment of *trust*. Of course, trust may well be the most non-negotiable deal-breaker in any deep therapeutic or psycho-spiritual undertaking.

An in-depth one-on-one adventure may be relatively appropriate, however, if these seekers have already worked holotropically in a previous milieu, perhaps a larger group breathwork setting. The best strategy would also be to include the same rigorous screening process, as we do for all Holotropic Breathwork sessions, to ascertain who might respond safely and positively to the kind of adventure we are about to propose.

In addition, it is clearly essential that the proposed holotropic therapist, who employs such a gentle, intimate, yet powerful practice, should have done a truly substantial amount of inner work on herself, as we have been thoroughly stressing throughout this inquiry. Obviously, having experienced Holotropic Breathwork regularly, or other in-depth therapeutic work in non-ordinary states of consciousness, would be paramount.

We should also mention the all-important consideration of the gender of the therapist in relation to that of the seeker. Work in expanded states of awareness—particularly in the revelations of deep, heretofore unconscious trauma—brings a special focus to this issue that may or may not be quite as essential in traditional verbal therapy.

Most of us feel that if the practitioner in this "one-on-one" scenario is a man, then it is more than likely not appropriate for him to attempt, without a woman support person present, the meta-ordinary states work with a seeker who is a woman. We should, of course, stress the importance of gay and lesbian seekers to bring with them a support person, of whatever gender, with whom they would feel the most safe and supported.

This issue of gender, in terms of emotional safety, is much less crucial in a large group session where, in a sense, so much work is done "under the spotlight" of numerous participants—both facilitators as well as breathers. So, in an ideal situation, a seeker will bring with her a trusted friend to be the sitter throughout the session. We can begin to see already an intriguing development in therapeutic creativity, as well as the requirement of a deep, heart-centered sensitivity in all dimensions of guide/seeker interaction...

So, if it feels *1000 percent right*, imagine: We have one hour, or perhaps an hour and a quarter. The seeker arrives. The holotropic therapist immediately brings on-line the three part holotropic structure: *preparation*, *session*, and *integration*. In addition, the *entire session* is framed within the APS—the *Awareness Positioning System*. This establishes the easily grasped working, powering dynamic of the session's progression and unfolding toward wholeness—the *horizontal*; the *vertical*; and the *self-inquiry*, "Is this feeling familiar? Have you ever felt it before?"

First 15 Minutes—Preparation: Our seeker, accompanied by her support person, or "sitter"—in this case, also a woman—checks in, reports how she is doing. After succinctly, but clearly presenting the strategy for the session, perhaps a few questions from the therapist are in order. She shares briefly what has happened since last session. What's the feeling? Remember, emotions are almost always the royal road to our power within. The therapist reports in, as well.

Then she asks the seeker if she would like to try something: She may sit in a chair or recline on the sofa—her choice. Next, the therapist invites her to turn within, eyes closed, and open to whatever she imagines her source of inspiration may be for her. If she is having a little trouble with this, the guide/therapist suggests that she play a game: *Imagine* that she has a perfect source of healing deep within herself—just imagine that this is so.

The guide shares that she will play a brief piece of beautiful music for the seeker. She asks the seeker to open inward, and "be with what is"—not trying to change anything—just notice whatever emerges into her awareness. She should, as much as possible, trust herself—there may be thoughts, feelings, tears—just be with whatever emerges—no need to change anything. She should attempt to trust this power she has found within, or has imagined is there—as best she can.

The guide lets her know she may say stop, or open her eyes and end the adventure at any time. She may "report in" whenever she wishes—always within the guide's framing and utilization of the *vertical/horizontal* dyad. The support person shares that she, the seeker, can be with this process lightly if she wishes, almost as though she is just playing a game. Or she may try just letting go, and open deeply to whatever may emerge.

The guide also shares with her, as a mantra, that she just *cannot* do it wrong. At any point, the seeker may also say "Stop." Here the seeker knows she can "report in" on what is happening. And if necessary, the guide can then help her to renegotiate the adventure strategy—returning inward, or remaining horizontal with the support person, continuing the process in a verbal interaction, until she the seeker feels as complete as she can be for this day. The guide lets her know she has many choices!

Next 15 minutes—Session: The therapist briefly guides the seeker inward, verbally, as the music begins softly. Near the end of her verbal guidance, she invites the seeker to open to the mystery of healing within, however she sees it. Perhaps the guide rings a soft chime or bell. She brings on-line a piece of music—something soft and beautiful—yet at the same time imbued with true power and a sense of gravitas.

She plays this for about 10 minutes–what we call "heart, or break-through music." Then she softly encourages the seeker to "be with what is"—not trying to change anything in any way, even if she feels that "nothing" is happening. Just be with the "nothing"—trust herself—she cannot do it wrong. If she wishes, she may report what is happening, or just stay inward non-verbally. The therapist/guide shares with her that she is "in charge"—she may stop and open her eyes at any time … be held by her friend—or even by both the friend and the guide as well, as she sees fit.

If emotions come, the guide supports the seeker appropriately—tissues, the seeker's hand in the guide's hand or her friend's, or both—a gentle hug, but only if it feels totally appropriate, and if the seeker has asked for it, or states that this is ok. Or a few soft, encouraging words are perfect: "You are doing fine; stay with it; trust yourself"—or something similar. At some point, the guide rings the bell softly and eases the music down—asking the seeker, when she is ready, to open his eyes and gently allow herself to come back into the room, to every-day consciousness.

The guide now asks the seeker how she is doing. How does she feel emotionally, physically? If there is a little tension in her body, the guide encourages her to very gently tighten up that part of her body for a moment, hold it, then let it go. She and the sitter always stay in touch with the seeker: "How are you feeling now?" The support duo stays with this until she reports that she feels she has returned to the hylotropic mode of consciousness—or "back."

Final 30 minutes Integration: The guide gives the seeker a pen and pad on which to write; and a blank sheet of paper with crayons, pastels, or watercolor paints. She shares with the inner voyager that, if she wishes, she may record, in whatever way she feels moved, what has happened in her session. The guide lets her know she is doing very well, and that she just cannot do it wrong.

This period of the integration lasts for about 10 minutes. For the next 10 minutes after this, the guide asks the seeker to share with her and her sitter what has happened. They just listen—be attentive, encouraging, and supportive. The therapist/guide *never "therapizes"*—or tells her what has happened, or interprets in any way the seeker's experience for her. There are two components the guide always employs: First, every interaction she initiates is motivated by three things: ***Support, Support, Support***. And second, all therapeutic interaction occurs within and is framed by the dynamics of the *Yoga of the Cross*, or the *Awareness Positioning System*.

The meta-view of this stage of the "therapy" is an *uplifting*, as one who would, with palms raised toward the sun, release a wild bird which has serendipitously decided to temporarily grace a human being with its ineffable presence. The operative trajectory is expansion, freedom, and a glorious self-empowerment.

The final 10 minutes is a celebration of the seeker's inner "walkabout." In this crucial phase, they all discuss a strategy whereby she knows she can have a follow-up phone consultation almost any time. The guide lets her know how well she has done. In addition she points out that it is totally normal for her to have left-over emotions and sensations in her body—and that she can trust herself.

It is critical to again, as in the beginning, to bring on line the APS—the Awareness Positioning System. Once more, help her to reframe within this metaphor what has occurred. What part was horizontal—generated from the external environment? What it was like to "take it vertical"?

Before the seeker departs for the next phase of her life adventure, the guide encourages her to practice engaging the *Awareness Positioning System* as often as she can remember to do it, especially in those myriad episodes of our everyday lives where we feel emotionally moved—one way or the other—by interaction with, as we say, "people, places, and things." In this way, the seeker begins to realize that what she previously thought was an episode of therapy was merely one chapter of a profound life adventure with tremendous potential to upgrade her universe experience in ways she can only imagine at this point.

For This Seeker and All Seekers: A Return to the "Upper World"

It is critically important to emphasize, at this point in our inquiry, that the vertical line of the cross—*above* the horizontal, external reality line— plays a role of paramount importance in this, or any kind of deep work in meta-ordinary states. In the dynamic of the cross, this is the dimension of existence characterized by the infinite possibilities inherent in opening to the power of a radical numinosity in our lives. This power is truly the alchemical mediator of profound psycho-spiritual transformation.

At this stage, a refocus on *numinosity* brings us all the way back to the beginning of our inquiry. Here we are reminded that, through one extremely important lens, our entire journey has focused on varying attributes comprising *language, method, and structure for numinosity* in the lives of seekers and, indeed every planetary citizen. As we pointed out, for many inner adventurers, this subject of numinosity may feel quite fresh or even totally new, particularly within the domain of one-on-one or group therapy.

The good news is that when these issues arise for seekers—and no doubt they will, sometimes quickly, sometimes slowly—these seekers will no longer be subjected to hearing from the therapist, "Well, that is not my area of expertise. For that, you should consult a priest or a minister."

After every nuance of numinosity we have presented and hopefully found useful in this written adventure, such a statement really may begin to sound laughable. Numinosity is an accessible, experientially realizable truth that, through Holotropic Breathwork and other deep methods capable of accessing expanded states of awareness, we *all* have the ability to bring on line and profoundly benefit from its deepest treasures in our lives.

Having emphasized again and yet again this crucial truth, we would suggest that a therapist engaged in individual or group therapy who wishes to support seekers with this modified, yet totally holotropic framework, should seriously consider utilizing the Awareness Positioning System. Having done this, it is critical that, to benefit from the most thorough, expanded, potential inherent in this profound modern alchemical adventure, a guide must ceaselessly be alert to capitalize on the *upper vertical arm, or dimension*, of the cross itself.

This prompting applies to each of us who feel passionate about helping to midwife the holotropic paradigm's blossoming into its most complete fruition as a force in world service. The topics we have touched upon through this text represent a wide open window on the power of the numinous to impact the lives of seekers engaged in virtually every psycho-spiritual discipline on the planet, at this or any future point in time.

In this inquiry, we have attempted to provide a language, method, and structure for the numinous dimensions of transformation, as well as existence itself. Our hope is that in some small way, this particular dispensation may impact humanity in a positive way. If this occurs, it certainly feels likely that it will owe its success to the power of what is known as *grace*. Grace, as we have pointed out previously, seems to be an unlimited gift of transformation that has the potential to emerge in any therapeutic environment. But beyond this, grace may ultimately even inform the intimate unfoldings of our everyday lives.

Many of us "people helpers," and a great many others as well, have had the insight that, without embracing the dimension of numinosity, our therapeutic support of others will always be limited in a vital way. Without *language, method, and structure* for numinosity, we ourselves may well have a much more arduous time reaching our fullest potential in the planetary and cosmic odyssey upon which we have all embarked.

By our embracing of the vital domain of numinosity as an absolutely essential component of in-depth transformation, the therapeutic adventure becomes equal to the deepest psycho-spiritual aspirations presented in virtually every dimension of the world perennial philosophical traditions. The strategy we have proposed at this stage of our inquiry is quite simple and straightforward. In fact, it seems to be an ideal framework for modern therapeutic environments interested in the addition of a numinous component to their repertoire. So let us return to our previous setting, and a closure of our holotropic, one-on-one therapy.

Once More: Into the Temple of Transformation

As the seeker sits there, ask her once more to close her eyes. Encourage her to imagine the cross, and in particular the *upper vertical arm*, representing her aspirations toward her source of inspiration. Remember, if she does not have such a source, encourage her to "make one up." Share with her that imagination is a powerful talisman of transformation—with tremendous, possibly even unlimited psycho-spiritual power.

Let her know that, when she is ready, she may let go of, or "offer up," whatever she has experienced that she wishes to be free from, or healed of. She does this by imagining a ritual act of sending this issue, or issues, "*up the line*," as we say, to whatever her envisioning is of that inner power, or source of inspiration, she may have imagined or discovered for herself.

After she has completed this, encourage her to reenact this ritual *offering up the line* whenever she feels moved to do so over the next few days and weeks—or for that matter, as long as she wants. You may share with her that it can be a beautiful, ongoing way to stay, as we say, "clear and clean" on a day-to-day basis. This may be useful *whenever* her Inner Healer brings into her awareness any aspect of the issue she may wish to transform in her life. You may also suggest that she might find it useful to keep a journal of this practice of "offering up the line"—noting feelings, insights, revelations, and whatever else she feels is relevant in her continued unfolding toward wholeness.

After this brief but crucial interlude, we once again focus on other, all-important components of the integration phase. The guide encourages the seeker, over the next few days or weeks, to do whatever she feels may be grounding for herself: a walk in nature, hanging out with loved ones or a pet, exercising vigorously, journaling, creating an altar for herself, reading an inspiring book, eating what are, for her, grounding foods—whatever she feels is *nurturing* for herself.

The most valuable thing is that she trust her deepest self—her Inner Healer, the power within. It is also important for her to know that she may contact you, the guide, at any time and that, if you are busy in that moment, you will respond as soon as you can. Nothing is as powerful as, in the manner Bruce Springsteen so beautifully sings, "just a little of that human touch."

This is it: a holotropic therapy. It reenacts a strategy thousands of years old, here and now, in this era, in a little over one hour—from a temple or deep forest to the twenty-fifth floor of a sky-scraper in a world megacity—or from a hotel ballroom floor to a one-person office, "far from the madding crowd."

One last caveat: As we mentioned earlier, the standard therapy practice of seeing one client after the other, with very little time in between, will have to be modified and made entirely flexible, were a holotropic therapy implemented in the manner we just described, or in any way, for that matter. It is always possible that a seeker will open to an emergence from her psyche that will not be tidy, as she attempts to follow the rule of, "Times up, see you next week."

It is absolutely essential, in this kind of work, that the integration process be supported until its full completion—as we say, within the larger field of incompletion. If a therapist cannot commit to this possibly open-ended structure of closure, then the holotropic endeavor should, of course, not be undertaken at all.

Remember, for all the reasons shared over and over through our holotropic mantras—the ones we have covered in such detail in previous chapters—it is critical that therapists themselves be psycho-spiritually prepared for this adventure. Please notice your own feelings as you read this. One might wish to be wary of any personal leanings toward irrational, ungrounded, heart-pounding excitement over the possibility of employing this strategy with the next client one sees.

Such over-excitement is most likely a sign that we perhaps need to settle down, consult our mentors and friends, and attend a few Holotropic Breathwork sessions, or supported sessions of some sort, in meta-ordinary states of consciousness. After this, perhaps we should "be still" for a while, as the mystics say.

Remember, we ourselves are the only ones who can mess this up—for all the reasons of impeccability we have stressed during this written adventure. The truth is, these pages are in no way whatsoever the holotropic landscape itself—only maps and notes from many other holotropic explorers and pioneers. We must take the inner journey ourselves—again, and then again. This is our truest credential.

The holotropic "mantras" we have repeated throughout the text will always be our beacons of truth, as well as a benchmark of our readiness to engage in this type of sacred holotropic adventure with another seeker. We are only as adept as the work we have done on ourselves. And nothing prepares us any better than a series of ongoing personal ego deaths to recognize what a sacred adventure deep work actually is—for ourselves, as well as for those we would support.

We hope that including this imperative guideline of rigorous self-inquiry to determine our readiness to proceed in this manner will shine a gentle, powerful, yet cautionary light on one of the most promising psycho-spiritual fruits of the holotropic paradigm many of us can now envision.

CHAPTER XX

Archetypal Astrology, COEXs, and the Ensoulment of the Universe

As we alluded to early on, it is impossible to imagine either a transpersonal or holotropic perspective without the inestimable power of archetypal astrology and the contribution of Stan's close friend and colleague Rick Tarnas. Their relationship spans almost the entire time Stan was at Esalen in Big Sur, where their fortunes became interwoven in a brilliant creative synergy. I recall few teachings of Stan's I have attended anywhere in the world in the past thirty years where he has not referred to their collaboration. In the vast majority of these lectures, he has gone into passionate depth about the marriage between his work and Rick's.

I first met Rick at a month-long seminar at Esalen on transpersonal approaches to addictions recovery in 1988. First of all, I really resonated with his heart-felt presence, his radiant mind, as well as how he taught. Before this, I had always considered astrology—the way I saw it in newspapers and New Age paperbacks—to be particularly uncompelling. But when he spoke, a whole new world opened up—one that made absolutely perfect sense.

As he shared his passion, I had one of those heart/soul/mind openings that occur serendipitously and rarely. But when they do, they presage tremendous consciousness shifts and openings that have the potential to change everything about the way we live in the world. It was as though I had *always* known what he said was valid. When this special moment occurs, I am always certain I am in the presence of a truth that will upgrade my life in ways I cannot even imagine.

What follows are the musings of a complete "lay person" in terms of astrological theory, in my own metaphor and what it means for me. Since that first meeting, I have heard hundreds of seekers relate something on the subject quite different from my own insights, yet ones that make at least as much sense as mine—most more so. I have also been mesmerized by many of Rick's presentations, all of which have been catalysts for further revelations. This initial experience was overwhelmingly validated when, a short while later, he drew up my chart for the first time.

Here was astrology as I had never known it. Although he honored the dimensions of signs and houses, his almost total focus was an envisioning of the *planets as archetypal forces*. It was one of the most profound revelatory experiences of my transformational journey. All of a sudden, something about the very nature of cosmic existence made sense. Or, more to the point, a sacred truth seemed to emerge from what, before this, I had only felt in the powerful, yet perhaps not quite graspable, psychedelic experiences I had undergone earlier in my life adventures.

The core revelation upholding this sense of rightness was his assertion that the universe is *ensouled*. This, of course, *was* something I had experienced in psychedelic adventures. But to hear it, in the context of a psycho-spiritual teaching from a brilliant friend of Stan's, gave this revelation a validity and a gravitas I had not known before.

Immediately after returning home, I set up a reading. We had a phone consultation, and he sent me a tape of it. This was a good thing, because there was no way I could have absorbed anything close to all the nuances of our conversation. Plus, it was clear to me—and he reported this would happen—as I periodically went back to the tape, I heard the truths therein differently each time. This, of course, reflects the fact that I was not the same person from one day to the next. This seems to be particularly true of all seekers, for whom the spiritual journey becomes an ever-shifting kaleidoscope of revelations, all reflecting that spiral toward wholeness that seems to be common to authentic transformation.

The core blessing for me was an overwhelming revelation of *validation* for who I was and my own particular life adventure. Previous to this time, every stage of my journey seemed colored by at least some sense that I was perhaps strange, or "doing life wrong." Transformation felt like a kind of random accumulation of insights based on not always related personal, perinatal, and transpersonal experiences. These experiences seemed to be organized haphazardly within systems to which I really just could not relate, such as traditional therapy and the continued tolling of the death knell of organized religion in the dark corners of my consciousness.

This new, overwhelming blast of validation shattered much of these old, crystallized patterns and thought forms. To put it in a metaphor we have been using regularly in this inquiry, I was suddenly catapulted into a deeper stratum of the *wellness model* of transformation. Many involved in the holotropic work who have gone through their own experiences of this "conversion experience"—through psychedelics, Holotropic Breathwork, deep mystical practice, or authentic shamanic ritual work—often report this sense of life validation, this shift from *wrongness* to *rightness*. This kind of work and revelation absolutely changes everything. They seem to be core to true healing—to in-depth self-validation and personal empowerment.

To return to our inquiry, just how does archetypal astrology fit into this category? The restrictions of space and time within the scope of this book, as well as my own sense of limitation to do the subject justice—justifies my not attempting to explore in any depth this priceless contribution to the holotropic perspective. For this, I refer you to Rick's work, particularly *Cosmos and Psyche*—where he guides the reader through world history via the astounding lens of archetypal astrology.

I also recommend wholeheartedly my close family friend and co-worker, Matthew Stelzner, who is a protégé of Rick's, and who has worked for years with us in the holotropic training, and has taught astrology modules throughout the world. I also deeply acknowledge Keiron Le Grice. He is an exceptional teacher—of astrology—but also of this discipline's efficacy within a holotropic perspective. This was born out when he led an astrology module in England that was part of the certification process in Grof Transpersonal Training. You may also remember my honoring him in the acknowledgments at the beginning of this book as the amazing editor of this treatise on the holotropic paradigm. In this context we should also mention Renn Butler's valuable contribution on this topic, *Pathways to Wholeness: Archetypal Astrology and the Transpersonal Journey*.

However, I will attempt a brief personal look at the value I see in astrology, in terms of the holotropic perspective. I apologize to my teachers in advance for any misrepresentations of their findings. Early in the text, we presented the extended cartography of the psyche: the biographical, perinatal, and transpersonal domains of consciousness.

We also mentioned the groundbreaking revelations Rick and Stan had at Esalen, in which, along with their comprehensive exploration into astrology, they recognized that the archetypes of the four outer planets correspond elegantly to the four matrices of the perinatal dimension. This would briefly be: Neptune, for the intrauterine experience; Saturn for the period of time when the fetus is stuck in the birth canal, before the cervix opens; Pluto, for the dimension of titanic life/death struggle after the cervix opens, which is characterized by sexual, aggressive, and even quasi-spiritual material; and finally, the archetype of Uranus, for psycho-spiritual death/rebirth and biological birth itself.

We also shared that the perinatal is a "gateway dimension," with a Janus-like, dual-directed gaze—one outward and upward, toward the transpersonal or archetypal dimension, and one forward, toward a human's biographical, or post-natal life in the world. We frequently hear from seekers that they have experienced one or other, or both these trajectories and powers of the perinatal. This depends on the path their Inner Healer presents for them in their journeys toward wholeness.

One experience may entail the journey of "coming in," or "down from" Being, from the macro-level of cosmic existence to the micro-level—or, in another metaphor, from the "All" toward individual manifestation. In this case, the perinatal would act as a kind of "down-stepping," a focusing of cosmic, or universal, energy toward the experience of the individual self, which would manifest in the womb and culminate at birth. The perinatal would, in this trajectory, be the field or dimension of this focusing, this down-stepping—this organizing of universal energies toward its experience as an individual human.

Or, it is also possible for seekers in deep work to experience the opposite trajectory. In this case, the individual, in her life on earth, makes a journey, guided by her Inner Healer, into the perinatal. There, she experiences deep, resonant levels of her particular manifestation as having a causal origin in the womb, then through the birth canal, then at birth, culminating as a human individual.

In another metaphor, she has the opportunity to experience the cosmic trajectory of Becoming, or moving from her personal incarnation toward an identification with wholeness, or Being—from the "micro" to the "macro," or as the *Individual* to *Oneness with all that is*. Through this process, the perinatal, as gateway, becomes an open window on the archetypal domain, where she confronts and identifies with the cosmic principles which are the expanded forms of her patterns and characteristics manifested in her biographical life.

In these two trajectories, the archetypes play an essential role—one, from Being to Becoming, as a focusing agent, a down-stepper of universal characteristics into their eventual human individual counterparts. On the other hand, the archetypes represent transformational functionaries of the individual journey—from Becoming to Being—from the individual to the cosmic level.

So, what role does astrology play in this dual trajectory of human to cosmic, or individual to universal—Becoming to Being or Being to Becoming? It is clear that, for many seekers, astrology can be an extremely revealing archetypal signpost. Yet for our inquiry into an evolutionary process of the human being in either of its evolutionary poises—Being to Becoming or Becoming to Being—even more, astrology is part of a tremendously powerful therapeutic system. In its therapeutic role, it has equal status and influence with Stan's contribution of COEX systems, or Systems of Condensed Experience, which we have covered already in some detail. As revolutionary dynamics for transformation, these two—archetypal astrology and COEXs—are intimately intertwined.

In our work, the integration of experiences from expanded states of awareness is probably best supported and framed by the use of COEXs. As we have shared, a *COEX is the link between dimensions of the psyche made readily discernible by seekers in expanded states of awareness.* As such, it plays a pivotal role in the practice of any holotropically-oriented healing strategy. It is an intra-psychic dynamic recognizable, by a seeker through deep work, as a pattern, gestalt, engram, (a concept from Scientology), chief feature, *samskara*, or thread of inherited past tendencies that she makes conscious during the healing process. These patterns can be experienced as, and characterized by, a powerful emotion, thought form or insight, spiritual impulse, or physical imprint in the body.

COEXs are powerful healing mechanisms because they can introduce the seeker to, and educate her on, a profound experience of *pattern* and the *reality of wholeness*, or the experience of life beyond ego, or the limited self. In our work through the years, seekers have become accustomed to naming their COEXs—a valuable consciousness-expanding, healing tool in itself—by the matrix of the perinatal which seems to be the most accurate wellspring of the nature of the particular manifesting pattern.

For example, a "second-matrix" COEX is frequently characterized by feelings of hopelessness, loss, aloneness, and a sense of being stuck. These characteristics come under the aegis of the archetype of Saturn. A "fourth-matrix" COEX includes feelings of liberation, freedom, awakening, and rebirth. These characteristics are part of the archetype of Uranus. A third matrix COEX would be centered in issues of power, aggression, and sexuality—all characteristics of the archetype of Pluto.

To return to astrology, and to thicken the plot, when we are born, every planetary archetype, including the sun and the moon, are in either a beneficial, challenging, or perhaps neutral relationship with each other, reflected in the positions of the corresponding planets. These relationships become clear when an astrologer "does the chart" for the seeker. The therapeutic value of the chart is multifold.

First of all, as we mentioned, it can be hugely validating. By this, I mean that when we see the relationship of archetypal forces influencing our lives—those patterns we have experienced over and over—how we have felt suddenly makes revelatory, experiential sense. By working with these perennial energies in a meta-ordinary state of consciousness, we free ourselves from the "power of pattern," or the COEXs that inform our unfolding life, and which we are also making conscious, as a "co-conspirator," if you will, with astrological configurations, during deep inner work.

What's more, making conscious a COEX in deep exploration seems to *simplify* the process of transformation. Briefly, we discover that, instead of having fifty things wrong with us, once we understand pattern, our issues become organized around a few COEXs. This reflects a graceful way that the Inner Healer or a power within orchestrates our transformational process.

This is the dance between pattern, or COEXs, and the play of the archetypes. To thicken the plot once more, we can understand the archetypal patterns behind our own COEXs by considering where the celestial bodies were at the time of our birth. The heavens are always in motion— the planets and all celestial bodies are moving at different speeds, in different orbits, creating different relationships with each other with an ever-morphing kaleidoscope of energies and powers that reflect what we are experiencing on a day-to-day basis. Yet we are not cursed. Provided we are willing to work in expanded states of awareness with the energies of COEXs—by recognizing them as patterns that elegantly connect the transpersonal, perinatal, and biographical domains—we can open to a whole new dimension of healing and wholeness not usually available in traditional psychological methods alone.

It is difficult to imagine any more powerful therapeutic mechanisms than the interaction between our archetypal-astrological configurations and our COEXs, or multi-dimensional patterns. Based on our discussion of the implementation of a holotropic perspective in more traditional settings, it seems it would be invaluable to include these dynamics. Even if the therapeutic endeavor in some of these settings precludes work in expanded states, an archetypal, astrological viewpoint can be implemented, which could have tremendous healing, consciousness expanding implications.

Obviously, it would be more difficult for the principles of the COEX to be utilized in a traditional setting. By their nature, they would be, for the most part, unavailable without work in rather deep meta-ordinary states of consciousness. However, it may be that, if there is the use of modified, or somewhat mitigated forms of working in expanded states, such as guided imagery with music, and the *Yoga of the Cross* dynamic, experientially relevant material from COEXs may become therapeutically available. The use of these mitigated forms of deep work are issues we recently previously explored.

The bottom line is, the COEX mechanism and its companion component, archetypal astrology, are invaluable tools to access, or to bring on line, tremendously effective reservoirs of deep personal and transpersonal power. The reasons for this are multiple. First and foremost, these tools open us to deeper causative levels of how and why we feel and react throughout our lives in the repetitive way we do. I am reminded of the Awareness Positioning System, and its alarm mechanism when encountering the presence of a troublesome pattern: "Opportunity to heal! Opportunity to heal!"

The second reason for the value of these mechanisms is that by uncovering a COEX in deep work, or by having our chart done regularly—not just for the birth, but for the ongoing transit shifts—we cease to feel victimized by life and by forces that we cannot understand, or by forces that feel beyond our control. In addition, one of the most beautiful aspects of working with deep, previously unavailable energies is that we can once again begin to make the shift from a *sickness* or *disease* model of the human psyche to a *wellness* model. This shift alone is revolutionarily transformative.

We are learning that every experience we make conscious from within our psyches—by the very factor of its coming into our awareness—is transformative. In addition, their emergence demonstrates the orchestration by our Inner Healer of a benevolent power of *wellness*—a *will toward goodness and love*—in our lives.

Consciousness, as we know, is the transformer—the inner healing power itself. Over time, we find ourselves open to, and searching for—not just what we think is wrong with us—but what constitutes *rightness*, or *goodness* itself. What emerges from our psyches can become occasions for tremendous celebration, no matter how challenging they may be, as they fully emerge into our awareness and are healed.

This is what we mean by a radical self-empowerment. We need no longer feel victimized by psychologies that say that what comes up from the depths of our psyche is inherently a sign of pathology. Nor do we need to fear or dread the power we imagine these deep reservoirs of unconscious energies have to sabotage the possibility of our fulfillment in our everyday lives. Instead, we can celebrate the uniqueness of who we are, as well as our interconnectedness with humanity, creation, and existence itself.

This celebration would include the ability to welcome our challenges, and to work with them consciously in multiple ways in expanded states of consciousness. We can also have the revelation that the psyche, the human experiment, is ultimately entirely motivated by a profound inner love and compassion. The Inner Healer—our power within—becomes a very real and true ally, with our best interests at heart. We are heir to the discovery that this love and compassion contain a tremendous power of radical freedom, which can liberate us from believing we will always be victims in a world or cosmos over which we have no control.

We become the inheritors of an infinite power within, greater and deeper than any trauma or negativity, and always up to the task of whatever challenge we may make conscious in our evolution toward wholeness. This is the promise of *radical self-empowerment*. This is the "gift of the ages" which we in modern times can embrace and celebrate, as we support each other on our individual paths toward freedom, power, and wholeness, one second at a time.

CHAPTER XXI

The Planet Through a Holotropic Lens

Mystics often seem to recognize that poetry is a language that best describes the mysteries that confound the intellect and beguile the spirit. Without question, the mystery of transformation plays havoc with the rational mind. In one sense, a Holotropic Paradigm begins with LSD, and Stan's mystical experience. It seems to reach its flowering, as well as its grounding, in the cultivation and dissemination of Holotropic Breathwork and its perspective.

Yet, through another lens, a holotropic archetype begins in the cauldron of mystic history, as far into the past as a numinous dimension has been recorded. Then, well, who can tell? Systematic deep work, of no matter what origin, teaches us not to get too enamored of our stories. For, no matter how we conceptualize the miraculous—that "about which naught can be said"—a story is all we have. And the two things we know of stories are that, one, they ever change; and, two, the story is never "the thing" in itself.

Yet for those of us on the holotropic journey, what a story we have been blessed to be a part of! We can celebrate that we each are one elegant line in a life epic with a glorious trajectory, if not exactly a happy ending. It does not have a happy ending, that we know of, because, well, the epic is just not finished! However, the uplifting trajectory already demonstrates that we each have the opportunity to discover both a treasure of blessings, as well as to live absolutely fulfilling lives.

A rich, fascinating "couplet" of this holotropic epic begins with Stan's skillful, yet artistic use of the term *holotropic* itself to characterize, not just what happens with entheogens or breathwork, but in what every being in every order of creation appears to be engaged. This is *moving toward wholeness*. To "riff on" well-known sayings—as musicians might say, we are "dancing the only dance there is"; "at play in the fields of the Mystery"; and "golfing, or whatever else, in the Kingdom."

Our path is holotropic—we are moving toward wholeness. We live, create, transform, die, and are reborn in a Becoming. What's more, just as

Stan experienced in the Prague laboratory on his first journey with LSD, we may be blessed at some point with an experience of Being. And from that poise, we appear to participate in the completion of the great circle described by moving toward wholeness. Remember, "moving toward" is the Becoming. And "wholeness" is Being. In this way, we may suggest that the holotropic perspective takes its rightful place in the "wisdom of the ages."

It is possible to discern an elegant, almost artistic trajectory within the development of a holotropic paradigm toward a future flowering. Through a mythic lens, this work of which we are a part seems to have been birthed from Being, like any number of Being's historic "golden children"—which are the methods that have helped shape humanity in this "moving toward wholeness." Even though it has only been in existence for a few decades, Holotropic Breathwork appears to have already become a vital, valid component of psycho-spiritual evolution in time and space—or the Becoming.

We may also imagine that its purpose in existence follows an elegant cycle, from the highest womb, or matrix, of creation, to its most inner, fundamental, and personal dynamis—what we call a power within, the Inner Healer. Through a mystic lens, this Inner Healer, this power within, is the spark, the soul, the true self, the atman—and a thousand other names from cultures throughout recorded time—to denote the sojourn of Being in the Becoming.

To put it simply, we are operating within a paradigm based on authentic personal empowerment and the natural urge of all beings to pursue an evolutionary path. Yet at some point on this epic journey, we may be blessed with the experience that personal power has become both the archetype of power and the universal creative womb of power itself. The work Stan and Christina have midwifed seems to flow in an integrative circle—from the spiritual/philosophical, to the fundamentally therapeutic, to the spiritual/philosophical once more. It could be said to follow a dynamic orbit of philosophy/spirit, to therapy-in-action as a psycho-spiritual evolution, and then upward toward Point Omega, or Being, once again.

The holotropic work also has a rather luminous pedigree. From Kashmir Shaivism to Tibetan Buddhism; from Taoism to the ancient shamanic traditions of the world; the evolutionary trajectory posed by Sri Aurobindo based on the Vedas and the Upanishads; the world mystery schools of death/rebirth; rites of passage; modern consciousness research; and the growing edge of science in dozens of disciplines, Holotropic Breathwork is graced with the "gifts of the ages."

On the Evolution of Personal Empowerment

We have touched upon dozens of blessings that individuals have experienced through systematic exploration using Holotropic Breathwork. Toward that end, a fundamental offering from this inquiry has been the discovery of our Inner Healer—a power within. But the very word *power* can be unsettling for many people. This makes sense, given the horrific abuses of power we have either experienced ourselves, witnessed in the world around us, or studied as a dark shadow in planetary history.

As we pointed out earlier, at a meta-level, power can be characterized as the *dynamis of creation*. We can witness and experience its expression in every level of our existence—from a macro-view of nature and cosmic forces, as well as a micro-view of human evolution. In a very real sense, it is the motivating principal force in existence. None of us can spell out definitively—either scientifically, philosophically, or logically—the blueprint of existence, or why and how we happen to be here now. This is the stuff of epic poems—of the fire of inspiration which radiates from every work of art that has mesmerized us down through time.

So, in honor of this great mystery, imagine that what follows is a kind of Greek chorus in the enacting of a universal play. Only, this chorus can also be a choir of those who have undertaken a holotropic journey—an adventure toward wholeness. It can be a song for those of us who have created, through our inner healing power, our Becoming—a conscious adventure toward a perfection of Being, or an apotheosis of the human experiment.

We can experience that *power without consciousness and love* is a force of sorrow, pain, and destruction in the world. There is no doubt that, throughout history as well as myth, the immortals' gift of power has been co-opted by multiple levels of the false self, or ego—both individually, in personal relationships, and globally, in the hellish abuses one culture wreaks upon another in a seemingly never-ending war for selfish, personal gain.

In the meantime, what we may term Mother Nature eternally manifests levels of power that dwarf what humans seem to be able to muster. Yet She appears to do this within a level of cosmic yet loving neutrality, as well as through the capricious, often overwhelming power of natural disasters. In spite of this capriciousness, Her power does not seem to mirror or manifest as the supremely selfish, egocentric human level, where country against country, race against race, and individuals against individuals, seem to be a horrific norm passed down for millennia.

Where are we in this vast play of creation? We can experience ourselves as participating in a grand, co-creative scheme of evolution. One of the most crucial stages of this evolution has been the casting of power onto the acutely focused stage of our awareness—both in its positive as well as its negative aspects. We, and perhaps every species in some way, feel only too well the blind use of power. Through another lens, we might suggest that we are perhaps the only species that *know* about the abuse of power, even though virtually every other species seems to be on the receiving end of such chaos.

But, for good or ill, power is an integral thread in the cosmic tapestry that winds its way through the human evolution toward wholeness—from Becoming to Being. It is a mighty force of mystery manifesting in the human experiment amid infinite attributes of a cosmic nature which seem to be understandable to us only in moments of great opening through some kind of deep work, or perhaps through a power of grace or serendipity.

The ultimate flowering of a right use of power can be one of the most noble events in a celebration of human evolution. But our gradual, often stumbling awakening to the essential nature of power itself is a dubiously successful adventure. We are all too aware of the destructive use of power by the rampant forces of our egos and the false selves that we voraciously, addictively nurture and manifest individually and collectively.

In this faltering procession of the human spirit, one of the grandest moments of all occurs along the evolutionary trajectory of what we are calling the ego death. As we have tried to meticulously outline, from this ego death, or dismantling of the false self, emerges an experience where will and power dance together in a cosmic dream of unfolding—an evolution toward wholeness once and for all imbued with the creative evolutionary power of love. This is an experience to which we have been referring, through a kaleidoscope of lenses, throughout this book.

This is what we mean by *radical self-empowerment*. Many seekers report that a true self-empowerment based on ego-less love is a crowning dynamic of the human experiment. For others, it is one of the most important forces in the universe. We can recognize it as a ubiquitous power—somehow interjected into the human scheme—as a sign-post and beacon—to let us know where we truly are on the road of our own personal and collective evolution.

Love is the one true barometer of how consciously we wield power itself—that tremendous, miraculous gift within that is the infinitely creative way-shower of our evolution toward wholeness. In this text, many feel we are referring to a pinnacle of human evolution—a recognition of a cosmic interplay between heart and will—where we cease to be "sorcerer's apprentices" as Disney's *Fantasia* so aptly demonstrated, and instead become co-creators with a great mystery. It seems also to be the Omega Point, the pinnacle for Teilhard de Chardin. And for one of my true inspirations in this life, Sri Aurobindo, it may be the descent of the Supermind, bringing with it the spiritualization of the entirety of the universe. This mystery is what Aurobindo is referring to in his masterpiece, *The Life Divine*. Metaphorically, it is a union of heaven and earth—the culmination of a cosmic passion play, an event that many feel is the ultimate purpose of human experience in the first place.

Through another lens, one of our purposes in incarnation seems to be to transform the earth field—from a vast, vicious struggle to satiate our self-centered, egoic needs, into a wondrous adventure characterized by a pair of sister-mantras: *Opportunity to Heal*; *Opportunity to Love*. It is in an earth field, seemingly itself transformed by human evolution toward wholeness, where these two mantras may become a song of all humanity. This may be the ultimate right use of power in our lives—both cosmically and personally. It seems to be a golden thread winding its way through this inquiry, and might be one of the crowning achievements of creation and humanity itself.

On Gratitude

Bill Wilson and his friends, who formulated the great modern Western yoga known as the Twelve Steps of Alcoholics Anonymous, were without a doubt "tapped in." By yoga, I do not mean a system of body postures and practices. I use the term from its original definition in Sanskrit, which means "to yoke," or "to join together." In the case of the Twelve Steps, we would be referring to a bringing together of the individual self with the one True Self, the All, the Higher Power, or the Great Spirit. Recovery pioneers definitely seemed to be channeling the wisdom of the ages. I cover this universal practice in another book, *The Wide Open Door: The Twelve Steps, Spiritual Tradition, and the New Psychology.*

But our interest now is not the entire practice. We are in the closing phase of our inquiry, which, if we had so chosen, could easily have been called a Holotropic Yoga. For a closure to our inquiry into self-empowerment and a Holotropic Paradigm, we may learn something very valuable from the *closing* step of the Twelve Step practice. The Twelfth Step reads: "Having had a spiritual awakening as the result of these steps, we sought to carry the message to other alcoholics, and to practice these principles in all our affairs."

In our work, a parallel reading of this final step might go something like this: *"Having had a spiritual awakening as the result of systematic inner work, and trusting the power of our Inner Healers, we sought to share what we have experienced—in service to others—and to continue to consciously undertake the journey toward wholeness as best we can."*

Why would we feel the need to "carry the message," the good news that real self-empowerment is possible and absolutely life-changing? Mystics for all time have asked similar questions, so we are in pretty fine company. For addicts and alcoholics, the yoga is simple: "We *have to* give it away—or pass it on—to keep it." For us, our lives depend on it. To stagnate, to isolate, to lapse into a selfish hoarding of a miracle, a gift, or blessing that came to us, not because of how special we are—but through the great mystery known as *grace*—this would be the seedbed of stagnation, and our downfall once more.

What a Twelve Step yoga professes has turned out to be absolutely true for me and my colleagues, as well as hundreds of seekers with whom we have shared this vision around the world. As we have said, the ego death is incremental—that is, for most of us, it is not a one-time issue. It is a powerful, central chord around which a life practice can be woven. It is called a "death" for a reason—because this is truly what it feels like—annihilation, obliteration, a painful dissolution, a rude ripping away of cherished thought forms and beliefs, ways of being in the world centered on our selves at the expense of those around us. The ego death hurts! Most of us report that patterns have powerful momentum—that just because they "give up the ghost" once or twice, we would be foolish to think they will not rear their ugly heads once more—just when we celebrate ourselves as being free.

This is what many of us love about a yoga of "passing it on," of giving away what we have received. We may think we are being saintly when we are in service. But in AA, they were so wise about the machinations of the ego, the false self. This ego-centered power will use anything it can to puff up—to become the king or the queen. Especially it will use those characteristics that we cherish about ourselves—how special we are to be great spiritual travelers, or to be in service like the yogis of old.

Yet, there is another way we may serve. We recognize the power of our egos to co-opt whatever there is about us we think makes us special. So, it is like this: in recognition of our own egoic machinations, *we serve to get free—not because we are saintly and good.* We serve to transform *ourselves.* It is a yoga! And we may be blessed, somewhere down the roads of whatever service our Inner Healer calls upon us to render, where another force emerges for us, and this one a grace too. This may be the beginnings of a real and true, unselfish love—where we start to give away what we have, because, well, it is spontaneously, irrevocably, absolutely the only action we can take.

When we have received these greatest gifts from our inner selves, the only true response seems to be *gratitude.* There just is no way we can feel equal to the magnitude of the blessings that have come our way. When they do come, at some point in our evolution there is only one response we can have: what else would we do? We absolutely must pass it on—we cease to be the doers of this service.

But a spirit of service consumes us in the fires of its own greater love—all while this unknown, unnameable power gives and loves, and gives some more. When we ourselves have received the great blessing of this gift—not what we have given up, but what spirit has chosen to pass through us—we can only continue to feel that one beautiful response to the magic and mystery of it all. We have received something so precious there is no way we could have orchestrated it for ourselves. And this feeling is, once again, the power of *gratitude*.

One of the most special and influential teachers of my life has been Brother David Steindl-Rast, a Benedictine monk who lives near Big Sur in California. I first met him through his close friends, Christina and Stan, at a month-long workshop at Esalen. He was a regular guest teacher in their groups. He said a number of things that have been beacons of light, or cornerstones of power, for me throughout my life since then. But the most important for me was what he had to say about *gratitude*.

Brother David shared that gratitude is a *power*. It is a dynamis of transformation. He said that just to *feel* gratitude is transformational—that it is a living force capable of changing us and upgrading our adventure toward wholeness. He went on to say that gratitude puts us in *right relationship* with the Great Mystery—that which is always, always, bigger and more mysterious than we can imagine. To regularly feel gratitude is humbling—a recognition of the power of grace in our lives.

Grace seems to be serendipitous. It is what happens for us way beyond what we feel our small selves can orchestrate. It is even beyond karma, having the power to transcend law with love. Thus, grace and gratitude become two dynamics of a simple yet exacting yoga. Just to stay with these two forces, according to Brother David, is sufficient to transform us in ways we can only imagine.

Therefore, we offer you a little of what has worked for us in the holotropic work—what in the Twelve Step programs we call, "sharing our own *experience, strength, and hope.*" After all, this is all we have to offer others. Here is what works for us: We could say, if your Inner Healers feel moved, that we are here to be of service. We will go down stream with you—to keep you safe—and to trust your deepest inner healing powers to know what is best for you. We will nourish and support your true selves as best we can, knowing that this is really all we can offer others on their roads to wholeness.

Lo and behold, in the meantime, we feel better. We transform. We are allowed to feel grace, gratitude, and humility. We get to be stuck—to die and be born again. We can travel what Bill Wilson calls the "Broad High-way." As Gandalf sang in the Lord of the Rings, "the road goes ever on and on—down from the place where it began…" wherever that was! And wherever it may be headed.

World Service: Sitting for the Planet

One final word on service, and then we are done, for this myth. In our holotropic circles, one may hear a strange concept tossed about. At first, many of us thought facilitators might just have a bit of a speech problem. The word we guessed they were going for was a cornerstone of the good, old new age. The word we thought they were trying to say, but just mispro-nouncing, was *synergy*. Only, the way we kept hearing it was *sittergy*. Then we realized we had heard it right. After we had done Holotropic Breath-work for a while, we realized nobody had made a mistake. Everyone was just being playful about a holotropic dynamic with the potential power to change the world.

Of course, they were talking about how important the sitter is in the holotropic dyad—the dynamic between sitter and breather. The sitter is the living, breathing representative of the magic of the Inner Healer. She can be a perfect example of the trust that facilitators have in the breather's own power within. We have seen hundreds and hundreds of times where the sitter—a new breather, not a therapist—but someone who has never, ever done any work on herself, sits for a well-traveled seeker—perhaps a psy-chiatrist, a massage therapist, a famous author, or a philanthropist.

This person, this sitter, "knows nothing," yet she is a miracle. It is through her *unknowing,* her trust in the Inner Healer, that she holds space, that the breather feels safe. We cannot tell you how many times we have heard breathers in the circles share how absolutely critical their sitter was for them in the transformation that occurred. Just *presence*—no big deal, right? Well, yes and no. In one sense, sitters do nothing. Just sit there, we say, even if you feel stupid. In another sense, they *still* do nothing. And it is this "nothing" that they do which is the miracle of the holotropic work. It is the "doing not doing" we honor.

So, this is the holotropic blueprint. At some point—actually quite fre-quently, especially when it is time to return to our everyday lives—we share a little about sittergy. Sometimes we make a suggestion. We recom-mend giving sitting a try with a family member. This is a big deal, because it is often in family, the World Cup of interpersonal dynamics, where we meddle, manipulate and continually express, in one way or another, that we really think we know what's best for others. We cannot help but take on the responsibility of being a fixer in our family. It only rarely dawns on any participant that sitting in the breathwork room is just a warm-up—yet also the manifestation of an archetype—for a dynamic that has the power to change the world.

Can we even imagine how different our relationships may be—all kinds of relationships—when we actually trust that these acquaintances already have a space within themselves that absolutely knows what is best for them? Most of our relationships are built on dependence, on fixing others, and on sharing quite assuredly our so-called valuable advice. But what if we turned this all around?

We have absolutely no idea how powerful sitting might be in *other* settings, just as it is in the breathwork room. The dynamic, where it seems as though the sitter is doing nothing, yet it turns out how important she actually is, *is the very same miracle that can happen in all our other relationships.* What happens? People feel *empowered.* Can you imagine: everyone around us—every one—beginning to have the space to trust themselves and experiencing us as sitters for them, not directors.

Usually this realization is not a nuclear blast. The dynamic of honoring those around us seems to operate on a much subtler level—gradually over a period of time. What makes the difference is that *we* are different. Whether it is our associates and loved ones—or the people who sell us our ticket at the movies—what is different is the thing we explored earlier called *presence.* Remember, we have no idea what impact our presence has in the lives of those with whom we interact. We cannot *make* any thing or any relationship or interaction with a stranger be different. We can only *allow* a difference to emerge. The results are not in our hands. However, the intention and the commitment are.

We can allow ourselves to stretch a bit, to every interaction we have during the day. Wherever, whenever. Imagine traveling: the bus station, the airport. Imagine the office, the grocery store. At first, everyone external to us seems the same, because most of us are unconsciously looking for support and power *outside* ourselves. But we do not have to worry if they intuit what is happening, or not: that we are "doing not doing"—just "sitting" for them, trusting them and the openness of the space between us and them. The bottom line is, we ourselves will change. We will be healed. And if we are in the healing process, if we really free others to truly find their own power within, then ultimately they change as well. They can eventually learn to trust their deepest selves.

Now imagine countries, diplomats, politicians—the whole human community opening to each other, and honoring each others' right to a sacrosanct internal power. Next, take a stretch, and imagine the great force we call Mother Nature. Imagine our planet Earth as a goddess—the unimaginable mystery of the cosmos in form. Now imagine that we sit for Her—for the Earth—for the world. Breathe this in, and "try it on," as we say.

We hold in our hearts and minds a tremendous power. It is most often not a power of conscious knowing. It is a power of un-knowing. It is not a power of knowledge. It is a power of *unlearning*. We say, go forth and sit. We say, go forth and unlearn. As Ram Das has said, we say go forth and be *nobody special*. Imagine a world in which this is the hidden practice, the yoga of honoring the self-empowerment of others. After all, that's how it starts.

Death or Death/Rebirth: The Battle of Our Time

We have discussed how, in homeopathy, we heal by intensification of the symptoms of an illness and how it is a pivotal holotropic dynamic. This fresh perspective is integral to our nurturing of a Wellness Model of evolution and transformation. It can also bolster us with a positive outlook on what may often seem to be a rather hopeless global dilemma.

This dilemma is that, as operators of "spaceship earth"—to borrow a phrase from Buckminster Fuller—we are facing crises with the imminent potential to destroy us all—humanity and perhaps even the earth itself. However, if we view the phantasmagoria of current global crises through a homeopathic lens, we may be able to discern a healing trend. This virtually hidden trajectory may provide the foundation of an era of global transformation and healing.

We have covered the meta-level of the perinatal dimension as the stages of individual transformation—the Hero's Journey of Joseph Campbell bringing together the myths from a thousand world cultures—singing the complementary notes of a universal paean. The parallels between the Hero's Journey and the perinatal dimension of the psyche are unmistakable. We have discussed the fertile, often terrifying power that the fetus undergoes—as a victim and perpetrator. It is the same for us in our regularly revisited archetypal journey through the realms of death and rebirth. We highlighted the overwhelming intensity one may feel, on the cusp between death and rebirth; the borders between titanic struggle and coming into the arms—loving or not—of whoever or whatever is waiting for us on the outside.

Archetypally, many of us know this place well in our inner search: the merging of the tremendous, sometimes frightening and terrible powers of aggression, sexuality and twisted spirituality. It might be an orgy of death-throes; a vast conflagration of the false self—a death of deaths, through pain of the body, mind, and soul. We may revisit the cessation of linear time once more in a fiery hell that feels never-ending. We may revel or cringe in the vast excesses of forbidden, sometime horrifying orgies of self-destruction, hell, or even our murderous intensions to wipe out all that's good and beautiful left in a world gone unimaginably, irrevocably awry. We may feel that we can only heal ourselves and a blighted world by the abject destruction of all that is.

In the moment of the most violent, sexually charged exhilaration—where we may become the lord or the goddess of some unholy under-world—our annihilation becomes complete. We are no longer the ones who pillage, rape, and burn. We are no longer the idol of our own self-created universe to be worshipped. In the final throws of this orgasmic self-worship, it is we who are pillaged. Here, the universe turns upside down. It is *ourselves* who are violated and burned. It is we who are left alone in the vast desert, beneath the fires of an ultraviolet downpour of hell-fire and disease. We no longer dispense death. It is we who die there—bereft, alone, and broken.

This is a turning point. It cannot be imagined. As they say, one would just have to *be there*. But it is in this moment of the end, when all hope is lost, when every machination of the ego has failed, having lost every piece of itself in the game of annihilation—when fire rains down, and lava rises like a flood—it is here that we die. Yet it is not just our personal death. It can be the death of all—every being, child, woman, and man. It can be the rape and destruction of Mother Nature; a war of gods and goddesses until none are left. It is intimately personal yet it is collective and all-encompassing. Here, there is no more hope—no last chance for redemption. All is lost.

It is in this moment that She may come—that great angel of our dreams, of our time: Kali together with Lakshmi; and the Morrigan side-by-side with Mary. The miracle transpires. We are rescued from hell. We awaken in a field of dreams, a valley of angels and hope, where trees and flowers sing a song of praise and love. We come into the arms of the Mother—the goddess—as a babe. A spirit of the cosmic forest glade we may become—free and clear and shining, our rebirth complete. As the ballad goes: "It's a new dawn. It's a new day."

This is how it happens in our work—but in a thousand metaphors beyond the paltry few we have mentioned. Yet each story is blessed—as powerful as any emotions are of magical rescue and freedom. We are often blessed with a shining light of power, like the fiery inspiration and consciousness burning from many a Goddess of Wisdom's visage. Our death/rebirth journey becomes the exodus of humanity—the great human/cosmic migration from death to rebirth. It is the destruction of the world blossoming into a blinding crystal, a verdant explosion of paradise. Once again, the world is saved from us, from itself.

These imaginings sing the song of what we are going through in these dark times. It is a ballad to the way we destroy our planet from around us— not just in meta-ordinary states, *but for real*. We realize as a human species that we face two deaths. It is up to us which one we choose. We can die the ego death and free ourselves. We may get the insight that, if enough of us do this, we just might "make it" as a species and as a planet. If we do not, then it is not just *our* dying on the mat in the breathwork room. It will be that our actions have literally destroyed this earth from beneath us and all around us.

This is the adamantine promise, the dream of this kind of inner work— that what we do, breathing deeply from the hotel ballroom floor—may actually be one of the most vital ways we can save our cosmic home. One way or the other, we *will* go through a death. But it is our choice: either the death from within, or the annihilation from without. Our earth home, this minute, hangs in the balance. The planet itself struggles and burns in the conflagration of the late third birth matrix, just as we individuals do.

May we make this an internal death! Some see it as a way to free the Mother—from within and from without. This is a sacred trust and a promise of this work, and many good works today. May we, each and all, experience the deepest power within—in the service of love—and not in thrall to our voracious egos. If we can make this shift, then we will have some powerful myths to add to the legacy of the gods and goddesses of this place and the rest of the living cosmos.

If we do not, we are but a cosmic waste dump. We are but a cloud of pollution drifting with no voice and no song through the trackless wastes of a dead sun we can no longer reach—of a moon which will no longer shine her goddess light on the children of a now dead humanity. We can do this work in a hotel, an office, a room in our home. From a ballroom floor, we can participate in freeing earth from that which has poisoned us individually and collectively for so long. We can begin to turn selfishness into love and darkness to light. This is the promise of transformation—one person at a time—one breath at a time.

In Ending ... a Beginning

Many of us feel that, once we really get rolling on a transformation fast-track, it seems almost useless to attempt to hold onto even one of our protean, lightning-like universe dreams. We all feel a bit silly as we dig in, establish a beach-head on a shore of consciousness, and make a stand for any theory or revelation. For, by the time we draw our intellectual sword to defend an insight, the insight seems to have evaporated. We sheepishly realize we have been flirted with once more. We have been seduced by a mystic will-o-the-wisp, a fairy light beguiling us, who, even as we search the night for her, has flitted away into the ancient forest of our past beliefs.

This is where a worldview like a holotropic paradigm emerges—a perspective that by its very nature has no boundaries, like the far horizons of consciousness itself that we can discover we are heir to. A journey toward wholeness feels, to many of us, never-ending. If we were to ever reach this goal, this space of wholeness, it seems that all we would need to do would be to look up once more, turn our gaze to another far horizon. There another wholeness would shine once again, seducing us like a mythic siren from the rocky shore of our dreams.

How many of us have felt—at least once—that we have experienced a culmination of Being—that we have completed our Becoming in some way? And when we have experienced this yet again and again—another Becoming and then another ultimate Being, the moving toward wholeness and then the wholeness once more—there seems there is nothing left to do but to surrender, to let go as wholeheartedly as we can. We find that our task would be to embrace yet again, with deep, wide-open arms and heart, the paradox of the ages: That Becoming and Being are not two poles of a linear trajectory, but more like spirals dancing on the ever-shifting frontiers of one penultimate dream of consciousness.

We are now opening to a meta-octave of the holotropic paradigm—one that ever defies institutionalization, one that plays hide-and-seek with every word written about it. Wholeness, unity, oneness, completion, Becoming and Being—these are wantonly untamable seductions. As in the ancient, mysterious indigenous cultures of the world, truth is a wild thing, a beast—a unicorn, vulture, sylph, salamander, a hind of Fairie. Pursue Her and She ever recedes.

We hear from the great ones that it is a good thing to be perplexed, confounded. We must let the universe turn inside out, and She is here—a consort, a playmate, an ally. We do what the Irish minstrel sage Van Morrison sings: "Let your soul and spirit fly into the mystic. And when that foghorn blows, you know I will be coming home ..."

Yet we write of the latest all-encompassing paradigm anyway—in full knowledge, or at least in the dream of a full knowledge—that our strivings may be but a candle light in the dark night—useful until the wax melts away. Then, behold, we reach out with our consciousness for another light, and another. We do this until that point of the great confounding, when we are left with nothing but a forever upturned gaze upon a truer light—beyond the moon, the stars, the sun—the eternally re-occurring, infinitely ever-present bursting of the Becoming from the womb of Being. And it is by the shining and whirling of this forever new-birthed cosmos that we chart our way once more.

Does this mean we do not chronicle what we feel in this millennial instant? Are we deluded to play with the words and the concepts of our human dimensions? Mystics seem to tell us that we can unveil all the paradigms we want, as long as we do not take ourselves too seriously—and as long as we remember that this is *still* the Becoming. In our world, there are billions who suffer. They need the words. They need beacon-fires shining from the mountains. It may be our task to write a few of these words. But so much more than words, they need actions, love, and the fruits of our own transformation passed on to others in whatever way we can, as often as we can give it up.

When we have awakened through the myriad episodes of our Becoming, to at least one way-station in the realm of Being, we must ask ourselves what do we do now. The answer we have heard from thousands all over the world is this: that our one task is to give back what we have received through the miracle of grace. Our job is to make the gift of our life count, at least for something, of the goodness with which we have been blessed.

Our personal fruit of this paradigm dream is true self-empowerment, in the middle of an ever-recurring ego death. But this power with which we have been graced is only meaningful if we pass it on. Many feel we must let the light that shines in us flow through us, radiate out to others. And when our light goes out, we must light another—let that one shine on, go out, then light another. Thus, like the signal fires of Middle Earth, we can, one after the other, allow that light to spread, and spread, until ... well, who can tell of such things?

And in the meantime? We need not make apologies for all our words, or our paradigms—our sandcastles on the beach, no matter how impeccable—no matter how ephemeral. We must celebrate, make room for every thought, for every dream, every treatise that claims that this is how it all is. So, it is in this spirit of unlearning, of unknowing—and yet of giving back—that we offer this text—what we call a holotropic paradigm. As we shared in the beginning, the truth is, most of us are just not that attached to whether this name—the holotropic paradigm—gets any traction in the current world lexicon. We are much more interested in the possibility that the principles we have shared may be of service in some small, at least temporary way, here in these wonder-filled crisis times of planet Earth.

May there be many wilder, deeper, truer, more compelling stories to surpass this ephemeral episode of human experience—this momentary candle, lit from the eternal flame, and blown out by the Mystery when its time is done.

Biography

Tav Sparks is an author and international workshop leader with over thirty years' experience supporting seekers therapeutically in non-ordinary states of consciousness. He and Cary Sparks are owner/directors of Grof Transpersonal Training, the only program offering world-wide certification in Holotropic Breathwork™. Since 1985, Tav has led numerous workshops internationally in Holotropic Breathwork and in transpersonal approaches to wellness and recovery.

His writing includes books, articles, screenplays, and poetry. Among his publications are *The Wide Open Door: The Twelve Steps, Spiritual Tradition, and the New Psychology*; *Movie Yoga: How Every Film Can Change Your Life*; and *Through Thunder: An Epic Poem of Death and Rebirth*. His groundbreaking article, "Transpersonal Treatment of Addictions: Radical Return to Roots," published in *ReVision: A Journal of Consciousness and Transformation*, in 1987, is considered to be the definitive work in the establishing of a transpersonal addictions recovery model. His treatise on the practice of Holotropic Breathwork, *Doing Not Doing: A Facilitator's Guide to Holotropic Focused Release Work*, has been used in every Holotropic Breathwork training program in the world since 1990.

For the past decade, one of his passions has been explicating and fostering a holotropic paradigm, and the dissemination of the holotropic approach within a variety of disciplines, including spiritual emergency; a universally applicable wellness model in recovery; and other therapeutic and psycho-spiritual support practices.

Index